ADVANCE PRAISE FOR *THE BOOK OF JAVASCRIPT, 2ND EDITION*

"Thau! has been demonstrating his JavaScript wisdom since before it was cool. Now, this new edition of his classic text makes JavaScript wizardry more accessible than ever for experts and beginners alike."
—JESSE JAMES GARRETT, CREATOR OF THE TERM "AJAX" AND AUTHOR OF *The Elements of User Experience*

"The fastest way to killer JavaScript chops!"
—STEWART BUTTERFIELD, CO-FOUNDER, FLICKR.COM

"The new version of *The Book of JavaScript* offers the same elegant simplicity, but now includes the whiz-bang popular advances like working with the DOM and Ajax."
—TED RHEINGOLD, TOP DOG, DOGSTER, INC. (DOGSTER.COM AND CATSTER.COM)

PRAISE FOR *THE BOOK OF JAVASCRIPT, 1ST EDITION*

"*The Book of JavaScript* shines. . . . [It's] an outstanding model for teaching language by example."
—WEB TECHNIQUES (NOW NEW ARCHITECT)

"A great introduction to JavaScript for beginners."
—JAVASCRIPT.COM

"*The Book of JavaScript* is ideal for people who are intimidated by the thought of writing code."
—FOREWORD MAGAZINE

"A practical, surprisingly easy guide to use, even for relative novices."
—THE MIDWEST BOOK REVIEW

"Thau's JavaScript tutorials at Webmonkey.com are so insanely popular, they've earned him a Plato-like following of devoted fans . . . Thau-mania is destined to grow to Elvis proportions."
—EVANY THOMAS, FORMER MANAGING EDITOR, WEBMONKEY.COM

THE BOOK of™
JAVASCRIPT
2ND EDITION

A PRACTICAL GUIDE TO *INTERACTIVE* WEB PAGES

by thau!

NO STARCH PRESS

San Francisco

Publisher: William Pollock
Associate Production Editor: Christina Samuell
Cover and Interior Design: Octopod Studios
Developmental Editors: Jim Compton, William Pollock, and Riley Hoffman
Technical Reviewer: Luke Knowland
Copyeditor: Publication Services, Inc.
Compositors: Riley Hoffman and Megan Dunchak
Proofreader: Stephanie Provines
Indexer: Nancy Guenther

For information on book distributors or translations, please contact No Starch Press, Inc. directly:

No Starch Press, Inc.
555 De Haro Street, Suite 250, San Francisco, CA 94107
phone: 415.863.9900; fax: 415.863.9950; info@nostarch.com; www.nostarch.com

Library of Congress Cataloging-in-Publication Data

```
Thau.
  The book of JavaScript : a practical guide to interactive Web pages / Thau!. -- 2nd ed.
      p. cm.
  Includes index.
  ISBN-13: 978-1-59327-106-0
  ISBN-10: 1-59327-106-9
  1. JavaScript (Computer program language)  I. Title.
QA76.73.J39T37 2006
005.13'3--dc22
                                    2006011786
```

I dedicate this revised edition of *The Book of JavaScript* to my wonderful wife Kirsten Menger-Anderson, who never failed to keep a straight face when I said, "It's almost done."

BRIEF CONTENTS

CONTENTS IN DETAIL

5
OPENING AND MANIPULATING WINDOWS   67

6
WRITING YOUR OWN JAVASCRIPT FUNCTIONS   83

7
PROVIDING AND RECEIVING INFORMATION
WITH FORMS   99

8
KEEPING TRACK OF INFORMATION WITH
ARRAYS AND LOOPS   123

11
VALIDATING FORMS, MASSAGING STRINGS, AND WORKING WITH SERVER-SIDE PROGRAMS 191

12
SAVING VISITOR INFORMATION WITH COOKIES 215

13
DYNAMIC HTML 233

14
AJAX BASICS 261

15
XML IN JAVASCRIPT AND AJAX 279

16
SERVER-SIDE AJAX 299

18
DEBUGGING JAVASCRIPT AND AJAX   363

A
ANSWERS TO ASSIGNMENTS   381

B
RESOURCES   405

C
REFERENCE TO JAVASCRIPT OBJECTS AND FUNCTIONS   411

D
CHAPTER 15'S ITALIAN TRANSLATOR
AND CHAPTER 17'S TO DO LIST APPLICATION 455

INDEX 469

FOREWORD

The first JavaScript I remember writing was a routine
to change two frames at the same time. I was the production specialist for HotWired, and it was shortly after
frames and JavaScript debuted, well before there was documentation for
either. Fortunately, it was also well before Internet Explorer 3.0 appeared on
the scene, so I only had to make sure my JavaScript worked for Netscape 2.0.
Even so, without a reference book to point out where possible pitfalls could be
or answer simple questions such as how to set variables that JavaScript would
like or how to make different windows talk to each other, it was one hell of a
challenge. And it was deeply satisfying when I got it to work correctly.

When Dave asked me to do the technical review of the second edition
of *The Book of JavaScript*, I couldn't have been more pleased or honored. The
deep satisfaction I felt when I wrote those first JavaScripts and they worked
correctly, and the deeper satisfaction I felt as more and more browsers were
released and I figured out how to write cross-browser and cross-platform
JavaScript, are the same feelings I got when I read Dave's explanations and
examples. He describes what a piece of code is going to do and how to think
about it, then lays out an example of code that makes sense—whether you're
a seasoned programmer or entirely new to JavaScript. On top of all that, he
takes a practical approach to programming, he's able to explain complex

problems in a way that doesn't make them sound daunting, and when you're done covering each topic, you feel like you've earned the knowledge. That's rare, and it's really, really refreshing.

Since the first edition of this book was published, there have been a few advancements in JavaScript, most notably the advent of Ajax. Ajax is a concept that makes even a few professional programmers' heads spin, but (not surprisingly) Dave manages to break down what Ajax is and what it isn't, explains when it makes sense to use it, and shows you how to do it.

If you're new to JavaScript, you win—you couldn't ask for a better person to teach you how to program. If you're an old hat at JavaScript and you're looking for a refresher course or wondering how to take advantage of Ajax, you win too.

Happy coding!

Luke Knowland
Interaction Designer, Six Apart
San Francisco

FOREWORD TO THE FIRST EDITION

I learned JavaScript completely on my own. There was no one to tell me about "event handlers" or how to set cookies. No one even explained what a variable is, let alone the best ways to name them. Of course I had reference books, but they were intimidating tomes, full of cryptic lists and tables, written by programmers for programmers.

David Thau is a remarkable combination of natural teacher and seasoned programmer. As a result, *The Book of JavaScript* not only teaches JavaScript thoroughly and enjoyably in a friendly, unintimidating tone, but it teaches programming as elegantly as any book I've seen. In fact, I've always thought of this as Thau's ulterior motive—he pretends he's just showing you how to make a rollover or validate the text in an HTML form, but before you know it you've learned how to code!

Perhaps the most telling thing I can say is that, reading this book, I can't help but wish I was learning JavaScript for the first time. If you are, then consider yourself lucky to have Thau as a teacher. You couldn't do better.

Happy JavaScripting!

Nadav Savio
Principal, Giant Ant Design
San Francisco

ACKNOWLEDGMENTS

This second edition of *The Book of JavaScript* took me much longer to complete than I could have imagined. I'd like to thank the entire No Starch Press staff for putting up with all the delays and surprise extra bits. I would especially like to thank Christina Samuell for moving the process along, William Pollock, Riley Hoffman, Jerome Colburn, and Stephanie Provines for extensive edits, and Luke Knowland for making sure all the code works and offering many excellent suggestions. I'd also like to thank my neighbor, Laurentino Padilla, for sweeping our sidewalk on Thursdays. Without him, this book would have taken even longer to finish.

INTRODUCTION

You are about to begin a journey through JavaScript—
a programming language that adds interactivity and
spark to web pages all over the Internet. This book,
written primarily for nonprogrammers, provides scripts
you can cut and paste for use on your website, but it also explains how they
work, so you'll soon be writing your own scripts. Each chapter focuses on
a few important JavaScript features, shows you how professional websites
incorporate those features, and gives you examples of how you might add
those features to your own web pages.

How This Book Is Organized

Before you dive in, here is a quick overview of what you'll learn as you make
your way through *The Book of JavaScript.*
Have fun!

Chapter 1: Welcome to JavaScript!

This chapter lays out the book's goals, introduces you to JavaScript and compares it to other tools, describes some of the nifty ways in which JavaScript can enhance your web pages, and walks you through writing your first JavaScript.

Chapter 2: Using Variables and Built-in Functions to Update Your Web Pages Automatically

Did you know that JavaScript can figure out what day it is and write the date to a web page? This chapter will show you how. Along the way you'll also learn how JavaScript remembers things using variables and performs actions using functions.

Chapter 3: Giving the Browsers What They Want

In this chapter you'll learn how to direct someone to a web page specifically designed for his or her browser. You'll figure out which browser the visitor is using, then you'll use if-then statements and their kin to point the visitor in the right direction.

Chapter 4: Working with Rollovers

This chapter covers everyone's favorite JavaScript trick—the image swap. You'll also learn how to trigger JavaScript based on a viewer's actions.

Chapter 5: Opening and Manipulating Windows

This chapter explains everything you need to know about opening new browser windows—another favorite JavaScript trick. You'll also learn how JavaScript writes HTML to the new windows, closes them, and moves them around on the screen.

Chapter 6: Writing Your Own JavaScript Functions

Functions are the major building blocks of any JavaScript program, so learning to write your own is a critical step toward JavaScript mastery. This chapter gives you the tools you'll need to write your own functions and put them to work.

Chapter 7: Providing and Receiving Information with Forms

This chapter shows you how JavaScript works with HTML forms to collect all kinds of information from your users and give them fancy ways to navigate your site.

Chapter 8: Keeping Track of Information with Arrays and Loops

JavaScript calls lists *arrays*, and they come in very handy. This chapter describes how JavaScript deals with these lists, whether they include all the images on a web page or all the friends in your address book.

Chapter 9: Timing Events

This chapter discusses setting events to occur at specific times. For example, you can open a window and then close it in five seconds, or you can write a clock that updates every second. Once you know how to do this, you can create games and other interactive applications based on timed events.

Chapter 10: Using Frames and Image Maps

How JavaScript works with HTML frames and image maps is the subject of this chapter. It covers topics including changing two or more frames at once and preventing your web page from getting trapped in someone else's frame set.

Chapter 11: Validating Forms, Massaging Strings, and Working with Server-Side Programs

This chapter shows you how to make sure people are filling out your HTML forms completely. Along the way, you'll learn fancy ways to check user input—for example, you'll learn how to check the formatting of an email address.

Chapter 12: Saving Visitor Information with Cookies

Cookies are bits of code that let your web pages save information a visitor has provided even after he or she turns off the computer. This allows your site to greet a guest by name whenever he visits (if he tells you his name, of course!).

Chapter 13: Dynamic HTML

This chapter introduces Dynamic HTML, a feature of newer browsers that lets you animate entire web pages.

Chapter 14: Ajax Basics

This chapter begins a trilogy of chapters on Ajax, a programming technique that helps you build websites that act like desktop applications. Here you'll be introduced to Ajax and most of the JavaScript you'll need to know to create Ajax applications.

Chapter 15: XML in JavaScript and Ajax

The *X* in Ajax stands for *XML*. This chapter describes how to represent information using the XML data-sharing standard and process XML documents using JavaScript.

Chapter 16: Server-Side Ajax

You'll wrap up your introduction to Ajax with instructions for writing programs that run on webservers. This chapter touches on the PHP programming language and shows you how PHP programs store files on webservers and contact other webservers for information.

Chapter 17: Putting It All Together in a Shared To Do List

In this chapter you'll apply everything you learned in the first 16 chapters and create a collaborative To Do list application. Not much new material will be introduced, but you'll see how everything we've covered so far fits together.

Chapter 18: Debugging JavaScript and Ajax

This chapter wraps things up by giving you tips for what to do when the JavaScript you've written isn't working correctly.

Appendix A: Answers to Assignments

Here you'll find answers to the assignments that end each chapter.

Appendix B: Resources
This appendix provides information about the many JavaScript and Ajax libraries you can use to further enhance your web pages.

Appendix C: Reference to JavaScript Objects and Functions
This appendix lists all of the objects and functions that comprise JavaScript.

Appendix D: Chapter 15's Italian Translator and Chapter 17's To Do List Application
The last appendix gives a couple of the book's longest code examples in their entirety.

Companion Website

The *Book of JavaScript* website (http://www.bookofjavascript.com) contains the code examples from each chapter, archived copies of many of the websites mentioned, and lots of script libraries and freeware. You'll find that each chapter has its own directory, complete with the example scripts and relevant images from that chapter, as well as the answer to that chapter's assignment. Here's a rundown of the directories.

/Chapter01, /Chapter02, and so on
Each chapter has its own directory. For example, the code examples from Chapter 1 are available at http://www.bookofjavascript.com/Chapter01.

/Freeware
This directory contains free software you may find useful, including:

- XAMPP webserver and PHP packages for Windows and Linux
- MAMP webserver and PHP packages for Macintosh
- Flock social web browser
- Venkman JavaScript debugger for Firefox
- Firefox 2.0 browser

/Libraries
This directory contains free JavaScript libraries you can cut and paste into your website, including:

- Prototype JavaScript Framework
- Webmonkey Cookie Library
- Sarissa XML Toolkit

/Websites
This directory contains HTML (including JavaScript) and images for many of the websites discussed in the book.

1

WELCOME TO JAVASCRIPT!

Welcome to *The Book of JavaScript*. JavaScript is one of the fastest and easiest ways to make your website truly dynamic— that is, interactive. If you want to spruce up tired-looking pages, you've got the right book.

This book will give you some ready-made JavaScripts you can implement immediately on your website, but, more importantly, it will take you step by step through sample scripts (both hypothetical and real-world examples) so that you understand how JavaScript works. With this understanding you can modify existing scripts to fit your specific needs as well as write scripts from scratch. Your knowledge of JavaScript will grow as you work through the book; each chapter introduces and explores in depth a new JavaScript topic by highlighting its application in real-life situations.

Is JavaScript for You?

If you want a quick, easy way to add interactivity to your website, if the thought of using complex programming languages intimidates you, or if you're interested in programming but simply don't know where to start, JavaScript is for you.

JavaScript, a programming language built into your web browser, is one of the best ways to add interactivity to your website because it's the only cross-browser language that works directly with web browsers. Other languages such as Java, Perl, PHP, and C don't have direct access to the images, forms, and windows that make up a web page.

JavaScript is also very easy to learn. You don't need any special hardware or software, you don't need access to a webserver, and you don't need a degree in computer science to get things working. All you need is a web browser and a text editor such as SimpleText or Notepad.

Finally, JavaScript is a complete programming language, so if you want to learn more about programming, it provides a great introduction. (If you don't give a hoot about programming, that's fine too. There are plenty of places—including this book and its companion website—where you can get prefab scripts to cut and paste right into your pages. But you'll get much more out of the book by using it as a tool for learning JavaScript programming.)

Is This Book for You?

This book assumes you don't have any programming background. Even if you have programmed before, you'll find enough that's new in JavaScript to keep you entertained. One of the best things about JavaScript is that you don't have to be a mega-expert to get it working on your web pages right away. You do need a working knowledge of HTML, however.

The Goals of This Book

The main goal of this book is to get you to the point of writing your own JavaScripts. An important tool in learning to write scripts is the ability to read other people's scripts. JavaScript is a sprawling language, and you can learn thousands of little tricks from other scripts. In fact, once you've finished this book, you'll find that viewing the source code of web pages that use JavaScript is the best way to increase your knowledge.

Each of the following chapters includes JavaScript techniques used in building professional sites. Along the way, I'll point out sites that use the technique described, and by viewing the source code of such sites you'll soon see there are many ways to script. Sometimes going through a site's code reveals interesting aspects of JavaScript that I don't cover in this book.

Beyond learning how to write your own JavaScript and read other people's scripts, I also want you to learn where to look for additional information on JavaScript. As I've noted, the best place to learn new techniques is to view the source code of web pages you find interesting. However, several websites also offer free JavaScripts. I'll be introducing some of these as we go along, but here are a few good examples to get you started:

- http://www.webmonkey.com/reference/javascript_code_library
- http://javascript.internet.com

- http://www.scriptsearch.com/JavaScript/Scripts
- http://www.javascriptsearch.com

Another good place to get information is a JavaScript reference book. *The Book of JavaScript* is primarily a tutorial for learning basic JavaScript and making your website interactive. It's not a complete guide to the language, which includes too many details for even a lengthy introduction to cover. If you're planning to become a true JavaScript master, I suggest picking up *JavaScript: The Definitive Guide* by David Flanagan (O'Reilly, 2006) after making your way through this book. The last 500 or so pages of Flanagan's book list every JavaScript command and the browsers in which it works.

What Can JavaScript Do?

JavaScript can add interactivity to your web pages in a number of ways. This book offers many examples of JavaScript's broad capabilities. The following are just two examples that illustrate what you can do with JavaScript.

The first example (Figure 1-1) is a flashing grid of colored squares (to get the full effect, browse to http://www.bookofjavascript.com/Chapter01/Fig01-01.html), created by a fellow named Taylor way back in 1996. Flashy, isn't it? In this example, a JavaScript function changes the color of a randomly chosen square in the grid every second or so.

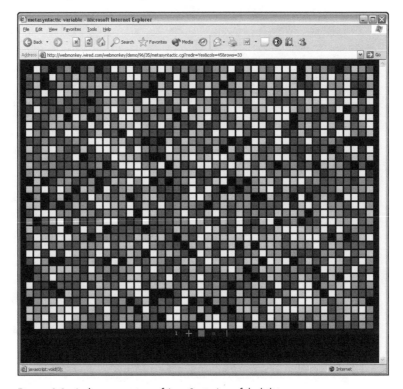

Figure 1-1: A demonstration of JavaScript's artful abilities

Mousing over one of the five icons below the squares (number, plus sign, square, letter, and horizontal line) tells the page to use a new set of images on the grid. For example, mousing over the number icon tells the JavaScript to start replacing the squares with 1s and 0s. This page illustrates four important JavaScript features you'll learn about throughout the book:

- How to change images on a web page
- How to affect web pages over time
- How to add randomness to web pages
- How to dynamically change what's happening on a web page based on an action taken by someone viewing the page

Although Taylor's demo is beautiful, it's not the most practical application of JavaScript. Figure 1-2 (available at http://www.bookofjavascript.com/ Chapter01/Fig01-02.html) shows you a much more practical use of JavaScript that calculates the weight of a fish based on its length. Enter the length and type of fish, and the JavaScript calculates the fish's weight. This fishy code demonstrates JavaScript's ability to read what a visitor has entered into a form, perform a mathematical calculation based on the input, and provide feedback by displaying the results in another part of the form. You may not find calculating a fish's weight a particularly useful application of JavaScript either, but you can use the same skills to calculate a monthly payment on a loan (Chapter 7), score a quiz (Chapter 10), or verify that a visitor has provided a valid email address (Chapter 11).

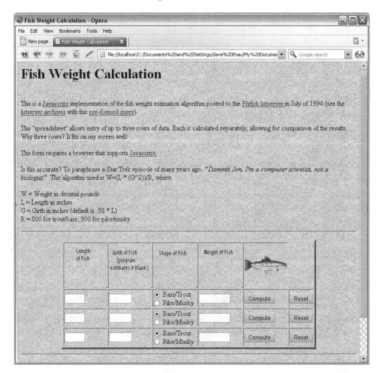

Figure 1-2: How much does my fish weigh?

These are just two examples of the many features JavaScript can add to your websites. Each chapter will cover at least one new application. If you want a preview of what you'll learn, read the first page or so of each chapter.

What Are the Alternatives to JavaScript?

Several other programming languages can add interactivity to web pages, but they all differ from JavaScript in important ways. The four main alternatives are CGI scripting, Java, VBScript, and Flash.

CGI Scripting

Before JavaScript, using CGI scripts was the only way to make web pages do more than hyperlink to other web pages containing fixed text. *CGI* stands for *Common Gateway Interface*. It's a protocol that allows a web browser running on your computer to communicate with programs running on webservers. It is most often used with HTML forms—pages where the user enters information and submits it for processing. For example, the user might see a web page containing places for entering the length and selecting the type of a fish, as well as a Compute button. When the user keys in the length, selects the type, and clicks the button, the information is sent to a CGI script on the server. The CGI script (which is probably written in a programming language like Perl, PHP, or C) receives the information, calculates the weight of the fish, and sends the answer, coded as an HTML page, back to the browser.

CGI scripts are very powerful, but because they reside on webservers, they have some drawbacks.

The Need for Back-and-Forth Communication

First, the connection between your web browser and the webserver limits the speed of your web page's interactivity. This may not sound like a big problem, but imagine the following scenario: You're filling out an order form with a dozen entry fields including name, address, and phone number (see Figure 1-3), but you forget to fill out the phone number and address fields. When you click the Submit button to send the information across the Internet to the webserver, the CGI script sees that you didn't fill out the form completely and sends a message back across the Internet requesting that you finish the job. This cycle could take quite a while over a slow connection. If you fill out the form incorrectly again, you have to wait through another cycle. People find this process tiresome, especially if they're customers who want their orders processed quickly.

With JavaScript, though, the programs you write run in the browser itself. This means that the browser can make sure you've filled out the form correctly before sending the form's contents to the webserver. JavaScript thus reduces the time your information spends traveling between the browser and the server.

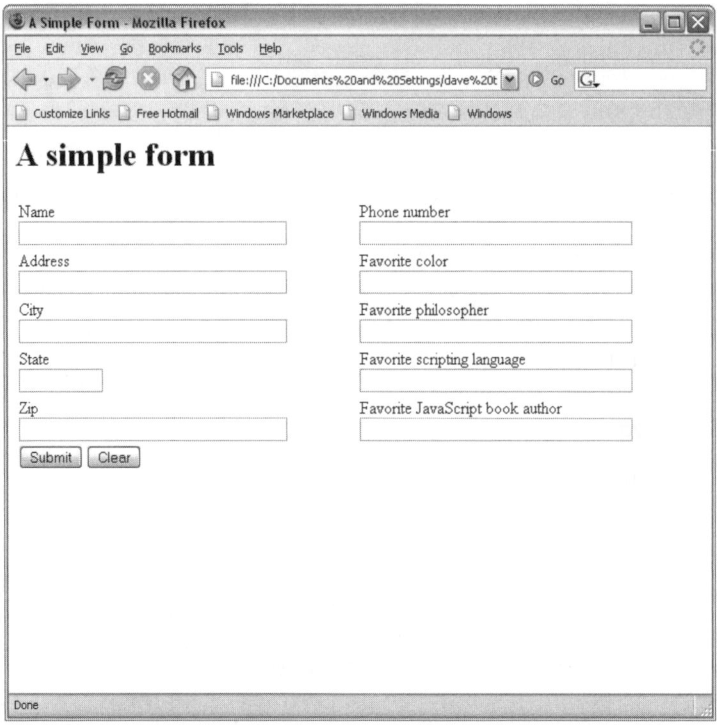

Figure 1-3: A simple order form

Server Overload by Concurrent Access

Another drawback to CGI scripts is that a webserver running a CGI program can get bogged down if too many people call the script simultaneously (for example, if too many fishermen decided to run the weight calculator and click the Compute button at the same time). Serving up HTML pages is pretty easy for a webserver. However, some CGI scripts take a long time to run on a machine, and each time someone calls the script, the server has to start up another copy of it. As more and more people try to run the script, the server slows down progressively. If a thousand people are trying to run the script at once, the server might take so long to respond that either the user or the browser gives up, thinking the server is dead. This problem doesn't exist in JavaScript because its scripts run on each visitor's web browser—not on the webserver.

Security Restrictions

A third problem with CGI scripts is that not everyone has access to the parts of a webserver that can run CGI scripts. Since a CGI script can conceivably crash a webserver or exploit security flaws, system administrators generally guard these areas, only allowing fellow administrators access. If you have Internet access through an Internet service provider (ISP), you may not be allowed to write CGI scripts. If you are designing web pages for a company, you may not be given access to the CGI-enabled areas of the webserver.

JavaScript, on the other hand, goes right into the HTML of a web page. If you can write a web page, you can put JavaScript in the page without permission from recalcitrant administrators.

VBScript

The language most similar to JavaScript is Microsoft's proprietary language, VBScript (*VB* stands for *Visual Basic*). Like JavaScript, VBScript runs on your web browser and adds interactivity to web pages. However, VBScript works only on computers running Internet Explorer (IE) on Microsoft Windows, so unless you want to restrict your readership to people who use IE on Windows, you should go with JavaScript.

Java

Although JavaScript and Java have similar names, they aren't the same. Netscape, now a part of AOL, initially created JavaScript to provide interactivity for web pages, whereas Sun Microsystems wrote Java as a general programming language that works on all kinds of operating systems.

Flash

Flash is a tool from Macromedia developed to add animation and interactivity to websites. Almost all modern browsers can view Flash animations or can easily download the Flash plug-in. Flash animations look great, and a basic Flash animation requires no programming skills at all. To create Flash animations, however, you must purchase a Flash product from Macromedia.

While some people consider Flash and JavaScript to be competitors, that's not the case. In fact, you can call JavaScript programs from Flash, and you can manipulate Flash animations using JavaScript. Web page designers will often blend the two, using Flash for animations and JavaScript for interactivity that does not involve animations. Flash animations can also be made more interactive using a language called ActionScript, which is almost exactly like JavaScript.

JavaScript's Limitations

Yes, JavaScript does have limitations, but these limitations are natural and unavoidable by-products of its main purpose: to add interactivity to your web pages.

JavaScript Can't Talk to Servers

One of JavaScript's drawbacks is also its main strength: It works entirely within the web browser. As we've seen, this cuts down on the amount of time your browser spends communicating with a webserver. On the other hand, this also means that JavaScript can't communicate with other machines and therefore can't handle some server tasks you may need to do.

For example, JavaScript can't aggregate information collected from your users. If you want to write a survey that asks your visitors a couple of questions, stores their answers in a database, and sends a thank-you email when they finish, you'll have to use a program that runs on your webserver. As we'll see in Chapter 7, JavaScript can make the survey run more smoothly, but once a visitor has finished filling out the questions, JavaScript can't store the information on the server, because it can't contact the server. In order to store the survey information, you need to use a program that runs on a webserver. Sending email with JavaScript is also impossible, because to send email JavaScript would have to contact a mail server. Again, you need a server-side program for this job.

Although JavaScript can't directly control programs that run on webservers, it can ask webservers to run programs, and it can send information to those programs. We'll see examples of that in Chapters 7 and 14, and we'll get a taste for writing server-side programs in Chapters 15 and 16.

JavaScript Can't Create Graphics

Another of JavaScript's limitations is that it can't create its own graphics. Whereas more complicated languages can draw pictures, JavaScript can only manipulate existing pictures (that is, GIF or JPEG files). Luckily, because JavaScript can manipulate created images in so many ways, you shouldn't find this too limiting.

JavaScript Works Differently in Different Browsers

Perhaps the most annoying problem with JavaScript is that it works somewhat differently in different browsers. JavaScript was introduced in 1996 by Netscape in version 2 of Netscape Navigator. Since then, JavaScript has changed, and every browser implements a slightly different version of it—often adding browser-specific features. Luckily, starting in the late 1990s, the European Computer Manufacturers Association (ECMA) began publishing standards for JavaScript, which they call ECMAScript. About 99 percent of all browsers being used today comply with at least version 3 of the ECMA standard. These include Internet Explorer version 5.5 and later, Netscape version 6 and later, Mozilla, Firefox, all versions of Safari, and Opera version 5 and later. Because almost all browsers currently in use adhere to version 3 of the ECMA standard, I'll be using that as the standard version of JavaScript in the book. Where incompatibilities between browsers arise, I'll point them out.

Getting Started

We're about ready to begin. To write JavaScripts, you need a web browser and a text editor. Any text editor will do: Notepad or WordPad in Windows and SimpleText on a Macintosh are the simplest choices. Microsoft Word or Corel's WordPerfect will work as well. You can also use a text editor such as BBEdit or HomeSite, which are designed to work with HTML and JavaScript.

Some tools for building websites will actually write JavaScript for you— for example, Adobe's Dreamweaver and GoLive. These tools work fine when you want to write JavaScripts for common features such as image rollovers and you know you'll never want to change them. Unfortunately, the JavaScript often ends up much longer than necessary, and you may find it difficult to understand and change to suit your needs. Unless you want a JavaScript that works exactly like one provided by the package you've purchased, you're often best off writing scripts by hand. Of course, you can also use one of these tools to figure out how you want your page to behave and then go back and rewrite the script to suit your specific needs.

NOTE *Always save documents as text only, and end their names with .html or .htm. If you're using Microsoft Word or WordPerfect and you don't save your documents as text-only HTML or HTM files, both programs will save your documents in formats web browsers can't read. If you try to open a web page you've written and the browser shows a lot of weird characters you didn't put in your document, go back and make sure you've saved it as text only.*

Where JavaScript Goes on Your Web Pages

Now let's get down to some JavaScript basics. Figure 1-4 shows you the thinnest possible skeleton of an HTML page with JavaScript.

```
<html>
<head>
<title>JavaScript Skeleton</title>
❶ <script type = "text/javascript">
// JavaScript can go here!
// But no HTML!
❷ </script>
</head>
<body>
<script type = "text/javascript">
// JavaScript can go here too!
// But no HTML!
</script>
</body>
</html>
```

Figure 1-4: An HTML page with JavaScript

In Figure 1-4, you can see the JavaScript between the `<script type = "text/javascript">` and `</script>` tags in ❶ and ❷.

Note that you can also start JavaScript with this `<script>` tag:

```
<script language = "JavaScript">
```

Although this will work in all browsers, it's better to stick to the official format:

```
<script type = "text/javascript">
```

If you feel like being extra clear, you can explicitly state which version of JavaScript your script will support. ECMAScript version 3 is also called JavaScript version 1.5. To tell a browser to run the JavaScript only if it understands JavaScript version 1.5, you can use this <script> tag:

```
<script type = "text/javascript" language = "JavaScript1.5">
```

Unfortunately, not all browsers check the language attribute for a version number, and the ones that don't check are, of course, the ones that don't understand JavaScript 1.5. So those browsers will happily try to run your JavaScript and will probably generate a JavaScript error. I'll talk more about ways to deal with older browsers in the next section and throughout the book. All in all, I recommend just sticking with <script type = "text/javascript">.

With one exception, which Chapter 4 will cover, all JavaScript goes between the open <script> and close </script> tags. Furthermore, you can't include any HTML between <script> and </script>. Between those tags, your browser assumes that everything it sees is JavaScript. If it sees HTML in there, or anything else it can't interpret as JavaScript, it gets confused and gives you an error message.

These JavaScript tags can go in either the head (between <head> and </head>) or the body (between <body> and </body>) of your HTML page. It doesn't matter too much where you put them, although you're generally best off putting as much JavaScript in the head as possible. That way you don't have to look for it all over your web pages.

One final thing worth mentioning here is that the lines that start with two slashes are JavaScript comments. The browser ignores any text that appears after two slashes. Documenting your work with comments is extremely important, because programming languages aren't easily understood. The script you're writing may make perfect sense while you're writing it, but a few days later, when you want to make a little modification, you might spend hours just figuring out what you wrote the first time. If you comment your code, you'll have a better chance to save yourself the hassle of remembering what you were thinking when you wrote that bizarre code at 2 AM in the midst of what seemed like an amazingly lucid caffeine haze.

Dealing with Older Browsers

There's a slight problem with the JavaScript skeleton in Figure 1-4 (besides the fact that it doesn't really have any JavaScript in it): Netscape didn't introduce the <script> tag until version 2.0 of Netscape Navigator, so any browser released before 1997 won't recognize the tag.

When a browser sees an HTML tag it doesn't understand, it just ignores that tag. That's generally a good thing. However, a browser that doesn't understand JavaScript will write your lines of JavaScript to the browser as text. Figure 1-5 shows how the JavaScript skeleton in Figure 1-4 would be displayed in an older browser.

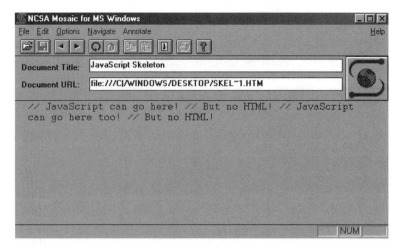

Figure 1-5: What Figure 1-4 would display in an older browser

Although more than 99 percent of the browsers in use today understand JavaScript, most popular sites (Google, for example) still add lines like ❶ and ❷ of Figure 1-6, to hide their JavaScript from browsers that don't understand JavaScript.

```
   <script type = "text/javascript">
❶  <!-- hide me from older browsers
   // JavaScript goes here
❷  // show me -->
   </script>
```

Figure 1-6: Hiding JavaScript from browsers that don't understand it

The important symbols are the <!-- code in ❶ and the // --> comments in ❷. These weird lines work because in HTML, the <!-- and --> are tags that mark the beginning and end of an entire block of comments. Older browsers that don't recognize the <script> tag see the comment markers and therefore don't try to display any of the JavaScript code between them. In JavaScript, on the other hand, <!-- is the beginning of a comment that reaches only to the end of that one line, so browsers that understand JavaScript don't ignore the rest of the JavaScript between ❶ and ❷. The words in the tags (hide me from older browsers and show me) aren't important; they're just there to help you understand the code better. You can make those whatever you want or just leave them out entirely. It's the <!-- and // --> tags that are important.

This trick may be a bit tough to understand at first. If so, don't worry—just remember to put the <!-- tag on its own line right after <script> and the // --> tag on its own line right before </script>, and people with older browsers will thank you.

Your First JavaScript

It's time to run your first JavaScript program. I'll explain the code in Figure 1-7 in the next chapter, so for now, just type the code into your text editor, save it as my_first_program.html, and then run it in your browser. If you don't want to type it all in, run the example at http://www.bookofjavascript.com/Chapter01/Fig01-07.html.

```
<html>
<head>
<title>JavaScript Skeleton</title>
</head>
<body>
<script type = "text/javascript">
<!-- hide me from older browsers
// say Hello, world!
➊ alert("Hello, world!");
// show me -->
</script>
</body>
</html>
```

Figure 1-7: Your first JavaScript program

When a browser reads this file, the JavaScript in ➊ instructs the browser to put up a little window with the words *Hello, world!* in it. Figure 1-8 shows you what this looks like in a web browser. Traditionally, this is the first script you write in any programming language. It gets you warmed up for the fun to come.

Figure 1-8: Window launched by the "Hello, world!" script

Summary

Congratulations—you're now on your way to becoming a bona fide JavaScripter! This chapter has given you all the basic tools you need and has shown you how to get a very basic JavaScript program running. If you followed everything here, you now know:

- Some of the great things JavaScript can do
- How JavaScript compares to CGI scripting, VBScript, Java, and Flash

- JavaScript's main limitations
- Where JavaScript goes on the page
- How to write JavaScript older browsers won't misunderstand

Assignment

Try typing Figure 1-7 into a text editor and running it in a web browser. You'll find the next chapter's assignments hard to do if you can't get Figure 1-7 to work.

If you're sure you've recreated Figure 1-7 exactly and it's not working, make sure you're saving the file as text only. You may also find it helpful to peruse Chapter 14, which discusses ways to fix broken code. Although you may not understand everything in that chapter, you may find some helpful tips.

If it's still not working, try running the version of Figure 1-7 at http://www.bookofjavascript.com/Chapter01/Fig01-07.html. If that doesn't work, you may be using a browser that doesn't support JavaScript, or your browser may be set to reject JavaScript. If you're sure you're using a browser that supports JavaScript (Netscape 2.0 and later versions, and Internet Explorer 3.0 and later), check your browser's options and make sure it's set to run JavaScript.

Once you're comfortable with the concepts covered in this chapter, you'll be ready to write some code!

2

USING VARIABLES AND BUILT-IN FUNCTIONS TO UPDATE YOUR WEB PAGES AUTOMATICALLY

With JavaScript you can update the content of your pages automatically—every day, every hour, or every second. In this chapter, I'll focus on a simple script that automatically changes the date on your web page.

Along the way you'll learn:

- How JavaScript uses variables to remember simple items such as names and numbers
- How JavaScript keeps track of more complicated items such as dates
- How to use JavaScript functions to write information to your web page

Before getting into the nuts and bolts of functions and variables, let's take a look at a couple of examples of web pages that automatically update themselves, starting with the European Space Agency (http://www.esa.int). As you can see in Figure 2-1, the ESA's home page shows you the current date. Rather than change the home page every day, the ESA uses JavaScript to change the date automatically.

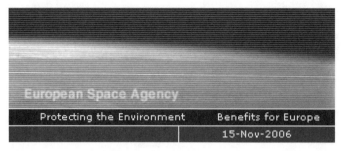

Figure 2-1: Using JavaScript to display the current date

An even more frequently updated page is the home page of the *Book of JavaScript* website (http://www.bookofjavascript.com), which updates the time as well as the date (see Figure 2-2). You don't have to sit in front of your computer, updating the dates and times on your websites. JavaScript can set you free! The ability to write HTML to web pages dynamically is one of JavaScript's most powerful features.

Figure 2-2: Dynamically updating the date and time

To understand how to update the date and time on the page, you'll first have to learn about variables, strings, and functions. Your homework assignment at the end of this chapter will be to figure out how to add seconds to the time.

Variables Store Information

Think back to those glorious days of algebra class when you learned about variables and equations. For example, if $x = 2$, $y = 3$, and $z = x + y$, then $z = 5$. In algebra, variables like x, y, and z store or hold the place of numbers. In JavaScript and other programming languages, variables also store other kinds of information.

Syntax of Variables

The *syntax* of variables (the set of rules for defining and using variables) is slightly different in JavaScript from what it was in your algebra class. Figure 2-3 illustrates the syntax of variables in JavaScript with a silly script that figures out how many seconds there are in a day.

NOTE   *Figure 2-3 does not write the results of the JavaScript to the web page—I'll explain how to do that in Figure 2-4.*

```
<html>
<head>
<title>Seconds in a Day</title>

<script type = "text/javascript">
<!-- hide me from older browsers
```

❶ `var seconds_per_minute = 60;`
   `var minutes_per_hour = 60;`
   `var hours_per_day = 24;`

❷ `var seconds_per_day = seconds_per_minute * minutes_per_hour * hours_per_day;`

   `// show me -->`
❸ `</script>`
   `</head>`
   `<body>`

   `<h1>Know how many seconds are in a day?</h1>`
   `<h2>I do!</h2>`

   `</body>`
   `</html>`

Figure 2-3: Defining and using variables

There's a lot going on here, so let's take it line by line. Line ❶ is a *statement* (a statement in JavaScript is like a sentence in English), and it says to JavaScript, "Create a variable called seconds_per_minute and set its value to 60." Notice that ❶ ends with a semicolon. Semicolons in JavaScript are like periods in English: They mark the end of a statement (for example, one that defines a variable, as above). As you see more and more statements, you'll get the hang of where to place semicolons.

The first word, var, introduces a variable for the first time—you don't need to use it after the first instance, no matter how many times you employ the variable in the script.

NOTE   *Many people don't use var in their code. Although most browsers let you get away without it, it's always a good idea to put var in front of a variable the first time you use it. (You'll see why when I talk about writing your own functions in Chapter 6.)*

Naming Variables

Notice that the variable name in ❶ is pretty long—unlike algebraic variables, it's not just a single letter like x, y, or z. When using variables in JavaScript (or any programming language), you should give them names that indicate what piece of information they hold. The variable in ❶ stores the number of seconds in a minute, so I've called it seconds_per_minute.

If you name your variables descriptively, your code will be easier to understand while you're writing it, and much easier to understand when you return to it later for revision or enhancement. Also, no matter which programming language you use, you'll spend about 50 percent of your coding time finding and getting rid of your mistakes. This is called *debugging*—and it's a lot easier to debug code when the variables have descriptive names. You'll learn more about debugging in Chapter 14.

There are four rules for naming variables in JavaScript:

1. The initial character must be a letter, an underscore, or a dollar sign, but subsequent characters may be numbers as well.

2. No spaces are allowed.

3. Variables are case sensitive, so `my_cat` is different from `My_Cat`, which in turn is different from `mY_cAt`. As far as the computer is concerned, each of these would represent a different variable—even if that's not what the programmer intended. (You'll see an example of this in the section "alert()" on page 22.) To avoid any potential problems with capitalization, I use lowercase for all my variables, with underscores (_) where there would be spaces in ordinary English.

4. You can't use reserved words. *Reserved words* are terms used by the JavaScript language itself. For instance, you've seen that the first time you use a variable, you should precede it with the word var. Because JavaScript uses the word var to introduce variables, you can't use var as a variable name. Different browsers have different reserved words, so the best thing to do is avoid naming variables with words that seem like terms JavaScript might use. Most reserved words are fairly short, so using longer, descriptive variable names keeps you fairly safe. I often call my variables things like `the_cat`, or `the_date` because there are no reserved words that start with the word *the*. If you have a JavaScript that you're *certain* is correct, but it isn't working for some reason, it might be because you've used a reserved word.

Arithmetic with Variables

Line ❷ in Figure 2-3 introduces a new variable called `seconds_per_day` and sets it equal to the product of the other three variables using an asterisk (*), which means multiplication. A plus sign (+) for addition, a minus sign (-) for subtraction, and a slash (/) for division represent the other major arithmetic functions.

When the browser finishes its calculations in our example, it reaches the end of the JavaScript in the head (❸) and goes down to the body of the HTML. There it sees two lines of HTML announcing that the page knows how many seconds there are in a day.

```
<h1>Know how many seconds are in a day?</h1>
<h2>I do!</h2>
```

So now you have a page that knows how many seconds there are in a day. Big deal, right? Wouldn't it be better if you could tell your visitors what the answer is? Well, you can, and it's not very hard.

Write Here Right Now: Displaying Results

JavaScript uses the write() function to write text to a web page. Figure 2-4 shows how to use write() to let your visitors know how many seconds there are in a day. (The new code is in bold.) Figure 2-5 shows the page this code displays.

```html
<html>
<head>
<title>Seconds in a Day</title>

<script type = "text/javascript">
<!-- hide me from older browsers

var seconds_per_minute = 60;
var minutes_per_hour = 60;
var hours_per_day = 24;

var seconds_per_day = seconds_per_minute * minutes_per_hour * hours_per_day;

// show me -->
</script>
</head>
<body>

<h1>My calculations show that . . .</h1>

<script type = "text/javascript">
<!-- hide me from older browsers

➊ window.document.write("there are ");
window.document.write(seconds_per_day);
window.document.write(" seconds in a day.");

// show me -->
</script>

</body>
</html>
```

Figure 2-4: Using write() to write to a web page

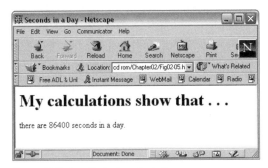

Figure 2-5: JavaScript's calculations

Line-by-Line Analysis of Figure 2-4

Line ❶ in Figure 2-4 writes the words *there are* to the web page (only the words between the quotes appear on the page). Don't worry about all the periods and what window and document really mean right now (I'll cover these topics in depth in Chapter 4, when we talk about image swaps). For now, just remember that if you want to write something to a web page, use `window.document.write("whatever");`, placing the text you want written to the page between the quotes. If you don't use quotes around your text, as in

```
window.document.write(seconds_per_day);
```

then JavaScript interprets the text between the parentheses as a variable and writes whatever is stored in the variable (in this case, seconds_per_day) to the web page (see Figure 2-6). If you accidentally ask JavaScript to write out a variable you haven't defined, you'll get a JavaScript error.

Be careful not to put quotes around variable names if you want JavaScript to know you're talking about a variable. If you add quotes around the seconds_per_day variable, like this:

```
window.document.write("seconds_per_day");
```

then JavaScript will write *seconds_per_day* to the web page. The way JavaScript knows the difference between variables and regular text is that regular text has quotes around it and a variable doesn't.

Strings

Any series of characters between quotes is called a *string*. (You'll be seeing lots of strings throughout this book.) Strings are a basic type of information, like numbers—and like numbers, you can assign them to variables.

To assign a string to a variable, you'd write something like this:

```
var my_name = "thau!";
```

The word thau! is the string assigned to the variable my_name.

You can stick strings together with a plus sign (+), as shown in the bolded section of Figure 2-6. This code demonstrates how to write output to your page using strings.

```
<html>
<head>
<title>Seconds in a Day</title>
<script type = "text/javascript">
<!-- hide me from older browsers

var seconds_per_minute = 60;
var minutes_per_hour = 60;
var hours_per_day = 24;

var seconds_per_day = seconds_per_minute * minutes_per_hour * hours_per_day;
```

```
// show me -->
</script>
</head>
<body>

<h1>My calculations show that . . .</h1>

<script type = "text/javascript">
<!-- hide me from older browsers
```
❶ `var first_part = "there are ";`
❷ `var last_part = " seconds in a day.";`
❸ `var whole_thing = first_part + seconds_per_day + last_part;`

```
window.document.write(whole_thing);

// show me -->
</script>

</body>
</html>
```

Figure 2-6: Putting strings together

Line-by-Line Analysis of Figure 2-6

Line ❶ in Figure 2-6,

```
var first_part = "there are ";
```

assigns the string "there are" to the variable first_part. Line ❷,

```
var last_part = " seconds in a day.";
```

sets the variable last_part to the string "seconds in a day." Line ❸ glues
together the values stored in first_part, seconds_per_day, and last_part.
The end result is that the variable whole_thing includes the whole string
you want to print to the page, *there are 86400 seconds in a day.* The
window.document.write() line then writes whole_thing to the web page.

NOTE   *The methods shown in Figures 2-4 and 2-6 are equally acceptable ways of writing*
there are 86400 seconds in a day. *However, there are times when storing strings
in variables and then assembling them with the plus sign (+) is clearly the best way
to go. We'll see a case of this when we finally get to putting the date on a page.*

More About Functions

Whereas variables store information, *functions* process that information.
     All functions take the form *functionName*(). Sometimes there's some-
thing in the parentheses and sometimes there isn't. You've already seen
one of JavaScript's many built-in functions, window.document.write(), which

writes whatever lies between the parentheses to the web page. Before diving into the date functions that you'll need to write the date to your web page, I'll talk about two interesting functions, just so you get the hang of how functions work.

alert()

One handy function is alert(), which puts a string into a little announcement box (also called an *alert box*). Figure 2-7 demonstrates how to call an alert(), and Figure 2-8 shows what the alert box looks like.

```
<html>
<head>
<title>An Alert Box</title>

<script type = "text/javascript">
<!-- hide me from older browsers
❶ alert("This page was written by thau!");
// show me -->
</script>

<body>
❷ <h1>To code, perchance to function</h1>
</body>
</html>
```

Figure 2-7: Creating an alert box

The first thing visitors see when they come to the page Figure 2-7 creates is an alert box announcing that I wrote the page (Figure 2-8). The alert box appears because of ❶, which tells JavaScript to execute its alert() function.

While the alert box is on the screen, the browser stops doing any work. Clicking OK in the alert box makes it go away and allows the browser to finish drawing the web page. In this case, that means writing the words *To code, perchance to function* to the page (❷).

Figure 2-8: The alert box

The alert() function is useful for troubleshooting when your JavaScript isn't working correctly. Let's say you've typed in Figure 2-6, but when you run the code, you see that you must have made a typo—it says there are 0 seconds in a day instead of 86400. You can use alert() to find out how the different variables are set before multiplication occurs. The script in Figure 2-9 contains an error that causes the script to say there are "undefined" seconds in a year; and to track down the error, I've added alert() function statements that tell you why this problem is occurring.

```
<html>
<head>
<title>Seconds in a Day</title>

<script type = "text/javascript">
<!-- hide me from older browsers

var seconds_per_minute = 60;
var minutes_per_hour = 60;
❶ var Hours_per_day = 24;
❷ alert("seconds per minute is: " + seconds_per_minute);
❸ alert("minutes per hour is: " + minutes_per_hour);
❹ alert("hours per day is: " + hours_per_day);
❺ var seconds_per_day = seconds_per_minute * minutes_per_hour * hours_per_day;


// show me -->
</script>
</head>
<body>

<h1>My calculations show that . . .</h1>

<script type = "text/javascript">
<!-- hide me from older browsers

var first_part = "there are ";
var last_part = " seconds in a day.";
var whole_thing = first_part + seconds_per_day + last_part;

window.document.write(whole_thing);

// show me -->
</script>

</body>
</html>
```

Figure 2-9: Using alert() to find out what's wrong

Line-by-Line Analysis of Figure 2-9

The problem with this script is in ❶. Notice the accidental capitalization of the first letter in Hours_per_day. This is what causes the script to misbehave. Line ❺ multiplies the other numbers by the variable hours_per_day, but hours_per_day was not set—remember, JavaScript considers it a different variable from Hours_per_day—so JavaScript thinks its value is either 0 or undefined, depending on your browser. Multiplying anything by 0 results in 0, so the script calculates that there are 0 seconds in a day. The same holds true for browsers that think hours_per_day is undefined. Multiplying anything by something undefined results in the answer being undefined, so the browser will report that there are undefined seconds in a day.

This script is short, making it easy to see the mistake. However, in longer scripts it's sometimes hard to figure out what's wrong. I've added ❷, ❸, and ❹ in this example to help diagnose the problem. Each of these statements puts a variable into an alert box. The alert in ❷ will say seconds_per_minute is: 60. The alert in ❹ will say hours_per_day is: 0, or, depending on your browser, the alert won't appear at all. Either way, you'll know there's a problem with the hours_per_day variable. If you can't figure out the mistake by reading the script, you'll find this type of information very valuable. Alerts are very useful debugging tools.

prompt()

Another helpful built-in function is prompt(), which asks your visitor for some information and then sets a variable equal to whatever your visitor types. Figure 2-10 shows how you might use prompt() to write a form letter.

```html
<html>
<head>
<title>A Form Letter</title>
<script type = "text/javascript">
<!-- hide me from older browsers
```
❶ `var the_name = prompt("What's your name?", "put your name here");`
```
// show me -->
</script>
</head>
<body>
```
❷ `<h1>Dear`
```
<script type = "text/javascript">
<!-- hide me from older browsers

document.write(the_name);

// show me -->
</script>

,</h1>

Thank you for coming to my web page.

</body>
</html>
```

Figure 2-10: Using prompt() to write a form letter

Notice that prompt() in ❶ has two strings inside the parentheses: "What's your name?" and "put your name here". If you run the code in Figure 2-10, you'll see a prompt box that resembles Figure 2-11. (I've used the Opera browser in this illustration; prompt boxes will look somewhat different in IE and other browsers.) If you type Rumpelstiltskin and click OK, the page responds with *Dear Rumpelstiltskin, Thank you for coming to my web page.*

Figure 2-11: Starting a form letter with a prompt box

The text above the box where your visitors will type their name ("What's your name?") is the first string in the prompt function; the text inside the box ("put your name here") is the second string. If you don't want anything inside the box, put two quotes ("") right next to each other in place of the second string to keep that space blank:

```
var the_name = prompt("What's your name?", "");
```

If you look at the JavaScript in the body (starting in ❷), you'll see how to use the variable the_name. First write the beginning of the heading to the page using normal HTML. Then launch into JavaScript and use document.write(the_name) to write whatever name the visitor typed into the prompt box for your page. If your visitor typed yertle the turtle into that box, *yertle the turtle* gets written to the page. Once the item in the_name is written, you close the JavaScript tag, write a comma and the rest of the heading using regular old HTML, and then continue with the form letter. Nifty, eh?

The prompt() function is handy because it enables your visitor to supply the variable information. In this case, after the user types a name into the prompt box in Figure 2-10 (thereby setting the variable the_name), your script can use the supplied information by calling that variable.

Parameters

The words inside the parentheses of functions are called *parameters*. The document.write() function requires one parameter: a string to write to your web page. The prompt() function takes two parameters: a string to write above the box and a string to write inside the box.

Parameters are the only aspect of a function you can control; they are your means of providing the function with the information it needs to do its job. With a prompt() function, for example, you can't change the color of the box, how many buttons it has, or anything else; in using a predefined prompt box, you've decided that you don't need to customize the box's appearance. You can only change the parameters it specifically provides—

namely, the text and heading of the prompt you want to display. You'll learn more about controlling what functions do when you write your own functions in Chapter 6.

Writing the Date to Your Web Page

Now that you know about variables and functions, you can print the date to your web page. To do so, you must first ask JavaScript to check the local time on your visitor's computer clock:

```
var now = new Date();
```

The first part of this line, var now =, should look familiar. It sets the variable now to some value. The second part, new Date(), is new; it creates an object.

Objects store data that require multiple pieces of information, such as a particular moment in time. For example, in JavaScript you need an object to describe *2:30 PM on Saturday, January 7, 2006, in San Francisco.* That's because it requires many different bits of information: the time, day, month, date, and year, as well as some representation (in relation to Greenwich Mean Time) of the user's local time. As you can imagine, working with an object is a bit more complicated than working with just a number or a string.

Because dates are so rich in information, JavaScript has a built-in Date object to contain those details. When you want the user's current date and time, you use new Date() to tell JavaScript to create a Date object with all the correct information.

NOTE   *You must capitalize the letter D in Date to tell JavaScript you want to use the built-in Date object. If you don't capitalize it, JavaScript won't know what kind of object you're trying to create, and you'll get an error message.*

Built-in Date Functions

Now that JavaScript has created your Date object, let's extract information from it using JavaScript's built-in date functions. To extract the current year, use the Date object's getYear() function:

```
var now = new Date();
var the_year = now.getYear();
```

Date and Time Methods

In the code above, the variable now is a Date object, and the function getYear() is a method of the Date object. *Methods* are simply functions that are built in to objects. For example, the getYear() function is built in to the Date object and gets the object's year. Because the function is part of the Date object, it is called a method. To use the getYear() method to get the year of the date stored in the variable now, you would write:

```
now.getYear()
```

Table 2-1 lists commonly used date methods. (You can find a complete list of date methods in Appendix C.)

Table 2-1: Commonly Used Date and Time Methods

Name	Description
getDate()	The day of the month as an integer from 1 to 31
getDay()	The day of the week as an integer where 0 is Sunday and 1 is Monday
getHours()	The hour as an integer between 0 and 23
getMinutes()	The minutes as an integer between 0 and 59
getMonth()	The month as an integer between 0 and 11 where 0 is January and 11 is December
getSeconds()	The seconds as an integer between 0 and 59
getTime()	The current time in milliseconds where 0 is January 1, 1970, 00:00:00
getYear()	The year, but this format differs from browser to browser

NOTE *Notice that* getMonth() *returns a number between 0 and 11; if you want to show the month to your site's visitors, to be user-friendly you should add 1 to the month after using* getMonth(), *as shown in* ❷ *in Figure 2-12.*

Internet Explorer and various versions of Netscape deal with years in different and strange ways:

- Some versions of Netscape, such as Netscape 4.0 for the Mac, always return the current year minus 1900. So if it's the year 2010, getYear() returns 110.

- Other versions of Netscape return the full four-digit year except when the year is in the twentieth century, in which case they return just the last two digits.

- Netscape 2.0 can't deal with dates before 1970 at all. Any date before January 1, 1970 is stored as December 31, 1969.

- In Internet Explorer, getYear() returns the full four-digit year if the year is after 1999 or before 1900. If the year is between 1900 and 1999, it returns the last two digits.

You'd figure a language created in 1995 wouldn't have the Y2K problem, but the ways of software developers are strange. Later in this chapter I'll show you how to fix this bug.

Code for Writing the Date and Time

Now let's put this all together. To get the day, month, and year, we use the getDate(), getMonth(), and getYear() methods. To get the hour and the minutes, we use getHours() and getMinutes().

Figure 2-12 shows you the complete code for writing the date and time (without seconds) to a web page, as seen on the *Book of JavaScript* home page.

```
<html>
<head><title>The Book of JavaScript</title>
<script type = "text/javascript">
<!-- hide me from older browsers
// get the Date object
//
❶ var date = new Date();

// get the information out of the Date object
//
var month = date.getMonth();
var day = date.getDate();
var year = date.getYear();
var hour = date.getHours();
var minutes = date.getMinutes();
❷ month = month + 1;  // because January is month 0
// fix the Y2K bug
//
❸ year = fixY2K(year);

// fix the minutes by adding a 0 in front if it's less than 10
//
❹ minutes = fixTime(minutes);

// create the date string
//
❺ var date_string = month + "/" + day + "/" + year;
❻ var time_string = hour + ":" + minutes;
❼ var date_time_string = "Today is " + date_string + ".  The time is now " +
    time_string + ".";

// This is the Y2K fixer function--don't worry about how this works,
// but if you want it in your scripts, you can cut and paste it.
//
function fixY2K(number) {
  if (number < 1000) {
    number = number + 1900;
  }
  return number;
}

// This is the time fixer function--don't worry about how this works either.
function fixTime(number) {
  if (number < 10) {
    number = "0" + number;
  }
  return number;
}

// show me -->
</script>
</head>
<body>
```

```
❽ <h1>Welcome to the Book of JavaScript Home Page!</h1>

   <script type = "text/javascript">
   <!-- hide me from older browsers
❾ document.write(date_time_string);
   // show me -->
   </script>
   </body>
   </html>
```

Figure 2-12: Writing the current date and time to a web page

Line-by-Line Analysis of Figure 2-12

Here are a few interesting things in this example.

Getting the Date and Time

The lines from ❶ up until ❷ get the current date and time from the visitor's computer clock and then use the appropriate date methods to extract the day, month, year, hours and minutes. Although I'm using a variable name date in ❶ to store the date, I could have used any variable name there: the_date, this_moment, the_present, or any valid variable name. Don't be fooled into thinking that a variable needs to have the same name as the corresponding JavaScript object; in this case, date just seems like a good name.

Making Minor Adjustments

Before building the strings we will write to the website, we need to make some little adjustments to the date information just collected. Here's how it works:

- Line ❷ adds 1 to the month because getMonth() thinks January is month 0.
- Line ❸ fixes the Y2K problem discussed earlier in the chapter, in which the getYear() method returns the wrong thing on some older browsers. If you feed fixY2K() the year returned by date.getYear(), it will return the correct year. The fixY2K() function is not a built-in JavaScript function. I had to write it myself. Don't worry about how the function works right now.
- Line ❹ fixes a minor formatting issue, using another function that's not built-in. If the script is called at 6 past the hour, date.getMinutes() returns 6. If you don't do something special with that 6, your time will look like 11:6 instead of 11:06. So fixTime() sticks a zero in front of a number if that number is less than 10. You can use fixTime() to fix the seconds too, for your homework assignment.

Getting the String Right

Now that we've made a few minor adjustments, it's time to build the strings. Line ❺ builds the string for the date. Here's the *wrong* way to do it:

```
var date_string = "month / day / year";
```

If you wrote your code this way, you'd get a line that says *Today is month / day / year*. Why? Remember that JavaScript doesn't look up variables if they're inside quotes. So place the variables outside the quote marks and glue everything together using plus signs (+):

```
var date_string = month + "/" + day + "/" + year;
```

This may look a little funny at first, but it's done so frequently that you'll soon grow used to it. Line ❻ creates the string to represent the time. It is very similar to ❺. Line ❼ puts ❺ and ❻ together to create the string that will be written to the website. Lines ❺ through ❼ could all have been written as one long line:

```
var date_time_string = "Today is " + month + "/" + day + "/" + year +
    ". The time is now " + hour + ":" + minutes + ".";
```

However, using three lines makes the code easier for people to read and understand. It's always best to write your code as if other people are going to read it.

What Are Those Other Functions?

The JavaScript between ❼ and ❽ defines the fixY2K() and fixTime() functions. Again, don't worry about these lines for now. We'll cover how to write your own functions in glorious detail in Chapter 6.

JavaScript and HTML

Make sure to place your JavaScript and HTML in the proper order. In Figure 2-12, the welcoming HTML in ❽ precedes the JavaScript that actually writes the date and time in ❾, since the browser first writes that text and then executes the JavaScript. With JavaScript, as with HTML, browsers read from the top of the page down. I've put document.write() in the body so that the actual date information will come after the welcome text. I've put the rest of the JavaScript at the head of the page to keep the body HTML cleaner.

Why document.write()?

Notice that the code in Figure 2-11 uses document.write() instead of window.document.write(). In general, it's fine to drop the word window and the first dot before the word document. In future chapters I'll tell you when the word window must be added.

How the European Space Agency Writes the Date to Its Page

The JavaScript used by the European Space Agency is very much like the code I used for the *Book of JavaScript* web page. One big difference between the two is that the ESA prints out the month using abbreviations like *Jan* and *Feb* for *January* and *February*. They do this using arrays, a topic discussed in Chapter 8, so in Figure 2-13 I've modified their code a bit to focus on topics covered so far.

```
<script type = "text/javascript">
var now = new Date();
var yyyy = now.getFullYear();
var mm = now.getMonth() + 1;
```
❶ `if (10 > mm) mm = '0' + mm;`
```
var dd = now.getDate();
```
❷ `if (10 > dd) dd = '0' + dd;`
```
document.write(dd + '-' + mm + '-' + yyyy);
</script>
```

Figure 2-13: How the European Space Agency writes the date to its page

Everything here should look very familiar to you, except for ❶ and ❷, which will make more sense after you've read Chapter 3. If anything else in the ESA script seems unclear to you, try doing the homework assignment. In fact, do the homework assignment even if it all seems extremely clear. The only way to really learn JavaScript is to do it. Go ahead, give that homework a shot! And enjoy!

Summary

This chapter was chock-full of JavaScript goodness. Here's a review of the most important points for you to understand:

- How to declare and use variables (use var the first time and use valid and descriptive variable names)
- How to write to web pages with document.write()
- How to get the current date from JavaScript with the Date object and its various methods

If you got all that, you're well on your way to becoming a JavaScript superstar. Try the following assignment to test your JavaScript skills.

Assignment

Change the script in Figure 2-12 so that it writes out the seconds as well as the hour and minutes.

If you're feeling like getting ahead of the game, you can try, for a big chunk of extra credit, to change the time from a 24-hour clock to a 12-hour clock. The getHours() method returns the hour as a number between 0 and 23. See if you can figure out how to adjust that time to be between 1 and 12. You'll have to use some tricks I haven't covered in this chapter. If you can't figure this out now, you'll be able to do it by the end of the next chapter.

3

GIVING THE BROWSERS
WHAT THEY WANT

Much to the dismay of web developers everywhere, different browsers implement JavaScript and HTML in slightly different ways. Wouldn't it be great if you could serve each browser exactly the content it could understand?

Fortunately, you can use JavaScript to determine which browser a visitor is using. You can then use that information to deliver content suitable for that specific browser, either by redirecting the visitor to a page containing content especially tailored for that browser or by writing your JavaScripts so that the same page does different things depending on the browser looking at it.

This chapter covers the three topics you need to understand to deliver browser-specific pages using redirects:

- How to determine which browser your visitor is using

- How to redirect the visitor to other pages automatically

- How to send the visitor to the page you want, depending on which browser he or she is using

As in Chapter 2, while learning how to handle an important web authoring task, you'll also be introduced to fundamental elements of the JavaScript language—in this case, if-then statements and related methods for implementing logical decision making in your scripts.

Let's first talk about determining which browser a visitor is using.

A Real-World Example of Browser Detection

Before we get into the details of how browser detection works, let's look at a real-world example.

Netscape, the company that brought you the Netscape Navigator browser, has a complicated home page with lots of interesting features. They've taken great pains to make their home page look good to most browsers, including early versions of their own browser. If you compare the Netscape home page seen with Netscape Navigator 4 (Figure 3-1) to the page seen using Navigator 8 (Figure 3-2), you'll notice some subtle differences. Among other things, the news blurb at the bottom of Figure 3-2 has a little navigational element in the lower-right corner. Clicking the numbers in that corner cycles you through different news blurbs. Figure 3-1 does not have these numbers, probably because there isn't a good way to provide this fancy functionality in the old Netscape Navigator.

Figure 3-1: Netscape Navigator 4 view of Netscape home page

Figure 3-2: Netscape Navigator 8 view of Netscape home page

How does Netscape show the numbers to only those browsers that can provide this feature? There are two steps. First you have to determine which browser your visitor is using. Once you know the browser, you know what JavaScript and HTML features it supports. Then you have to figure out how to control what the person will see based on the known capabilities of the browser.

Browser Detection Methods

A browser is identified by its name (Netscape, Firefox, Internet Explorer, and so on) combined with its version number. Your JavaScript needs to determine both of these items. There are two ways to approach this task: a quick but rough method and a slightly less quick but more accurate method.

Quick-but-Rough Browser Detection

In general, the line

```
var browser_name = navigator.appName;
```

determines who made the browser. If the user is using a Netscape browser, the variable `browser_name` will be set to the string `"Netscape"`. If it's a Microsoft Internet Explorer browser, `browser_name` will be set to `"Microsoft Internet Explorer"`. Every JavaScript-enabled browser must have the variable `navigator.appName`. If you use Opera, `navigator.appName` equals `"Opera"`. Unfortunately, some browsers travel incognito. For example, the `navigator.appName` for Firefox is `"Netscape"`. The JavaScript in Firefox is the same as that for Netscape browsers, so in general, it's fine to treat Firefox browsers as Netscape browsers. But, as you can see, if you want to be sure about the browser being used, you can't rely on `naviagor.appName`.

There's a similar rough method for determining the browser version being used: `navigator.appVersion`. Unfortunately, `navigator.appVersion` isn't just a number but a sometimes cryptic string that varies from browser to browser. For example, the Macintosh browser Safari has this nice, simple `navigator.appVersion` string: `"5.0"`. By contrast, Internet Explorer 6.0 running under Windows XP has a `navigator.appVersion` that looks like this: `"4.0 (compatible; MSIE 6.0; Windows NT 5.1; .NET CLR 1.1.4322)"`. To see the `navigator.appVersion` string for your browser, type this into the browser's address box (where you normally enter web addresses):

```
javascript:alert(navigator.appVersion)
```

If you care only about whether a person is using a 4.0 browser or later, you can pick out the version numbers from those `navigator.appVersion` strings with the `parseFloat()` command, which looks at the string and grabs the first item that resembles a *floating-point number* (a number that contains a decimal point). Thus the line

```
var browser_version = parseFloat(navigator.appVersion);
```

sets the variable `browser_version` to the first number in the `navigator.appVersion` string. For most browsers, this will be the actual version number. For Internet Explorer, it will be 4.0 for any version of the browser 4.0 or later. You can see why I call this method rough.

More Accurate Browser Detection

JavaScript has another variable that contains information about the browser being used: `navigator.userAgent`. This variable identifies both the manufacturer of the browser and its version. As it did with `navigator.appVersion`, however, the formatting of the string varies from browser to browser.

Because the `navigator.userAgent` strings are different from each other, there is no simple way to extract the information you want. Fortunately, people have already written *browser sniffers*: bits of JavaScript that will do all the hard work of browser identification for you. You can find brwsniff.js, which I downloaded from http://jsbrwsniff.sourceforge.net, at http:// www.bookofjavascript.com/Chapter03.

To use this file, put it in the same folder as the web page containing your JavaScript. Then, put this line in the header of your web page:

```
<script type = "text/javascript" src = "brwsniff.js"></script>
```

This tells JavaScript to add the contents of the file named brwsniff.js to your web page. Now you can use the JavaScript stored in that file.

To use the JavaScript in brwsniff.js to determine the name and version of the browser being used to view your web page, add these lines of JavaScript:

```
❶ var browser_info = getBrowser();
❷ var browser_name = browserInfo[0];
❸ var browser_version = browserInfo[1];
```

Line ❶ calls a function in brwsniff.js that reads the `navigator.userAgent` string and compares it to all the different browser version strings it knows. Once it determines the name and version of the browser, the function loads this information into a variable called `browser_info`. All the variables we've seen so far store one piece of information—a string or a number, for example. This `browser_info` variable is an *array*, a type of variable designed to hold multiple items of related information. You'll learn how to work with arrays in Chapter 8. For now it's enough to know that an array is a variable that can store more than one piece of information. Line ❷ puts the first bit of information stored in the array into a variable called `browser_name`. Line ❸ puts the second piece of information stored in `browser_info` into a variable named `browser_version`. Used together, these two variables tell you what kind of browser is viewing the web page. Try the web page in Figure 3-3 on your own browser.

NOTE   *This `<script>` tag does not require the `<!--` and `//-->` to hide it from older browsers because there is no code between the opening and closing tags.*

The quick but rough method of browser detection should work for most situations, especially when you don't need to know exactly which browser is being used. For the cases in which you do need the exact name and version, you should use a browser sniffer like the one just described.

```
<html>
<head>
<title>I Know Which Browser You're Using!</title>
<script type = "text/javascript" src = "brwsniff.js"></script>
</head>
<body>
<script type = "text/javascript">
<!-- hide me from older browsers

var browser_info = getBrowser();
var browser_name = browser_info[0];
var browser_version = browser_info[1];
document.write ("You're using " + browser_name + " version " +
    browser_version);

// show me -->
</script>
</body>
</html>
```

Figure 3-3: Finding the browser version number with a browser sniffer

Redirecting Visitors to Other Pages

Now that you understand browser detection, you can tailor your site to provide information specific to each browser. There are two main ways to do this. First, you can use document.write(), which we saw in the last chapter, to display one message on your page if the site visitor is using Netscape Navigator 4, and a different message on the same page for Internet Explorer 6.0. Alternatively, you can redirect your visitors to separate pages specifically tailored to different browsers. To redirect visitors to another page, you'd write something like this:

```
window.location.href = "http://www.mywebsite.com/page_for_netscape4.html";
```

When JavaScript sees a line like this, it loads the page with the specified URL into the browser.

NOTE   *Are you wondering "What's with all these periods in commands like window.location.href and navigator.appName?" Never fear. I'll address these when I discuss image swaps and dot notation in Chapter 4.*

In general, it's probably best to use document.write() instead of redirecting the user. Because there are so many browsers, trying to maintain a different page for each one can quickly become burdensome. However, if you just want to redirect someone with an older browser to a page that tells them to upgrade, redirection is probably the best way to go.

if-then Statements

Now that you know which browser your visitor is using, you need to learn how to tell JavaScript to write different things depending on the browser being used—in other words, how to implement a *logical test*, choosing between different actions based on specific information. *Branching* is a fundamental technique in any programming or scripting language. Be sure to read this section if you're not already familiar with the concept.

To alter your web pages based on the browser a visitor is using, you tell JavaScript something like, "*If* the visitor is using Internet Explorer, then write this IE-tailored content."

An if-then statement in JavaScript looks like this:

```
if (navigator.appName == "Microsoft Internet Explorer")
{
  // write IE-specific content
  document.write("Welcome, Internet Explorer user!");
}
```

Here's the basic structure of an if-then statement:

```
if (some test)
{
  statement_1;
  statement_2;
  statement_3;
  ...
}
```

NOTE *JavaScript is unforgiving:* if *must be lowercase, and you must put parentheses around the test that follows it.*

The test that appears between the parentheses must be either true or false. If the variable navigator.appName equals "Microsoft Internet Explorer", the test between the parentheses is true, and the statements located between the curly brackets are executed. If the variable doesn't equal "Microsoft Internet Explorer", the test between the parentheses is false, and the statements between the curly brackets aren't executed.

Boolean Expressions

The test in the parentheses after if is a *Boolean expression*—an expression that's either true or false. In JavaScript, a Boolean expression is usually a statement about the values of one or more variables. Table 3-1 lists some of the symbols you'll be using to form Boolean expressions in JavaScript.

NOTE *Boolean expressions are named after George Boole (1815–1864), who invented a way to express logical statements in mathematical form.*

Table 3-1: Symbols in Boolean Expressions

Test	Meaning	Example (All of These Are True)
<	Less than	1 < 3
>	Greater than	3 > 1
==	The same as (equal)	"happy" == "happy", 3 == 3
!=	Different from (not equal)	"happy" != "crabby", 3 != 2
<=	Less than or equal to	2 <= 3, 2 <= 2
>=	Greater than or equal to	3 >= 1, 3 >= 3

Notice in Table 3-1 that you must use two equal signs when you want JavaScript to test for equality in an `if-then` statement Boolean expression. In fact, accidentally using one equal sign instead of two in an `if-then` statement is probably *the* major cause of mind-blowing programming errors. As you learned in Chapter 2, a single equal sign is used to assign a value to a variable. So if you accidentally use only one equal sign, JavaScript thinks you mean to set the variable on the left of the equal sign to the value of whatever is on the right of the equal sign, and it will act as if the test result is always true.

Here's an example of the trauma that this mistake can cause. Say you want to write a JavaScript that puts *Happy Birthday, Mom!* on your web page when it's your mother's birthday. If her birthday were August 6, you might write something like Figure 3-4 (which contains the dreaded error).

If you try this script, you'll see that it *always* prints *Happy Birthday, Mom!* to the web page, which is great for Mom, but probably not what you want.

```
<script type = "text/javascript">
<!-- hide me from older browsers

var today = new Date();
var day = today.getDate();
❶ var month = today.getMonth();

❷ if (month = 7) // remember, January is month 0, so August is month 7
{
❸   if (day = 6)
    {
❹     document.write("<h1>Happy Birthday, Mom!</h1>");
    }
}

// show me -->
</script>
```

Figure 3-4: Mom's birthday greeting—broken version

The script starts off correctly. When JavaScript sees ❶, it sets the variable month to whatever month it is. If you're running the script in March, it sets month to 2. The problem arises in the next line, though:

```
if (month = 7)
```

Here JavaScript sees one equal sign and thinks you want to *set* the variable month to the value 7. The script does what you're telling it to do, and then acts as if your test is true.

Since the result is true, JavaScript moves to the curly brackets, where it finds ❸, another if-then statement that incorrectly uses one equal sign instead of two. This line sets the variable day to the value 6 and again results in a true statement. JavaScript then moves to the second set of curly brackets, where it sees that it's supposed to ❹ write <h1>Happy Birthday, Mom!</h1>, which it does—every time someone visits the page (see Figure 3-5).

Figure 3-5: Mom's birthday greeting

NOTE *I remember the difference between one and two equal signs by thinking* is *the same as* instead of *equals* when I'm doing an if-then test, and remembering that *is the same as* translates into two equal signs.

Nesting

Figure 3-4 is the first example I've used of *nesting*—one if-then statement inside another. Although it sometimes makes sense to nest your if-then statements, things get confusing if you start to get three or more levels deep (one if-then statement inside the curly brackets of another if-then statement, which itself is inside the curly brackets of a third if-then statement).

Try to write your code so that it doesn't need more than two levels of nesting. If you find yourself with if-then statements more than two levels deep, it often means that you're doing something complicated enough to justify writing a new function to handle some of the complexity. (More on that in Chapter 6.)

if-then-else Statements

There are a couple of fancier versions of the if-then statement. The first is the if-then-else statement:

```
if (navigator.appName == "Microsoft Internet Explorer")
{
  // write IE-specific content
```

```
    document.write("Welcome, Internet Explorer user!");
}
else
{
  // write netscape specific content
  document.write("Welcome, Netscape user!");
}
```

This reads nicely in English if you read *else* as *otherwise*: "If they're using Internet Explorer, show them IE-specific content, otherwise send them Netscape-specific content."

if-then-else-if Statements

The above code assumes that there are only two browser manufacturers in the world, when in fact there are a multitude. We can solve this problem with an if-then-else-if statement that, if a visitor has a browser other than Netscape or Internet Explorer, displays content regarding unknown browsers.

```
if (navigator.appName == "Netscape")
{
  // write netscape-specific content
  document.write("Welcome, Netscape user!");
}
else if (navigator.appName == "Microsoft Internet Explorer")
{
  // write IE-specific content
  document.write("Welcome, Internet Explorer user!");
}
else
{
  // write unknown browser content
  document.write("Welcome, user of a fancy unknown browser!");
}
```

This code reads in English as: "If they're using Netscape, send them Netscape-specific content; if they're using Internet Explorer, send them IE-specific content. Otherwise send them a message about having a mysterious browser."

When and Where to Place Curly Brackets

Notice in the examples above that curly brackets (braces) mark the beginning and end of the body of an if-then statement, enclosing the part where you tell JavaScript what action(s) to take. You'll also notice that I place my beginning and ending curly brackets on their own lines, like this:

```
if (something == something_else)
{
  blah_blah_blah;
}
```

This is my style, one that I think makes it easier to align pairs of beginning and ending brackets. Other people prefer this slightly more compact style:

```
if (something == something_else) {
  blah_blah_blah;
}
```

It's up to you to choose where you put the curly brackets. Many studies have tried to figure out which formatting style is most readable or which avoids bugs. When you get right down to it, just decide what you think looks good and go with that.

Sometimes curly brackets are not needed in an if-then statement, such as when the body of the statement has only one line. For example, this is legal:

```
if (something == something_else)
  alert("they're equal");
else
  alert("they're different!");
```

Since each of the "then" parts of the clause is only one line (the alert functions), the curly brackets around these statements are optional. However, it's always a good idea to include the braces anyway, because you might want to add a second line to that else clause. If you do add a second line to the else clause and forget to put the brackets around the two lines, your script won't work.

With curly brackets, the previous example would look like this:

```
if (something == something_else)
{
  alert("they're equal");
}
else
{
  alert("they're different!");
}
```

Or, if you prefer the more compact style:

```
if (something == something_else) {
  alert("they're equal");
} else {
  alert("they're different!");
}
```

OR and AND

The if-then statements we've seen so far are pretty simple. You might, however, want to add more conditions to an if-then statement (for example, "If Joe is in high school *and* is not doing his homework, then tell him to get to work"). To add more conditions to an if-then statement, use the *OR* and *AND operators*.

OR

Suppose you want to give different greetings to people who come to your site, depending on who they are. You could, as in Figure 3-6, use a prompt box to ask for a visitor's name (Figure 3-7) and then use an if-then statement to determine which greeting to give.

```
<script type = "text/javascript">
<!-- hide me from older browsers

var the_name = prompt("What's your name?", "");
if (the_name == "thau")
{
  document.write("Welcome back, thau! Long time no see!");
} else {
  document.write("Greetings, " + the_name + ". Good to see you.");
}

// show me -->
</script>
```

Figure 3-6: Asking for a visitor's name with the prompt box

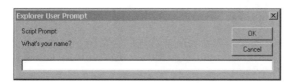

Figure 3-7: The prompt box asking for a visitor's name

This example greets thau with "Welcome back, thau! Long time no see!" (Figure 3-8) and everyone else with "Greetings, *Name*. Good to see you."

Figure 3-8: thau's greeting

To greet others the same way you greet thau, you could use a series of if-then statements as in Figure 3-9.

```
if (the_name == "thau")
{
  document.write("Welcome back, thau! Long time no see!");
}
else if (the_name == "dave")
{
  document.write("Welcome back, dave! Long time no see!");
}
```

```
else if (the_name == "pugsly")
{
  document.write("Welcome back, pugsly! Long time no see!");
}
else if (the_name == "gomez")
{
  document.write("Welcome back, gomez! Long time no see!");
}
else
{
  document.write("Greetings, " + the_name + ". Good to see you.");
}
```

Figure 3-9: Personalized greetings with a series of if-then statements

This would work, but there's a lot of waste here: We repeat basically the same document.write() line four times. What we really want to say is something like: "If the_name is *thau,* or *dave,* or *pugsly,* or *gomez,* give the 'Long time no see' greeting." JavaScript has a feature called the OR operator, which comes in handy here. Figure 3-10 shows OR in use:

```
if ((the_name == "thau") || (the_name == "dave") ||
    (the_name == "pugsly") || (the_name == "gomez"))
{
  document.write("Welcome back, " + the_name + "! Long time no see!");
}
```

Figure 3-10: The OR operator

The OR operator is represented by two vertical lines (||), called *bars.* You will usually be able to type the bar (|) character as the shifted backslash (\) key on your keyboard.

NOTE   *Although each of the Boolean tests in Figure 3-10 (for example, the_name == "thau") has its own parentheses, these aren't strictly necessary. However, the set of parentheses around all four Boolean tests is required, and it's a good idea to include the other parentheses for legibility's sake.*

AND

AND, another important operator, is represented by two ampersands (&&). Figure 3-11 shows this operator in use.

```
var age = prompt("How old are you?", "");
var drinking = prompt("Are you drinking alcohol (yes or no)?", "yes");

if ((age < 21) && (drinking == "yes"))
{
  document.write("Beat it!");
}
else
```

```
{
  document.write("Enjoy the show!");
}
```

Figure 3-11: The AND operator

When bars start using robot bouncers that run on JavaScript, this is the kind of code they'll be running. The script asks a person's age and whether he or she is drinking alcohol (Figure 3-12).

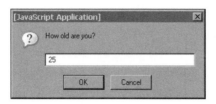

Figure 3-12: The bouncer's questions

If the person is under 21 and is drinking alcohol, the bouncer tells him or her to beat it. Otherwise, the visitor is perfectly legal and is welcome to stay (Figure 3-13). (Never mind the fake IDs for now.)

Figure 3-13: The bouncer's response

Putting It All Together

Here's a script containing most of what's been presented in the chapter so far. The script in Figure 3-14 redirects users to one page if they're using an older version of Netscape (version 4 or earlier), another page if they're using an older version of Internet Explorer (version 5.5 or earlier), a third page for browsers it's unfamiliar with, and a fourth page for modern browsers it knows about.

I've broken the code into two blocks of <script> tags. The first sets up the variables and the second does the redirection.

NOTE   *It's a good idea to declare variables at the top of your script. That way, if you want to change a variable later, you won't have to go hunting through a lot of HTML and JavaScript to find it.*

```
<html><head><title>Redirection</title>
<script type = "text/javascript" src = "brwsniff.js"></script>
<script type = "text/javascript">
<!-- hide me from older browsers
```

```
var browser_info = getBrowser();
var browser_name = browser_info[0];
var browser_version = browser_info[1];
var this_browser = "unknown";
if (browser_name == "msie")
{
  if (browser_version < 5.5)
  {
    this_browser = "old Microsoft";
  }
  else
  {
    this_browser = "modern";
  }
} // end if browser_name == Microsoft
if (browser_name == "netscape")
  {
  if (browser_version < 6.0)
  {
    this_browser = "old Netscape";
  }
  else
  {
    this_browser = "modern";
  }
} // end if browser_name == Netscape

// show me -->
</script>
</head><body>
<SCRIPT type = "text/javascript">
<!-- hide me from older browsers
if (this_browser == "old Netscape")
{
  window.location = "archaic_netscape_index.html";
} else if (this_browser == "old Microsoft")  {

  window.location.href = "archaic_ie.html";
} else if (this_browser == "modern")
{
  window.location.href = "modern_browser.html";
}

// show me -->
</script>
<h1>Unknown Browser</h1>
Sorry, but this page only works for browsers Netscape 6.0 and later, and
Internet Explorer 5.5 and later.
</body>
</html>
```

Figure 3-14: Complete redirection code

A Few More Details About Boolean Expressions

There are just a few more things you need to know about Boolean expressions before you can call yourself a Boolean master. You already know that you can create an if-then statement using code like this:

```
if (name == "thau") {
  alert("Hello, thau!");
}
```

This says, "If it is true that the variable name contains the string thau, put up an alert saying *Hello, thau!*" What you may not know is that you can store the value true or false in a variable and use it later. So, I could have done this instead:

```
var thisIsThau = (name == "thau");
if (thisIsThau == true) {
  alert("Hello, thau!");
}
```

The first line tests to see whether the variable name contains the string "thau". If it does, the test is true. This true value is stored in the variable thisIsThau. You can then test to see whether the variable thisIsThau is true, as seen in the subsequent if-then statement. This can be shortened a bit to this:

```
var thisIsThau = (name == "thau");
if (thisIsThau) {
  alert("Hello, thau!");
}
```

Notice that I'm not explicitly checking to see whether thisIsThau contains the value true. Instead, I'm just putting the variable inside the if-then test parentheses. The if-then rule states, "If the thing inside the parentheses is true, do the action in the curly brackets." In this case, the variable isThisThau will be true if the variable name contains the value "thau".

If you wanted to do something in the case where the string stored in name was something other than "thau" you could do this:

```
var thisIsThau = (name == "thau");
if (thisIsThau == false) {
  alert("Hello, somebody other than thau!");
}
```

Here, we're checking to see whether the value stored inside thisIsThau is false, which it will be if the comparison of name and "thau" turned out to be false in the line above (for example, if name equaled "pugsly").

The final shortcut involves using the special character !, which means *not*.

```
var thisIsThau = (name == "thau");
if (!thisIsThau) {
  alert("Hello, somebody other than thau!");
}
```

The expression means "if thisIsThau is not true, then do the stuff in the curly brackets." These Boolean shortcuts are used quite frequently in the scripts I've seen on the Web, so you should take some time to get used to them.

How Netscape Provides Browser-Specific Content

Now we've covered just about everything you need to know to understand how Netscape serves up the browser-specific content illustrated at the beginning of the chapter (Figures 3-1 and 3-2). Here is a somewhat simplified and modified version of the JavaScript on Netscape's home page:

```
<script type = "text/javascript">
❶ var agent = navigator.userAgent.toLowerCase();
❷ var major = parseInt(navigator.appVersion);
  var minor = parseFloat(navigator.appVersion);
❸ var ns = ((agent.indexOf('mozilla') != -1) &&
     (agent.indexOf('compatible') == -1));
❹ var ns4 = (ns && (major == 4));
  var ns7 = (ns && (agent.indexOf('netscape/7') != -1) );
  var ie = (agent.indexOf("msie") != -1);
  var ie4 = (ie && (this.major >= 4));
  var ie6 = (ie && (agent.indexOf("msie 6.0") != -1));
  var op3 = (agent.indexOf("opera") != -1);
</script>
```

Next comes all of the HTML. Inside the HTML, when you want to decide whether or not to write something based on the browser being used, you do something like this:

```
<script type = "text/javascript">
❺  if (!ns4) document.write('<td>the stuff that puts in the numbers</td>');
   </script>
```

The script starts by using the userAgent and appVersion variables to determine the type of browser being used. Notice the use of parseInt() in ❷. This function works just like parseFloat(), except that it pulls the first integer out of a string, rather than the first floating-point number. This will set the variable major to a number like 4, 5, or 6.

The next line (❸) is jam-packed with information, so take it slow. The first thing to notice is the use of the indexOf() function. We'll see more of indexOf() in Chapter 11 when we work with strings. The main thing to know here is that indexOf() checks to see whether a string contains another string. To see if the word mozilla is part of the string stored in agent, we use agent.indexOf('mozilla'). If mozilla is in the agent string, indexOf() will return some number other than −1. If mozilla is not part of the agent string, indexOf() will return −1. This can get a little confusing, so make sure you understand that last rule.

Now, looking at ❸, we see that there are two main parts. The first part checks to see whether some application of the indexOf() function gives a result different from −1. The next part checks to see if another application of the indexOf() function gives a result that equals −1. If the first part is true, *and* the second part is also true, then the whole thing is true, and the value true is stored in the variable ns. If either of the comparisons is false, then the whole thing will be false, and the value false will be stored in ns. Remember the bouncer's test:

```
if ((age < 21) && (drinking == "yes"))
```

If both statements were true—the person was under 21, *and* the person was drinking—the person got bounced. If either part was not true, then they were okay.

With all that in mind, let's look to see what the two comparisons in ❸ are. The first one will return the value true if indexOf() finds the string mozilla in the variable agent. Take a long, hard look at the expression:

```
agent.indexOf('mozilla') != -1
```

Remember, if the string stored in variable agent contains the string mozilla, indexOf() will return a value not equal to −1. So this test will be true if the navigator.userAgent has the word mozilla (upper- or lowercase) in it.

The next part makes sure that the navigator.userAgent does not contain the string compatible. This is because many browsers say they are Mozilla compatible, and they'll have both the words mozilla and compatible in their navigator.userAgent string. Netscape just has the word mozilla in its string. The end result of ❸ is that the variable ns will be true if the navigator.userAgent contains the string mozilla but not the string compatible.

The next lines figure out which version of Netscape this might be. Consider ❹:

```
var ns4 = (ns && (major == 4));
```

This line says, "If the variable ns is true, and the variable major has a value of 4, then put the value true in the variable ns4." If it's not true *both* that the variable ns is true *and* that the variable major is 4, then ns4 will be false. The other lines perform similar tests for Navigator 7 and other browsers. Each one is a little different from the others, so make sure you take some time to understand all of them.

Once the browser is known, the decision whether or not to display the browser-specific feature (namely, the page number navigation links) happens later in the code. Right at the place where you either write something to the web page or not, depending on the browser being used, you use a line like ❺:

```
if (!ns4) document.write('<td>the stuff that puts in the numbers</td>');
```

This says, "If this is not a Netscape 4 browser, write the code that puts in the navigation element." The variable ns will be true if the earlier code determined that it was a Netscape 4 browser being used, and false otherwise. Remember that this code must go between <script> and </script> tags.

Except for the part of the script that determines the type of browser being used, the Netscape code is fairly simple. If you want to avoid the complexities involved in determining the browser being used, use one of the browser sniffer packages available for free on the Web, incorporating the software into your page using JavaScript statements similar to those shown in the section "More Accurate Browser Detection" on page 36.

Summary

Here are the things you should remember from this chapter:

- JavaScript's tools for identifying a visitor's browser (navigator.appName, navigator.appVersion, and navigator.userAgent)
- How if-then, if-then-else, and if-then-else-if statements work
- How Boolean expressions work
- How to redirect your visitors to other web pages
- How to import JavaScript from another file

Did you get all that? If so, here's an assignment for you.

Assignment

Write a web page that asks for a visitor's name. If the visitor is someone you like, send him to your favorite page. If it's someone you don't know, send him to a different page. And if it's someone you don't like, send him to yet another page.

4

WORKING WITH ROLLOVERS

You've seen rollovers a million times. You mouse over an image, and the image changes. You mouse off the image, and the image changes back to its original state. Rollovers are an easy way to make your site more interactive.

This chapter will show you how to create a good rollover. This involves:

- Telling JavaScript to detect the mouse event that will trigger an image swap
- Telling JavaScript which of several images to swap in, based on the mouse event
- Replacing the old image with a new one

I'll also teach you a new way to detect which browser a visitor is using.

A Real-World Example of Rollovers

To begin, let's take a look at rollovers in action. *Tin House* (http://www.tinhouse.com), one of my favorite literary journals, has a little house on its home page that helps you navigate the site. When you first come to the page, all the lights in the house are off (Figure 4-1); rolling over different parts of the house lights those areas up (Figure 4-2). It may be a little silly, but I like it.

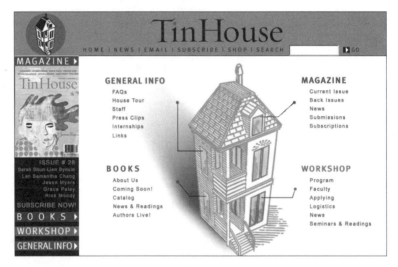

Figure 4-1: Tin House *home page before mousing over the house*

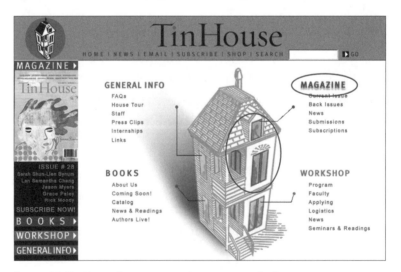

Figure 4-2: Tin House *home page with mouse over the house*

The *Book of JavaScript* home page also has a relatively straightforward and uncomplicated implementation of an image swap. If you mouse over the graphic that says *Turn it over!* the image of the front cover of the book will change to show the back of the book (see Figures 4-3 and 4-4). Mouse off the *Turn it over!* image again and the book image switches back to the front cover.

There are many ways to script a rollover. Because rollovers don't work in old browsers, or when people turn JavaScript off, creating them also involves browser detection, so in this chapter you'll learn more ways to tailor JavaScripts to the visitor's browser.

You'll also learn how quotation marks are handled in JavaScript and how the hierarchical framework of a web page, known as the *Document Object Model (DOM)*, is reflected in JavaScript syntax.

Figure 4-3: An image from the Book of JavaScript home page before mouseover

Figure 4-4: The same image after mouseover

Triggering Events

So far all the JavaScript we've seen is triggered when a web page loads into a browser. But JavaScript can also be *event driven.*

Event-driven JavaScript waits for your visitor to take a particular action, such as mousing over an image, before it reacts. The key to coding event-driven JavaScript is to know the names of events and how to use them.

Event Types

With JavaScript's help, different parts of your web page can detect different events. For example, a pull-down menu can know when it has changed (see Chapter 7); a window when it has closed (see Chapter 5); and a link when a visitor has clicked on it. In this chapter I'll focus on link events.

A link can detect many kinds of events, all of which involve interactions with the mouse. The link can detect when your mouse moves over it and when your mouse moves off of it. The link knows when you click down on it, and whether, while you're over the link, you lift your finger back off the button after clicking down. The link also knows whether the mouse moves while over the link.

Like the other kinds of interactions that we'll cover in later chapters, all of these events are captured in the same way: using an *event handler.*

onClick

Figure 4-5 shows the basic format of a link that calls an alert after a visitor clicks it.

Before adding JavaScript:

```
<a href = "http://www.bookofjavascript.com/">Visit the Book of JavaScript
    website</a>
```

After adding JavaScript:

```
<a href = "http://www.bookofjavascript.com/"
  onClick = "alert('Off to the Book of JavaScript!');">Visit the Book of
    JavaScript website</a>
```

Figure 4-5: A link that calls an alert

Try putting the link with the onClick into one of your own web pages. When you click the link, an alert box should come up and say *Off to the Book of JavaScript!* (Figure 4-6). When you click OK in the box, the page should load the *Book of JavaScript* website.

Figure 4-6: The event-driven "Off to the Book of JavaScript!" alert box

Notice that, aside from the addition of onClick, this enhanced link is almost exactly like the normal link. The onClick event handler says, "When this link is clicked, pop up an alert."

onMouseOver and onMouseOut

Two other link events are onMouseOver and onMouseOut. Moving the mouse over a link triggers onMouseOver, as shown in Figure 4-7.

```
<a href = "#" onMouseOver = "alert('Mayday! Mouse overboard!');">board</a>
```

Figure 4-7: onMouseOver

As you can see, moving the mouse over the link triggers onMouseOver. The code for onMouseOut looks like the onMouseOver code (except for the handler name) and is triggered when the mouse moves off of the link. You can use onMouseOut, onMouseOver, and onClick in the same link, as in Figure 4-8.

```
<a href = "#"
  onMouseOver = "alert('Mayday! Mouse overboard!');"
  onMouseOut = "alert('Hooray! Mouse off of board!!');"
  onClick = "return false;">
board
</a>
```

Figure 4-8: onMouseOut, onMouseOver, and onClick in the same link

Mousing over this link results in an alert box showing the words *Mayday! Mouse overboard!* (Figure 4-9). Pressing ENTER to get rid of the first alert and moving your mouse off the link results in another alert box that contains the words *Hooray! Mouse off of board!!* If you click the link instead of moving your mouse off it, nothing will happen, because of the return false; code in the onClick.

Figure 4-9: An alert box produced by mousing over a link

onMouseMove, onMouseUp, and onMouseDown

The onMouseMove, onMouseUp, and onMouseDown event handlers work much like the others. Try them yourself and see. The onMouseMove event handler is called whenever the mouse is moved while it is over the link. The onMouseDown event handler is triggered when a mouse button is pressed down while the mouse is over a link. Similarly, the onMouseUp event handler is triggered when the mouse button is lifted up again. An onClick event handler is triggered whenever an onMouseDown event is followed by an onMouseUp event.

Quotes in JavaScript

This example also demonstrates a new wrinkle in JavaScript syntax. Inside the double quotes of the onClick (Figure 4-8) is a complete line of JavaScript, semicolon and all. In previous chapters, we've placed all of our JavaScript between opening <script> and closing </script> tags. The only exception to this rule is when JavaScript is inside the quotes of an event. Your browser will assume that anything within these quotes is JavaScript, so you shouldn't put <script> and </script> tags in there.

Also note that the quotes in the alert are single quotes ('). If these were double quotes ("), JavaScript wouldn't be able to figure out which quotes go with what. For example, if you wrote

```
onClick = "alert("Off to the Book of JavaScript!");"
```

JavaScript would think that the second double quote closed the first one, which would confuse it and result in an error. Make sure that if you have quotes inside quotes, one set is double and the other is single.

Apostrophes can also pose problems. For example, let's say you want the alert in Figure 4-7 to say

```
Here's the Book of JavaScript page. You're gonna love it!
```

You would want the JavaScript to resemble this:

```
onClick = "alert('Here's the Book of JavaScript page. You're gonna love it!');"
```

Unfortunately, JavaScript reads the apostrophes in Here's and You're as single quotes inside single quotes and gets confused. If you really want those apostrophes, *escape* them with a backslash (\), like this:

```
onClick = "alert('Here\'s the Book of JavaScript page. You\'re gonna love it!');"
```

Putting a backslash before a special character, such as a quote, tells JavaScript to print the item rather than interpret it.

Clicking the Link to Nowhere

You may have noticed that the links in Figures 4-7 and 4-8 have an unusual form for the href attribute:

```
<a href = '#'>
```

This hash mark (#) in an href means, "Go to the top of this page." I've included it there because most browsers expect something to be inside the quotes after the href, usually a URL. In Figure 4-5, for example, the tag is

```
<a href = "http://www.bookofjavascript.com/">
```

In HTML, href is a required attribute of the anchor (<a>) tag, or link. href is an abbreviation for *hypertext reference*, and it's required because, as far as HTML is concerned, the whole purpose of a link is to send the user somewhere else when the link is clicked, so the browser needs to be told where to go. Usually that's another page, but in this case you are not trying to go anywhere. I might have just put nothing inside the quotes (href = ""), but different browsers will do different things in that case, and it's usually something weird. Give it a try in your favorite browser. To avoid weird behaviors, it's best to put the # sign inside an href when you don't want the link to go anywhere when clicked.

The link in Figure 4-8 had a second way of ensuring that the link didn't go anywhere when clicked: onClick = "return false;". Placing return false; in the quotes after an onClick tells JavaScript to prevent the browser from following the URL inside the link's href. This can be quite useful for dealing with people who have JavaScript turned off in their browsers. For example, if someone with JavaScript turned off clicks the link in Figure 4-10, the browser will ignore the onClick and happily follow the URL inside the href. This URL might go to a web page that describes the wonders of JavaScript and tells the user how to turn JavaScript on. People who already have JavaScript turned on will be treated to the contents of the onClick. They will see an alert box, and then the return false inside the onClick will prevent the browser from following the URL in the href. Although very few people turn JavaScript off (fewer than 1 percent of browsers), it never hurts to take them into consideration.

```
<a href = "please_turn_js_on.html" onClick =
    "alert('I\'m glad you have JavaScript turned on!'); return false;">Click me</a>
```

Figure 4-10: Links for people with JavaScript turned off

More Interesting Actions

You can do more with event handlers than simply triggering alert boxes. Figure 4-11, for instance, uses an event handler to customize a page's background color.

```
<a href = "#"
  onClick = "var the_color = prompt('red or blue?','');
    window.document.bgColor = the_color;
    return false;">
change background</a>
```

Figure 4-11: Customizing background color

When you click this link, a prompt box asks whether you want to change the background to red or blue. When you type your response, the background changes to that color. In fact, you can type whatever you want into that prompt box, and your browser will try to guess the color you mean. (You can even do a kind of personality exam by typing your name into the prompt and seeing what color your browser thinks you are. When I type thau into the prompt, the background turns pea green.)

This example demonstrates two new facts about JavaScript. First, notice that the onClick triggers three separate JavaScript statements. You can put as many lines of JavaScript as you want between the onClick's quotes, although if you put too much in there, the HTML starts to look messy.

Second, notice that you can change the background color of a page by setting window.document.bgColor to the color you desire. To make the background of a page red, you'd type:

```
window.document.bgColor = 'red';
```

In the example, we're setting the background color to any color the user enters into the prompt box. I'll say more about window.document.bgColor soon.

Swapping Images

Using JavaScript, you can change or swap images on your web pages, making buttons light up, images animate, and features explain themselves. Before you tell JavaScript to swap an image, you have to tell it what image to swap by naming the image. Figure 4-12 shows you how.

Before JavaScript:

```
<img src = "happy_face.gif">
```

After JavaScript:

```
<img src = "happy_face.gif" name = "my_image">
```

Figure 4-12: Naming an image

In this example, I've put an image of a happy face on the page and named it my_image.

NOTE   *You can name an image whatever you like, but the name can't contain spaces.*

Once you've named an image, it's easy to tell JavaScript to swap it with a new one. Let's say you have an image named my_image. To create an image swap, tell JavaScript you want to change the src of that image to another.gif:

```
window.document.my_image.src = "another.gif";
```

Figure 4-13 shows the code for a very basic page with an image and a link; click the link, and the image changes to happy_face.gif (Figure 4-14).

```
<html><head><title>Simple Image Swap</title></head>
<body>
<img src = "sad_face.gif" name = "my_image">
<br>
<a href = "#"
  onClick = "window.document.my_image.src = 'happy_face.gif';
```

```
    return false;">make my day!</a>
</body>
</html>
```

Figure 4-13: JavaScript for a basic image swap

Figure 4-14: Swapping a sad face for a happy one

Working with Multiple Images

If you have more than one image on a page, you should give each one a different name. Figure 4-15 has two images and two links. The first link tells JavaScript to swap the image called my_first_image (the sad face) with happy_face.gif. The second link tells JavaScript to swap the image called my_second_image (a circle) with square.gif. The result is shown in Figure 4-16.

NOTE *When using more than one image, you must name your images differently. If you accidentally give two images the same name, the swap won't work.*

```
<html><head><title>Two Image Swaps</title></head>
<body>
<img src = "sad_face.gif" name = "my_first_image"><br>
<img src = "circle.gif" name = "my_second_image">
<br>
<a href = "#"
  onClick = "window.document.my_first_image.src = 'happy_face.gif';
    return false;">make my day!</a>
<br>
<a href = "#"
  onClick = "window.document.my_second_image.src = 'square.gif';
    return false;">square the circle!</a>
</body>
</html>
```

Figure 4-15: JavaScript for swapping two images

NOTE *Image swapping doesn't work in browsers earlier than Internet Explorer 4.0 or Netscape 3.0. Furthermore, if you're trying to replace a small image with a bigger one, or a big image with a smaller one, browsers earlier than Netscape 4.61 and Internet Explorer 4.0 will squash or stretch the new image to fit the space the old one occupied. Later versions of these browsers adjust the page to fit the bigger or smaller image.*

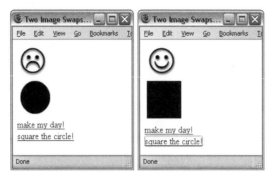

Figure 4-16: Swapping two images

What's with All the Dots?

You may wonder why JavaScript refers to my_image as window.document.my_image and not just as my_image. You may also wonder why you would use window .document.my_image.src when you want to change the src of that image. In short, what's with all the dots?

The answer has to do with how your browser looks at your web page.

Figure 4-17 shows the hierarchical organization of a web page as JavaScript understands it—through the Document Object Model (DOM). At the top of the DOM is the window that contains the web page you're viewing. That window contains the navigator, document, and location objects. Each of these objects has a lot of information in it, and by changing one you can change what happens on your web page.

The dots in a line of JavaScript separate hierarchical levels of objects. When JavaScript sees a series of objects separated by dots, it goes to the last object in the series. So, for example, the phrase window.location tells JavaScript to find the location object inside the current window. Similarly, the line window.document.my_image.src tells JavaScript to find the source file (src) of the image named my_image within the document object in the current window. The current window is the one in which the JavaScript is located.

The document Object

The document object lists all the images, links, forms, and other stuff on a web page. To code an image swap, we must tell JavaScript to find the document object in the window, then locate the image object we would like to change in the document object's list, and finally change the image's src. In JavaScript terms (where happy_face.gif is the image we're swapping in), this is how it looks:

```
window.document.my_image.src = "happy_face.gif";
```

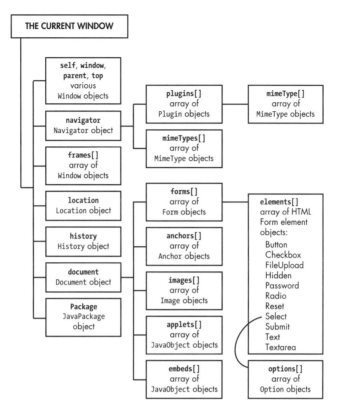

Figure 4-17: DOM's hierarchical organization

Object Properties

An object's *properties* are the bits of information that describe the object, such as its height, width, and src (the name of the file that the image displays). Some properties, such as the src of an image, can be changed, and others can't. As we've seen, changing the src property of an image object changes which file is displayed:

```
window.document.my_image.src = "happy_face.gif";
```

Other properties, like the image's height and width, are read-only and cannot be changed.

The document object contains the image objects, and it has its own properties. For example, the background color of the document object is called bgColor. That's why we could change the background color of our document using window.document.bgColor = 'red'. The image and document objects are just two of many objects we'll be seeing throughout the book. Each JavaScript object has its own set of properties. Appendix C provides a list of many JavaScript objects and their properties.

Finally, Rollovers!

Now that we know how to tell JavaScript how to do an image swap and how to trigger JavaScript based on a user event with onClick, onMouseOver, and onMouseOut, we can create a rollover. Just stick an onMouseOver and onMouseOut inside an image tag, like this:

```
<img src = "sad_face.gif" name = "my_first_image"
  onMouseOver = "window.document.my_first_image.src = 'happy_face.gif';"
  onMouseOut = "window.document.my_first_image.src = 'sad_face.gif';"
>
```

See how that works? When first loaded, the image shows the sad_face.gif because that's what the image tag calls.

```
<img src = "sad_face.gif" name = "my_first_image"...
```

Then, when the mouse moves over the image, the link around it captures the onMouseOver, and the image swaps to happy_face.gif, like so:

```
onMouseOver = "window.document.my_first_image.src = 'happy_face.gif';"
```

When the mouse moves off the image again, the link captures the onMouseOut event, which causes JavaScript to swap sad_face.gif back into the image:

```
onMouseOut = "window.document.my_first_image.src = 'sad_face.gif';"
```

Alternatively, the onMouseOut and onMouseOver could have gone inside an HTML link, as we've done with onClick in earlier examples. Because there are still a few people using browsers that don't allow onMouseOut and onMouseOver handlers inside <img> tags, it's not a bad idea to put them in a link surrounding the image:

```
<a href = "#"
  onMouseOver = "window.document.my_first_image.src = 'happy_face.gif';"
  onMouseOut = "window.document.my_first_image.src = 'sad_face.gif';">
<img src = "sad_face.gif" name = "my_first_image" border = "0">
</a>
```

Image Preloading

That's pretty much all there is to your basic image swap. As usual, there's something that makes the process a little more difficult. When you do an image swap as I've described, the image that's swapped in downloads only when your visitor mouses over the image. If your network connection is slow or the image is big, there's a delay between the mouseover and the image swap.

The way around this potential download delay is to *preload* your images—grabbing them all before they're needed and saving them in the browser's cache. When the mouse moves over a rollover image, the browser first looks to see whether the swap image is in its cache. If the image is there, the browser doesn't need to download the image, and the swap occurs quickly.

There are hundreds of image preloading scripts, and they're all basically the same. Rather than write your own, you can download one of the free ones and paste it into your page (Webmonkey has a good one at http://www .hotwired.com/webmonkey/reference/javascript_code_library/wm_pl_img). Let's go over the basics of how preloads work so you'll recognize them when you see them.

There are two parts to a preload. First, you create a new image object. The line

```
var new_image = new Image();
```

creates a new image object that has no information. It doesn't have a GIF or JPEG associated with it, nor does it have a height or width. If you know the height and width of the image, you can do this:

```
var new_image = new Image(width, height);
```

Giving JavaScript information about the size of the image helps the browser allocate memory for the image; it doesn't have much impact on how users experience your web page.

Once you've created this new object,

```
new_image.src = "my_good_image.gif";
```

forces the browser to download an image into its cache by setting the image object's src. When the image is in the browser's cache, it can be swapped for another image without any download delays. Figure 4-18 incorporates a preload with the rollover we saw in the last example.

```
<html><head><title>Preloaded Rollover</title>
<script type = "text/javascript">
<!-- hide me from older browsers

var some_image = new Image();
some_image.src = "happy_face.gif";

// show me -->
</script>
```

```
</head>
<body>
<img src = "sad_face.gif" name = "my_first_image"
  onMouseOver = "window.document.my_first_image.src = 'happy_face.gif';"
  onMouseOut = "window.document.my_first_image.src = 'sad_face.gif';">
</body>
</html>
```

Figure 4-18: Image preload and rollover

How the *Tin House* Rollovers Work

At the beginning of the chapter, I mentioned the home page of *Tin House*. Its image swap JavaScript is quite simple and will give you an idea of how easy it is to add a little JavaScript to your site. The Tin House rollover involves four images: the top, middle, left, and right parts of the bottom floor of the house. These images are placed in an HTML table to create the complete image of the house. Figure 4-19 shows you the (abbreviated) code for the top floor.

```
❶ <a href = "general_info/submission.html"
❷   onMouseOver = "attic3.src='images/index/home_attic3b.gif';"
❸   onMouseOut = "attic3.src='images/index/home_attic3.gif';">
❹     <img src = "images/index/home_attic3.gif" name =
      "attic3" width = "289" height = "68" border = "0" alt =
      "General Information: Our history, our glory, and our guidelines.">
  </a>
```

Figure 4-19: Rollover from the Tin House *home page*

This should look very familiar by now. Line ❹ describes the image. Notice that *Tin House* puts width, height, border, and alt attributes inside their image tag as well as the name attribute used to do the image swap. The height and width attributes tell web browsers how much space to reserve for the image. The alt attribute does two important things. First, some browsers don't display images. This might be because the person is on a slow connection and has turned images off in their browser, or because they using are a device that can read web pages to them, or perhaps it's a search engine visiting your web page, looking for stuff to add to its index. The alt attribute in an image provides information about that image in all of these situations. In addition, the alt attribute is used by some browsers even when images are being displayed. Recent versions of Internet Explorer, for example, will display the alt text in a yellow box when you leave your mouse over an image for more than a second or two.

Getting back to the JavaScript, you can see that *Tin House* has put its onMouseOver (❷) and onMouseOut (❸) inside an HTML link (❶). As we've seen, the onMouseOver and onMouseOut event handlers can go either in the image itself, or in a link surrounding the image, as *Tin House* has done.

Summary

In this chapter you've learned:

- How to trigger events, such as `onMouseOver` and `onMouseOut`
- How to nullify a link with `return false` inside `onClick`
- How to change the background color of a page
- How to swap images
- How to preload images so that they'll swap in more quickly
- How the DOM uses dots to separate objects into hierarchies

Now that you know the basics of image swapping, you can perform lots of tricks. You can make an image vanish by swapping in one that's the same color as the page background. You can make images composed of explanatory text and place them next to the feature they describe. There's no end to the fun you can have with image swaps.

As always, we'll be revisiting many of these points in later chapters, so you'll become more and more familiar with them. To make sure you understand how they work, try the following assignment.

Assignment

Figures 4-20 and 4-21 show you a page which does two image swaps simultaneously. Notice that mousing over the text on the bottom of the screen changes the words from *turn over* to *turn back* and swaps the book's front cover with its back cover. The words, like the book covers, are images, and they are swapped using the techniques we've learned in this chapter. Your assignment is to write a similar page where mousing over one image causes two images to change.

Figure 4-20: The Chapter 4 assignment page before the rollover

Figure 4-21: The Chapter 4 assignment page after the rollover

5

OPENING AND MANIPULATING WINDOWS

JavaScript gives you the ability to open multiple browser windows and control what's inside them. JavaScript can also change where windows are located on your visitor's screen. You can use the windows you open to present a slide show or some help information or to build a remote control device for your site.

In this chapter, you'll learn how to:

- Open new windows with JavaScript
- Make those windows look the way you'd like
- Position the windows on your visitor's screen
- Swap images inside windows you've opened

Real-World Examples of Opening Windows to Further Information

Let's begin with a quick look at two examples of windows linked from home pages. The Network for Good (http://www.networkforgood.org) is one of the best charity resources on the Web. At the top and bottom of its page, it has links to a Help window (Figure 5-1). Click either link, and a window with answers to frequently asked questions pops up. Notice that this window is smaller than the Network for Good home page and has no menu bar across the top. Also notice the familiar close box button in the upper-right corner of the Help window. Clicking that box closes the window.

Figure 5-1: Opening a window to further information

The *Book of JavaScript* web page (http://www.bookofjavascript.com) has an About the Author link (Figure 5-2), which acts similarly. Clicking this link opens a smaller window that provides more information about me, the author. At the bottom of the window is a button that closes the window.

Help windows like these can vastly improve a visitor's experience of your site. Rather than clicking to a new web page, waiting for the download, and then having to click back to the original page if she wants to refer to it for a moment, the user will find that these windows display your information very quickly and without browser navigation, and it will be possible for her to see both pages at once and switch quickly between them.

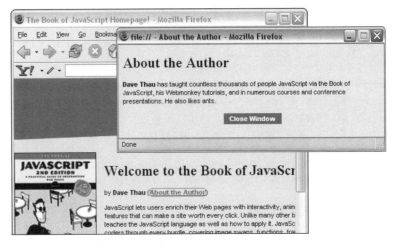

Figure 5-2: A small helper window

Working with Windows as Objects

Because windows are objects, you manipulate them just as you would any object (see Chapter 2 for a discussion of objects and methods), by using JavaScript's dot notation to apply one of the available methods to the window object you name:

```
window_name.method_name();
```

This chapter introduces the methods that JavaScript provides for the most important window operations, along with useful properties you can specify for a window object.

Opening Windows

To open a window, use the open() method, which opens a window that has the characteristics you specify as parameters inside its parentheses:

```
var window_name =
    window.open("some_url", "html_name", "feature1,feature2,feature3,...");
```

In this example, I've set up a variable called window_name to refer to the window we're opening. When I want to use JavaScript to change or manipulate what's inside the window, I'll refer to this window as window_name. Here window_name is just a variable—you could use any valid JavaScript variable name, such as fido, in its place if you so desired (see Chapter 2 for variable naming rules).

Manipulating the Appearance of New Windows

The three parameters of the window.open() command control the new window's characteristics.

The URL Parameter

The first parameter is the URL of the page you want to appear inside the window when the window opens. If you'd like to open a window with the *Book of JavaScript* website, inside the <script> tags you'd write:

```
var window_name =
    window.open("http://www.bookofjavascript.com/", "html_name");
```

The HTML Name Parameter

The HTML name of the window (the second parameter inside the parentheses) is useful only if you want to load a page into the window when the user clicks an HTML link on a different page. For example, if you open a window using window.open() and use the second parameter to name the window my_window, you can then use an HTML link to load a page into your new window. To do this, put the HTML name of the new window into the target attribute of the link. For example, clicking the following link loads the Webmonkey site into my_window:

```
<a href = "http://www.webmonkey.com/" target =
    "my_window">Put Webmonkey into my new window!</a>
```

You can also use the target element of the link tag to open windows without using JavaScript. For example, if a visitor clicks a link like the one above and you *haven't* already opened a window named my_window with JavaScript, your browser opens a new window and loads the link. The downside to opening a window without using JavaScript is that you have no control over what the window looks like, and you can't change it once you've opened it (except by loading another page into it from a link).

The Features Parameter

The third parameter in the window.open() command is a list of features that let you control what the new window will look like. This is where things start to get fun. Figure 5-3 illustrates the parts of each browser window that JavaScript allows you to control.

The features parameter lets you open a new window that includes all, some, or none of these features. If you leave out the third parameter (that is, you list just the first two parameters and nothing more—not even empty quotes), the window you open will have all the features you see in Figure 5-3 and will be the same size as the previous window. However, if you list any of the features in the third parameter, only the listed features appear in the window you open. So if you open a window with the command

```
var book_of_javascript_window =
    window.open("http://www.bookofjavascript.com/","book_of_javascript", "resizable");
```

you'll get a resizable window with the *Book of JavaScript* site in it. This window will be the same size as the window from which you opened it, but will lack the menu bar, status bar, scroll bars, and other features (see Figure 5-4).

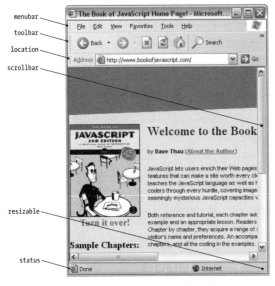

menubar
toolbar
location
scrollbar
resizable
status

Figure 5-3: Browser window features you can control with JavaScript

Figure 5-4: The Book of JavaScript *site in a window without features*

If you want more than one feature, you can list them inside the quotes, separated by commas. *Make sure to leave all spaces out of this string.* For some reason, spaces inside a feature string cause some browsers to draw your windows incorrectly. Here's an example of a window with two features (height and width) specified:

```
var pictures =
    window.open("http://bookofjavascript.com", "book_of_javascript","width=605,height=350" );
```

Figure 5-5 shows the result.

Figure 5-5: The Book of JavaScript *window opened with a height of 350 pixels and a width of 605 pixels*

Table 5-1 lists all the different window.open() features you can play with. Try experimenting with different ones to see what they do. Except for the features that deal with pixels (for example, height), all you have to do is type the feature name inside the third parameter's quotes. Some of the features apply to a specific browser—the directories feature, for example, works only on Netscape.

Table 5-1: JavaScript Window Features

Feature	Effect
directories	Adds buttons such as What's New and What's Cool to the menu bar. Some browsers ignore this feature. Others add different buttons.
height = X	Adjusts the height of the window to X pixels.
left = X	Places the new window's left border X pixels from the left edge of the screen.
location	Adds a location bar, where the site visitor can enter URLs.
menubar	Adds a menu bar.
resizable	Controls whether the visitor can resize the window; all Mac windows are resizable even if you leave this feature out.
scrollbars	Adds scroll bars if the contents of the page are bigger than the window.
status	Adds a status bar to the bottom of the window. Use the status property of the window object, discussed later in this chapter, to define what will be displayed in the status bar.
toolbar	Adds a standard toolbar with buttons such as back, forward, and stop. Which buttons are added depends on the browser being used.
top = X	Places the window's top border X pixels from the top edge of the screen.
width = X	Adjusts the window width to X pixels.

Some Browsers and Computers Open Windows Differently

The process of opening windows differs slightly depending on the browser and computer being used. For example, JavaScript windows in Mozilla, Safari, and Opera browsers are always resizable, so even if you leave that feature out of the string, the window remains resizable. Another difference is that you can't hide the menu bar on a Macintosh.

Closing Windows

If you've opened a window called my_window and want to close it later in the script, use the close() method:

```
my_window.close();
```

You'll recall from Chapter 4 that the word window refers to the window containing the JavaScript. This means you can also use JavaScript to close the window that's actually running the JavaScript, like this:

```
window.close();
```

This is exactly how the About the Author window on the *Book of JavaScript* page works. If you view the source code on the page that loads into one of the help windows, you'll see it has a button toward the bottom, labeled *Close Window*. If that button were a link, the script would look like this:

```
<a href = "#" onClick = "window.close(); return false;">Close Window</a>
```

Figure 5-6 shows how to do the same thing with a button instead of a link.

```
<form><input type = "button" value = "Close Window" onClick =
    "window.close();"></form>
```

Figure 5-6: Using a button to close a help window

The primary difference between the code in Figure 5-6 and the simple link I described is that Figure 5-6 uses a button instead of a link. The button is a form element that takes an onClick, just as a link does.

Using the Right Name: How Windows See Themselves and Each Other

Every window is a bit egocentric and thinks of itself as window. Let's say you open a web page titled *The Original Window*. Now let's say that window opens a second window, new_window.html (titled *The New Window*), using JavaScript, like this:

```
var new_window =
    window.open("new_window.html","new_window","height=100,width=100");
```

These two windows see each other in different ways. The original window thinks the new window is called new_window. The new window, however, thinks of itself as window. This means if you want to close the *new* window using JavaScript inside the *original* window, you'd write this code:

```
new_window.close();
```

But to close the new window using JavaScript inside the *new* window, you'd write the following in new_window.html:

```
window.close();
```

This window-centrism is one of the aspects of object-oriented programming that makes it interesting. It's like dealing with distinct individuals who have different perspectives on the world.

Moving Windows to the Front or Back of the Screen

Of course, once you've opened a window, you can do much more than just close it. You can move it to the front of the screen (on top of the other windows) or to the back of the screen (behind all the other windows). The focus() method brings a window forward, and blur() puts the window in back. The focus() method is especially useful when you have a window that should always appear at the front of a screen. For example, if I wanted a small navigation window to appear over the intro page, I could make all the links using this technique:

```
<a href = "#" onClick =
    "navigation = window.open('http://www.bookofjavascript.com/nav.html','navigation',
    'width=605,height=350' );navigation.focus(); return false;">Navigation Window</a>
```

This line opens the navigation window and brings it up to the front.

NOTE   *Notice that I didn't put the word* var *before the* navigation *variable when I called* window.open()*. If you use* var *inside a link, JavaScript will forget the name of the window once it executes the rest of the JavaScript commands in the* onClick*. The reason for this will be clearer after you read Chapter 6.*

Window Properties

So far we've seen four methods for the window object: open(), close(), focus(), and blur(). Later in the chapter, we'll explore two somewhat more complicated methods, resizeto() and move(), *both* of which involve a little math. First, however, let's look at some window properties that come in handy from time to time.

The status Property

One of the most useful (and most abused) properties is the window's status. The value of this property defines what appears in the window's status bar (see Figure 5-3). One common status is the URL of a link you are mousing over.

You can use the status property to change what appears in the status bar. You may have noticed that some people put a kind of marquee in this area, scrolling across the bottom with messages like *Buy our stuff! Buy our stuff!* I don't want to encourage status bar abuse, so I'm not going to teach you exactly how to do that, but you can use these JavaScript techniques to create a similar effect. To change what appears in the status bar of a window, use a <body> tag like this:

```
<body onLoad = "window.status = 'hi there!';">
```

This tag tells JavaScript to change the contents of the window's status bar after the page has been fully loaded into the browser.

You might want to use the status property to inform visitors about the site they'll see if they click a link. For example, if you have a link to a very graphics-intensive site, the words *Warning: This site has a lot of graphics* could appear in the status bar when the visitor mouses over the link. You can set this up with an onMouseOver:

```
<a href = "http://www.myheavygraphicsite.com/" onMouseOver =
    "window.status='Warning: This site has a lot of graphics'; return true;">
    My Heavy Graphic Site</a>
```

Notice the return true after the window.status command. This is similar to the return false I put at the end of my onClick in rollover links (see Chapter 4), and it does almost the same thing. When the user performs an onMouseOver, return true prevents the URL from appearing in the status bar. If you don't put it there, the words *Warning: This site has a lot of graphics* flash briefly in the status bar; then the link's URL quickly replaces them before the warning can be seen.

NOTE   *You might be asking, "Why is it return false in the case of onClick and return true in the case of onMouseOver?" That's a good question, and unfortunately there's no good answer—that's just how it is. The best you can do is memorize which goes with which.*

The opener Property

When one window opens a new window, the new window remembers its parent (the original window) using the opener property. An opened window can access its parent through this property and then manipulate the parent. For example, if you want a link in the new window to change the contents of the status bar in the original window, you'd include the following code inside a link in the new window:

```
<a href = "#" onClick =
    "var my_parent = window.opener; my_parent.status='howdy'; return false;">
    put howdy into the status bar of the original window</a>
```

The first statement inside the onClick says, "Find the window that opened me, and set the variable my_parent to point to that window." The second statement changes the status property of that window to howdy.

Alternatively, you could combine the lines:

```
<a href = "#" onClick =
    "window.opener.status = 'howdy'; return false;"> put howdy into the status
    bar of the original window</a>
```

The opener property is very useful if you want to have a remote control that affects the contents of the original window. The remote control file (available at http://www.bookofjavascript.com/Chapter05/the_remote.html) offers an example of this. Figure 5-7 shows the code that triggers the remote control.

```
<html>
<head>
<title>The Controlled Window</title>
<script type = "text/javascript">
<!-- hide me from older browsers
// open the control panel window
var control_window =
    window.open("the_remote.html","control_window","width=100,height=100");
// show me -->
</script>
</head>
<body>
Use the remote control to send various web pages to this window.
</body>
</html>
```

Figure 5-7: The code for the window that calls the remote control

NOTE *Some people install pop-up blocking software on their computers or set their browsers to block pop-up windows. Because the JavaScript in Figure 5-7 opens a window automatically (without the user having to click a link), it qualifies as a pop-up window, and computers that block pop-ups will prevent the window from opening. If the above JavaScript doesn't work on your computer, it may be because you have blocked pop-ups.*

The code in Figure 5-7 opens a window and loads the web page called the_remote.html, which is shown in Figure 5-8. Figure 5-9 shows you the code for the_remote.html.

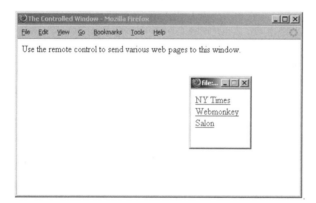

Figure 5-8: The page that calls the remote control, and the remote control itself

```
<html>
<head>
<title>Remote Control</title>
</head>
<body>
❶ <a href = "#"
   onClick = "window.opener.location.href='http://www.nytimes.com/';
   window.focus();">NY Times</a><br>
```

```
<a href = "#"
  onClick = "window.opener.location.href='http://www.webmonkey.com/';
    window.focus();">Webmonkey</a><br>
<a href = "#"
  onClick = "window.opener.location.href='http://www.salon.com/';
    window.focus();">Salon</a><br>
</body>
</html>
```

Figure 5-9: The remote control code

Figure 5-9 includes code for a typical link using an `onClick` (❶). When a visitor clicks the New York Times link, JavaScript looks up `window.opener` (the window that opened the remote control) and then changes its `location` to http://www.nytimes.com. Then, because of the `window.focus()`, JavaScript brings the remote control window to the front of the screen. Notice that because this JavaScript is running inside the remote control window, we use `window.focus()` rather than `control_window.focus()`.

More Window Methods

You've seen four window methods so far: `open()`, `close()`, `focus()`, and `blur()`. Let's look at two more that come in handy from time to time: resizing and moving windows.

Resizing Windows

Modern browsers provide two different ways your JavaScript can resize a window. The `window.resizeTo()` method resizes a window to a given width and height. To change a small window into one that's 500 pixels wide and 200 pixels high, you'd use the following script:

```
window.resizeTo(500,200);
```

Alternatively, you can change the size of a window by a specific amount using `window.resizeBy()`. The `window.resizeBy()` method takes two numbers: how much the width of the window should change and how much the height should change. The code

```
window.resizeBy(10, -5);
```

makes a browser 10 pixels wider and 5 pixels shorter.

Moving Windows

The `window.moveTo()` method moves a window to an absolute position on the screen. If you want the window in the upper-left corner of the user's screen, you'd type:

```
window.moveTo(0,0);
```

The first number is the number of pixels from the left border of the screen you want the window's upper-left corner to appear, and the second number is the number of pixels from the top of the screen.

An alternative to `window.moveTo()` is `window.moveBy()`. If you want to move a window 5 pixels to the right and 10 pixels down from its current position, you'd type:

```
window.moveBy(5,10);
```

The first number is the number of pixels to the right you want to move the window, and the second is the number of pixels down. If you want to move the window 10 pixels up and 5 to the left, just use negative numbers:

```
window.moveBy(-5,-10);
```

Be careful not to move a window entirely off a user's screen. To ensure against this possibility, you have to know the size of the user's screen. The two properties that indicate this are:

```
window.screen.availHeight
window.screen.availWidth
```

Figure 5-10 shows how you can use `window.screen.availHeight` and `window.screen.availWidth` to move a window to the center of the screen. This script centers the window on any screen, regardless of its size.

```
<html>
<head>
<title>Center Window</title>
<script type = "text/javascript">
<!-- hide me from older browsers

// set some variables
❶ var window_height = 200;
❷ var window_width = 200;

// make the window smallish
❸ window.resizeTo(window_height, window_width);

// find out how big the screen is
var height = window.screen.availHeight;
❹ var width = window.screen.availWidth;

// get the left position
// it'll be half of the screen
// minus half of the window width
var left_point = parseInt(width / 2) - parseInt(window_width / 2);

// get the top position
```

```
    // similar calculation as for the left position
❺ var top_point = parseInt(height/2) - parseInt(window_height / 2);

    // move the window
    //
❻ window.moveTo(left_point, top_point);

    // show me -->
    </script>
    </head>
    <body>
    <h1>Hi!</h1>
    </body>
    </html>
```

Figure 5-10: Code for moving a window to the center of the screen

Lines ❶ through ❸ resize the window to 200 by 200 pixels. Once that's done, the script uses window.screen.availHeight and window.screen.availWidth to figure out how high and wide the screen is. After determining those values, the script does some calculations to figure out where the upper-left corner of the window should go. Let's look at the formula to calculate the left-hand position of the window:

```
var left_point = parseInt(width / 2) - parseInt(window_width / 2);
```

The first part of this formula determines the screen's midpoint by dividing the width of the screen by two (we've defined the variable width in ❹). The parseInt() command ensures that the resulting number is an integer. Knowing the screen's midpoint isn't enough to center the window, however, because window.moveTo() sets the *left border* of the window you're moving. If you move the left border of the window into the center of the screen, the window will be too far to the right. To get the window to the center of the screen, we have to move it over to the left. The second part of the formula, subtracting parseInt(window_width / 2), figures out how far to move the window to the left: half the window's width (see Figure 5-11).

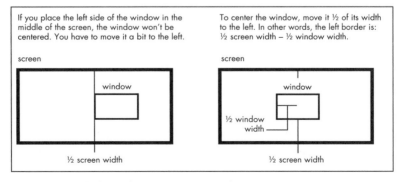

Figure 5-11: Calculating how to center a window

Line ❺ performs a similar calculation to determine where to set the top of the window. Once we've determined the window's correct top and left position, we use the `window.moveTo()` command to move it (❻).

NOTE   *In Internet Explorer, the `moveTo()` method works only when it is moving the window containing the JavaScript. In other words, if you have opened a window named `my_window`, you can't move that window using `my_window.moveTo(100,100)`. You can still use `window.moveTo(100,100)` to move the window that contains the JavaScript calling the `moveTo()` method.*

Summary

In this chapter you've learned:

- How to open new windows with `window.open()`
- How to incorporate various standard browser elements in the new window using the `feature` parameter
- How to close the windows you've opened with `window_name.close()`
- How to move windows to the front of the screen with `window.focus()`
- How to send windows to the back of the screen with `window.blur()`
- How to change the message in the window's status bar by setting `window.status`
- How a window you've opened can affect the previous window with `window.opener`
- How to resize windows with `window.resizeTo()` and `window.resizeBy()`
- How to move windows with `window.moveTo()` and `window.moveBy()`

Congratulations! Now that you know how to swap images and mess with windows, you can handle about 75 percent of what most web professionals do with JavaScript. The next few chapters will cover some details of JavaScript as a programming language, and then we'll be ready for the *really* fancy stuff.

Assignment

We've learned how to change the contents of the status bar of a window we've opened using JavaScript:

```
var my_window = window.open("http://www.nostarch.com","my_window");
my_window.status = "I'm in the new window's status bar!";
```

We can use a similar technique to swap an image in a window we've opened using JavaScript. Remember, the code to swap an image looks like this, where `the_image` is the name of an image on the page:

```
window.document.the_image.src = "new_image.gif"
```

To swap an image in another window, just replace `window` in the script with the name of the window containing the image.

Your homework assignment is to write a page (let's call it the main page) that contains two links. Write some JavaScript so that when the main page opens, it also opens a little window containing an image. When clicked, the two links on the main page swap different images into the little window. Figures 5-12 and 5-13 demonstrate what I mean.

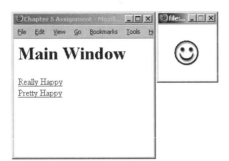

Figure 5-12: After opening the main window

Figure 5-13: After clicking the Really Happy link

This assignment is a bit tricky, but give it your best shot before looking at the solution in Appendix A.

6

WRITING YOUR OWN JAVASCRIPT FUNCTIONS

In this chapter we're going to focus on a programming concept—writing your own functions. Knowing how to write your own functions will improve almost any JavaScript you create. In fact, you'll see how custom-made functions can enhance several of the JavaScript tricks you've already learned.

In this chapter, you'll learn how to:

- Write your own functions
- Use homemade functions to improve your code
- Write functions you can cut and paste into whatever pages you want

We'll be using homemade functions in every chapter from now on, so pay extra-close attention to what's going on in this chapter. You'll be glad you did.

Functions as Shortcuts

Functions aren't anything new. You've already seen a number of functions that come built in to JavaScript. The alert() function, for example, takes whatever text you put inside the parentheses and displays an alert box with that text.

In its simplest form, *function* is just a shorthand name for a series of JavaScript instructions. When you call the alert() function, JavaScript understands it as a command to carry out some task, such as opening a window that has an OK button and a close button and putting some text in the window.

The functions you create act as shorthand as well. Let's say you want to write a link that opens a small window and then centers that window on the screen if the visitor is using Netscape 4.0 or above.

You *could* write a link resembling Figure 6-1 (most of the code in it is similar to Figure 5-10).

```
<a href = "#"
  onClick = "if ((parseInt(navigator.appVersion) > 3) &&
          (navigator.appName == 'Netscape')) {
    var the_window =
      window.open('http://www.nostarch.com/',
          'the_window','height=200,width=200');
    var screen_height = window.screen.availHeight;
    var screen_width = window.screen.availWidth;
    var left_point = parseInt(screen_width / 2) - 100;
    var top_point = parseInt(screen_height / 2) - 100;
    the_window.moveTo(left_point, top_point);
} return false;">Click me to open a small centered window</a>
```

Figure 6-1: A link that opens a small window and centers it in Netscape 4 and above— this won't work in Internet Explorer (see note at the end of Chapter 5)

However, it is not a good idea to write a link in this way: There's too much JavaScript embedded in the HTML. This makes HTML hard to follow, even for people who know JavaScript. Furthermore, if you want two or three links on your page, your HTML becomes even uglier and your page's download time increases. Even more problematic, if you want to change the code to affect window size or centering, you have to make the change everywhere you put the link.

The solution to these problems is to give all the JavaScript in Figure 6-1 a name and then simply call that name when you want to open and center a window. That's exactly what homemade functions are for: They allow you to call a set of JavaScript instructions (the function) just by using its name.

Basic Structure of JavaScript Functions

Figure 6-2 shows you the skeleton of a homemade function.

```
function functionName()
{
    a line of JavaScript;
    another line of JavaScript;
    more lines of JavaScript;
}
```

Figure 6-2: The basic structure of a homemade function

A function definition starts with the word function. When JavaScript sees that word, it knows you're about to define the subsequent bunch of JavaScript as a function.

Naming Your Functions

Next comes the function's name. The rules for naming a function are similar to those for naming a variable. The first character must be a letter; the rest of the characters can include letters, numbers, dashes, and underscores. No other characters, including spaces, are allowed. Like variables, function names are case sensitive, so JavaScript will consider a function called feedTheCat() to be different from a function called FeedTheCat().

Make sure you don't give a function and a variable the same name. If you have a variable called my_cat and a function called my_cat, JavaScript will forget either what the function's supposed to do or what value you've stored in the my_cat variable. Because of this weird behavior, and because function names are case sensitive, it makes sense to have a different convention for naming functions than for naming variables. For variables I use lowercase letters with underscores, and for functions I use what's called *in-caps* or *camel-caps notation*. Names in this notation style consist of strings of words without spaces, in which every word except the first is initial-capitalized, as in openAndCenterTheWindow(), myCat(), and printDate(). In-caps notation is a pretty common convention and should serve you well.

Parentheses and Curly Brackets

A pair of parentheses follows the function's name. For now, you won't be entering anything between them, but they're still necessary.

After the parentheses you need a pair of curly brackets. Between these brackets you'll write the JavaScript that will run when the function is called.

An Example of a Simple Function

Figure 6-3 shows you how the window-centering code in Figure 5-10 looks rewritten as a web page containing a function. Notice that the link calling the function (❶) has the same form as a link that calls a built-in JavaScript function—the function name appears inside an onClick.

```
<html>
<head>
<title>Getting Centered</title>
<script type = "text/javascript">
<!-- hide me from older browsers
function openAndCenterWindow()
{
  if ((parseInt(navigator.appVersion) > 3) &&
          (navigator.appName == "Netscape")) {
    var the_window =
      window.open('http://www.nostarch.com/',
          'the_window','height=200,width=200');

    var screen_height = window.screen.availHeight;
    var screen_width = window.screen.availWidth;
    var left_point = parseInt(screen_width / 2) - 100;
    var top_point = parseInt(screen_height / 2) - 100;
    the_window.moveTo(left_point, top_point);
  }
}
// show me -->
</script>
</head>
<body>
❶ <a href = "#" onClick =
    "openAndCenterWindow(); return false;">Click me to open a small
    centered window</a>
</body>
</html>
```

Figure 6-3: Opening and centering a window using a function

Next, notice that I've put the JavaScript declaring the function in the head of the page. You can declare functions in either the head or the body of an HTML page, but I like to declare my functions in the head because that way I don't have to search for them all over the page.

Finally, it's important to remember that the browser reads the page from the top down. When it sees the word function, it remembers the function name and the lines of JavaScript you've associated with that name. However, the JavaScript between the curly brackets doesn't actually execute until the onClick in the link calls the function. When we start putting more than one function on a web page, you'll see why it's important to keep this in mind.

Writing Flexible Functions

The code in Figure 6-3 does a good job of opening and centering a window containing No Starch Press's home page. But what if you wanted another link to open and center a different window with a different URL in it—Webmonkey's, for example?

One approach would be to write a second function that looks just like the first one, the only difference being that you'd replace the line

```
var the_window =
    window.open('http://www.nostarch.com/','the_window','height=200,width=200');
```

with the line

```
var the_window =
    window.open('http://www.webmonkey.com/','the_window','height=200,width=200');
```

This would work fine, but it's not a good idea to have two functions that do almost exactly the same thing. First of all, it's wasteful. If you could write one function that worked regardless of the URL, you'd save both typing and download time. Even more important, if you want to change how you're doing the centering, you'll have to change two functions instead of just one.

Using Parameters

Luckily, there's a way to make your function more flexible. The trick is to add a parameter. Remember, the alert() function takes one parameter—the words you want to appear in the alert box. You can write the openAndCenterWindow() function to take a parameter, too. In this case, the parameter would be the URL of the web page you want to appear in the window. In general, a function's parameter is whatever item of information the function needs in order to do its job—text to be displayed, a URL to link to, or whatever. Many functions use multiple parameters.

The code in Figure 6-4 shows how to add a parameter to your function and how to call the function with this parameter.

```
<html>
<head>
<title>Getting Centered Functionally</title>
<script type = "text/javascript">
<!-- hide me from older browsers
function openAndCenterWindow(the_url)
{
  if ((parseInt(navigator.appVersion) > 3) &&
        (navigator.appName == "Netscape"))
  {
❶    var the_window =
        window.open(the_url,'the_window','height=200,width=200');
      var screen_height = window.screen.availHeight;
      var screen_width = window.screen.availWidth;
      var left_point = parseInt(screen_width / 2) - 100;
      var top_point = parseInt(screen_height / 2) - 100;
      the_window.moveTo(left_point, top_point);
  }
}
```

```
     // show me -->
     </script>
     </head>
     <body>
❷   <a href = "#"
       onClick = "openAndCenterWindow('http://www.webmonkey.com/'); return false;">
         Click me to put the Webmonkey home page in a small centered window</a>
     <p><a href = "#"
       onClick = "openAndCenterWindow('http://www.nostarch.com/'); return false;">
         Click me to put the No Starch Press home page in a small centered window</a>

     </body>
     </html>
```

Figure 6-4: Opening and centering a window with a parameter

Line-by-Line Analysis of Figure 6-4

The tag for Webmonkey,

```
<a href = "#" onClick =
    "openAndCenterWindow('http://www.webmonkey.com/'); return false;">Click me
    to put the Webmonkey home page in a small centered window</a>
```

calls the function with the URL for Webmonkey in parentheses (see the result in Figure 6-5). Here Webmonkey's URL goes into the function just as the words go into the alert() function, but instead of any random string, it's a URL.

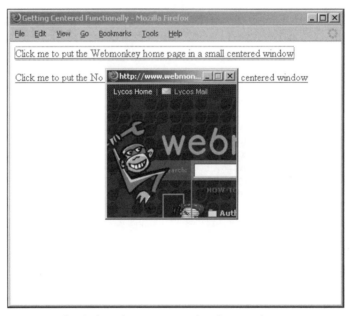

Figure 6-5: The Webmonkey site, opened and centered

Similarly, the tag

```
<a href = "#"
  onClick = "openAndCenterWindow('http://www.nostarch.com/'); return false;">
    Click me to put the No Starch Press home page in a small centered window</a>
```

calls the function with the URL for No Starch Press.

Now let's look at the function itself. Only two lines differ from those in Figure 6-3. The first line of the function now looks like this:

```
function openAndCenterWindow(the_url)
```

Notice that a word appears inside the parentheses now. This term is a variable, storing whatever value you'll use when you call the function. So if the line

```
openAndCenterWindow("happy happy!");
```

calls the function, the variable the_url holds the value "happy happy!".

When we call the function in Figure 6-4 as follows, the variable the_url holds the value "http://www.nostarch.com/":

```
<a href = "#"
  onClick = "openAndCenterWindow('http://www.nostarch.com/'); return false;">
    Click me to put the No Starch Press home page in a small centered window</a>
```

The second line in the function that differs from Figure 6-3 is ❷, which opens the window. In Figure 6-3 we opened the window with a web page:

```
var the_window =
        window.open('http://www.nostarch.com/', 'the_window',
          'height=200,width=200');
```

In Figure 6-4 we open the window with the variable that was set when the function was called:

```
var the_window =
        window.open(the_url, 'the_window', 'height=200,width=200');
```

JavaScript sees the variable the_url and knows it's a variable because no quotes surround it. If the function has 'http://www.nostarch.com/' inside the parentheses, like this

```
openAndCenterWindow('http://www.nostarch.com/');
```

the variable the_url has the value http://www.nostarch.com/, so the window opens with the No Starch Press home page. Figure 6-6 shows you graphically what's going on here.

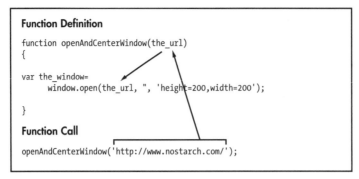

```
Function Definition
function openAndCenterWindow(the_url)
{

var the_window=
    window.open(the_url, ", 'height=200,width=200');

}
Function Call
openAndCenterWindow('http://www.nostarch.com/');
```

Figure 6-6: Passing parameters

Using More Than One Parameter

Sometimes you want to change more than one thing each time you call a function. The built-in JavaScript function prompt(), for example, can change two sets of words: the words that appear above the text box and those that appear within it. When we call prompt() as follows, we pass in two parameters, separated by a comma:

```
var the_answer = prompt("What's your favorite color?","yellow?");
```

The method window.open(), discussed in the last chapter, provides an example of three parameters: the URL you want to open inside the window, the name of the window, and the window's features.

The functions you write can also take more than one parameter. Let's say you want to write a function to display a web page in a square window. You might write a function that finds the name of the page and the length of one of the sides of a window. Figure 6-7 shows you what this would look like.

```
    <html>
    <head>
    <title>Square Windows</title>
    <script type = "text/javascript">
    <!-- hide me from older browsers
❶ function openSquareWindow(the_url, the_length)
    {
        var the_features = "width=" + the_length + ",height=" + the_length;
        var the_window = window.open(the_url, "", the_features);
    }
    // show me -->
    </script>
    </head>
    <body>
❷ <a href = "#"
      onClick = "openSquareWindow('http://www.webmonkey.com/', 400); return false;">
        Open the Webmonkey home page in a big square window</a><br>
```

```
<a href = "#"
   onClick = "openSquareWindow('http://www.nostarch.com/', 100); return false;">
     Open the No Starch Press home page in a small square window</a><br>
</body>
</html>
```

Figure 6-7: Writing functions that take more than one parameter

Notice that in ❶ two variables now appear between the parentheses following the function name: the_url and the_length. In ❷ we're calling the function as we would call prompt(), with two parameters separated by a comma. Calling the function sets the first variable in the function definition to the first parameter, so in the case of ❷, the_url is set to http://www.webmonkey.com/. Similarly, the second variable in the function definition is set to the second parameter in the function call. If we call the function as in ❷, the_length is set to 400. Figure 6-8 depicts the results of calling functions with two parameters.

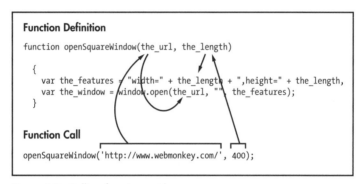

Figure 6-8: Calling functions with two parameters

Getting Information from Functions

You can also write functions that give information back to you. Consider the prompt() function:

```
var the_answer = prompt("What's your name?","Ishmael");
```

When a user types his or her name into the prompt box and clicks OK, the name goes into the variable the_answer. In programming parlance, you'd say that the function prompt() *returns* the words typed into the prompt box. The functions you write can return values as well. Figure 6-9 shows a very simple example of how to make a function return values.

```
<html>
<head>
<title>Date Printer</title>
<script type = "text/javascript">
<!-- hide me from older browsers
function getNiceDate()
```

```
{
    var now = new Date();
    var the_month = now.getMonth() + 1; // remember, January is month 0
    var the_day = now.getDate();
    var the_year = now.getYear();
❶  var the_nice_date = the_month + "/" + the_day + "/" + the_year;
❷  return the_nice_date;
}
// show me -->
</script>
</head>
<body>
Hello! Today is
<script type = "text/javascript">
<!-- hide me from older browsers
❸ var today = getNiceDate();
document.write(today);
// show me -->
</script>
</head>
</body>
</html>
```

Figure 6-9: A script with a simple function that returns a value

Line-by-Line Analysis of Figure 6-9

Most of the function should be familiar by now. The first four lines create a new Date object and carry out a few method calls to get information from that object. Line ❶ takes the information gathered and creates a nicely formatted date. Notice that the line is

```
var the_nice_date = the_month + "/" + the_day + "/" + the_year;
```

and not

```
var the_nice_date = "the_month/the_day/the_year";
```

The latter won't work, because JavaScript won't recognize the_month, the_day, or the_year as variables if they appear inside quotes. The correct version of this line takes the variables out of the quotes and puts them together with slashes using the plus (+) sign. In the incorrect version, the quotation marks stop JavaScript from interpreting the names as variables, so the web page would display *Hello! Today is the_month/the_day/ the_year*. Line ❷ tells JavaScript to exit the function and return the value of the_nice_date to whatever variable is waiting for it. In this case, the variable is today in ❸. Whenever JavaScript sees the word return in a function, it exits the function and outputs whatever value comes after return.

Line ❸ calls the function getNiceDate(), which returns a nicely formatted date. The code document.write(today) then puts the date on the web page, as shown in Figure 6-10.

Figure 6-10: Returning the date

Dealing with Y2K

Figure 6-9 works fine, but it has a little problem. Remember our discussion of the Y2K problem in the getYear() method of the Date object ("Writing the Date to Your Web Page" on page 26)? Different browsers deal with years differently. In some versions of Netscape, getYear() returns the year minus 1900. So if it's the year 2010, getYear() returns 110. Other versions return the full four-digit year if the year is before 1900 or after 1999. Different versions of Internet Explorer give different results for the same date as well.

The way to deal with this problem is to see whether the year returned by getYear()is less than 1000. If so, your visitor is using a browser that subtracts 1900 from the date if it's after 1899. In this case, you can get the correct four-digit year by adding 1900 to the date. You'll find a concise form for all this convoluted logic in the JavaScript function Y2K(), shown in Figure 6-11.

```
function Y2K(the_date)
{
    if (the_date < 1000)
    {
        the_date = the_date + 1900;
    }
    return the_date;
}
```

Figure 6-11: Dealing with the Y2K problem

This function adds 1900 to the year if it is less than 1000. You can drop the Y2K() function into the script shown in Figure 6-8 to deal with its Y2K problem. Figure 6-12 demonstrates how the two look together.

```
<html>
<head>
<title>Date Printer</title>
<script type = "text/javascript">
<!-- hide me from older browsers
function getNiceDate()
{
    var now = new Date();
    var the_month = now.getMonth()+1; // remember, January is month 0
    var the_day = now.getDate();
❶  var the_year = now.getYear();
❷  var the_fixed_year = Y2K(the_year);
    var the_nice_date = the_month + "/" + the_day + "/" + the_fixed_year;
```

```
            return the_nice_date;
    }
❸ function Y2K(the_date)
    {
        if (the_date < 1000)
        {
            the_date = the_date + 1900;
        }
        return the_date;
    }
    // show me -->
    </script>
    </head>
    <body>
    Hello! Today is
    <script type = "text/javascript">
    <!-- hide me from older browsers
    var today = getNiceDate();
    document.write(today);
    // show me -->
    </script>
    </head>
    </body>
    </html>
```

Figure 6-12: The script in Figure 6-9 with the Y2K fix

Line-by-Line Analysis of Figure 6-12

Line ❶ in Figure 6-12 uses the getYear() method to get the year, and ❷ calls the function Y2K() on the year to fix it up. The variable the_fixed_year is set to whatever Y2K() returns. The JavaScript in Figure 6-12 actually defines the function Y2K() after the getNiceDate() function. It might seem strange that getNiceDate() can call Y2K() even though Y2K() is defined after getNiceDate(). Remember, though, that when you define functions, you're just telling JavaScript their names and what they do, so the order in which you define your functions doesn't matter as long as you define them all before you call any of them from HTML.

Defining Variables Properly

The getNiceDate() function in Figure 6-12 calls the year variable the_year. However, when you look at how the Y2K() function appears in ❸, you'll see that it calls whatever passes into it the_date. Since we're calling Y2K(the_year), JavaScript looks up the value of the_year and then sends that value to the Y2K() function. The Y2K() function stores that value in the variable the_date. In other words, the functions getNiceDate() and Y2K() have two different names for the same value. It's as if the functions are different countries where people speak different languages. If you try to talk about the_year inside the Y2K() function, it won't know what you're saying, and you'll get an error. Figure 6-13 shows you a graphical representation of how this works.

```
function getNiceDate()
{
  var now = new Date();
  var the_month = now.getMonth()+1; // remember, Jan is month 0
  var the_day = now.getDate();
  var the_year = now.getYear();
  var the_fixed_year = Y2K(the_year);
  var the_nice_date = the_month + "/" + the_day + "/" + the_fixed_year;
  return the_nice_date;
}
function Y2K(the_date)
{
      if(the_date < 1000)
      {
            the_date = the_date + 1900;
      }
      return the_date;
}
```

Let's say now.getYear() returns 110, meaning that it's 2010 and your visitor is using IE. This means that the_year = 110 inside the getNiceDate() function.

Here we're passing the_year into the Y2K() function. First, JavaScript figures out that the_year is a variable equal to 110. Then it passes the value 110 to the Y2K() function.

Inside the Y2K() function, the variable the_date takes the value 110, because that's what we passed into the function.

Now the_date gets changed to 2010.

The value of the_date is returned to the awaiting variable.

The awaiting variable is the_fixed_year. So now the_fixed_year has the value 2010.

Figure 6-13: How variables work in different functions

Why can't the Y2K() function access the variable the_year in getNiceDate()? Because when you first defined the_year, you put the word var in front of it:

```
var the_year = now.getYear();
```

The word var tells JavaScript to create the variable only for the function where it's defined. If you'd omitted var when defining the_year, you could access that variable inside the Y2K() function. You might think that freedom would be a good thing. Why shouldn't you access the_year anywhere in the program—why hide it inside getNiceDate()? The reason is that if you don't hide variables inside functions, you will soon drive yourself crazy. Having one function change a variable that was declared in another function is a major cause of difficult-to-debug problems. The idea of protecting variables declared inside functions is such an important programming concept that it gets its own name: *encapsulation.*

Consider the example in Figure 6-14 to see the headaches you'll avoid if you define your variables with var:

```
<html>
<head>
<title>Bad Encapsulation</title>
<script type = "text/javascript">
<!-- hide me from older browsers

function getNames()
{
    the_name = prompt("What's your name?","");
    dog_name = getDogName();
    alert(the_name + " has a dog named " + dog_name);
}
```

```
function getDogName()
{
    the_name = prompt("What's your dog's name?","");
    return the_name;
}

// show me -->
</script>
</head>
<body>
<a href = "#" onClick = "getNames(); return false;">Click here for a survey</a>
</body>
</html>
```

Figure 6-14: The dangers of variables without var

If I run this example and input thau when the prompt asks for a name and fido when the prompt asks for a dog's name, we end up with an alert that says *fido has a dog named fido*. Somewhere along the line, the program forgot that my name was thau and replaced it with fido.

This happened because both getNames() and getDogName() use a variable called the_name. Function getNames() saves the user's name in the variable the_name. Then function getDogName() saves the dog's name in the_name. If I had used var when declaring the variable the_name in the getDogName() function, JavaScript would have understood that the variable is specific to that function and would have left alone all the_name variables in other functions. Because I didn't use var when I set the variable the_name inside the getDogName() function, I unintentionally replaced the contents of the_name with the dog's name. When getDogName() exits and the alert comes up, we see the dog's name:

```
alert (the_name + " has a dog named " + dog_name);
```

If I had used var inside the getDogName() function, *thau has a dog named fido* would have come up. As your JavaScripts get longer, you're likely to use the same variable in different functions. Without var, it's very difficult to track down what's going wrong in these functions, so save yourself the headache with a little preparation.

Using var to hide variables inside functions also allows you to write functions that you can cut and paste into other scripts. If you define all your variables with var, you don't have to worry about whether a function you've written will mess up another function when you paste it into a different page. Otherwise you can't tell whether some variable in a program shares a variable name with your function.

Summary

There's an art to figuring out when to use a function and knowing the best way to write one. In general, the best time to use a function is for a simple task you need to execute more than once. For example, patching the Y2K bug in JavaScript is a task you may have to do repeatedly, so it's a good idea to create a function to handle it. As we see more complicated examples of JavaScript later in the book, you'll get a sense for what should go into functions. And, of course, as you view the source code on all the great web pages you see, you'll notice how various JavaScripters use functions.

Almost all complicated JavaScripts use at least one homemade function. In this chapter, you've seen how to write simple functions with no parameters and more complicated functions that take parameters and return values. If you found all of this a bit tricky, don't worry. You'll have many more opportunities to learn how to use functions in JavaScript.

Assignment

Write a page with three images on it, each of them a navigational icon leading to another website. Each time the user mouses over a navigational icon, it should do an image swap, and a new window should open with an appropriate URL. For example, the three images could be of an apple, a monkey, and a sun. (See http://www.bookofjavascript.com/Chapter06.) When the user mouses over the sun icon, the image could swap to a happy sun, and a window with the Sun Microsystems home page could open up. Create this effect using a function that takes three parameters: the image to swap, the new image to put in its place, and the URL to open in the new window. For example, if the user mouses over the sun icon, the image should look like this:

```
<img src = "normal_sun.gif" name = "sun" border = "0"
  onMouseOver =
    "fancySwap(window.document.sun,'hilight_sun.gif','http://www.sun.com/');"
  onMouseOut = "window.document.sun.src='normal_sun.gif';">
```

The first parameter in the function fancySwap() is the location of the image you want to swap. Notice that the image has the name sun. This means JavaScript will refer to this image as window.document.sun. The second parameter is the name of the GIF file to swap into the image called sun. The third parameter is the URL that should open in the new window. The function you write will start as follows:

```
function fancySwap(the_image_tag, the_new_image, the_url)
{
    you fill in here . . .
}
```

The lines of code you write will carry out the image swap (using what you learned in Chapter 4) and open a new window with the_url (using what you learned in Chapter 5).

NOTE   *As described in Chapter 5, if the user has a pop-up blocker, the code may not work.*

Good luck—this is a tough one!

7

PROVIDING AND RECEIVING INFORMATION WITH FORMS

So far I've shown you a few ways to get information from your visitors. You can ask questions with the `prompt()` function, and you can use `onClick` to tell when they click a link or `onMouseOver` to detect when they move over a link. In this chapter, you'll learn a plethora of ways to collect and display information using HTML forms and JavaScript. You can rely on forms and JavaScript to create very interactive sites that might include surveys and quizzes, calculators, games, and novel navigational tools.

In this chapter you'll learn how to:

- Create HTML forms
- Use JavaScript to read a form a visitor has filled out
- Use JavaScript to fill out a form automatically
- Use forms as navigational tools

Real-World Examples of Forms

Forms can gather all sorts of input, including demographic information such as age and gender, answers to quizzes and polls, and numbers for tricky equations. The mortgage monthly payment calculator shown in Figure 7-1 offers an example of the latter. The form gives you places for the amount, interest rate, and length of a loan. If you enter all this information and click the submit button (which says *calculate monthly payment*), JavaScript reads the information off the form, performs a calculation, and displays the results in the monthly payment box.

Figure 7-1: This mortgage calculator uses a form that presents input fields.

You can also use forms as navigational tools. The home page for Doctors Without Borders (http://www.doctorswithoutborders.org, shown in Figure 7-2) has a pull-down menu that functions as a navigational tool. Click the menu, pull down to highlight the name of the country you'd like information about, and release the mouse—JavaScript tells the browser to take you to the page.

Figure 7-2: The Doctors Without Borders home page uses a pull-down menu that acts as a navigational form.

As a third example, the *Book of JavaScript* home page also has a pull-down menu that functions as a navigational tool (Figure 7-3). Click the menu, pull down to highlight the name of the chapter you'd like to visit, and release the mouse—JavaScript directs your browser to a page of information about that chapter. Figure 7-3 shows the navigation element on the *Book of JavaScript* home page.

Figure 7-3: The Book of JavaScript *home page's navigation element*

All three examples work in the same general way: HTML draws the forms in Figures 7-1 and 7-3 on the web page, and JavaScript reads the information that the visitor fills in. Most forms that use JavaScript follow this pattern. Let's look first at how to write forms to your web page with HTML.

Form Basics

Figure 7-4 shows a simple form displayed in a browser, and Figure 7-5 shows the HTML behind that form.

Figure 7-4: A simple HTML form

```
<html>
<head>
<title>A Very Basic HTML Form</title>
</head>
<body>
❶ <form>
❷ Name: <input type = "text"> <br>
❸ Age: <input type = "text"> <br>
```

```
❹ </form>
   </body>
   </html>
```

Figure 7-5: HTML code for the basic form shown in Figure 7-4

Text Fields

As you can see in Figure 7-4, the HTML in Figure 7-5 draws two text boxes on the screen. A visitor to your site can click inside the text boxes and type a name and age.

Notice that the form is constructed of normal HTML. Like most HTML, the form must go between the <body> and </body> tags. The form begins with a <form> tag and ends with a </form> tag (❶ and ❹). Between the <form> tags you'll see the *elements* of the form (❷ and ❸), the parts that hold information. In this chapter, you'll encounter a variety of different form elements, each with special characteristics. The elements in ❷ and ❸ are called *text fields*. These allow the user to type a line of text in a field. Later you'll learn how JavaScript reads the user's typed input.

The part of ❷ and ❸ that tells the browser to draw a text field is the <input> tag:

```
<input type = "text">
```

The <input> tag tells the browser to create an input field of type text. You can embellish the text field a bit—for example, you can make the text box bigger by setting its size:

```
<input type = "text" size = "40">
```

The size of the text field is roughly equal to the number of characters that can fit inside the field.

You can also tell the browser to place some words in the text box. For example, if you want the words Type your name here to appear inside the text box, enter this:

```
<input type = "text" value = "Type your name here">
```

By setting the value of the text box, you determine what goes inside it. Remember the term value—it will come in handy later.

Buttons, Checkboxes, and Radio Buttons

In addition to text fields, you can put buttons, checkboxes, and radio buttons in your forms. Figure 7-6 shows you what each of these elements looks like, and Figure 7-7 shows you the HTML used to draw Figure 7-6.

Figure 7-6: A checkbox, radio buttons, and a button

The Checkbox

The code in ❶ of Figure 7-7 shows you the HTML for a single checkbox. If you want the box checked by default in the above example, put the word checked inside the element tag, like this:

```
<input type = "checkbox" checked>
```

You'll encounter the word checked again, so remember it.

```
<html>
<head>
<title>Checkboxes, Radio Buttons, and Buttons</title>
</head>
<body>
<h1>Tell me about your dog</h1>
<form>
<p>Name: <input type = "text">
<p>Would you like your dog to get our daily newsletter?
❶ <p><input type = "checkbox"> yes
<p>How old is your dog? <br>
❷ <input type = "radio" name = "age">between 0 and 1 years<br>
❸ <input type = "radio" name = "age">between 1 and 3 years<br>
❹ <input type = "radio" name = "age">between 3 and 7 years<br>
❺ <input type = "radio" name = "age">older than 7 years<br>
<p>
❻ <input type = "button" value = "I'm done">

</form>
</body>
</html>
```

Figure 7-7: The HTML for a checkbox, radio buttons, and a button

The Radio Button

The next type of input element is the radio button. Radio buttons differ from checkboxes in that they're meant to come in groups of mutually exclusive radio buttons. Since a dog cannot be between 0 and 1 *and* between 1 and 3 years old, a group of radio buttons is a good way to input the dog's age range. The way to put radio buttons into a group is to give them all the same name attribute. In Figure 7-7 I've given the radio buttons the same name (❷ through ❺) so that a visitor can only choose one of them. Because all these buttons share the name age, you can only turn on one at a time. For example, if the visitor chooses the first radio button and then the third one, that action deselects the first radio button. If you want the page to open with a radio button already chosen, use the word checked, just as with checkboxes:

```
<input type = "radio" name = "age" checked>
```

The Button

The final type of input element demonstrated in Figure 7-7 is the button:

```
input type = "button"
```

This input type creates a rectangular button. If you want some words to appear inside the button, set the button's value as in ❻. Right now the button doesn't perform any function, but soon we'll learn how to attach an action to it.

Select Elements

All the form elements we've discussed so far are input elements. The next two elements, pull-down menus and scrolling lists, have a slightly different format. Figure 7-8 shows what these elements look like, and Figure 7-9 shows the HTML used to write that page.

Figure 7-8: A pull-down menu and a scrolling list

Pull-down menus start with a <select> tag (❶) and end with a </select> tag (❸). An <option> tag (❷) precedes each item in the pull-down menu. You don't have to put each option on its own line, but doing that makes for cleaner-looking HTML.

```
<html>
<head>
<title>A Pull-Down Menu and a List</title>
</head>
<body>
<form>
Your dog's gender:<br>
<select>
<option>Male</option>
<option>Female</option>
</select>
<p>
Your dog's favorite food: <br>
❶ <select size = "3">
❷ <option>beef</option>
<option>chicken</option>
<option>fish</option>
<option>pork</option>
<option>rawhide</option>
<option>lettuce</option>
<option>cactus</option>
❸ </select>

</form>
</body>
</html>
```

Figure 7-9: HTML for a pull-down menu and a scrolling list

Sometimes you want one of the options to appear as the default when the page loads. To do that, put the word selected inside the <option> tag. If you want the word Female to appear in the gender pull-down menu when the page loads, you would write this:

```
<option selected>Female</option>
```

The main difference between scrolling lists and pull-down menus is that scrolling lists have size set inside the <select> tag, as in ❶. Setting the size determines how many options appear in the list. In ❶, since we're setting size to 3, three options appear in the list. To see more options, a visitor can use the scroll bar on the side of the list.

If you want to give your visitors the ability to choose multiple options, put the word multiple inside the <select> tag, like this:

```
<select size = "3" multiple>
```

This allows a visitor on a PC to choose more than one item by holding down the CTRL key (the apple key for Macintosh users) and clicking multiple options.

Textareas

If you want to let your visitors input more than one line of text, you'll have to use the textarea form element, which scrolls to let your visitors type as much information as they like. Figure 7-10 shows you what a textarea looks like in the browser, and Figure 7-11 shows you the HTML used to draw the textarea.

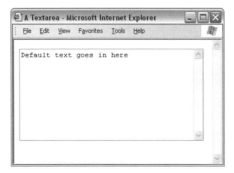

Figure 7-10: The textarea form element

Any text that goes between the <textarea> and </textarea> tags appears inside the textarea when the browser renders the page. You can control the size of the textarea by setting its rows and columns. As with the text box, these numbers roughly reflect the number of characters a visitor can enter in the textarea: The rows number controls the textarea's height, and cols controls the width.

```
<html>
<head>
<title>A Textarea</title>
</head>
<body>
<form>
<textarea rows = "10" cols = "40">
Default text goes in here
</textarea>
</form>
</body>
</html>
```

Figure 7-11: The HTML for a textarea

Final Form Comments

This section has covered much of what you need to know about writing HTML forms for the purpose of this book. You'll find other details about forms in any good HTML manual.

Forms and JavaScript

Once you have a form on your web page, you can use JavaScript to read information from that form and display information in it. The mortgage monthly payment calculator, for example, reads the principal, interest rate, and other information the user types into the form, calculates a monthly payment based on this information, and then writes the result to the form.

Naming Form Elements

Before you can read from or write to an element of your form, you need to tell JavaScript which form element you're talking about by naming your form and its elements. The code in Figure 7-12 demonstrates how to name forms (❶) and their elements (❷ and ❸). Notice that you can't name the <option> tag (❹). Figure 7-13 shows the simple form this code displays.

```
   <html>
   <head>
   <title>A Form with Names</title>
   </head>
   <body>
   <h1>A Form with Names</h1>
❶ <form name = "my_form">
❷ Age: <input type = "text" name = "the_age_field">
   Gender:
❸ <select name = "the_gender">
❹ <option>male</option>
   <option>female</option>
   </select>
   </form>
   </body>
   </html>
```

Figure 7-12: A form with names

When naming form elements, you should follow the same principles as in naming an image tag for an image swap: Do not use spaces, make sure no other HTML element has the same name, and don't use names that are also HTML tags. For example, don't name a text field body, because <body> is an HTML tag. (Some browsers work fine if you do this, but others will give visitors a JavaScript error.) You can name buttons, checkboxes, textareas, and radio buttons just as you name text fields and selects.

Figure 7-13: The form in Figure 7-12

Naming Radio Buttons

Radio buttons are a special case. Since all radio buttons that belong to a group receive the same name, we can't use the name to figure out which radio button the visitor selected. Putting value = "something" inside a radio button tag lets us differentiate between different radio buttons in the same set (see Figure 7-14).

```
<html>
<head>
<title>Values Inside Radio Buttons</title>
</head>
<body>
<form name = "radio_button_form">
How old is your dog? <br>
<input type = "radio" name = "age" value = "puppy">between 0 and 1 years<br>
<input type = "radio" name = "age" value = "young">between 1 and 3 years<br>
<input type = "radio" name = "age" value = "middle_age">between 3 and 7 years<br>
<input type = "radio" name = "age" value = "older">older than 7 years<br>
</form>
</body>
</html>
```

Figure 7-14: Putting values inside radio buttons

I've named each radio button age to show that it's part of the age group, but each one has its own value. How JavaScript determines which radio button the user has selected will be discussed later in this chapter.

Naming Options

The same holds true for the <option> tag in <select> form elements. Although options don't receive names, they do take values. In order to use JavaScript to determine what a visitor has chosen from a pull-down menu, you need to put values inside the options. Figure 7-15 shows a variant on the code in Figure 7-12, with values added to the <option> tags.

In Figure 7-15, the <select> tag still gets a name (❶), and the <option> tags get values (❷ and ❸). When you use JavaScript to determine which option a user selected, the value of the option will be what you retrieve. If the visitor selects the Female option, you'll retrieve the value female because of the value = "female" inside that option.

```
     <html>
     <head>
     <title>A Form with Values Inside the Option Tags</title>
     </head>
     <body>
     <h1>A Form with Names</h1>
     <form name = "my_form">
     Age: <input type = "text" name = "the_age_field">
     Gender:
❶   <select name = "the_gender">
```

```
❷ <option value = "male">Male</option>
❸ <option value = "female">Female</option>
   </select>
   </form>
   </body>
   </html>
```

Figure 7-15: Values inside <option> tags

Reading and Setting Form Elements

Once your form and form elements have names, JavaScript can easily find out what your visitors have typed into the form elements. Just tell JavaScript the form and element for which you want information.

Reading Information from Text Fields

If you want to see what value a user has typed into the text field named the_age_field (❷) in Figure 7-12, use this:

```
window.document.my_form.the_age_field.value
```

This line tells JavaScript to look in the window, locate its document, find the form called my_form inside the document, find the form element called the_age_field inside that form, and read its value. Figure 7-16 shows how to build a simple calculator using form elements as inputs.

```
   <html>
   <head>
   <title>A Very Simple Calculator</title>
   <script type = "text/javascript">
   <!-- hide me from older browsers
   function multiplyTheFields()
   {
❶ var number_one = window.document.the_form.field_one.value;
❷ var number_two = window.document.the_form.field_two.value;
❸ var product = number_one * number_two;
❹ alert(number_one + " times " + number_two + " is: " + product);
   }
   // show me -->
   </script>
   </head>
   <body>
❺ <form name = "the_form">
❻ Number 1: <input type = "text" name = "field_one"> <br>
❼ Number 2: <input type = "text" name = "field_two"> <br>
❽ <a href = "#" onClick = "multiplyTheFields(); return false;">Multiply them!</a>
   </form>
   </body>
   </html>
```

Figure 7-16: A very simple calculator

This example presents two text fields and a link. When a visitor puts numbers in the text fields and clicks the link (Figure 7-17), an alert box appears, showing the product of those numbers (Figure 7-18). The link in ❽ calls the function multiplyTheFields() when a user clicks it.

Figure 7-17: The multiplying calculator

Figure 7-18: Displaying the results

The function multiplyTheFields() does all the work. The code in ❶ of Figure 7-16 looks up the value of the text field field_one (❻) inside the form my_form, located in the document of the window. It then stores this value in the variable number_one. The same thing happens in ❷, except this time JavaScript looks at the text field named field_two (❼) and stores it in the variable number_two. Once JavaScript reads the values of the two text fields, it multiplies them (❸) and puts the result inside an alert box (❹).

Setting the Value of a Text Field

One difference between Figure 7-17 and the mortgage calculator in Figure 7-1 is that the results of the mortgage calculator are displayed in a text field instead of in an alert box. To put an item inside a text field using JavaScript, simply set the value of the text field to whatever you want to write inside it.

If Figure 7-16 had a third text field named the_answer, we could put the product of the other numbers into it using this line:

```
window.document.the_form.the_answer.value = product;
```

Here we're telling JavaScript to set the value of the text field named the_answer, located inside the form called the_form, to the value product. Figure 7-19 shows what this looks like in a browser, and Figure 7-20 lists the complete code.

The only differences between Figures 7-20 and 7-16 are the addition of a new text field called the_answer (❷) and the changed location of the output from an alert box to inside the_answer (❶).

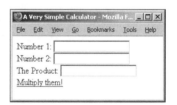

Figure 7-19: Putting the results of the calculation in a text field

```
<html>
<head>
<title>A Very Simple Calculator</title>
<script type = "text/javascript">
<!-- hide me from older browsers
function multiplyTheFields()
{
    var number_one = window.document.the_form.field_one.value;
    var number_two = window.document.the_form.field_two.value;
    var product = number_one * number_two;
❶    window.document.the_form.the_answer.value = product;
}
// show me -->
</script>
</head>
<body>
<form name = "the_form">
Number 1: <input type = "text" name = "field_one"> <br>
Number 2: <input type = "text" name = "field_two"> <br>
❷ The Product: <input type = "text" name = "the_answer"> <br>
<a href = "#" onClick = "multiplyTheFields(); return false;">Multiply them!</a>
</form>
</body>
</html>
```

Figure 7-20: The code for Figure 7-19

Figure 7-20 should give you a basic idea of how the mortgage monthly payment calculator works. I won't go into the guts of the mortgage calculator, but if you'd like to see the mathematics behind your monthly mortgage payment, browse to http://www.bookofjavascript.com/Websites/Mortgage. This might be a little tough to understand until you read the next chapter, though, so tread lightly.

Textareas

You can set and read a textarea, the form element that lets you enter more than one line of text, just as you can a text field. For example, if you have a textarea named my_text_area inside a form called my_form, you can enter some words like this:

```
window.document.my_form.my_text_area.value =
    "Here's the story of a lovely lady...";
```

If your visitor types some input in the textarea, you can read it using this:

```
var the_visitor_input = window.document.my_form.my_text_area.value;
```

Checkboxes

Checkboxes differ from text fields and textareas. Instead of having a value as text fields and textareas do, they have a Boolean attribute called checked (see Chapter 3 for discussion of Booleans).

If a user has clicked a checkbox so that an × or check mark appears in it, then checked equals true. If the checkbox is not on, then checked equals false (remember—because true and false are Booleans, they don't take quotes). The quiz illustrated in Figure 7-21 shows how to use the checked property of checkboxes. Figure 7-22 shows the code.

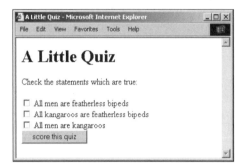

Figure 7-21: A short JavaScript quiz

When a user clicks the button form element at the bottom of the window in Figure 7-21, it calls the scoreQuiz() function. Line ❶ in Figure 7-22 then creates a variable called correct and sets its value to 0. This variable keeps track of how many answers the visitor answered correctly. The code in ❷ and ❸ gives the visitor one point if he or she clicked the checkbox next to the first question; ❷ fetches the value of the checked property in the first checkbox and compares this value to the word true. If the user selects the checkbox, its checked value is true, so ❸ executes, adding a 1 to the variable correct, and ❹ does the same thing for the second question.

The if-then statement in ❺ is slightly different from the other two. It says that if the checked property of the third checkbox is false (that is, the visitor hasn't selected the checkbox), then JavaScript should add 1 to correct.

Finally, ❻ tells visitors how well they did.

```
<html>
<head>
<title>A Little Quiz</title>
<script type = "text/javascript">
<!-- hide me from older browsers
function scoreQuiz()
{
❶    var correct = 0;
❷    if (window.document.the_form.question1.checked == true) {
❸        correct = correct + 1;
     }
❹    if (window.document.the_form.question2.checked == true) {
         correct = correct + 1;
```

```
        }
❺       if (window.document.the_form.question3.checked == false) {
            correct = correct + 1;
        }
❻       alert("You got " + correct + " answers right!");
    }
    // show me -->
    </script>
    </head>
    <body>
    <h1>A Little Quiz</h1>
    Check the statements which are true:
    <form name = "the_form">
    <input type = "checkbox" name =
        "question1"> All men are featherless bipeds<br>
    <input type = "checkbox" name =
        "question2"> All kangaroos are featherless bipeds<br>
    <input type = "checkbox" name = "question3"> All men are kangaroos<br>
    <input type = "button" value = "score this quiz" onClick = "scoreQuiz();">
    </form>
    </body>
    </html>
```

Figure 7-22: The code for the quiz

To show visitors the correct answers after they click the score button in Figure 7-21, we could use the scoreQuiz() function to determine the value of each checkbox by setting its checked property to true or false. Figure 7-23 updates the scoreQuiz() function to give the correct answers.

In Figure 7-23, I add an else to each if-then clause, which sets the checkbox to the correct answer if the visitor gets the answer wrong. The first if-then clause, starting with ❶, reads in plain English, "If the visitor checks the first checkbox, the answer is correct, so add 1 to the variable correct. Otherwise, check the first checkbox to indicate the correct answer." If the visitor guessed wrong, ❷ selects the first checkbox by setting its checked property to true.

```
function scoreQuiz()
{
    var correct = 0;
❶   if (window.document.the_form.question1.checked == true) {
        correct = correct + 1;
    } else {
❷       window.document.the_form.question1.checked = true;
    }
    if (window.document.the_form.question2.checked == true)
    {
        correct = correct + 1;
    } else {
        window.document.the_form.question2.checked = true;
    }
    if (window.document.the_form.question3.checked == false) {
        correct = correct + 1;
    } else {
```

```
        window.document.the_form.question3.checked = false;
    }
    alert("You got " + correct +
        " answers right! The correct answers are now shown.");
}
```

Figure 7-23: The scoreQuiz() function from Figure 7-22, changed to show the correct answers

Radio Buttons

The code for reading and setting radio buttons is slightly more complicated than for text fields and checkboxes. Because all the radio buttons in a group have the same name, you can't just ask about the settings for a radio button with a certain name—JavaScript won't know which button you mean.

To overcome this difficulty, JavaScript puts all of the radio buttons with the same name in a list. Each radio button in the list is given a number. The first radio button in the group is number 0, the second is 1, the third is 2, and so on. (Most programming languages start counting from 0—you just have to get used to this.)

To refer to a radio button, use the notation radio_button_name[item_number]. For example, if you have four radio buttons named age, the first one will be age[0], the second will be age[1], the third age[2], and the fourth age[3].

To see whether a visitor has chosen a certain radio button, look at its checked property, just as with checkboxes. Let's say you have four radio buttons named age in a form called radio_button_form, as in Figure 7-14. To test whether your visitor has selected the first radio button in the age group, write something like this:

```
if (window.document.radio_button_form.age[0].checked == true)
{
    alert("the first radio button was selected!");
}
```

This is much the same method that you would use for a checkbox. The only difference is that you must refer to the first radio button in the age group as age[0], whereas with a checkbox you can just give its name.

Once you know how to determine whether a radio button is checked, it's easy to understand how to select a radio button with JavaScript. With checkboxes, you use something like this:

```
window.document.form_name.checkbox_name.checked = true;
```

With radio buttons, you tell JavaScript which radio button you mean by referring to its list number. To select the first radio button of a set called age, input this:

```
window.document.form_name.age[0].checked = true;
```

Pull-Down Menus and Scrollable Lists

JavaScript can read and set pull-down menus and scrollable lists as it does radio buttons, with two main differences. First, while radio buttons have a checked property, pull-down menus and scrollable lists have a comparable property called selected. Second, the list that keeps track of the options in a pull-down menu or scrollable list differs from that for a radio button. As discussed in the section on reading and setting radio buttons, when a browser sees a group of radio buttons, it creates a list with the same name as the set of radio buttons. In Figure 7-12, we named the radio button set gender, so the browser calls the list gender. The first element of this list is called gender[0].

In contrast, a pull-down menu or scrollable list has the options property, a list of all the options in the pull-down or scrollable list, which can tell you what's selected in that menu or list. In the list for the simple pull-down shown in Figure 7-24, male is the first element (item number 0) and female the second (item number 1).

```
<form name = "my_form">
<select name = "the_gender">
<option value = "male">Male</option>
<option value = "female">Female</option>
</select>
</form>
```

Figure 7-24: A simple pull-down menu

Thus the following lines tell you whether a visitor has selected the first option in the list (male):

```
if (window.document.my_form.the_gender.options[0].selected == true)
{
    alert("It's a boy!)";
}
```

You can also select an option:

```
window.document.my_form.the_gender.options[1].selected = true;
```

Executing this line of JavaScript would select the female option in the pull-down menu.

Sometimes you have a long list of options in a pull-down menu, and you just want to know which one the visitor has selected. Happily, pull-down menus and scrollable lists have a value property that contains the value of the selected option.

Let's say you have a pull-down menu like the one in Figure 7-24. To figure out quickly whether a visitor chose *male* or *female* in this pull-down menu, you write something like this:

```
var chosen_gender = window.document.my_form.the_gender.value;
```

If you want to know the index number of the option selected, rather than its value, you can use the select's `selectedIndex` property, like this:

```
var chosen_gender_index = window.document.my_form.the_gender.selectedIndex;
```

If your site visitor has selected the first option in the list, `selectedIndex` will be 0.

I'll show you a way to shorten these last two examples when we discuss using pull-down menus as navigation tools. But before that, you need to know a little more about forms in general.

Handling Events Using Form Elements

So far, all the functions in this chapter have been triggered by a visitor clicking a link or button.

Each type of form element has its own list of triggering events. As demonstrated in Figure 7-22, button elements can use `onClick` to call a function when someone clicks the button. However, not all form elements take `onClick`. Table 7-1 shows you some of the events that different form elements handle. You'll find a complete list in Appendix C.

Table 7-1: Some Events That Different Form Elements Can Handle

Form Element	Event	What Triggers the Event
Button	onClick	Self-explanatory
Checkbox	onClick	Self-explanatory
Radio button	onClick	Self-explanatory
Text field	onChange	Change the contents of the text field and then click out of the field (anywhere else on the web page)
Textarea	onChange	Change what's in the textarea and then click out of it
Select	onChange	Change a selection in the pull-down menu or list
Form	onSubmit	Press ENTER inside a text field or click a submit button

Note that text fields, textareas, and selects can trigger events only when someone changes them. If a user clicks on a pull-down menu and then chooses an already selected option, that doesn't trigger the `onChange` event. Similarly, if someone clicks a text field and then clicks somewhere else without changing anything in the text field, `onChange` won't register this action.

Notice also that the form element takes an event called `onSubmit`. A form is *submitted* when the user presses the ENTER key with the cursor in a text field or when the user clicks a submit button. Figure 7-25 shows you how to build a very simple browser using a form with an `onSubmit` event.

```
<html>
<head>
<title>A Simple Browser</title>
</head>
<body>
```

Type a URL and then either click the submit button or just press ENTER.

```
❶ <form name = "the_form"
     onSubmit =
       "window.location = window.document.the_form.the_url.value; return false;">
   <input type = "text" name = "the_url" value = "http://">
❷ <input type = "submit" value = "Go there!">
   </form>
   </body>
   </html>
```

Figure 7-25: Using onSubmit inside a form

The `<form>` tag in ❶ shows you what `onSubmit` does. In this case, the `onSubmit` says, "Whenever someone submits this form, look into the form element called `the_url` and send this person to the URL there." This happens when a visitor presses ENTER in the text field or clicks the submit button (❷). The `return false` that appears at the end of ❶ prevents the web browser from taking control away from JavaScript when the form is submitted. Without it, the JavaScript command never executes.

Make this a Shortcut

You might have noticed that the `<form>` tag in ❶ of Figure 7-25 is a little long. You can shorten it by replacing most of the part identifying the form, `window.document.the_form`, with the word `this`, which refers to the thing that contains it. For example, in ❶ of Figure 7-25, the code that looks for the value of `the_url` is located inside the `<form>` tag. That means you can replace all the code identifying the `<form>` tag with the word `this`—in other words, you can write ❶ in Figure 7-25 as follows:

```
<form name = "the_form" onSubmit = "window.location = this.the_url.value;">
```

I've replaced the elements that identify the form, `window.document.the_form`, with `this`, because `this` is inside the `<form>` tag. Though it's sometimes hard to know what `this` will be, in general it refers to whichever HTML tag contains it.

Here's another example. Imagine we've written a function called `checkEmail()` that makes sure an email address entered into a form is valid (we'll be doing this in Chapter 11). The form and text box used to collect the email address could look like this:

```
<form name = "the_form">
<input type = "text" name = "email"
  onChange = "checkEmail(window.document.the_form.email.value);"/>
</form>
```

However, the elements `window.document.the_form.email` inside the `onChange` simply identify the text field that the `onChange` is part of. Because the text field is sending its own `value` to the `checkEmail()` function, the `onChange` of the text field can be rewritten like this:

```
onChange = "checkEmail(this.value);">
```

Here, the term this replaces window.document.the_form.email because this appears inside the text field.

Using Pull-Down Menus as Navigational Tools

Now you're ready to create a navigational pull-down menu like the one Doctors Without Borders uses, shown in Figure 7-2. Figure 7-26 shows you what such a tool typically looks like, and Figure 7-27 gives you the script.

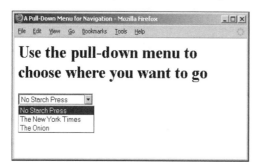

Figure 7-26: A simple navigation tool

You should understand most of the script in Figure 7-27 by now. The onChange in ❶ is the only tricky part (remember that <select> tags take the onChange event). When the onChange happens, it calls the function visitSite(), which receives this.value.

```
<html>
<head>
<title>A Pull-Down Menu for Navigation</title>
<script type = "text/javascript">
<!-- hide me from older browsers
function visitSite(the_site)
{
    window.location = the_site;
}
// show me -->
</script>
</head>
<body>
<h1>Use the pull-down menu to choose where you want to go</h1>
<form name = "the_form">
❶ <select name = "the_select" onChange = "visitSite(this.value);">
<option value = "http://www.nostarch.com">No Starch Press</option>
<option value = "http://www.nytimes.com">The New York Times</option>
<option value = "http://www.theonion.com">The Onion</option>
</select></form>
</body>
</html>
```

Figure 7-27: Using pull-down menus as navigation tools

One Last Forms Shortcut

Sometimes you just want to find out whether a given radio button has been selected. As we've seen, you can do that with a line like this:

```
if (window.document.radio_button_form.age[0].checked == true)
{
    alert("The first radio button was selected!");
}
```

This line is pretty long. It can be shortened if you add an id attribute to your form elements—like so:

```
<input type = "radio" name = "age" id = "age1" value = "puppy">0 to 1 <br>
<input type = "radio" name = "age" id = "age2" value = "young">1 to 3 <br>
<input type = "radio" name = "age" id = "age3" value = "middle">3 to 7<br>
```

The contents of the id attribute can be whatever you want, as long as you don't give two elements the same id. Once you've given each of your form elements an id, you can refer to an element by its id using the method getElementById():

```
var myElement = window.document.getElementById("age1");
if (myElement.checked == true) {
    alert("The first radio button was selected!");
}
```

Or, more concisely:

```
if (document.getElementById("age1").checked == true) {
    alert("The first radio button was selected!");
}
```

The id attribute can go into any HTML element, not just forms. If an <img> tag has an id, it can be referenced using the same getElementById() method. Some people prefer getElementById() over using the names of the elements, as I've been doing in the rest of the book, and there are good reasons to use it. First, you can access a form element without knowing which form the element is in. This can be handy if you have many forms on a page. Second, getElementById() is the only way to manipulate certain parts of HTML. This will come up in Chapter 13, where you'll learn about Dynamic HTML.

I prefer to use element names rather than id attributes because of the frequent need to integrate JavaScript with CGI scripts (see Chapter 11). Websites often send the contents of forms to server-side programs that do things like adding information to a database or sending email to site users. These programs rely on the names of the form elements, rather than their id attributes. To get full functionality from web forms, you need to give the elements names. And since you have to give the elements names anyway, you may as well use the names when manipulating the forms with JavaScript.

As you study other people's JavaScripts, you'll see both names and ids being used. They are equally valid, and which one you use will depend on the situation and your preferences.

How the Doctors Without Borders Pull-Down Navigation Tool Works

The Doctors Without Borders pull-down navigation code is very similar to the JavaScript you saw in Figure 7-27. Figure 7-28 shows you their code, modified to save space:

```
<script type = "text/javascript">
<!-- hide me from older browsers
function gotosite(site) {
    if (site != "") {
self.location = site; }
}
// show me -->
</script>
<SELECT class = textbox onchange = javascript:gotosite(this.value); name =
    select>
<OPTION selected>Select Country</OPTION>
<OPTION value=/news/afghanistan.cfm>Afghanistan
<OPTION value=/news/algeria.cfm>Algeria
<OPTION value=/news/angola.cfm>Angola
</SELECT>
```

❶

Figure 7-28: Code for the Doctors Without Borders pull-down navigation tool

The only big difference between the code in Figure 7-27 and the Doctors Without Borders code in Figure 7-28 is the if-then clause starting in ❶. This extra test is necessary because the first option in their pull-down contains no value—it's just a header. If a visitor selects an option with no value, the value property of the select is set to "". So ❶ in Figure 7-28 checks to see whether the visitor selected the first option of the list. If so, the function does not send the visitor anywhere.

Summary

We covered a lot of ground in this chapter. If you missed any item in the following list, go back and take another look. You should now know:

- How to write HTML forms
- How to read information entered into a form
- How to write your own content to a form
- How to trigger functions from all the form elements

- How to use the word `this` as a shortcut
- How to use the `id` attribute and the `getElementById()` method to access HTML elements

Most form hassles involve the various form elements. Take a look at Appendix C for a complete review of what kinds of events the different elements trigger and what information your JavaScript can discover from them.

Assignment

Write a clock that tells the time in San Francisco, New York, London, and Tokyo. The clock should have a text field for the time, a button to update the clock, and four radio buttons, each for a different time zone. When you click one of the radio buttons, the correct time should appear in the text field. When you click the update button, the clock should update with the time from the zone you've selected with the radio buttons. Figure 7-29 shows an example.

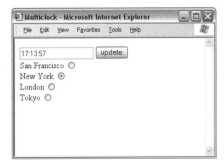

Figure 7-29: Updating the time for different cities

First you'll need some information about looking up time. Remember from Chapter 2 how to get the current hour:

```
var now = new Date();
var the_hour = now.getHours();
```

The `Date` object has a few methods that come in handy for dealing with different time zones. In this case, use `getUTCHours()`, `getUTCMinutes()`, and `getUTCSeconds()`. These methods tell you the hour, minutes, and seconds in Coordinated Universal Time (UTC), which has replaced Greenwich Mean Time as the world standard.

London time is the same as UTC time. New York time is five hours behind London time, California time is eight hours behind London time, and Tokyo time is nine hours ahead of London time.

As always, the answer is in Appendix A, but you'll learn a lot more if you give the assignment a good try before looking there. It's not an easy assignment, so don't be surprised if it takes longer than an hour to get it exactly right.

8

KEEPING TRACK OF INFORMATION WITH ARRAYS AND LOOPS

The last chapter showed you how JavaScript stores radio buttons and pull-down menu options in lists. In programmer's parlance, lists are called *arrays*. This chapter will teach you how to create your own arrays and use them to keep track of large amounts of information.

In this chapter, you'll learn how to:

- Use JavaScript's built-in arrays to control your HTML
- Create new arrays of your own information
- Use loops to search through arrays for information

Real-World Examples of Arrays

JavaScript's built-in arrays are useful in a wide variety of applications. One of the sites I work on, http://www.antweb.org, uses JavaScript's built-in arrays to show users which species of ants live in various counties in the

San Francisco Bay Area (see Figure 8-1). At the bottom of the list of counties is a Select All checkbox. Clicking this box causes all the other checkboxes to become checked. This trick is easy to script because the checkboxes are stored in an array, allowing me to use JavaScript to check off each one. Browse to http://www.bookofjavascript.com/Websites/AntWeb to see this in action.

Figure 8-1: AntWeb checkboxes

Creating your own arrays can be useful as well. The *Book of JavaScript* website employs arrays to show visitors a series of JavaScript programming tips. In the textarea in Figure 8-2, you'll see one of a dozen programming tips that rotate through this box. I store these tips in a JavaScript array and rotate through the array to put different tips into the textarea. The same principle applies to making a timed slide show, which we'll see in the next chapter.

Figure 8-2: Rotating programming tips on the Book of JavaScript home page

JavaScript's Built-In Arrays

When a web browser reads an HTML page, it automatically creates a number of arrays. In the previous chapter we saw that JavaScript creates an array for each set of radio buttons with the same name. If you create a set of radio buttons named age inside a form named the_form, you can refer to the first radio button in the set like this:

```
window.document.the_form.age[0]
```

JavaScript also creates an array for the options in each pull-down menu and scrollable list. Here's how you could access the second option in a pull-down menu named gender:

```
window.document.the_form.gender.options[1]
```

These are just two of JavaScript's automatically created arrays. Browsers also automatically create an array of all the image objects on a web page, called images. The same holds true for form elements (the array of form elements is called elements). In Figure 8-3 (part of the Document Object Model), you can see which elements (the boxes with the words *array of* in them) get automatically created arrays.

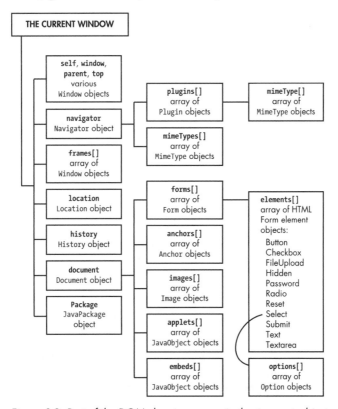

Figure 8-3: Part of the DOM showing arrays in the document object

Each of these arrays is built based on how the page's creator has written its HTML. In the images array, for example, the first image on a web page is called images[0], the second is images[1], and so on. If you use the images array, you don't have to name your images to swap them (as in "Swapping Images" on page 58). For example, you can swap the first image on a web page with an image called happy.gif with this line:

```
window.document.images[0].src = 'happy.gif';
```

Why would you want to use built-in arrays instead of just naming HTML elements? Sometimes you have no choice. As we saw in Chapter 7, because all the radio buttons in a set have the same name, you can access them only using the built-in array.

Built-in arrays are also useful when you have many elements on a page. If you have a web page with 100 images, naming them all becomes tedious. Instead, you can just refer to each image by its number (for a set of 100 images, the numbers would be 0 to 99).

The best thing about arrays, however, is that a little bit of JavaScript can act on each element in the array—a great time-saving feature if you have a 100-element array. In the AntWeb example, clicking one checkbox (Select All) checks all the individual county checkboxes. It doesn't matter whether you have a lone checkbox or a thousand of them—the code is the same.

To control an entire array as the AntWeb script does, your code needs to determine how many elements the array contains and then go through each element in the array, performing whatever action you want on it. AntWeb, for example, figures out how many checkboxes there are and then checks each one.

Figuring Out How Many Items an Array Contains

In all modern JavaScript-enabled browsers, an array's length property contains the number of elements in an array. For example, the script in Figure 8-4 figures out how many images a web page holds.

```
<script type = "text/javascript">
<!-- hide me from older browsers
❶ var num_images = window.document.images.length;
alert("There are " + num_images + " images on this page. ");
// show me -->
</script>
```

Figure 8-4: How many images a web page contains

Drop this JavaScript into the bottom of a web page with images, and you'll see how it works. The critical line is ❶, which tells JavaScript to create a variable called num_images and set it to the number of images in the built-in images array. If the page has 10 images, num_images will equal 10.

Going Through Arrays

Once you know how many elements are in an array, you need to write some code that goes through each element. If you have a list of four checkboxes and want to check them all, you could write a script like Figure 8-5.

```
<html>
<head>
<title>Checking Four Checkboxes</title>
```

```
<script type = "text/javascript">
<!-- hide me from older browsers
function checkFour()
{
    window.document.the_form.elements[0].checked = true;
    window.document.the_form.elements[1].checked = true;
    window.document.the_form.elements[2].checked = true;
    window.document.the_form.elements[3].checked = true;
}
// show me -->
</script>
</head>
<body>
<form name = "the_form">
<input type = "checkbox"> One <br>
<input type = "checkbox"> Two <br>
<input type = "checkbox"> Three <br>
<input type = "checkbox"> Four <br>
<input type = "button" value = "check 'em" onClick = "checkFour();"> <br>
</form>
</body>
</html>
```

Figure 8-5: Checking four checkboxes

The checkFour() function in this script goes through each of the four checkboxes and sets its checked property to true (see the result in Figure 8-6). But this code is not the best solution, since it only works for four checkboxes. To work with *five* checkboxes, you'd have to add another line to the function.

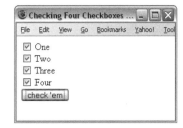

Figure 8-6: The checkboxes checked

With 1,000 checkboxes the function would end up 1,000 lines long, each line identical to the one before it except for the number between brackets. Writing this would be very tedious.

Worse, sometimes, when a page is dynamically generated (see Chapter 13), you don't know how many checkboxes will appear on a page. In this case, it would be impossible to write a function like the one in Figure 8-5.

You can avoid both these problems with a loop. A *loop* allows you to execute the same JavaScript statements multiple times with slight variations. For example, a loop could execute the following line 1,000 times, changing the number in the brackets each time.

```
window.document.the_form.elements[0].checked = true;
```

while Loops

One kind of loop is called a while loop. In plain English, this translates to "While such-and-such is true, do the following." Figure 8-7 shows a while loop that prints the word *happy* three times.

```
<html>
<head>
<title>I'm Happy and I Know It</title>
</head>
<body>
I'm <br>
<script type = "text/javascript">
<!-- hide me from older browsers
❶ var index = 0;
❷ while (index < 3)
❸ {
❹   window.document.writeln("happy<br>");
❺   index = index + 1;
❻ }
❼ // show me -->
</script>
and I know it!
</body>
</html>
```

Figure 8-7: Printing the word happy *three times with a* while *loop*

Loops are a very common programming technique. They may seem strange the first couple of times you see them, but they are so common that after a while you'll understand them on sight.

The typical while loop starts with a variable set to zero, as in ❶ of Figure 8-7. The variable index is just like any other variable.

Once you've set this variable, the while loop begins. Line ❷ reads, "While the variable index is less than three, execute the JavaScript between the curly brackets (❸ and ❻)." The format of this line is important. The word while must be lowercase, and the Boolean test index < 3 must fall between parentheses.

When JavaScript sees ❷, it checks whether the variable index has a value less than 3. If so, the script runs the lines between the curly brackets ❸ and ❻. When we start, index is 0, which is less than 3, so the script executes the two lines between ❸ and ❻. Line ❹ writes the word *happy* to the web page, and ❺ adds one to index, changing it from 0 to 1.

Once we execute ❺ and reach the curly bracket in ❻, JavaScript jumps back to ❷ to see if index is still less than three. This is the nature of the while loop. Every time JavaScript reaches a loop's closing curly bracket (❻), it jumps back to the beginning of the loop (❷) to see whether the test in the parentheses is still true. Because 1 is less than 3, JavaScript executes ❹, which prints *happy* again; it then executes ❺, adding 1 to index (which now has a value of 2).

Again, because we're in a while loop, JavaScript jumps from ❻ to ❷ and checks to see whether index is still less than 3. It is, so ❹ and ❺ execute again. The word *happy* appears a third time, and the script increments index from 2 to 3.

Once again, JavaScript jumps from ❻ to ❷ and checks to see whether index is less than 3. This time, however, index is equal to 3, so the test (index < 3) is not true. The while loop stops and JavaScript jumps to ❼, the line after the closing curly bracket.

Many people have a hard time with looping, so make sure you understand how it works. You may find it helpful to translate ❷ into plain English: "While index is less than 3, write *happy* and add 1 to index."

while Loops and Arrays

Now that you know how while loops work, you can apply them to arrays. Look back at the function in Figure 8-5, and notice that each of the four lines is more or less the same:

```
window.document.the_form.elements[some_number].checked = true;
```

The only difference is the number between the square brackets. Now think about the variable index in Figure 8-7. Its value increases by 1 each time the script goes through the loop. This feature makes the index variable ideal for accessing each element in an array. Figure 8-8 uses index to create a more flexible version of Figure 8-5.

```
    <html>
    <head>
    <title>Checking Four Checkboxes</title>
    <script type = "text/javascript">
    <!-- hide me from older browsers
    function checkFour()
    {
❶    var index = 0;
❷    while (index < 4)
❸    {
❹        window.document.the_form.elements[index].checked = true;
❺        index = index + 1;
❻    }
❼ }
    // show me -->
    </script>
    </head>
    <body>
    <form name = "the_form">
    <input type = "checkbox"> One <br>
    <input type = "checkbox"> Two <br>
    <input type = "checkbox"> Three <br>
    <input type = "checkbox"> Four <br>
    <input type = "button" value = "check 'em" onClick = "checkFour();"> <br>
```

```
    </form>
  </body>
</html>
```

Figure 8-8: Using a loop to check four checkboxes

The critical line is ❹ , which says, "Set form element number index to true." The first time through the loop, index is 0, so ❹ checks the first form element (the first checkbox). Then ❺ adds 1 to index, changing index from 0 to 1. JavaScript reaches ❻ and jumps back to ❷ , executes ❹ and ❺ because index is less than 4, and repeats the process until index equals 4. When index equals 4 and JavaScript jumps to ❷ , the while loop ends (because index is no longer less than 4) and JavaScript jumps to ❼ , the line after the closing curly bracket.

Combining while loops and arrays is extremely common, so make sure you comprehend the process. The advantage of this kind of code is that it works whether you have just a few checkboxes or a few thousand. To get the code to work for, say, 4,000 checkboxes, you would just change the number in ❷ from 4 to 4,000. The loop will then run 4,000 times, starting with 0 and finally ending when index equals 4,000.

Going Off the Deep End

The script in Figure 8-8 looks at the values of form elements 0 through 3, which are the four checkboxes at the start of the form. The next form element in the figure is the button. All input elements have a checked value, although it doesn't really do anything for a button, so

```
window.document.the_form.elements[4].checked
```

will always be false. But what about this:

```
window.document.the_form.elements[5].checked
```

Here, we're asking JavaScript to look at the checked value of whatever is stored in the sixth spot in the elements array. Sadly, there's nothing there; there are only five elements in this form, so JavaScript will respond with the special word undefined. Then, when you ask JavaScript to find the checked value of this undefined thing, it gets confused and you get a JavaScript error.

You can prevent this kind of error by making sure that the values stored in the array are defined, like this:

```
if (window.document.the_form.elements[5] != undefined) {
    var checked_value = window.document.the_form.elements[5].checked;
}
```

Notice that there are no quotes around the word undefined. It's a special word like true and false.

Using array.length in Your Loop

The code in Figure 8-8 works well, but it could use one improvement. In general, it's best to have as few literal numbers in your code as possible: Using specific numbers tends to make code apply only in specific situations. In Figure 8-8, for example, ❷ works only when exactly four checkboxes appear on the page. If you add another checkbox to the web page, you'll have to remember to change the 4 in ❷ to 5. Rather than rely on your memory, you should let the computer do the remembering. You can rewrite ❷ like this:

```
while (index < window.document.the_form.elements.length)
```

The expression `window.document.the_form.elements.length` always equals the number of form elements on a page, since adding another checkbox automatically increases the length of the `elements` array.

An Incremental Shortcut

Lines like ❺ in Figure 8-8 are used so frequently that programmers have come up with the shorthand `index++` to replace `index = index + 1`. That's the variable `index` followed by two plus signs (++), and it saves you the hassle of typing `index` twice. We'll be seeing many other shortcuts like this later.

Beware of Infinite Loops

You should avoid one common loop mistake like the plague. It's so common that it has a name: the infinite loop. Infinite loops happen when your code enters a loop it can never exit. Figure 8-9 shows you the classic error.

```
var index = 0;
while (index < 10)
{
    window.document.write("I am infinite! <br>");
}
```

Figure 8-9: The classic infinite loop—don't try this at home

Running this script will make you sad, so please don't try it. If you do run it, the script will endlessly write *I am infinite!* to the page. To stop the script from running, you'd have to quit the browser, which isn't always easy when you're stuck in an infinite loop.

This loop is infinite because I forgot to add 1 to `index` after writing "I am infinite!" The `index` variable starts at 0 and never changes, so `index < 10` is always true. Since the test `while (index < 10)` is always true, the loop continues until you exit the browser.

The only way to avoid accidentally writing an infinite loop is to exercise caution. Whenever you write a loop, make sure the loop will exit at some point.

for Loops

Another type of loop is the for loop. You format while and for loops differently, but they do the same things. Which loop you use is largely a matter of preference. Though for loops look a little more confusing at first, they are more compact.

Figure 8-10 compares a while loop and a for loop that perform exactly the same task.

```
   // while loop
❶ var index = 0;
❷ while (index < 10)
   {
       window.document.writeln("hello<br>");
❸      index++;
   }
   // for loop
❹ for (var index = 0; index < 10; index++)
   {
       window.document.writeln("hello<br>");
   }
```

Figure 8-10: Comparing a while loop and a for loop

Both of the loops in Figure 8-10 write the word hello to a web page ten times. The main difference between them is that ❶, ❷, and ❸ in the while loop collapse into ❹ in the for loop. The format of a for loop is as follows:

```
for (initializer; test; incrementer)
{
    // some JavaScript
}
```

All for loops start with the word for, followed by parentheses containing three pieces of JavaScript, separated by semicolons. The first piece is a statement that is said to *initialize* the loop. Usually this statement declares an index variable and sets it to the starting number. In ❹ of Figure 8-10, the initializer of the for loop is var index = 0 (the same as ❶ in the while loop). The second parameter of a for loop is the *test*, which, if true, means that the loop will execute one more time and then test again. In ❹ of Figure 8-10, the test is index < 10 (the same as ❷ in the while loop). The final piece is the *incrementer*, a statement that changes the condition each time the loop repeats, usually by adding a number to the index variable (like ❸ in the while loop).

Whether you use while loops or for loops is a matter of taste. You can write for loops in fewer lines, but while loops are a bit easier to read. Some people prefer for loops because they lower the risk of accidentally getting into an infinite loop. In a while loop, you can easily neglect to put index++ inside the curly brackets. In a for loop, it's hard to forget to put this element inside the parentheses because you always have three expressions there.

How AntWeb Checks Off All the Checkboxes

Figure 8-11 shows a stripped-down version of how AntWeb uses loops to check off all the checkboxes when a visitor clicks Select All.

I've taken out AntWeb's HTML formatting, along with the repetitive code for several of the counties, but the checkAll() function is exactly the same as AntWeb's. To see the complete AntWeb page in all its formatting glory, browse to http://www.bookofjavascript.com/Websites/AntWeb.

```
<html>
<head>
<title>AntWeb's Use of Arrays and Loops</title>
</head>
<body>
❶ <form name = "bayAreaSearchForm">
❷ <input type = "checkbox" name = "counties" value = "alameda">Alameda<br>
   <input type = "checkbox" name = "counties" value =
       "contra costa">Contra Costa<br>
   <input type = "checkbox" name = "counties" value = "marin">Marin<br>
❸ <input type = "checkbox" name = "selectall"
     onClick = "selectAll(window.document.bayAreaSearchForm);">Select All<br>
   </form>
   <script type = "text/javascript">
   <!-- hide me from older browsers
❹ function selectAll(thisForm) {
❺     var count = thisForm.counties.length;
❻     var checkedVal = thisForm.selectall.checked;
❼     for (var loop = 0; loop < count; loop++) {
❽         thisForm.counties[loop].checked = checkedVal;
       }
   }
   // show me -->
   </script>
   }
   </body>
   </html>
```

Figure 8-11: AntWeb's use of arrays and loops

Line-by-Line Analysis of Figure 8-11

The first few lines in Figure 8-11 describe the form that contains the checkboxes. Line ❶ names the form bayAreaSearchForm, and ❷ and the two lines after it describe each of the checkboxes. Line ❸ describes the checkbox that causes the other checkboxes to become checked. This checkbox is named selectall; clicking it calls the function selectAll(), which starts in ❹. Notice in ❸ that when the function is called, the name of the form to act on is passed to the function. In ❹, that form is named thisForm inside the function. The nice thing about this is that the selectAll function will work on any page, and for any form. You just need to pass the form into the function, as is done when the function is called in ❸. Line ❺, the first line in the function's body, stores the number of elements in the form into a variable named count. There are four elements in this form—the three county checkboxes and the Select All checkbox—so count will be 4.

Line ❻ stores the checked value of the selectall checkbox: either true, if the checkbox was just checked, or false, if it was unchecked. The real fun begins with the loop, starting in ❼. The first time through the loop, the variable named loop will have a value of 0, so thisForm.counties[loop] in ❽ will point to the first element in the bayAreaSearch form—the first checkbox. The second time through the loop, the value of loop will be 1, so thisForm.counties[loop] will point to the second checkbox. The loop occurs four times, once for each checkbox.

You may be thinking that testing the fourth checkbox is a bit unnecessary, and you would be correct. The fourth time through the loop, the script is just setting the fourth checkbox to checkVal, which already stores the value of the fourth checkbox. Hence, the script is just setting the value of the fourth checkbox to whatever the value already is. If I wanted to avoid this unnecessary step, I could have changed the loop to this:

```
for (var loop = 0; loop < count; loop++) {
❶    if (thisForm.counties[loop].name != 'selectAll') {
         thisForm.counties[loop].checked = checkedVal;
     }
}
```

Here, ❶ looks at the name of the checkbox. If it is anything other than 'selectAll', the JavaScript will change the checked value of the checkbox. I decided to leave that out because the unnecessary effort taken by JavaScript to change the checked value of a checkbox is less than the effort that would be required to examine the name of a checkbox and see whether it is selectAll each time through the script. With the types of tasks JavaScript is generally used for, efficiency decisions like this don't really save very much time. However, if you notice that your script is taking a long time to run, make sure code inside your loops does not take too long. Slow code that runs once in a script isn't too bad. Slow code that runs 1,000 times because it's in a loop might slow things down noticeably.

Creating Your Own Arrays

Arrays are so handy that you'll often want to create your own. A phone book, for example, is an array of names and phone numbers. You can think of a survey as an array of questions; an array can also store the answers a visitor enters. A slide show is an array of pictures shown in sequence.

Happily, JavaScript lets you create your own arrays. If you know what you want to store in the array when you create it, use a line like the following:

```
var rainbow_colors =
    new Array("red", "orange", "yellow", "green", "blue", "indigo", "violet");
```

This line creates a variable called `rainbow_colors` that stores an array of colors. The words `new Array()` tell JavaScript to create a new `Array` object, just as `new Date()` created a new `Date` object back in Chapter 2. To put values in your new array, simply list them in the parentheses.

Everything you've learned about JavaScript's built-in arrays also applies to arrays you create yourself. Figure 8-12 uses the `rainbow_colors` array to create a psychedelic strobe effect on a web page.

```
<html>
<head>
<title>Strobe</title>
<script type = "text/javascript">
<!-- hide me from older browsers
function strobeIt()
{
❶   var rainbow_colors =
        new Array("red", "orange", "yellow", "green", "blue", "indigo", "violet");
    var index = 0;
❷   while (index < rainbow_colors.length)
    {
❸     window.document.bgColor = rainbow_colors[index];
❹     index++;
    }
}
// show me -->
</script>
</head>
<body>
<form>
<input type = "button" value = "strobe" onClick = "strobeIt();">
</form>
</body>
</html>
```

Figure 8-12: A psychedelic strobe effect

Line-by-Line Analysis of Figure 8-12

Line ❶ in Figure 8-12 creates the array and ❷ sets up the loop, saying, "While index is less than the number of items in the array, execute the JavaScript between the curly brackets." The first time through the loop, `index` is 0, so when ❸ looks up `rainbow_colors[index]`, it gets the first item in the array, the value red. Line ❸ assigns this value to `window.document.bgColor`, which sets the background color to red. Once the script has set this color, ❹ adds 1 to `index`, and the loop begins again. Next time through, `index` will be 1, so ❸ will make the background color orange, ❹ then adds 1 to `index`, making it 2, and back through the loop we go. If you have a very fast computer, the background may strobe too quickly for you to see it. In this case, add a few more colors to the array in ❶.

How the *Book of JavaScript* Tip Box Works

The *Book of JavaScript* website has a little textarea that shows various programming tips. The script keeps these tips in an array and then uses JavaScript to loop through the array, showing one tip at a time. Each tip stays in the textarea for 3.5 seconds before the next one appears. I should confess that I got the idea for this tip box from something that the search engine Ask.com (http://www.ask.com, formerly known as Ask Jeeves) once had on its home page. In fact, I will present two different versions of the code. The first version, shown in Figure 8-13, is very similar to the code Ask.com originally used. The second version, which you'll see in Figure 8-14, is a bit simpler (though not necessarily better).

The code in Figure 8-13 is similar to code from Ask.com and contains many little tricks that I haven't yet covered. It starts out simply enough with ❶, which says, "After the page has loaded, call the function startScroll()." The first line in the JavaScript tags, ❷, creates an array called tips and loads it with a bunch of familiar programming adages. Line ❸ creates a variable called num_tips and sets it equal to the number of tips in the tips array.

```
    <html>
    <head>
    <title>Arrays and Loops a la Ask.com</title>
    </head>
❶  <body onLoad = "startScroll();">
    <script type = "text/javascript">
    <!-- hide me from older browsers
❷  var tips = new Array("Don't forget to comment your code.", "Beware of infinite
       loops.", "Program so that other humans can understand what you're doing.");
❸  var num_tips = tips.length;
    var index = 0;
❹  while ((num_tips > 0)  && (tips[num_tips-1] == ""))
       {
          --num_tips;
       }
    function startScroll() {
❺     if (num_tips != null) {
❻        if (window.document.tip_form) {
❼           window.document.tip_form.tip_box.value = tips[index++];
❽           if (index > num_tips - 1)
             {
❾               index = 0;
             }
          }
❿        setTimeout("startScroll()", 3500);
       }
    }
    // show me -->
    </script>
    <form name = "tip_form">
    <textarea name = "tip_box" rows = "3" cols = "30"></textarea>
```

```
</form>
</body>
</html>
```

Figure 8-13: Ask.com-style use of arrays and loops

Checking for Blank Statements

The next couple of lines exhibit "paranoid" programming style. Paranoid programmers make sure everything is perfect before they execute a line of code that's going to affect the user experience. Line ❹ and the line following it, for example, make sure no blank statements (two quotation marks with nothing between them) appear at the end of the tips array. Who knows why that would happen—but just in case, ❹ checks the last element in the array. If it's not blank, the loop ends. If it is blank, the line below it executes, reducing num_tips by 1. The loop then checks to see whether the second to last element is blank. If it's not, the loop ends. If it is, that line runs again, reducing num_tips by 1 once more. Notice that you can subtract one from a variable with the syntax *variable_name--*. You can also use *++variable_name* and *--variable_name* as shown.

Checking the Last Element in the Array

You might be wondering how ❹ checks the last element of the array. Remember, num_tips equals the number of items in the array. If the array has three items, num_tips equals three. However, because the first element in the array is zero, the last element in an array will be two—the length of the array minus one. To look at the last element of an array, use the following line:

```
var last_element = the_array[the_array.length - 1];
```

If the array contains three elements, the_array.length equals 3, and the_array.length minus 1 equals 2, which is the number JavaScript uses to reference the last element in the array. You may be thinking, "There's no way I'd ever figure that out!" But don't worry—this kind of array mathematics becomes second nature after you've done it a few times.

Testing the Limits of Arrays

You may have noticed that before ❹ checks to see whether the last element in the array is a blank string, it makes sure there is at least one tip in the array. If there are no elements in the array, num_tips will equal 0. If that's the case, then the second part of the while loop would be checking to see whether tips[0 - 1] == "", or doing the math, tips[-1]. Because arrays start at 0, there will never be a value in position -1, so there's really no reason to check what's in that position. When you have two parts to a test that contains and, both parts must be true for the whole thing to be true. JavaScript is smart enough to not bother checking the second part of a test with an and if the first part is false. Why bother testing the second part if it already knows the whole thing will be false?

The startScroll() Function

In the startScroll() function, we find more programming paranoia. Line ❺ checks to see whether the variable count actually has a setting. If not, its value is the special word null. Line ❻ exhibits even more paranoia. Ask.com makes sure the form named rotate has been drawn to the page by checking to see whether the form named document.tip_form exists. If it does not exist, document.tip_form is false, and the lines between the brackets of the if-then statement won't execute. I have never encountered any browsers that support JavaScript but not forms. If they're out there, however, ❻ makes sure JavaScript won't try to write to a form that doesn't exist.

Line ❼ looks up a tip in the array and writes it into the textarea. This line tells JavaScript to find the form named tip_form and the form element named tip_box and sets its value to whatever appears on the right side of the equal sign. The latter requires some explanation. Instead of just looking up the value of element index in the text array and then adding 1 to index, as in

```
document.tip_form.tip_box.value = tips[index];
index++;
```

line ❼ looks up the value of element index and adds 1 to index right there:

```
document.tip_form.tip_box.value = tips[index++];
```

This is legal and saves some space, but it's a little hard to read.

Going back to the notation introduced earlier, if Ask.com had done this,

```
document.tip_form.tip_box.value = tips[++index];
```

putting the plus signs in front of index, the JavaScript would add 1 to index and then look for the value of tips[index]. It's the same as this line:

```
index++;
document.tip_form.tip_box.value = tips[index];
```

It's rare to see people messing around with the location of the double plus and minus operators. But if you run into this while looking at source code, you'll know what's going on.

The next two lines, ❽ and ❾, are important for any program that continuously loops through an array. The JavaScript writes a tip in the textarea, then moves on to the next tip in the array, until it runs out of tips. Once that happens, the program should return to the first question in the array and start all over. Lines ❽ and ❾ make this happen. Line ❽ determines whether the last question has appeared. If the variable index is more than num_tips - 1, we've reached the end of the array. Remember, ❸ set num_tips to the length of the array, so num_tips - 1 is the position of the array's last element. If index is greater than num_tips - 1, we've reached the array's end, and ❾ executes. It sets the variable index back to 0, so the next time the script puts tips[index] into the textarea, index will indicate the first question in the array.

Finally, ❿ determines how fast the questions change in the textarea. The next chapter will talk more about how the code in ❿ works. For now, you just need to know that it translates as, "In 3.5 seconds, call the function startScroll() again." Each time the script calls startScroll(), the function puts a new question in the textarea and increments index by 1.

A Streamlined Version

The code in Figure 8-13 is a bit confusing. Figure 8-14 shows you a streamlined version that still works under most conditions.

Although the code in this version is more streamlined, it's not necessarily better. Paranoia is a good thing in programming. The more checks you put in, the less likely your visitors are to encounter a JavaScript error. Given the choice between the approaches demonstrated in Figures 8-13 and 8-14, I'd recommend the former because it's more robust. The code in Figure 8-14 is merely easier to understand.

```
<html>
<head>
<title>Arrays and Loops</title>
</head>
<body onLoad = "scroll();">

<script type = "text/javascript">
<!-- hide me from older browsers
var tips = new Array("Don't forget to comment your code.", "Beware of infinite
    loops.", "Program so that other humans can understand what you're doing.");
var index = 0;
function scroll() {
    document.tip_form.tip_box.value = tips[index];
    index++;
    if (index == tips.length)
    {
        index = 0;
    }
    setTimeout("scroll()", 3500);
}
// show me -->
</script>
<form name = "tip_form">
<textarea name = "tip_box" rows = "3" cols = "30">
</form>
</body>
</html>
```

Figure 8-14: A more streamlined version of the code in Figure 8-13

Loops Can Nest

Just as you can nest if-then statements inside other if-then statements, you can also put loops inside other loops. For example, Figure 8-15 shows you a script that writes a solid rectangle of Xs to a web page, five Xs high and ten Xs wide (see the result in Figure 8-16). Although this script doesn't do anything useful, it offers an idea of how nesting loops work.

```
❶ for (first_loop = 0; first_loop < 5; first_loop++) {
❷   for (second_loop = 0; second_loop < 10; second_loop++) {
❸     window.document.writeln("X");
    }
❹   window.document.writeln("<br>");
}
```

Figure 8-15: A simple example of nesting loops

Line ❶ in Figure 8-15 sets up a loop that will be executed five times. Each time through that loop, the second, or *inner*, loop (❷ and ❸) runs. That loop writes the letter X to the web page ten times. After the inner loop has run, ❹ in the outer loop writes a <br> to the web page, creating a line break. After ❹ runs, the loop in ❶ runs again. This happens five times. Each time loop ❶ runs, loop ❷ writes a line of ten Xs, then ❹ writes a <br>. Loops inside loops can seem puzzling at first, but they can come in handy.

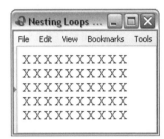

Figure 8-16: The rectangle of Xs created with nested loops in Figure 8-15

Creating Arrays As You Go Along

If you're giving someone a quiz and want to store the answers in an array, you must create an array even though you don't know what values it will store. In such cases, you'll need to build your array piece by piece.

Start by creating an empty array, as in this line:

```
var the_answers = new Array();
```

This tells JavaScript to create a new array called the_answers, leaving it empty.

Once you've created the array, you can load values into it, like this:

```
the_answers[0] = "yes";
the_answers[1] = "no";
the_answers[2] = "maybe";
```

The first line puts the word *yes* into the first slot of the array, the next puts *no* into the second slot, and the third line puts *maybe* into the third slot. You can store values in an array in any order. Reversing the three lines above wouldn't make any difference. The word *maybe* goes into the third slot of the array because the number 2 appears between the square brackets. Figure 8-17 demonstrates how to use this technique to create a Mad Lib, that party game.

```
<html>
<head>
<title>Mad Lib</title>
</head>
<body>

<script type = "text/javascript">
<!-- hide me from older browsers

❶ alert("This is a Mad Lib! Please fill in the blanks appropriately.");
❷ var answers = new Array();
❸ answers[0] = prompt("an animal","bear");
   answers[1] = prompt("an adjective","happy");
   answers[2] = prompt("a past tense verb","kissed");
   answers[3] = prompt("an object","tree");

❹ var the_string = "";
❺ the_string = the_string + "Once upon a time there was a " + answers[0];
   the_string = the_string + " who was very " + answers[1] + ".";
   the_string = the_string + " In fact, he was so " + answers[1];
   the_string = the_string + " that he " + answers[2] + " a " + answers[3] ".";

❻ window.document.writeln(the_string);

// show me -->
</script>
</body>
</html>
```

Figure 8-17: A short Mad Lib

It's not a very long Mad Lib, but you get the idea. When someone comes to this page, the alert in ❶ greets the visitor. After the alert, the script creates a new, empty array in ❷. The next few lines, starting with ❸, fill the array. Each of these lines uses the prompt() function to ask a question (and display a default answer) and then loads the visitor's answer into the array. The first answer goes into array position 0, the next into array position 1, and so on.

By the time the script reaches ❹, the visitor has filled the array's first four positions. Line ❹ initializes a variable that stores the contents of the Mad Lib. The next few lines, starting with ❺, build this string. Each line adds content to the string. Line ❺ adds "Once upon a time there was a *user answer.*" The next line appends "who was very *user answer*" to the end of the string. Line ❻ writes the complete string to the web page.

Associative Arrays

All the arrays we've seen so far have stored values according to their numerical position in the array. An *associative array* uses strings instead of numbers to store values. For example, the following lines create a phone book with an associative array:

```
var phone_book = new Array();
phone_book["dave thau"] = "(415) 555-5555";
phone_book["information"] = "(415) 555-1212";
```

The first line creates a new, empty array, as we've seen before. The next two lines put two associations into the array. The first associates the string dave thau with another string, (415) 555-5555. The second associates the string information with the number to dial for Information. To retrieve that number, you would look it up using a line like this:

```
var information_number = phone_book["information"];
```

This tells JavaScript to look in the array phone_book for the value associated with the string information. The string used to retrieve the association must precisely match the string used to store it. Retrieving thau's phone number with the line

```
var thau = phone_book["thau"];
```

won't work if you originally stored the information as

```
phone_book["dave thau"] = "(415) 555-5555";
```

Figure 8-18 shows how to use an associative array for a functional phone book, and Figure 8-19 shows the page displayed by this code.

```
  <html>
  <head>
  <title>Phone Book</title>

  <script type = "text/javascript">
  <!-- hide me from older browsers
❶ var phone_book = new Array();
```

```
❷ phone_book["blank"] = "";
  phone_book["happy"] = "(555) 555-1111";
  phone_book["sleepy"] = "(555) 555-2222";
  phone_book["sneezy"] = "(555) 555-3333";
  phone_book["sleazy"] = "(555) 555-4444";
  phone_book["sneery"] = "(555) 555-5555";
  phone_book["bleary"] = "(555) 555-6666";
  phone_book["tweaked"] = "(555) 555-7777";
❸ function displayNumber(the_phone_book, entry)
  {
❹     var the_number = the_phone_book[entry];
❺     window.document.the_form.number_box.value = the_number;
  }
  // show me -->
  </script>
  </head>
  <body>
  <h1>The Dwarves of Multimedia Gulch</h1>
❻ <form name = "the_form">
  <b>Name:</b>
❼ <select onChange =
      "displayNumber(phone_book,this.options[this.selectedIndex].value);">
❽ <option value = "blank">-- Choose a Dwarf --</option>
  <option value = "happy">Happy</option>
  <option value = "sleepy">Sleepy</option>
  <option value = "sneezy">Sneezy</option>
  <option value = "sleazy">Sleazy</option>
  <option value = "sneery">Sneery</option>
  <option value = "bleary">Bleary</option>
  <option value = "tweaked">Tweaked</option>
  </select>
  <p>
  <b>Number:</b>
  <input type = "text" name = "number_box" value = "">
  </form>
  </body>
  </html>
```

Figure 8-18: Creating a phone book using an associative array

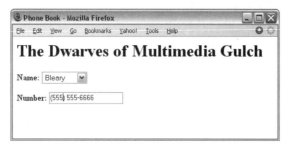

Figure 8-19: The phone book page generated by the
code in Figure 8-18

Line-by-Line Analysis of Figure 8-18

When a browser loads this page, it shows a pull-down menu with some names and a text box that displays a phone number (Figure 8-19). Selecting a name puts that person's phone number in the text box. This neat little application doesn't take too much work to implement.

The script starts by creating a new array called phone_book in ❶ and then filling it with the values in lines ❷ down. Note that the first element in the array deals with the header line in the pull-down menu (❽). If someone selects *Choose a Dwarf* in the pull-down menu, that will put a blank string in the phone number box.

After building the phone_book array, ❸ defines a function as displayNumber(). This function takes two parameters: an array that holds the phone book we want to use and a name we want to look up in the phone book. Line ❹ looks up the name in the phone book and stores it in the_number. Line ❺ puts the_number in the text box.

Line ❻ starts the form and names it the_form. Line ❼ is a bit more complicated; it defines the pull-down menu and describes what should happen when a visitor changes the value there. Changing the pull-down menu selection triggers the onChange event, which calls the displayNumber() function. As described earlier, displayNumber() takes two parameters: the phone book and the name to look up. In this case, we have just one phone book, called phone_book. Later we might expand this script to include several phone books—for example, one for friends, called friends_book; one for business, called business_book; and one for favorite shops, called shop_book. Because we can decide which phone book to use whenever we call the displayNumber() function, switching books is easy. If we wanted to use the business_book phone book, we'd just call the function like this:

```
<select onChange =
    "displayNumber(business_book, this.options[selectedIndex].value);">
```

The second parameter in the function is the name to look up. If we choose Happy, the person listed first in ❽ of Figure 8-18, the value happy passes to the function.

Play around with this example and make sure you understand how the displayNumber() function works and how the values in ❼ enter the function.

Summary

This chapter has introduced the last two fundamental ideas behind all programming languages: arrays and loops. Now that you've learned about variables, if-then statements, functions, loops, and arrays, you've learned all of the basic aspects of computer programming—so be happy! From now on, everything we learn is specific to how JavaScript works with the browser. All the tough programming nitty-gritty is behind us.

Before you leave this chapter, make sure you've learned how to:

- Create a new array
- Access elements in an array
- Use loops to go through an array's elements
- Use both for and while loops
- Nest loops
- Use associative arrays

Assignment

To make sure you understand everything in this chapter, try this assignment.

Write a script that creates bar charts. This script should first ask a visitor how many bars to include in the chart. If the visitor wants four bars, the script should then ask for four numbers, ranging from 1 to 10, and draw a bar for each. Figures 8-20 through 8-22 demonstrate what I mean. To draw the bars, create a square GIF, or use square.gif, which is available at http://www.bookofjavascript.com/Chapter08/square.gif. If someone wants a bar that's ten squares high, use a loop to write

```
window.document.writeln("<img src='square.gif'>")
```

ten times to the page. This is another tough assignment, so give yourself plenty of time to do it.

Figure 8-20: Asking visitors how many bars they want

Figure 8-21: Asking for bar values

Figure 8-22: The bar chart

9

TIMING EVENTS

Precise timing of events on your web pages transforms them from static documents to true multimedia applications. If you can time events, you can pace slide shows, create timed games, and control when visitors may perform different actions. In later chapters we'll see how timing events can animate your entire site.

In this chapter, you'll learn how to:

- Control when events happen on your web page
- Build clocks that update in real time
- Create slide shows that move at whatever pace you want

Real-World Examples of Timing Events

We've already seen a few examples of web pages that use event timing. In the last chapter, we saw how visitors to the *Book of JavaScript* web page get a new programming tip every 3.5 seconds. Space.com has a clock that counts down to the next known launch into outer space, available at http://www.space.com/missionlaunches/launches/next_launch.html. The *Book of JavaScript* home page (Figure 9-1) has a clock that shows you how long you've been on the page. Both of these timers update every second.

Figure 9-1: Timer on the Book of JavaScript *home page*

Timing events is not difficult. In fact, you only need to know two commands: setTimeout() and clearTimeout().

Setting an Alarm with setTimeout()

The built-in JavaScript function setTimeout() tells JavaScript to run a JavaScript command at some time in the future. The function takes two parameters: a JavaScript command and the time (in milliseconds) to wait before running it. For example, the following line causes an alert box to pop up after a visitor has been on a page for three seconds:

```
setTimeout("alert('You have been on this page for 3 seconds!');", 3000);
```

The first setTimeout parameter contains the JavaScript statement to execute. This statement must be enclosed by quotes and, like all JavaScript statements, end with a semicolon. Notice that the string to be displayed by the alert command appears between single quotes rather than double quotes (see "Quotes in JavaScript" on page 55).

The second parameter tells JavaScript to execute the first parameter in 3,000 milliseconds, which is three seconds (there are 1,000 milliseconds in a second). Figure 9-2 puts this line in the context of a full web page.

```
<html>
<head>
<title>A Three-Second Alert</title>
<script type = "text/javascript">
<!-- hide me from older browsers
setTimeout("alert('You have been on this page for 3 seconds!');", 3000);
// show me -->
</script>
</head>
<body>
<h1>A page so interesting you have to force yourself to stop reading it by
    having an alert tell you when you've spent too much time. </h1>
</body>
</html>
```

Figure 9-2: A three-second alert

Canceling an Alarm with clearTimeout()

Sometimes you'll want to cancel a setTimeout(). Imagine a riddle game in which a player has 10 seconds to guess the riddle's answer. If players don't answer the riddle correctly in 10 seconds, they are sent to a page that gives them the answer. If they do figure out the answer in time, they are congratulated. You could write this game by setting a setTimeout() to send players to the answer page in 10 seconds. If they answer the riddle correctly before the 10 seconds expire, you need to cancel the setTimeout() so they don't end up on the answer page.

To cancel a setTimeout(), you first need to name the time-out by storing it in a variable:

```
var my_timeout = setTimeout("goToAnswerPage();", 10000);
```

This line creates a time-out called my_timeout. Unless clearTimeout() cancels the time-out, JavaScript will call the function goToAnswerPage() in 10 seconds. To cancel the time-out when the player answers the riddle correctly, use this line:

```
clearTimeout(my_timeout);
```

This looks up the time-out called my_timeout and cancels it. Figure 9-3 shows a working version of the riddle game.

```
<html>
<head>
<title>A Riddle Game</title>
<script type = "text/javascript">
<!-- hide me from older browsers
❶ var my_timeout = setTimeout("goToAnswerPage();", 10000);
❷ function goToAnswerPage()
   {
       alert("Sorry!");
       window.location = "answer.html";
   }

❸ function checkAnswer(the_answer, the_timeout)
   {
❹    if (the_answer == "a newspaper")
      {
❺        clearTimeout(the_timeout);
❻        alert("Congratulations! You got it right!");
      }
   }
// show me -->
</script>
</head>
<body>
<h1>Riddle Me This</h1>
What is black, white, and read all over?<br>
```

```
❼ <form onSubmit =
       "checkAnswer(this.the_answer.value, my_timeout); return false;">
   <input type = "text" name = "the_answer">
   <input type = "submit" value = "answer">
   </form>
   </body>
   </html>
```

Figure 9-3: A riddle game

Line-by-Line Analysis of Figure 9-3

Line ❶ initiates setTimeout(). Ten seconds later, unless clearTimeout() cancels the time-out called my_timeout, the function goToAnswerPage(), defined in ❷, is called. This function calls up an alert box and sends the player to answer.html. Line ❸ defines checkAnswer(), the function called when the player submits an answer (❼). checkAnswer() takes two parameters: the answer that the player submits and the time-out to cancel if the answer is correct. The first line of the function, ❹, checks the answer. If it's correct, ❺ cancels the time-out, which stops JavaScript from calling the goToAnswerPage() function, and ❻ congratulates the player. If ❼, which calls the checkAnswer() function when the player submits the form, seems unfamiliar, look at "Handling Events Using Form Elements" on page 116, which discusses the onSubmit event. Figure 9-4 shows the riddle game in action.

NOTE   *If you want to run this script, you'll need to create the answer.html page, which is just a normal web page with the riddle's answer on it.*

Figure 9-4: What the riddle game looks like

Repeating Timed Actions

You've already seen examples of repeating timed actions. The tip box discussed in the section "How the Book of JavaScript Tip Box Works" on page 136 displays each tip for 3.5 seconds, and the text box that tells you how long you've been on the page updates every second. Both of these examples use the same mechanism.

As you have just seen in Chapter 8, the usual way to get JavaScript to perform an action repeatedly is to put the action into a loop. Unfortunately, we can't use a while or for loop for repeated timed events. The while and for loops run too quickly, and there's no good way to slow them down. Even if you could slow them, there's no way to time these loops accurately, because they run at different speeds on different computers. It might take an old computer two seconds to print *hello* to a web page 1,000 times, while a newer computer might take just a tenth of a second. What's more, your visitor won't be able to do anything else in the browser while the loop is running.

Instead of using a for or while loop, you can let JavaScript accurately time your loop by writing a function to set a time-out that calls the same function again. Using setTimeout() and clearTimeout(), the function can control exactly how far in the future it gets called. The simple timing loop in Figure 9-5 should make this clearer.

```
<html>
<head>
<title>A Simple Timing Loop</title>
<script type = "text/javascript">
<!-- hide me from older browsers
❶ var the_timeout;
❷ function upDate()
   {
❸    var the_number = window.document.the_form.the_text.value;
❹    the_number = parseInt(the_number) + 1;
❺    window.document.the_form.the_text.value = the_number;
❻    the_timeout = setTimeout("upDate();", 1000);
   }
// show me -->
</script>
</head>
<body>
<form name = "the_form">
❼ <input type = "text" name = "the_text" value = "0"><br>
❽ <input type = "button" value = "start timer" onClick = "upDate();">
❾ <input type = "button" value = "stop timer" onClick =
"clearTimeout(the_timeout);">
</form>
</body>
</html>
```

Figure 9-5: A simple timing loop

This simple timing loop (❶ through ❻) forms the basis for the ones we'll see later in this chapter (and in Chapter 13).

The HTML in Figure 9-5 creates a form with three elements: a text box to hold the timer number and two buttons (see Figure 9-6). When a user clicks the start timer button, the number in the text box (❼) starts to increase by 1 every second. It will keep increasing until the visitor clicks the stop timer button.

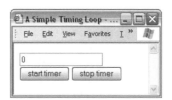

Figure 9-6: What the page coded in Figure 9-5 looks like in a browser

Line-by-Line Analysis of Figure 9-5

The key part of this script is the upDate() function starting in ❷. When a user clicks the start timer button, the button's onClick event (❽) calls the upDate() function. This function adds 1 to the contents of the text box (❸ through ❺) and then sets a time-out (the_timeout) in ❻ to call itself in one second. After executing ❻, the script is done, and control goes back to the browser until 1 second passes; then the time-out goes off and calls the upDate() function again. The upDate() function adds 1 to the contents of the text box and again sets the_timeout to call upDate() in 1 second. This cycle of calling the upDate() function, adding 1 to the contents, and setting another time-out to call the function in 1 second continues until a visitor clicks the stop timer button in ❾. The stop timer button's onClick event executes the statement clearTimeout(the_timeout) and cancels the most recently set time-out, stopping the upDate() function from running again. Table 9-1 charts this basic loop cycle.

Table 9-1: The Timing Loop Cycle

Step	Event
1	A user clicks the start timer button, triggering the upDate() function for the first time.
2	upDate() adds 1 to the number shown in the text box.
3	upDate() sets a time-out to trigger upDate() in 1 second. The time-out is named the_timeout.
4	If the user hasn't clicked the stop timer button, then after 1 second passes, the_timeout goes off and upDate() gets triggered as in step 2.
5	The user clicks the stop timer button, which calls clearTimeout(the_timeout).
6	clearTimeout(the_timeout) cancels the time-out set in step 3.
7	Because the last time-out was canceled, upDate() doesn't get called again, so the cycle stops.

The rest of this chapter covers a few applications of this basic timing loop. Don't worry if any of the structure of Figure 9-5 confuses you. You'll get used to it after seeing a few more examples.

Using parseInt() with Form Elements

All modern browsers treat the contents of form elements as strings. When the text box in Figure 9-5 has the number 2 in it, browsers read this as the string '2'. Ordinarily, this wouldn't be too much of a problem. However, remember that the plus (+) operator has two meanings. When you use the plus between two numbers, it adds them: 1 + 2 yields 3. But when you use the plus between strings, it concatenates them: '1' + '2' yields '12'. Because browsers read the contents of form elements as strings, they would just stick a 1 at the end of whatever number appears in the timer text box, which would show 0, 01, 011, 0111, and so on. This is not what we're looking for.

The built-in JavaScript function parseInt() in ❹ overcomes this problem by converting strings and numbers with decimal points into integers. For example, the lines

```
var first_number = '2';
var second_number = first_number + 1;
```

result in the variable second_number holding the value "21", while the lines

```
var first_number = '2';
var second_number = parseInt(first_number) + 1;
```

result in the variable second_number holding the value 3—parseInt(first_number) converts the string '2' to the number 2.

Calling parseInt() with a value that has no numbers in it results in a NaN (not a number) value. You can use JavaScript's isNaN() function to make sure parseInt() returns a number. The following scrap of code asks for a person's age and makes sure he or she has entered a number:

```
var the_age = prompt("How old are you?", "your age here");
if (isNaN(parseInt(the_age)))
{
    alert("That's not a number!");
}
```

Clearing Out a Time-Out Before You Set a New One

If you've tried running the code in Figure 9-5, you might have noticed that clicking the start timer button multiple times causes the timer to run more quickly. This happens because each time you click the button, it starts a timer that runs once a second. If you click the button twice, you have two timers that run once a second, which means the value in the text box updates twice a second. To keep this from happening, change the start timer button's onClick to clear the time-out before setting it again. In other words, change ❽ to the following:

```
<input type = "button" value = "start timer"
  onClick = "clearTimeout(the_timeout); upDate();">
```

Declaring Variables That Hold Time-Outs Outside Functions

You may have noticed that ❶ in Figure 9-5 declares a variable outside the function that uses it, even though I told you in Chapter 6 to declare variables using var inside the functions that use them. Variables that hold time-outs are one exception to this rule, because you don't actually want to hide them. Remember that inside a function the word var means "This variable only exists inside this function." If we declared the_timeout inside the upDate() function in Figure 9-5, we wouldn't be able to clear the time-out using the stop timer button, because the button isn't located inside the function. Declaring the_timeout with var outside all functions allows any JavaScript on the page (including the JavaScript inside the `onClick` of the stop timer button) to access and change `the_timeout`.

Building a Clock with Timing Loops

Clocks are one obvious application of timing loops. Figure 9-7 provides the code for a simple clock, and Figure 9-8 shows the resulting page in a browser. See if you can understand what's going on before you read the analysis. Start by looking at the form in the body of the page.

```
<html><head><title>A JavaScript Clock</title>
<script type = "text/javascript">
<!-- hide me from older browsers
❶ var the_timeout;
   function writeTime() {
     // get a Date object
❷   var today = new Date();
     // ask the object for some information
❸   var hours = today.getHours();
     var minutes = today.getMinutes();

     var seconds = today.getSeconds();
     // make the minutes and seconds look right
❹   minutes = fixTime(minutes);
     seconds = fixTime(seconds);
     // put together the time string and write it out
❺   var the_time = hours + ":" + minutes + ":" + seconds;
❻   window.document.the_form.the_text.value = the_time;
     // run this function again in a second
❼   the_timeout = setTimeout('writeTime();',1000);
   }
❽ function fixTime(the_time) {
       if (the_time < 10)
       {
           the_time = "0" + the_time;
       }
       return the_time;
   }
   // show me -->
</script>
</head>
<body>
The time is now:
<form name = "the_form">
<input type = "text" name = "the_text">
<input type = "button" value = "Start the Clock" onClick = "writeTime();">
<input type = "button" value = "Stop the Clock"
  onClick = "clearTimeout(the_timeout);">
</form>
</body>
</html>
```

Figure 9-7: Code for a JavaScript clock

Figure 9-8: The JavaScript clock running in Firefox

Line-by-Line Analysis of Figure 9-7

The heart of Figure 9-7's script is the writeTime() function. Every second, this function figures out the current time, puts the time in the text field, and then sets a time-out to run writeTime() a second later (see Figure 9-8).

As usual, the script starts by declaring the variable that will hold the time-outs (❶). Next comes the writeTime() function, which creates a new Date object in ❷ (remember that a new Date object holds the current date and time). Line ❸ and the two lines following it get the hours, minutes, and seconds from the Date object using the getHours(), getMinutes(), and getSeconds() methods. This code hearkens back to the section "Writing the Date to Your Web Page" on page 26, which discussed how the *Book of JavaScript* web page updates the date and time.

Line ❹ in Figure 9-7 is the only really new part of this script. If you look back at Table 2-1, you'll see that getMinutes() and getSeconds() each return an integer from 1 to 59. If it's two minutes and three seconds past 9 AM, the variable hours in ❸ will be 9, minutes will be 2, and seconds will be 3. But putting these numbers together to display the time would create the string 9:2:3 instead of 9:02:03. Line ❹ takes care of this little problem by sending the minutes and seconds variables to a function I've written called fixTime(). The fixTime() function in ❽ takes a number as its parameter and puts 0 before the number if it is less than 10 (so 2 becomes 02). Make sure you understand how the fixTime() and writeTime() functions work together. It's a good example of how one function can call on another to do its dirty work.

Once fixTime() fixes the minutes and the seconds by inserting zero where appropriate, ❺ creates the time string, and ❻ writes it into the text box. Finally, ❼ sets the time-out that will call writeTime() again in one second. When writeTime() is called again, it creates a new Date object, gets the information out of it, fixes the minutes and seconds if necessary, writes the new time into the text box, and sets the time-out again. The whole process starts when a visitor clicks the Start the Clock button and ends when the visitor clicks the Stop the Clock button, which cancels the most recently set time-out.

How the *Book of JavaScript* Website's Timer Works

The timer on the *Book of JavaScript* website works similarly to the clock, but with a few twists added. Figure 9-9 shows the code.

```
      <html>
      <head>
      <title>How Long You've Been on the Page</title>
      <script type = "text/javascript">
      <!-- hide me from older browsers
❶     function setTimeSinceArriving(start_time, update_time) {
❷         if (start_time == 0) {
❸             start_time = getCurrentMillisecs();
          }

❹         var millisecs = getCurrentMillisecs();
❺         var milliSecondsOnPage = millisecs - start_time;
❻         var secondsOnPage = Math.round(milliSecondsOnPage / 1000);
❼         document.timeForm.timeSince.value = secondsOnPage;
❽         setTimeout("setTimeSinceArriving(" + start_time + "," + update_time + ")",
              update_time);
      }

      function getCurrentMillisecs() {
        var now = new Date();
❾     var millisecs = now.getTime();
        return millisecs;
      }

      // show me -->
      </script>
      </head>
❿     <body onLoad = "setTimeSinceArriving(0, 500)">
      <form name = "timeForm">
      Seconds you've been on this page:
      <input type = "text" name = "timeSince" size = "10">
      </body>
      </html>
```

Figure 9-9: Code to show how long you've been on a page

The fun starts with the onLoad in the <body> tag in ❿ . This onLoad calls the function setTimeSinceArriving() and passes it two parameters: 0, which indicates that this is the first time the function is being called, and 500, the number of milliseconds to pass to the setTimeout() function—in other words, the time between calls to the setTimeSinceArriving() function.

The setTimeSinceArriving() function is defined at the top of the page, starting with ❶ . The function first checks to see whether this is the first time it has been called by checking whether start_time equals 0 (❷). This happens only when the function is called from the onLoad in the body. If this is the first call to the function, ❸ changes start_time to equal a number that represents the time when the function was called.

For historical reasons, JavaScript (along with other programming languages) considers 12 AM, January 1, 1970, to be the beginning of time. In ❾ the function getCurrentMillisecs() calculates the number of milliseconds from this starting point using the getTime() method of the Date object. Just as you can call getHour() to get the hour from a Date object, you can call getTime() to get the number of milliseconds between January 1, 1970 and the time stored in the Date object.

Converting the date to a number in this way lets you compare two dates by comparing two simple numbers. If you didn't convert to milliseconds, and you had very close dates, you'd have to compare each part of the dates separately. For example, to make sure that January 1, 1970, 1 AM did indeed fall earlier than January 1, 1970, 2 AM, you'd have to check the years, then the months, then the days, then the hours. The difference between these two dates doesn't become apparent until you compare their hours. Converting both dates into milliseconds means you compare just the milliseconds. Messing around with dates is one of the biggest hassles in programming, so if this procedure seems awkward, you're right.

Getting back to the program, ❸ sets the start_time variable to the time when the function is first called. Line ❹ then gets the current time in milliseconds again. The first time the function is called, this will be almost exactly the same number as was calculated in ❸. The next time the function is called, however, it will be different. This is because ❸ executes only the first time the function is called, while ❹ is called every time the function runs.

Lines ❺ and ❻ do a little math to get the seconds between the numbers generated in ❸ and ❹. Line ❺ takes the difference between the two times and gives you a number in milliseconds. Line ❻ divides that number by 1,000 to get seconds and rounds it to the nearest whole number. Next, ❼ puts this number in the form element to display the information on the page, and ❽ calls setTimeout() to call the function again in 500 milliseconds.

The number 500 comes from ❿, the first time the function is called. You may be wondering why the function is being called every 500 milliseconds if it updates the timer only every second. Wouldn't it make more sense to call the function every second? It would, except that the JavaScript timer isn't perfect. If you are running many programs on your computer, or just a couple, but one is doing some heavy calculations, the JavaScript timer may be a little slow. If we asked JavaScript to call the function every second, it might be a little late. If this happens the timer might skip a second—jumping from 3 seconds to 5 seconds, for example. To reduce the chance of this, it helps to ask JavaScript to check its clock twice a second, just to make sure it's accurate. This is yet another example of paranoid programming.

How Space.com's Countdown Script Works

Space.com's countdown script (Figure 9-10) is a bit more complicated than the one on the *Book of JavaScript* website. However, aside from the calculations involved in determining the time until the next launch, it functions very similarly.

```
<script language = "JavaScript">
<!-- hide me from older browsers
// change your event date event here
❶ var eventdate = new Date("December 6, 2005 00:00:00 EST");
```

```
                // set to 0 to turn clock off or set to 1 to turn clock on
❷ var clock_on = 1;
❸ function toSt(n) {
        s = ""
        if(n<10) s += "0"
        return s+n.toString();
    }
❹ function countdown() {
        if (clock_on) {
            cl = document.clock;
            d = new Date();
❺          count = Math.floor((eventdate.getTime()-d.getTime())/1000);
❻        if(count <= 0) {
                {cl.days.value = "----";
                cl.hours.value = "--";
                cl.mins.value = "--";
                cl.secs.value = "--";
❼              return;
            }
❽          cl.secs.value=toSt(count%60);
            count=Math.floor(count/60);
            cl.mins.value=toSt(count%60);
            count=Math.floor(count/60);
            cl.hours.value=toSt(count%24);
            count=Math.floor(count/24);
            cl.days.value=count;
❾        setTimeout("countdown()",500);
        }
    }
    // show me -->
    </script>
❿ <form name = "clock">
    <input name = "days" size = "5" type = "text"><br>
    <input name = "hours" size = "5" type = "text"><br>
    <input name = "mins" size = "5" type = "text"><br>
    <input name = "secs" size = "5" type = "text">
    </form>
```

Figure 9-10: Space.com's countdown script

Line ❶ sets the date of the next space launch (as of the date I accessed this code; you'd see a different date if you selected **View ▸ Source** to look at the code now). Up until now, we've seen how to get the current date. Line ❶ shows you how to set the Date object to a specific date. The number after 2005 is the time of the launch, where EST stands for Eastern Standard Time. Line ❷, as mentioned in the comment above it, is set to 0 if there is no upcoming launch. As we'll see later, setting a value to 0 is like setting it equal to false.

The script gets started when the countdown() function (❹) is called using onLoad inside the web page's body:

```
<body marginwidth = "0" marginheight = "0" leftmargin = "0" topmargin = "0"
  onload = "PageLoad('spaceflight');countdown();">
```

When we discussed if-then statements in Chapter 3, I omitted a little trick. You can use 0 as a substitute for the term false. So if the clock_on variable is set to 0, the test if (clock_on) will be false. If clock_on is any other value, such as 1, the test if (clock_on) will be true. This is another example of programmers being lazy people—why type false, when you can just type 0?

The next couple of lines set a couple of variables: c1 points to the form that holds the countdown values (⑩), and d contains the current date information. I've taken some of the formatting out of the form, starting in ⑩, but otherwise it's the same as on the Space.com page.

The next line of the countdown() function uses the getTime() method of the Date object to calculate the number of seconds between the current time and the time of the next launch. Remember that getTime() gives you the number of milliseconds between the date represented in the object and January 1, 1970, and there are 1,000 milliseconds in a second. Line ❺ subtracts the current date from the launch date and then divides that number by 1,000 to get the number of seconds. The Math.floor() method takes the number you get from the division and rounds it down to the nearest whole number. That way, you get 2 seconds rather than 2.821 seconds.

The next block of code puts dashes in the form elements if the launch date has already passed. The launch date has passed when the current date is bigger than the launch date. In this case, the count variable in ❺ will be less than 0. There's a very small chance that you'll have reached the page right when the rocket is launching. Line ❻ treats this as if you missed the launch.

Notice the return in ❼. Recall from Chapter 6 that return causes JavaScript to exit the function (returning any value that follows the word return; in this case we don't need a return value). Putting the return in the if clause, as Space.com has done, forces the JavaScript to stop executing the rest of the countdown() function after putting dashes in the form elements. Although this works, it's considered bad style to put return statements in the middle of functions, because doing that can make it hard to determine the circumstances under which specific lines in your function will be executed. If part of a function is in an if clause, you know the conditions under which that part of the function will be run. In small functions like this, it doesn't make too much difference, but in general, it's best to avoid having return in the middle of functions. As an alternative, Space.com could rewrite the countdown() function using an if-else statement, like this:

```
function countdown() {
  // stuff before the if clause
  if (count <= 0) {
    // put in the dashes
  } else {
    // do the rest of the function
  }
}
```

Note that if there is no value to return, a function doesn't need to say return at the end.

Calculating Times

When Space.com displays the time until the next launch on the web page, the time is split into the number of days, hours, minutes, and seconds until launch. JavaScript does this using a mathematical operator that most people don't know about: MOD, or modulus. The *MOD operator* is represented in JavaScript by the percent sign (%), and it calculates the remainder of a division. Here are some examples:

5 % 2 = 1 (5 divided by 2 is 2, with 1 left over)

19 % 5 = 4 (19 divided by 5 is 3, with 4 left over)

1 % 3 = 1 (1 divided by 3 is 0, with 1 left over)

The MOD operator is useful when you need to break down one number into several components (for example, when you have the difference in seconds between two times and you want to break that into days, hours, minutes, and seconds). Lines ❽ until ❾ use MOD to do exactly that. Let's say there are 3,930 seconds until launch—in other words, the count variable equals 3,930. We want to separate that number into days, hours, minutes, and seconds until launch. Line ❽ uses MOD to figure out what should go in the seconds form element. The expression count%60 means count mod 60. The value of count, 3,930, divided by 60 is 65, with 30 left over. This new value, 30, gets run through the toSt() function, which puts a 0 in front of the number if it's less than 10, and the result goes into the seconds box.

Next, Space.com figures out what should be in the minutes box. To calculate how many minutes there are in count, the next line divides count by 60 seconds, and rounds down. After this calculation, count now equals 65. In other words, there are 65 minutes in 3,930 seconds. The countdown() function then mods 65 with 60 to get the number to display in the minutes box. Because 65/60 = 1, with 5 left over, 5 is run through the toSt() function, and the result is put into the minutes box. At this point, you should be ready to follow the rest of these calculations.

After making the calculations and putting the generated values into their appropriate form elements, the function uses setTimeout() to call itself in half a second and the timing loop proceeds as we've seen in the other examples in this chapter.

Global Variables and Constants

Before finishing with the Space.com example, I'd like to point out one more important coding style issue. Notice that the variable declarations in ❶ and ❷ in the Space.com script don't appear inside a specific function. As with the time-outs described earlier, this means that any function in the script can access the variables. For example, ❺ in the countdown() function accesses eventdate, even though eventdate was declared outside the function. Variables declared outside JavaScript functions are called *global variables*. In general, global variables should be avoided. They tend to introduce hard-to-debug errors into code. These errors occur when multiple functions alter the value of the global variable at various points in the script, making it difficult to figure out what part of your script set a variable to a certain value. When your variables are declared with the word var inside a function, you know that only that function can alter the value of the variable. If the variable does not contain the value you think it should when you run the JavaScript, you can narrow your focus down to the function in which the variable is declared to debug the problem.

Other than time-outs, the one situation where global variables are a good idea is when the value of the variable never changes while the script is running. A variable like this is called a *constant*, and ❶ and ❷ in the Space.com script are a perfect example. While the script is running, the eventdate and clock_on values never change, so you don't have to worry about confusion arising when multiple functions change the variable values. The question of when a variable should be declared outside of a function, and therefore be available to all functions, boils down to this rule of thumb: If a variable never changes and is required in multiple functions, then you should declare it (using var) outside the functions; otherwise, you should declare the variable inside one function, and if other functions need it, pass it to those functions as a parameter, as described in Chapter 6.

A Timed Slide Show

A slide show is another good application of timed loops. Figure 9-11 shows you how to combine arrays and timing loops to create a looping slide show. Again, look the script over before diving into the explanation.

```
   <html>
   <head>
   <title>A Timed Slide Show</title>
   <script type = "text/javascript">
   <!-- hide me from older browsers
❶ var the_images = new Array();
❷ the_images[0] = new Image();
❸ the_images[0].src = "one.jpg";
   the_images[1] = new Image();
   the_images[1].src = "two.jpg";
   the_images[2] = new Image();
   the_images[2].src = "three.jpg";
❹ var the_timeout;
❺ var index = 0;
   function rotateImage()
   {
❻   window.document.my_image.src = the_images[index].src;
     index++;
❼   if (index >= the_images.length)
       {
           index = 0;
       }
```

```
❽    the_timeout = setTimeout("rotateImage();", 1000);
    }
    // show me -->
    </script>
    </head>
    <body>
❾  <img name = "my_image" src = "one.jpg">
    <form>
    <input type = "button" value = "Start the Show"
      onClick = "clearTimeout(the_timeout); rotateImage();">
    <input type = "button" value = "Stop the Show"
      onClick = "clearTimeout(the_timeout);">
    </form>
    </body>
    </html>
```

Figure 9-11: A timed slide show

Line-by-Line Analysis of Figure 9-11

The first few lines set up the array containing the images we'll put in the slide show. Line ❶ creates the new array, ❷ sets the first item in the array equal to an image object, and ❸ sets the src of that image object to the first picture of the slide show. Lines ❷ and ❸ are just like the lines used to preload images before an image swap (see "Image Preloading" on page 62). The next few lines load the rest of the images.

After the images have loaded, ❹ and ❺ set up two variables for use in the timing loop. Line ❹ declares the_timeout, which keeps track of each time-out, and ❺ keeps track of which image in the slide show to bring up next time the script calls rotateImage(). Keep in mind that declaring the index variable outside the rotateImage() function, as I've done here in ❺, is not the safest programming practice—it's just easier and quicker than the safe solution. A safer version of rotateImage() will be described subsequently.

Next comes the rotateImage() function, which swaps in a new image and then calls itself in one second. The first line of the function (❻) does the image swap. It looks up the value of index, finds the src of the element numbered index in the the_images array, and swaps in that image for my_image (the image in ❾).

After swapping the image, the function adds 1 to the index variable. The next time rotateImage() gets called, it looks up the next item in the array and swaps in that item. We have to make sure the number stored in index doesn't exceed the number of images stored in the the_images array. The if-then statement starting in ❼ takes care of this issue by ensuring that if index has incremented past the number of items in the array, it will be set back to 0 (corresponding to the first image in the the_images array). The last line in the function (❽) should be old hat by now. This line sets a time-out to call the rotateImage() function in one second.

The slide show starts when a visitor presses the button that calls rotateImage() and ends when the user presses the Stop the Show button, canceling the most recently set time-out.

A Safer Version of rotateImage()

If you're not interested in perfecting your coding style, you can skip this section; it's a bit advanced. However, if you want to be a supersafe coder, read on.

At a couple of points in this book, I've mentioned that it's best to declare variables inside the functions that use them. As we saw earlier in the chapter, this won't work for variables that hold time-outs, as in ❹ of Figure 9-11. But in ❺ of Figure 9-11, the variable index, declared outside the function, does not hold a time-out. The only part of the script that uses the index variable is the rotateImage() function—so I really should be declaring index inside the rotateImage() function. Unfortunately, as you'll see in Figure 9-12, I can't.

Why Declaring a Variable Outside a Function Is Unsafe

Before I describe how to get around this problem, let me first show you in more detail why declaring index outside rotateImage() is unsafe.

Let's say your script has two functions: rotateImage(), which performs the slide show, and beersOnTheWall(), which counts down from 99. If both rotateImage() and beersOnTheWall() depend on the variable index, and you don't declare index inside the functions, both functions will be looking at the same number—whatever index holds. This is awkward, because you'd probably want index to start at 99 for the beersOnTheWall() function and 0 for the rotateImage() function. You'd also want index to decrease by 1 each time through beersOnTheWall(), but increase by 1 each time through rotateImage(). Having both functions look at the same variable just won't work.

The easy, though dangerous, solution to the problem would be to make sure rotateImage() and beersOnTheWall() use different variables. For example, rotateImage() could use the variable index and beersOnTheWall() could use beers. This solution might work in a short script, especially if nobody else is going to change it. However, if the script is lengthy, if more than one person will modify it, or if the script will be changed and expanded frequently, you can't assume the people changing your script will all know they shouldn't name any new variable index. If someone accidentally does create another variable named index, the rotateImage() function probably won't work, because rotateImage() will expect a particular index value, and the newly created index will probably contain another value.

Why You Can't Put var Inside a Timing Loop

Using var and declaring variables inside the functions that use them is the safest, simplest solution to this problem. Unfortunately, this solution doesn't work exactly right in timing loops. To see why, look at the function in Figure 9-12.

```
    function rotateImage()
    {
❶      var index = 0;
        window.document.my_image.src = the_images[index].src;
        index++;
        if (index >= the_images.length)
        {
            index = 0;
        }
        the_timeout = setTimeout("rotateImage();", 1000);
    }
```

Figure 9-12: A faulty rotateImage() function

The addition of ❶ in Figure 9-12 is the only change to Figure 9-11's rotateImage() function. This line declares the variable index inside rotateImage(), thereby avoiding the problem of having two functions look at the same variable. Unfortunately, each time rotateImage() gets called, index gets set to 0 again. This means only the first image of the_images would ever show up.

The Solution

Figure 9-13 shows the only really safe way to use setTimeout() to call a function that takes a parameter. It's a bit complex, so look closely at it before reading the explanation.

```
    <html>
    <head>
    <title>A Timed Slide Show</title>
    <script type = "text/javascript">
    <!-- hide me from older browsers
    var the_images = new Array();
    the_images[0] = new Image();
    the_images[0].src = "one.jpg";
    the_images[1] = new Image();
    the_images[1].src = "two.jpg";
    the_images[2] = new Image();
    the_images[2].src = "three.jpg";
    var the_timeout;
❶  function rotateImage(index)
    {
        window.document.my_image.src = the_images[index].src;
❷      index++;
        if (index >= the_images.length)
        {
            index = 0;
        }
❸      var the_function_string = "rotateImage(" + index + ");";
❹      the_timeout = setTimeout(the_function_string, 1000);
    }
```

```
// show me -->
</script>
</head>
<body>
<img name = "my_image" src = "one.jpg">
<form>
❺ <input type = "button" value = "start the show" onClick = "rotateImage(0);">
<input type = "button" value = "stop the show"
   onClick = "clearTimeout(the_timeout);">
</form>
</body>
</html>
```

Figure 9-13: Coding timing loops the safe way

This safer version of `rotateImage()` never really declares the problematic variable `index` at all. Instead, `rotateImage()` is called with a parameter—the number of the image that should appear. Line ❶ shows how `rotateImage()` has changed to accept this parameter. Calling `rotateImage(0)` in ❺ calls `rotateIndex()` and sets `index` to `0` in ❶. The first line in the body of the function then swaps the image stored in position 0 of `the_images` with the image on the page. If `rotateImage(1)` was called instead of `rotateImage(0)`, the second image in `the_images` would have been swapped into the page, `rotateImage(2)` swaps in the third image, and so on.

The Hitch

Of course, there is a hitch. After incrementing `index` in ❷, as we did in Figure 9-13, it would make sense to call `rotateImage()` again in a `setTimeout` like this:

```
the_timeout = setTimeout("rotateImage(index);",1000);
```

Unfortunately, this triggers a JavaScript error. When one second passes and the `rotateImage(index)` command executes, JavaScript tries to remember what the variable `index` holds, then calls `rotateImage()` with that value. However, at this point, as far as JavaScript knows, no variable `index` exists. The variable `index` exists only inside the function. The `setTimeout()` in the above line looks up the variable before calling the function, and since nothing called `index` exists outside the function, JavaScript gives the visitor an error message.

The Solution to the Hitch

The way out of this bizarre situation is demonstrated in ❸ and ❹ of Figure 9-13. Line ❸ creates the command that the `setTimeout()` will call in one second. Instead of using the command

```
"rotateImage(index);"
```

line ❸ pulls the word `index` out of the quotes, forcing JavaScript to look up the value of the variable `index` and put that value into the command. If you have `index` set to `2`, for example, ❸ writes the command that goes into the `setTimeout()` as follows:

```
"rotateImage(2);"
```

Line ❸ may seem confusing, so make sure you understand why it's written that way. Because JavaScript calls `rotateImage()` with the number 2 instead of the variable `index`, it doesn't need to look up the value of any variable when the command runs in one second. Instead, `rotateImage()` receives the number 2, and the function proceeds normally.

Once ❸ creates the string that holds the command for the time-out to call, ❹ performs the `setTimeout()`.

What's the moral of this story? It's a bad idea to use `setTimeout()` to call a function with a variable between its parentheses, as in

```
timeout = setTimeout("rotateImage(index);",1000);
```

because you never know what `index` will be when you call the function in the future or even whether `index` will exist then. If you do use a function inside a `setTimeout()` and that function takes a parameter, use a line such as ❸ to place the value of the variable into the function.

Why image_array Is Declared Outside the rotateImage() Function

Since `rotateImage()` is the only function that makes use of `image_array`, why not declare it inside the `rotateImage()` function? Well, I could have, and if I was being supersafe, I might have. However, re-creating the array every time it calls the function—possibly hundreds or thousands of times—seems wasteful. As written, Figure 9-12 creates the array only once. It's pretty safe to declare `image_array` outside the function that uses it because the script probably won't ever change this array. Because the values in `image_array` aren't likely to change, I don't have to worry much about one function changing a value in the array contrary to the needs of another function.

This section has focused entirely on programming style. The code shown in Figure 9-11 will serve you perfectly well in many situations, and you may prefer it for short scripts because it's more comprehensible. The code shown in Figure 9-13 is better for complex scripts and for those scripts that you or others will change frequently.

Summary

If you have mastered this chapter, you now know the following:

- How setTimeout() causes a JavaScript statement to execute in the future
- How to use clearTimeout() to cancel a time-out
- How to create a timed loop by writing a function that sets a time-out that calls the same function
- How to use parseInt() to convert a string to a number, and why you might have to do this

If you read the part about coding timing loops the safe way in "A Safer Version of rotateImage()" on page 163, you also know how to write a timing loop that calls a function taking parameters.

To make sure you understand timing loops and how to cancel them, try the following assignment.

Assignment

Try enhancing the slide show in Figure 9-11 so that mousing over the image stops the slide show and mousing off the image resumes the slide show. It's a bit trickier than it sounds.

10

USING FRAMES AND IMAGE MAPS

Frames divide a web page into different sections and are useful for navigation and page layout. *Image maps* are images that contain multiple HTML links. Clicking different parts of an image map brings your visitors to different web pages. JavaScript can enhance both of these HTML features by allowing you to manipulate the contents of frames using image maps and links in other frames.

In this chapter you'll learn how to:

- Create basic frames
- Use JavaScript to control the contents of frames
- Use JavaScript to change two frames at once
- Use frames to share information between web pages
- Create basic image maps
- Use JavaScript to add functionality to your image maps

A Real-World Example of Frames and Image Maps

A page that is still my favorite example of integrating image maps, frames, and JavaScript appeared on the *Salon* website a few years ago: It presents a book about eating bugs (see Figure 10-1). The version I will describe may be found at http://www.bookofjavascript.com/Websites/Salon/frame.html. The current version of the page is available at http://www.salon.com/wlust/pass/1999/02/bugs/frame. Mousing over the map highlights that area of the world and swaps in two pictures: one of the insects that people there eat, and another of them preparing the insect for a meal.

Figure 10-1: Salon's bug-eating pictorial

This page is divided into four frames. One frame holds the map of the world on the left, a second frame holds the picture, a third holds the user instructions at the top of the page, and a fourth frame holds a caption describing the picture. The world map is an image map; JavaScript causes the frames to change when a visitor mouses over any area of the map. Later in the chapter you'll see some of the code that creates this set of frames and activates the image map.

Frames

If you're already familiar with frames—what they are and how they are used to build web pages—and don't need a review of the basics, you can skip to the section "Frames and JavaScript" on page 172 to learn how the language works with them.

Frame Basics

A web page with frames is actually a set of HTML pages displayed simultaneously. If a page has two frames, it displays two HTML pages, one for each frame. In addition to the HTML pages that provide the content in the frames, another page describes how to display these HTML pages. Figure 10-2 shows the HTML for a simple web page with frames. Figure 10-3 shows what the resulting page looks like in a browser.

```
index.html
<html>
<head>
<title>A Simple Frame Set</title>
</head>
❶ <frameset cols = "30%, *">
❷ <frame src = "navigation.html" name = "nav">
   <frame src = "content.html" name = "contents">
❸ </frameset>
</html>

navigation.html
<html><head><title>Nav</title></head>
<body>
<h1>News navigation</h1>
<a href = "http://www.wired.com" target = "contents">Wired News</a><br>
<a href = "http://www.news.com" target = "contents">C|Net News</a><br>
❹ <a href = "http://www.newsoftheweird.com" target = "contents">News of the
Weird</a><br>
</body></html>

content.html
<html><head><title>News</title></head>
<body>
<h1>Choose a link on the left to see some news.</h1>
</body></html>
```

Figure 10-2: Code for a simple web page with frames

The code in Figure 10-2 consists of three separate HTML pages. The first page, index.html, describes how the other two pages should appear on the screen. The second page, navigation.html, is on the left side of the screen in Figure 10-3, and the third page, content.html, is on the right side. Clicking any of the links on the left side loads the corresponding web page on the right side of the screen.

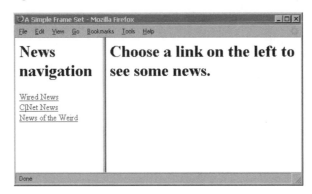

Figure 10-3: A simple web page with frames

The pages in Figure 10-3 are set next to each other because ❶ in Figure 10-2 tells the browser to set up two frames, arrange them in columns, and make the first column take up 30 percent of the page and the second column the rest of the page. Adding more percentages (their sum can't exceed 100) to the cols element adds more frames to the page. Alternatively, using the rows element stacks frames on top of each other. You can tweak frame sets in dozens of ways. Any good book about HTML devotes a chapter to them.

The two lines after ❶ tell the browser which HTML pages to load into each frame. Line ❷ loads navigation.html into the first frame (named nav), and the next line loads content.html into the second frame (named contents). Line ❸ closes the frame set. Notice that you don't use <body> tags in defining a frame set.

The next two HTML pages are standard web pages. The first page, navigation.html, contains three links, each leading to a news site. Clicking a link loads the contents into the contents frame, because each link contains the element target = "contents" (see ❹). We'll see shortly how to use JavaScript to do the same thing.

Frames and JavaScript

In HTML, the only way an action in one frame can change the contents of another is through standard HTML links. Fortunately, JavaScript allows you to expand your repertoire of frame tricks immensely. The JavaScript in Figure 10-4, for example, makes the contents of the right frame change when a visitor mouses over one of the links on the left. The pages index.html and content.html are the same as in Figure 10-2; only navigation.html has changed.

```
navigation.html
<html><head><title>Nav</title>
<script type = "text/javascript">
<!-- hide me from older browsers
❶ function changeContents(the_url)
   {
❷    var content_frame = parent.contents;
❸    content_frame.location = the_url;
   }
// show me -->
</script>
</head>
<body>
<h1> News navigation</h1>
<a href = "http://www.wired.com"
  onMouseOver = "changeContents('http://www.wired.com');
">Wired News</a><br>
<a href = "http://www.news.com"
  onMouseOver = "changeContents('http://www.news.com');
">C|Net News</a><br>
❹ <a href = "http://www.newsoftheweird.com"
  onMouseOver = "changeContents('http://www.newsoftheweird.com');
">News of the Weird</a><br>
</body></html>
```

Figure 10-4: Using JavaScript to change a frame with a mouseover

Line-by-Line Analysis of Figure 10-4

The key to this script is the function changeContents(). When a visitor mouses over the News of the Weird link, ❹ calls changeContents() and sends it the string "http://www.newsoftheweird.com".

The changeContents() function starts in ❶, where the_url is set to whatever string passes into the function. Line ❷ tells JavaScript to look for the thing named contents inside its parent (the frame set containing a frame is the frame's parent—see Figure 10-5), and sets the variable content_frame to point to the contents frame.

You refer to frames in JavaScript the same way you refer to windows. Just as you can change the page shown in a window by referring to its URL like this:

```
window_name.location = "http://www.newsoftheweird.com";
```

you can change the page shown in a frame like this:

```
the_frame.location = "http://www.newsoftheweird.com";
```

This is precisely what ❸ in Figure 10-4 does. After ❷ assigns content_frame to point to the frame we want to change, ❸ changes that frame's location by setting content_frame.location to the_url.

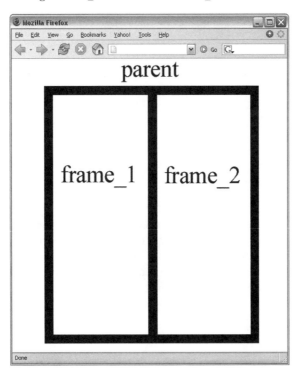

Figure 10-5: A graphical representation of frames and their parents

Frames and Image Swaps

In the Chapter 5 assignment, I described how clicking a JavaScript-enhanced link in one window can change an image in another window. Because JavaScript treats frames and windows similarly, the same trick enables a link in one frame to change an image in another.

As a refresher, Figure 10-6 contains the code necessary to swap an image in one window by clicking a link in a second window. Figure 10-7 shows how the same trick works with frames.

```
first_page.html
<html>
<head>
<title>Control Panel</title>
<script type = "text/javascript">
<!-- hide me from older browsers
❶ var image_window =
      window.open("image_page.html","image_window","width=100,height=100");
   // show me -->
   </script>
   </head>
   <body>
❷ <a href = "#" onClick =
     "image_window.document.the_image.src = 'sad.gif'; return false;">sad</a>
   <br>
❸ <a href = "#" onClick =
     "image_window.document.the_image.src = 'happy.gif'; return false;">happy</a>
   </body>
   </html>


image_page.html
<html><head><title>The Image Page</title></head>
<body>
❹ <img src = "happy.gif" name = "the_image">
   </body>
   </html>
```

Figure 10-6: Swapping an image in one window with a link in another

Figure 10-6 consists of two HTML pages. The first page, first_page.html, starts by launching a new window in ❶ and calling it image_window. This window will open to image_page.html, which has only one item in it—an image of a happy face, named the_image (❹). When someone clicks the link in ❷, JavaScript looks for the window called image_window and looks in its document for the_image. Once it finds the_image, it changes its src to sad.gif. The link in ❸ changes the image back to happy.gif.

```
frameset.html
<html>
<head>
<title>Image Swapping in Frames</title>
</head>
<frameset rows = "30%, *">
```

```
<frame src = "navigation.html" name = "navigate">
<frame src = "image_page.html" name = "image_frame">
</frameset>
</html>
```

navigation.html
```
<html>
<head>
<title>Control Panel</title>
</head>
<body>
```
❶ ```
<a href = "#" onClick =
   "parent.image_frame.document.the_image.src = 'sad.gif'; return false;">sad</a>

<a href = "#" onClick = "parent.image_frame.document.the_image.src =
   'happy.gif'; return false;">happy</a>
</body>
</html>
```

**image_page.html**
```
<html><head><title>The Image Page</title></head>
<body>
```
❷ ```
<img src = "happy.gif" name = "the_image">
</body>
</html>
```

Figure 10-7: Swapping an image in one frame with a link in another

Figure 10-7 does the same thing with frames instead of windows. The page frameset.html in Figure 10-7 sets up the page illustrated in Figure 10-8; it has navigation.html in the top frame (which takes up 30 percent of the window) and image_page.html in the bottom frame with happy.gif (called the_image in ❷). Line ❶ is the link in the top frame that changes happy.gif in the bottom frame to sad.gif. The critical part of ❶ is

```
parent.image_frame.document.the_image.src = 'sad.gif';
```

which is similar to ❷ in Figure 10-6:

```
image_window.document.the_image.src = 'sad.gif';
```

The only difference is that in Figure 10-6 we refer directly to the window image_window, while in Figure 10-7 we tell the JavaScript in the navigation.html to go up to its parent and then down to the frame image_frame. Figure 10-8 shows the code in Figure 10-7 at work.

Figure 10-8: Interframe image swapping in action

Changing the Contents of Two Frames at Once

In some situations, you may want to change the contents of two or more frames at once. In *Salon*'s bug-eating piece, for example, mousing over part of the world in the map frame changes the contents of all three frames.

Figure 10-9 contains the JavaScript for a simple example of changing more than one frame: a Spanish-language tutorial. As you can see in Figure 10-10, clicking a Spanish word in one frame shows you an image of what that word means in a second frame and puts the translation of the word into English inside a form element in a third frame.

```
frameset.html
<html>
<head>
<title>Changing Two Frames at Once</title>
</head>
❶ <frameset cols = "30%, 30%, *">
<frame src = "navigation.html" name = "navigate">
<frame src = "form_page.html" name = "form_frame">
<frame src = "image_page.html" name = "image_frame">
</frameset>
</html>


navigation.html
<html>
<head>
<title>Navigation Frame</title>
<script type = "text/javascript">
<!-- hide me from older browsers

function changeFrames(new_image, new_words)
{
❷    parent.image_frame.document.the_image.src = new_image;
❸    parent.form_frame.document.the_form.the_name.value = new_words;
}
// show me -->
</script>
</head>
<body>
❹ <a href = "#"
   onClick = "changeFrames('apple.gif','apple'); return false;">manzana</a>
<br>
<a href = "#"
   onClick = "changeFrames('orange.gif','orange'); return false;">naranja</a>
</body>
</html>


form_page.html
<html><head><title>The Form Page</title></head>
<body>
<form name = "the_form">
<input type = "text" name = "the_name">
```

```
</form>
</body>
</html>

image_page.html
<html><head><title>The Image Page</title></head>
<body>
❺ <img src = "blank.gif" name = "the_image">
</body>
</html>
```

Figure 10-9: Changing two frames at once

Figure 10-10: A simple Spanish tutorial—after clicking the word
manzana

Line-by-Line Analysis of Figure 10-9

The tutorial consists of four HTML pages. The first, frameset.html, describes the layout of the frames (❶).

In the first frame, navigation.html contains the JavaScript function and the links that change the contents of the other two frames. The function changeFrames() takes the parameters new_image, the name of the image to swap in the third frame, and new_words, the words to put into the form element in the second frame. Line ❷ performs the image swap by telling JavaScript to find the parent of the navigation frame (frameset.html), then the frame image_frame inside the frame set, and, inside that frame, the image named the_image (❺). Once JavaScript has found the_image, changeFrames() changes the_image.src to whatever new_image was set to when the script called the function. Line ❸ changes the contents of the text box in form_frame in a similar fashion.

Clicking the *manzana* link in the navigation frame (❹) calls the changeFrames() function, with apple.gif as the image to swap in and *apple* as the word to go into the form. Although changeFrames() only changes two frames, you could easily expand it to change as many frames as the frame set holds.

Frames Inside Frames

Sometimes you need to mix side-by-side frames with stacked frames. For example, the page shown in Figure 10-11 has one wide frame on top and two narrower frames next to each other, below the wider top frame. You would achieve this effect by creating one frame set with two frames, one on top of the other, and loading the bottom frame with a second frame set that has two frames next to each other. Figure 10-12 shows the code for Figure 10-11.

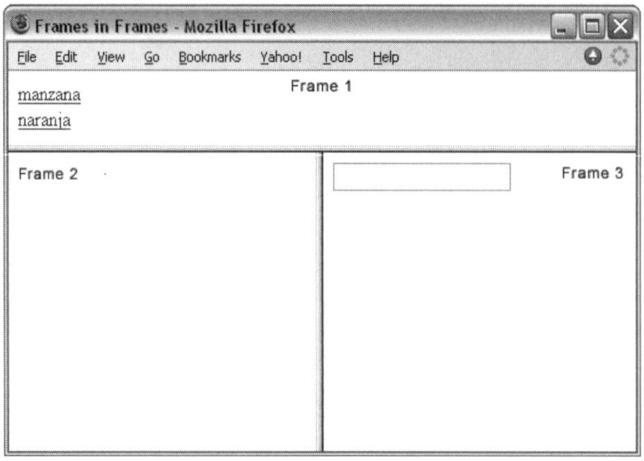

Figure 10-11: Frames inside frames

```
index.html
<html>
<head><title>Frames in Frames</title></head>
❶ <frameset rows = "20%,*">
❷     <frame src = "navigation.html" name = "navigate">
❸     <frame src = "bottom_frame.html" name = "bottom">
</frameset>
</html>


bottom_frame.html
<html>
<head><title>Bottom Frames</title></head>
❹ <frameset cols = "50%,*">
      <frame src = "image_page.html" name = "image_frame">
      <frame src = "form_page.html" name = "form_frame">
</frameset>
</html>
```

Figure 10-12: The frame set for Figure 10-11

The pages navigation.html, image_page.html, and form_page.html invoked by the code in Figure 10-12 function in the same way as the corresponding pages in Figure 10-9.

The first frame set (call it the outer frame set) sets up two frames, one on top of the other (❶). The top frame (❷) holds navigation.html, which contains the navigation links and the JavaScript that controls how the links affect the other frames. The bottom frame (❸) loads bottom_frame.html, which holds the second frame set (call it the inner frame set). This frame set (❹) creates two frames: The left frame contains image_page.html, and the right frame contains form_page.html. Each of these pages could also have a frame set, since you can nest frame sets infinitely. Be careful, though—having more than one level of frame sets quickly boggles the minds of even the best web page producers.

JavaScript and Frames Inside Frames

As long as you have only one frame set, JavaScript in one frame can influence any other frame by referring to it as `parent.frame_name`. Matters get a bit more complicated if you have nested frame sets. Consider frame 3 in Figure 10-11. The parent of this frame is the inner frame set (bottom_frame.html), containing frames 2 and 3. The appropriate JavaScript in frame 3 could influence frame 2 using `parent.image_frame`. For example, to change the URL shown in frame 2, frame 3 could run the following script:

```
parent.image_frame.location = "http://www.webmonkey.com";
```

But how can JavaScript in frame 3 change the contents of frame 1? The inner frame set (which contains frames 2 and 3) doesn't "know" anything about frame 1 because it's located in another frame set. The outer frame set (index.html), however, does "know" about frame 1 and the inner frame set because it set them up. So in order for a frame in the inner frame set to affect a frame in the outer frame set, the inner frame must ask the outer frame set to find the frame to change. In this case, you could control frame 1 by calling the parent of frame 3's parent:

```
parent.parent.top_frame.location = "http://www.webmonkey.com";
```

Running this script in frame 3 changes the URL displayed in frame 1. The line in frame 3 tells JavaScript to go up to frame 3's parent, the inner frame set; find that frame set's parent, the frame set in frameset.html; and then find the frame `top_frame` inside that frame set.

Alternatively, you can have frame 3 refer directly to the outermost frame set by using the word `top` in your script:

```
top.navigate.location = "http://www.webmonkey.com";
```

This tells JavaScript to find the topmost frame set and look for the frame named `navigate` inside that frame set. The top object contains everything in the web browser window, so if there are frame sets on the page, top refers to the outermost frame set. If there are no frames in the browser, top means the same thing as `window`.

Whether you use top or a chain of parents to deal with nested frame sets depends on the circumstances. If you have a link in a frame buried four frame sets deep that you want to affect a frame on the top level, using top probably makes sense. If you want the link in the buried frame set to affect a frame in its own frame set, parent is the way to go.

Frame Busting

Some sites use frames to keep you in their site even when you think you're leaving it. For example, when you do an image search on Google, the result appears on a page that has Google's upper frame (see Figure 10-13). Google allows its users to get rid of the top frame by clicking a link, but you might not want your web page showing up in a Google frame at all. To prevent this from happening, insert the script shown in Figure 10-14 in the header of your page.

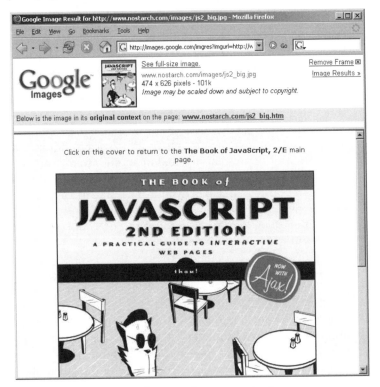

Figure 10-13: Google uses frames to keep you in its site

Line ❶ checks to see whether the HTML page containing this JavaScript is the top frame of the frame hierarchy (remember, self means *this page*). Line ❶ translates to "If this page is not on top, perform the statements between the curly brackets." If the HTML page is not on top, it's inside an alien frame set. To escape the frame set, the page puts itself on top by setting the top.location of the window to self.location (❷) which stores the URL of a web page.

```
<script type = "text/javascript">>
<!-- hide me from older browsers
❶ if (self != top)
  {
❷   top.location = self.location;
  }
// show me -->
</script>
```

Figure 10-14: Frame-busting code

Using Frames to Store Information

Web pages have lousy memories. Unless you've done something fancy, the moment a visitor leaves your web page, the page forgets any information it has collected. If, for example, you have a long quiz and you want to tell a visitor his or her score at the end, you'll find it tough to break the quiz into several pages—the second page can't keep track of which answers the visitor gave on the first page.

There are a few ways around this problem. If you want to store the information for a long time on your visitor's computer, cookies are the way to go (see Chapter 12). But if you only want to save the information briefly, there's a neat trick using frames to store information between pages.

The trick involves setting up an invisible frame containing a JavaScript function with an array that saves the information from each page as your visitors move from page to page inside your site. When you need to retrieve the information, simply access an array in the invisible frame. Figure 10-15 lists four web pages to show how you would do this for a quiz. Figure 10-16 shows you what the code in Figure 10-15 generates.

```
   frameset.html
   <html>
   <head>
   <title>A Quiz</title>
   </head>
❶ <frameset rows = "100%,*" frameborder = "0">
❷ <frame src = "quiz_page_1.html" noresize>
❸ <frame src = "secret_code.html" name = "tracker" noresize>
   </frameset>
   </html>


   secret_code.html
   <html>
   <head>
   <title>A Quiz</title>
   <script type = "text/javascript">>
   <!-- hide me from older browsers
❹ var answers = new Array();
❺ function score(answers)
   {
       var correct = 0;
       var correct_answers = new Array("true","true","false","true");
       for (var loop = 0; loop < correct_answers.length; loop++)
       {
           if (answers[loop] == correct_answers[loop])
           {
               correct++;
           }
       }
       percent_correct = (correct/4) * 100;
       alert("You got " + percent_correct + " percent right!");
   }
   // show me -->
```

```
</script>
</head>
<body>
Nothing to see here!
</body>
</html>
```

quiz_page_1.html
```
<html>
<head>
<title>Quiz Page 1</title>
</head>
<body>
Answer the following true/false questions:
<p>
<form>
A chicken is a bird.<br>
<input type = "radio" name = "bird"
  onClick = "parent.tracker.answers[0]='true';">True<br>
<input type = "radio" name = "bird"
  onClick = "parent.tracker.answers[0]='false';">False<br>
<p>
A skink is a lizard.<br>
<input type = "radio" name = "skink"
  onClick = "parent.tracker.answers[1]='true';">True<br>
<input type = "radio" name = "skink"
  onClick = "parent.tracker.answers[1]='false';">False<br>
<p>
</form>
<p>
```
❻ ```<a href = "quiz_page_2.html">Next Page</a>```
```
</body>
</html>
```

quiz_page_2.html
```
<html>
<head>

<title>Quiz Page 2</title>
</head>
<body>
Answer the following true/false questions:
<p>
<form>
A whale is a fish.<br>
<input type = "radio" name = "whale"
  onClick = "parent.tracker.answers[2]='true';">True<br>
<input type = "radio" name = "whale"
  onClick = "parent.tracker.answers[2]='false';">False<br>
<p>
A human is a primate.<br>
<input type = "radio" name = "human"
  onClick = "parent.tracker.answers[3]='true';">True<br>
<input type = "radio" name = "human"
  onClick = "parent.tracker.answers[3]='false';">False<br>
```

```
   <p>
❼ <input type = "button" value = "Score the Quiz"
     onClick = "parent.tracker.score(parent.tracker.answers);">
   </form>
   </body>
   </html>
```

Figure 10-15: Preserving information between pages with frames

As you can see in Figure 10-16, the quiz doesn't look as if it's in frames. In fact, it has two frames, but one is invisible. The visible frame holds two true/false questions and a link to go to the next page (Figure 10-17). Although clicking the link apparently brings the visitor to a completely new web page, it's actually the same page with new contents in the visible frame.

Figure 10-16: Page 1 of the quiz generated by Figure 10-15

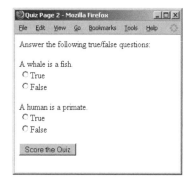

Figure 10-17: Page 2 of the quiz generated by Figure 10-15

Line-by-Line Analysis of Figure 10-15

The invisible frame stores the visitor's answers as he or she moves from page to page. If you didn't put the quiz in frames, the browser would forget the visitor's answers each time it loaded a new web page. Here's how the invisible frame stores information.

The first page in Figure 10-15, frameset.html, sets up the frames as we've seen before, but with a few changes. Line ❶ describes two frames. The first one takes up 100 percent of the window, making it seem as if the page has no second frame. We've set frameborder, which controls the thickness of the line between the two frames, to 0 to eliminate any trace of the invisible frame.

Lines ❷ and ❸ contain another new element: noresize. This attribute to the <frame> tag tells the browser to prevent visitors from resizing the frames. Without this element, a visitor might accidentally click the bottom of the window and pull the hidden frame up. Putting noresize inside the <frame> tags prevents this from happening. Also note that the invisible frame, called tracker, holds the HTML page secret_code.html—this is where we'll be storing the information. Because the frame is hidden, visitors can't see the contents of secret_code.html.

The next page, secret_code.html, holds the visitor's answers in the answers array (❹) and scores the quiz at the end.

The scoring function starts in ❺. This function creates an array called correct_answers, which holds the correct answers and loops through the array, comparing each correct answer with the answer the visitor gave. If the answers match, the script increments the variable correct. Once the script has checked all the answers, the function calculates what percentage the visitor got right and announces the score in an alert.

The two quiz pages show how the script stores the visitors' answers in the invisible frame and how it calls the score() function.

The page quiz_page_1.html contains a form with two quiz questions and a link. Each quiz question is true or false; the visitor answers by clicking the appropriate radio button. Clicking the True radio button on the first question runs the following code:

```
parent.tracker.answers[0]='true';
```

This line goes to the frame tracker in the page's parent (that is, the frame set) and stores the string 'true' in the first slot (answers[0]) of the array. Clicking the False radio button on the second question runs the following code and then stores the string 'false' in the second slot of the answers array:

```
parent.tracker.answers[1]='false';
```

Clicking the link in ❻ loads the new page, quiz_page_2.html, into the visible frame. The invisible frame, however, sticks around, storing the values from the last page. It keeps the visitor's answers to the two questions on quiz_page_2.html in the third and fourth slots in the answers array. Clicking the Score the Quiz button in ❼ calls the following code:

```
parent.tracker.score(parent.tracker.answers);
```

This line invokes the score() function found inside the tracker frame. The function takes an array containing the visitor's answers as a parameter. Because the tracker frame stores the answers array, the script can pass the array to the score function by referring to parent.tracker.answers.

This example uses practically every major element of programming this book has covered to date, so take a long look at it and make sure you understand everything that's going on. I've introduced two major new concepts:

- One frame refers to a variable stored in another frame with parent.*other_frame.variable*, as in parent.tracker.answers
- One frame calls a function declared in another frame with parent.*other_frame.function*(), as in parent.tracker.score()

Image Maps

JavaScript allows you to expand the capabilities of image maps by letting you call JavaScript statements when users click, mouse over, or mouse off different parts of an image map.

Image Map Basics

To construct an image map, you need an image and a map that describes which parts of the image should link to which URLs. Figure 10-18 shows you part of the code for the image map that *Salon* uses in its bug-eating piece. Figure 10-19 shows you what this HTML looks like in a browser. Clicking any of the dark areas in the image brings you to a web page about that area.

```
      <html>
      <head>
      <title>Image Map Example</title>
      </head>
      <body>
❶    <img src = "left.gif" isMap useMap = "#left">
❷    <MAP name = "left">
❸    <AREA coords = "9,23,41,42"
❹        href = "http://www.salon.com/wlust/pass/1999/02/bugs/us.html"
❺        shape = "RECT">
      <AREA coords = "26,42,75,64"
          href = "http://www.salon.com/wlust/pass/1999/02/bugs/us.html"
          shape = "RECT">
      <AREA coords = "28,65,55,78"
          href = "http://www.salon.com/wlust/pass/1999/02/bugs/mexico.html"
          shape = "RECT">
      <AREA coords = "58,70,78,86"
          href = "http://www.salon.com/wlust/pass/1999/02/bugs/venezuela.html"
          shape = "RECT">
      <AREA coords = "51,88,63,103"
          href = "http://www.salon.com/wlust/pass/1999/02/bugs/peru.html"
          shape = "RECT">
❻    </MAP>
      </body>
      </html>
```

Figure 10-18: Part of Salon'*s bug-eating image map*

Line ❶ in Figure 10-18 tells the browser to display left.gif and associate it with the map called left. The element isMap tells the browser this is an image map, and the element useMap tells the browser which map to use.

The rest of the page defines the map. Line ❷ starts the definition and gives the map a name, ❸ through ❺ define the different regions of the map (each called an AREA), and ❻ ends the map definition. Three elements define each area: shape, coordinates, and URL link. In *Salon*'s image, each area is rectangular (❺). Line ❹ associates the first area with a URL that discusses bug eating in the United States, and ❸ defines which part of the image this area covers. The four numbers are the *x* (horizontal) and *y* (vertical) coordinates of the upper-left corner and the *x* and *y* coordinates of the lower-right corner, in pixels. So the first area in Figure 10-19 goes from the (9, 23) point of the image to the (41, 42) point of the image, where the numbers represent the number of pixels from the upper-left corner (see Figure 10-20).

Figure 10-19: Window displayed by the HTML in Figure 10-18

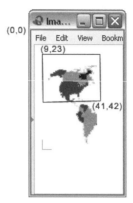

Figure 10-20: Graphical representation of the area described by ❸ through ❺ in Figure 10-18

Image Maps and JavaScript

Adding JavaScript to an image map is just like adding JavaScript to an HTML link. The area tag can handle `onClick`, `onMouseOver`, and (in the 4.0 and later browsers) `onMouseOut` events. For example, if you want an alert box to pop up when a visitor moves the mouse over Alaska, you could rewrite the first area in Figure 10-18 as follows:

```
<AREA coords = "9,23,41,42"
    href = "http://www.salon.com/wlust/pass/1999/02/bugs/us.html"
    onMouseOver = "alert('It's cooooold in Alaska!');"
    shape = "RECT">
```

Adding `onClick` and `onMouseOut` is equally simple.

How *Salon's* Bug-Eating Script Works

Because *Salon*'s bug-eating piece involves so many pages (see Figure 10-1 for what the page looks like in a browser), the code in Figures 10-21 through 10-23 describes only the frame set and navigation pages. One large difference between the code in these figures and *Salon*'s actual code is that *Salon* has divided its image map into three separate images to minimize download times. Figures 10-21 through 10-23 assume the site has just one image. To see how the code for handling three separate images differs, look at the scripts available at http://www.bookofjavascript.com/Websites/Salon.

```
index.html
<html>
<HEAD>
<TITLE>Salon | Wanderlust: Man Eating Bugs</TITLE>
```

```
                  </HEAD>
❶ <FRAMESET frameborder = no border = 0 COLS = "280,*">
❷ <FRAMESET frameborder = no border = 0 ROWS = "165,*">
      <FRAME SRC = "nav.html" NORESIZE SCROLLING = "no" border = "0" NAME = "map">
      <FRAME SRC = "teaser.html" NORESIZE SCROLLING = "no" border = "0" NAME =
         "teaser">
   </FRAMESET>
   <FRAME SRC = "eatbug.html" NORESIZE SCROLLING = "no" border = "0" NAME =
      "thePicture">
</FRAMESET>
</html>
```

Figure 10-21: Salon's bug-eating script—frame set

```
nav.html
<html>
<head>
<title>Image Map Example</title>
<script type = "text/javascript">>
<!-- hide me from older browsers
❶ var hold = "notta";
❷ function changeMe(theMap,theOne,theBug) {
❸   window.document.left.src = theMap;
❹   if (hold == theOne)
     {
❺       return;
     } else {
❻       parent.thePicture.location = theOne;
❼       parent.teaser.location = theBug;
❽       hold = theOne;
     }
   }
// show me --></script></head>
```

*Figure 10-22: Salon's bug-eating script—navigation page head containing changeMe()
function*

The top page of the site, index.html, uses two frame sets to describe three
frames. The frame on the left, called map, contains the image map; the one
below the map, called teaser, contains a little picture and some text; and the
third frame on the right, called thePicture, contains a bigger image of the
appropriate bug. The content of all three frames changes when a visitor
mouses over part of the map.

```
   <body>
❶ <img src = "left.gif" name = "left" isMap useMap = "#left">
   <MAP name = "left">
❷ <AREA coords = "9,23,41,42" shape = "RECT" href = "us.html"
❸    target = "thePicture"
❹    onmouseOver = "changeMe('us.gif','us.html','usteaser.html');"
❺    onMouseOut = "window.document.left.src='left.gif';">
```

```
<AREA coords = "26,42,75,64" shape = "RECT" href = "us.html"
    target = "thePicture"
    onmouseOver = "changeMe('us.gif','us.html','usteaser.html');"
    onMouseOut = "window.document.left.src='left.gif';">
<AREA coords = "28,65,55,78" shape = "RECT" href = "mexico.html"
    target = "thePicture"
    onmouseOver = "changeMe('mexico.gif','mexico.html','mteaser.html');"
    onMouseOut = "window.document.left.src='left.gif';">
</MAP>
</body>
</html>
```

Figure 10-23: Salon's bug-eating script—navigation page body containing images

Salon's Nested Frames

Salon nested its frames using a different method than the one I described in the section "JavaScript and Frames Inside Frames" on page 179. Instead of having a frame call in a second file containing a frame set, as in ❸ in Figure 10-12, *Salon* puts a second frame set right inside the first one (❷ in Figure 10-21). This works fine in HTML, but it confuses JavaScript a little, as we'll see.

Salon's Image Map

Most of the action happens in the frame containing the map, defined in nav.html in Figure 10-23, starting with ❶. This line puts the image of the world map on the page and tells the browser to use the image map left. Line ❷ sets the coordinates for the first region of the left image map and the URL link. Line ❸ targets the frame thePicture (on the right side of the screen), and ❷ tells the browser to load us.html into thePicture when a visitor clicks on the region. Lines ❹ and ❺ tell the browser what to do when a visitor moves the mouse over or out of this region. Mousing over a region calls the changeMe() function, which changes the contents of the frames appropriately.

The changeMe() Function

Function changeMe(), shown in Figure 10-22 starting in ❷, changes the contents of the frames. It takes three parameters: theMap, the name of a new map to swap with the standard one; theOne, the name of the page that holds the big image to swap into thePicture frame; and theBug, the name of the page with the teaser information to swap into the teaser frame. Each region of the map calls changeMe() with a different map, thePicture page, and teaser page. For example, the mouseOver() in ❹ of Figure 10-23 calls changeMe() like this:

```
changeMe('us.gif','us.html','usteaser.html');
```

This tells changeMe() to swap the us.gif map into one frame, us.html into another frame, and usteaser.html into a third frame.

Line ❸ in Figure 10-22 swaps the map of the world with another map with the appropriate region colored green—us.gif, for example. Line ❹ then checks to see whether the visitor has actually chosen a new area. If the visitor mouses over Alaska and then moves over to the continental United States, the picture in thePicture frame shouldn't change. The variable hold, declared in ❶, keeps track of the currently selected region. The if-else statement in ❹ checks to see whether the page to load into thePicture frame is already loaded there. If it is, the function just returns (❺) and no more swaps happen. Whenever JavaScript sees the word return inside a function, it leaves that function. Putting a return inside an if-then statement, as in ❺, is a handy way to quit in the middle of a function.

If the visitor has moused over a new area, the else part of the clause runs. Line ❻ puts the page theOne into the frame named thePicture, and ❼ puts the page theBug into the frame named teaser.

Summary

Enhanced with JavaScript's ability to change the contents of web pages, frames and image maps add functionality that would otherwise be impossible. The examples shown here just scratch the surface of what you can do with JavaScript, frames, and image maps. Keep practicing and playing with them, and you're bound to come up with amazing designs.

If you've read this whole chapter, you should know how to:

- Create frames
- Trigger image swaps in one frame with an event in another one
- Change the contents of a form in one frame following an event in another one
- Change the URL shown in a frame using both JavaScript and HTML
- Change more than one frame at the same time
- Deal with nested frames
- Use frames to save information after a visitor leaves a web page
- Create an image map
- Add JavaScript to image maps
- Say *apple* in Spanish

If you have all of that down, you should feel very powerful. Here's an assignment to test your knowledge.

Assignment

Create your own browser page using forms and frames. The page should have at least two frames: a frame with a text box that allows a visitor to type in a URL, and a frame that shows the URL after submission of the form. Figure 10-24 shows an example of what I mean, but you can build a browser page to suit your taste. In addition to providing a location box, the browser page in Figure 10-24 uses *Salon*'s image map to display various URLs in the display frame.

Figure 10-24: A homemade browser

11

VALIDATING FORMS, MASSAGING STRINGS, AND WORKING WITH SERVER-SIDE PROGRAMS

Web developers can add interactivity to their sites with code that runs on either the web browser or the webserver. JavaScript works inside web browsers, and everything we've seen so far adds interactivity to web pages by making the browser perform fancy JavaScript tricks. Web developers can also make their pages more interactive by using CGI scripts, Java servlets, .NET applications, and other scripting tools. Although the use of these tools is outside the scope of this book, it's important to know how JavaScript can be used to enhance these *server-side programs*.

One of the most common ways to use JavaScript along with server-side programs is as a *form validator*. Making sure that visitors have filled out a form correctly before sending it to a server-side program speeds up the process immensely by cutting down on the number of times they have to submit forms to your webserver.

In this chapter you'll learn how to:

- Make sure visitors fill out HTML forms correctly
- Make sure they have formatted strings (email addresses, for example) correctly
- Make JavaScript work with server-side programs

A Real-World Example of Form Validation

Before saving the information you've entered in a form, many sites use JavaScript to make sure you've filled out the form correctly. When you sign up for Dictionary.com's Word of the Day, for example, you must provide your name, a correctly formatted email address, and several other pieces of information. Before Dictionary.com saves your information, it checks your email address for correct formatting and tells you if it sees any mistakes (see Figure 11-1). Later in the chapter, after you've learned the basics of JavaScript form validation, we'll look at the code that implements this feature in the Dictionary.com site.

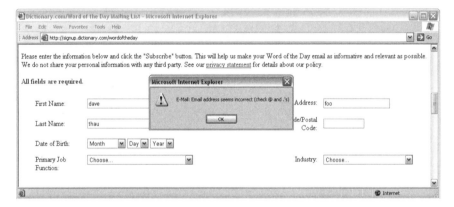

Figure 11-1: Dictionary.com's form validator in action

Making Sure a Visitor Has Filled Out a Form Element

Making sure a visitor has supplied all the mandatory information in an HTML form is the most basic type of form validation. If you want to require your visitors to provide a name and age, you need a JavaScript function to make sure they've entered this information before the form goes to the server-side program.

Chapter 7 covers almost everything you need to know to do this. If you're feeling unsure about how JavaScript and forms work together, review Chapter 7 before reading on. If you feel confident, look at Figure 11-2, which checks whether a user has filled out the mandatory form elements, and see whether you can figure out the code before reading the line-by-line analysis.

```
    <html>
    <head>
    <title>Checking Mandatory Fields</title>
    <script type = "text/javascript">
    <!-- hide me from older browsers
    function checkMandatory()
    {
❶   var error_string = "";
        // check the text field
❷   if (window.document.the_form.the_text.value == "")
    {
            error_string += "You must give your name.\n";
    }
        // check the scrollable list
❸   if (window.document.the_form.state.selectedIndex < 0)
    {
            error_string += "You must select a state.\n";
    }
        // check the radio buttons
❹   var rad_select = "no";
❺   for (var loop = 0; loop < window.document.the_form.gender.length; loop++)
    {
❻       if (window.document.the_form.gender[loop].checked == true)
            {
                rad_select = "yes";
            }
    }
❼   if (rad_select == "no")
    {
            error_string += "You must select a gender.\n";
    }
❽   if (error_string == "")
    {
        return true;
    } else {
        error_string = "We found the following omissions in your form: \n" +
            error_string;
❾       alert(error_string);
        return false;
    }
    }
    // show me -->
    </script>
    </head>
    <form name = "the_form" action = "" method = "post"
❿    onSubmit = "var the_result = checkMandatory(); return the_result;">
    Name:<input type = "text" name = "the_text">
    <br>
    State you live in:<br>
    <select name = "state" size = "3">
    <option value = "alabama">Alabama</option>
    <option value = "arizona">Arizona</option>
    <option value = "california">California</option>
    <option value = "colorado">Colorado</option>
    <option value = "connecticut">Connecticut</option>
```

```
<option value = "delaware">Delaware</option>
<option value = "illinois">Illinois</option>
</select>
<p>
Gender:<br>
<input type = "radio" name = "gender">Female<br>
<input type = "radio" name = "gender">Male<br>
<p>
<input type = "submit" value = "Submit me!">
</form>
</body>
</html>
```

Figure 11-2: Making sure your visitor has filled in mandatory fields

Line-by-Line Analysis of Figure 11-2

The validation begins in ❿, which calls checkMandatory() after your visitor
clicks the Submit me! button. If there are any empty form elements, an alert
box pops up explaining what needs filling out. (Figure 11-3 shows you what
happens if the visitor hasn't filled out any of the form elements before
clicking the button.)

In brief, the checkMandatory() function works by returning the value true if
the visitor has filled out all the fields, false if something's missing. If the function returns false, the script sets the variable the_result to false in ❿. As you
learned in Chapter 7, browsers won't submit a form if a JavaScript returns
false inside the onSubmit handler.

The checkMandatory() function checks each of the form elements and, if
the user fails to fill out an element, adds a phrase describing the error to the
error_string variable, declared in ❶. Once the function has made all the
checks, the error_string will contain a blurb for each form element not
filled in, or it will be blank if the user has entered all the elements.

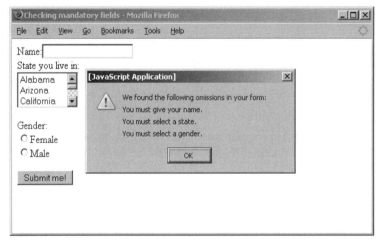

*Figure 11-3: The message displayed when your visitor hasn't filled in any of
the elements*

Checking Text Fields and Scrollable Lists

The first check is in ❷, where the function determines whether there's anything in the name field. If not, it adds some text to the error_string variable. Notice the use of the plus and equal signs (+=) in the body of the if-then statement in ❷. A statement such as a += b is short for a = a + b. When dealing with strings, += tells the function to add the following item to the end of the variable. The body of ❷ adds the string "You must give your name.\n" to the variable error_string (the \n at the end creates a line break inthe alert box). Line ❸ checks the scrollable list to see whether the user has selected anything. If the visitor has selected a state, selectedIndex equals the position of the selected element: 0 with the first option selected, 1 with the second option selected, and so on. If the visitor has not selected a state, selectedIndex equals −1. If the selectedIndex of this form element is less than 0, the script adds the appropriate message to error_string.

Checking Radio Buttons

The trickiest type of form element to check is the radio button. To check whether a user has selected a particular radio button, you have to loop through all the buttons in a series and check them one at a time. In Figure 11-2, ❹ declares the variable rad_select to keep track of whether the guest has chosen a radio button. Initially, the function sets rad_select to "no". If the function encounters a selected radio button as it loops through them, it sets rad_select to "yes" to show that it's found a selected radio button.

The loop begins in ❺ and is the standard loop for checking a list of radio buttons. The loop might look strange at first, but if you study it long enough to understand what's going on, it soon becomes second nature.

The variable loop starts at 0 and goes until it has checked the last radio button named gender. Each time through the loop, ❻ checks to see whether the radio button has been selected and, if it has, changes rad_select from "no" to "yes". After the loop has looked at all the radio buttons, ❼ checks whether rad_select is still "no". If it is, the visitor hasn't selected any of the radio buttons, so the script adds the appropriate error message to error_string.

Checking error_string

Now that all the checks are done, ❽ determines whether any error messages have been added to error_string. If not, error_string still equals the null string (""), which is what ❶ set it to. If error_string is null, no error messages have been added, which means the form is complete and can be sent to the server-side program that will process the input values in some way.

In a real-world web application, the server-side program would be specified in the action of the <form> tag. To send the form to that program, the onSubmit in ❿ must return true. If nothing has been added to error_string, the if-then statement starting in ❽ returns true, which sets the variable the_result in ❿ to true. Thus the onSubmit returns true, and the form is submitted.

In the example script in Figure 11-2, the action does not specify any server-side program. If there were a program there, it would probably store the information in a database somewhere and thank the user for filling out the survey. In this case, since there is no server-side program, the page just reloads, clearing the values entered into the form.

If the error_string contains something, meaning that the form is incomplete, the script adds We found the following omissions in your form: and a line break to the front of error_string and puts the string in an alert box (❾). After the visitor clicks OK in that box, checkMandatory() returns false, setting the_result to false in ❿. As a result, the onSubmit then returns false, the form does not go to the server-side program, and the page doesn't reload.

Much of the code in Figure 11-2 applies to all form validation scripts. The main differences between form validation scripts arise from the types of input values they need to check. If, for example, you wanted a script to test a form element for a valid email address, you'd add some code to do that check in the checkMandatory() function. In order to write that code, however, you have to know a bit about analyzing strings.

String Handling

You'll often want to verify that a string has a certain format—that an email address looks valid, or a date is formatted the way you want, or perhaps that a credit card number passes a basic validity test. There are two ways to verify string formats: using *string methods*, which break strings apart and analyze them, and using a technique called *regular expressions* to define patterns of strings as valid or invalid.

Breaking Strings Apart

To verify string formats by breaking them apart, you need these five useful string methods: indexOf(), lastIndexOf(), charAt(), substring(), and split(). I'll cover each method and show how to use them to verify an email address or date. The credit card script is long, so I don't discuss it here, but you'll find a good example at http://www.bookofjavascript.com/Libraries/ Form_validators/Netscape's_suite/index.html.

indexOf() and lastIndexOf()

The indexOf() method finds the location of a specified set of characters (called a *substring*) inside a string and tells you at what position the substring starts (the first character of a string is in position 0, the second in position 1, and so on). If the string doesn't contain the specified substring, indexOf() returns −1.

Complementing indexOf(), the lastIndexOf() method gives you the position of the last occurrence of a character or substring. Table 11-1 shows the value of various calls to indexOf() and lastIndexOf() when the variable the_word holds the string superduper (var the_word = "superduper").

Table 11-1: Some Example Calls to `indexOf()`

Call to `indexOf()`	Result	Reason
the_word.indexOf("s")	0	The letter *s* is in position 0 of the_word.
the_word.indexOf("u")	1	The letter *u* is in position 1 of the_word.
the_word.indexOf("dupe")	5	The substring dupe starts at position 5 in superduper.
the_word.indexOf("z")	-1	There's no *z* in superduper.
the_word.lastIndexOf("u")	6	The last *u* is in position 6 of the_word.

Figure 11-4, which checks an email address for valid formatting, illustrates a more realistic use of indexOf() and lastIndexOf().

```
<html><head><title>Validating an Email Address</title>
<script type = "text/javascript">
<!-- hide me from older browsers
function checkEmail(the_email)
{
❶   var the_at = the_email.indexOf("@");
❷   var the_dot = the_email.lastIndexOf(".");
❸   var a_space = the_email.indexOf(" ");
❹   if ((the_at != -1) &&  // if there's an '@'
❺       (the_at != 0) &&  // and it's not at position 0
❻       (the_dot != -1) && // and there's a '.'
❼       (the_dot > the_at + 1) &&  // and something between the '@' and '.'
❽       (the_dot < the_email.length - 1) && // and something after the '.'
❾       (a_space == -1))  // and there are no spaces
     {
          alert("Looks good to me!");
          return true;
     } else {
          alert("Sorry, your email address is invalid!");
          return false;
     }
}
// show me -->
</script>
</head>
<body>
<form method = "POST" action = ""
❿   onSubmit = "var result = checkEmail(this.emailbox.value); return result;">
Email Address: <input type = "text" name = "emailbox"><br>
<input type = "submit" value = "Submit me!">
</form>
</body>
</html>
```

Figure 11-4: Validating an email address

Line-by-Line Analysis of Figure 11-4

When the form is submitted, the onSubmit in ⑩ calls the checkEmail() function and sends it the contents of the emailbox form element. If the visitor filled out the form correctly (that is, with a correctly formatted email address), checkEmail() returns true, the form is submitted, and the page reloads. If the form has been completed incorrectly, the function returns false, the form is not submitted, and the page doesn't reload.

The checkEmail() function works by checking for six basic formatting rules all email addresses must follow:

1. There must be an @ sign.
2. The @ sign can't be the first character.
3. There must be a period in the address.
4. There must be at least one character between the @ and the last period.
5. There must be at least one character between the last period and the email's end.
6. There can be no blank spaces in the address.

To test all six rules, we need a few pieces of information. Lines ❶ through ❸ determine the location of the first @ sign, the location of the last period, and the location of the first space (if any) in the string. Lines ❹ through ❾ check to see whether the address violates any of the six rules. Because these lines are ANDed (&&) together (see the section "AND" on page 44 if you've forgotten about the && operator), they must *all* be true to trigger the first result clause of the if-then-else statement (which tells the visitor he or she filled out the form correctly). If any of the tests turns up false, that triggers the else part of the if-then-else statement, telling the visitor he or she entered the email address incorrectly.

Table 11-2 shows you each rule and the line that tests it.

Table 11-2: Checking Email Addresses

Line	Rule	Comment
❹	1	If there's an @ sign, the_at doesn't equal –1.
❺	2	If the @ sign is not the first character, the_at is greater than 0.
❻	3	If there's a period, the_dot doesn't equal –1.
❼	4	If there's something between the @ sign and the last period, the_dot is greater than the_at +1.
❽	5	If a period is the last character, the_dot equals the_email.length –1.
❾	6	If there are no spaces, a_space equals –1.

charAt()

The charAt() method finds the position of a specific character inside a string. To find the character in the first position of the string stored in the_word, you'd type something like this:

```
var the_character = the_word.charAt(1);
```

Table 11-3 shows some more examples of charAt() at work. Let's say the_word holds superduper again.

Table 11-3: Some Example Calls to charAt()

Call to indexOf()	Result	Reason
the_word.charAt(0)	"s"	The letter s is in position 0 of the_word.
the_word.charAt(1)	"u"	The letter u is in position 1 of the_word.
the_word.charAt(the_word.length-1)	"r"	The last character position is the_word.length-1.
the_word.charAt(100)	""	There's no position 100 in superduper.

Finding the last character in a string is a bit tricky. After you find out how many characters are in a string using string_name.length, you have to remember to subtract 1 from the length, since the first character of a string is at position 0. Thus the last character will be in position the_word.length-1.

Checking Strings Character by Character

The charAt() method is useful for analyzing strings on a character-by-character basis. Figure 11-5 lists a function that makes sure a string contains no characters that are illegal in email addresses (!#$%^&*()/:;,+). You can add this function to the email checker to make sure the address doesn't contain any illegal characters.

```
  function hasIllegalCharacters(test_string, illegal_string)
  {
❶   var is_illegal = false;
❷   var the_char = "";
❸   for (var loop = 0; loop < illegal_string.length; loop++)
    {
❹     the_char = illegal_string.charAt(loop);
❺     if (test_string.indexOf(the_char) != -1)
      {
❻       is_illegal = true;
      }
    }
❼   return is_illegal;
  }
```

Figure 11-5: Using charAt() with a loop

The hasIllegalCharacters() function takes two parameters: a string to check for illegal characters and a string that lists which characters are illegal. To add this to the email checking script in Figure 11-4, drop in the function hasIllegalCharacters() and call it as follows:

```
var bad_news = "!#$%^&*()/:;,+";
var the_email = "happy@javascript.is.my.friend.com";
var is_bad = hasIllegalCharacters(the_email, bad_news);
```

After `hasIllegalCharacters()` has done its work, is_bad will be true if one or more of the bad characters appear in the string or false if the string is fine. To use `hasIllegalCharacters()` in Figure 11-4, you also need to add an (is_bad == true) clause to the if-then statement starting in ❹ of Figure 11-4.

NOTE *If you use this code, make sure to pass hasIllegalCharacters() the email address you want checked—happy@javascript.is.my.friend.com is just an example.*

The two parameters in `hasIllegalChararcters()` are test_string, the string we're checking for illegal characters, and illegal_string, the string that lists the illegal characters. The function goes through each character in illegal_string and determines whether test_string contains that character. The loop in ❸ does most of the work, going from the first character of illegal_string (0) to the last (one less than illegal_string.length). Each time through the loop, ❸ sets the_char to a different character in illegal_string. Line ❸ checks to see whether the character stored in the_char is in the test_string string. If it's not, indexOf() returns -1. If the bad character appears in the string, indexOf() returns something other than -1 and ❻ changes is_illegal (❶) from false to true. At the end of the loop, is_illegal will be true if the script has found a bad character and false if it hasn't. The last line of the function (❼) returns this value.

substring()

The substring() method is just like charAt() except that it can grab entire substrings from a word, not just individual characters. The format is as follows:

```
var the_substring = the_string.substring(from, until);
```

Here from is the position of the first character of the substring, and until is, strangely enough, one greater than the last position of the substring. In other words, the substring grabs characters from the first parameter of the call up to, but not including, the second parameter of the call. Here it is in use:

```
  var the_string = "superduper";
❶ var where = the_string.substring(1,3);
❷ var who = the_string.substring(0,5);
```

Line ❶ sets where to up because the letter u is in position 1 of the string and the letter e is in position 3. Line ❷ sets who to super because the letter s is in position 0 and the letter d is in position 5.

You can use substring() with indexOf() to break strings apart. Figure 11-6 shows how to use substring() and indexOf() to take an email address and separate the person's username from the domain of the address.

```
<html><head><title>Username Yanker</title>
<script type = "text/javascript">>
<!-- hide me from older browsers
```

```
    function getUserName(the_string)
    {
❶   var the_at = the_string.indexOf('@');
❷   if (the_at == -1)
    {
        alert("You must type in a valid email address");
    } else {
❸          var user_name = the_string.substring(0, the_at);
           alert("The username is " + user_name);
    }
    }
    // show me -->
    </script>
    </head>
    <body>
    <form onSubmit = "getUserName(this.the_email.value); return false;">
    Email: <input type = "text" name = "the_email"><br>
    </form>
    </body>
    </html>
```

Figure 11-6: indexOf() and substring() working together

The script calls the getUserName() function when the visitor submits the form. Line ❶ uses indexOf() to find the position of the @ sign and ❷ warns the visitor if the @ sign is missing. If there is an @ sign, ❸ uses substring() to get everything from the beginning of the string to the @ sign. Remember that the second parameter of substring() is one *past* the last position you want to grab.

Combining indexOf() and substring() in this way is quite common. Sometimes you have to use them together more than once to get what you want. For example, to grab the domain name out of a URL, you have to use indexOf() and substring() twice. Figure 11-7 shows you the scrap of code that does this.

```
    var the_url = "http://www.webmonkey.com/javascript/";
❶ var two_slashes = the_url.indexOf('//');
❷ var all_but_lead = the_url.substring(two_slashes+2, the_url.length);
❸ var next_slash = all_but_lead.indexOf('/');
❹ var the_domain = all_but_lead.substring(0,next_slash);
```

Figure 11-7: Grabbing the domain from a URL

This code first locates the two slashes at the beginning of the string. The variable two_slashes holds the value 5 because the two slashes start at position 5. Line ❷ grabs everything two characters from the beginning of the two slashes until the end of the string. When it's done, all_but_lead will hold "www.webmonkey.com/javascript". Line ❸ looks at that string and finds the next slash; then ❹ grabs everything from the start of all_but_lead to the next slash, resulting in "www.webmonkey.com".

If it makes you feel any better, string handling is a pain in most languages. It's just something you have to get used to. An even more complicated use of substring() that performs simple checks on credit card numbers is available at http://www.bookofjavascript.com/Libraries/Form_validators/ Netscape's_suite/ccnums.html.

NOTE *Figure 11-7 only works for URLs with a slash (/) as their last character. You'll find a more general version of this code at http://www.bookofjavascript.com/Libraries/ Form_validators/isValidUrl().*

split()

The split() method makes extracting the domain name from a URL a little easier. The split() method uses a character or group of characters to divide a string into a bunch of substrings, then loads the substrings into an array, as in the following example:

```
var my_friends = "eenie,meenie,miney,mo";
var friend_array = my_friends.split(",");
```

This splits the my_friends string along its commas, creating an array called friend_array in which element 0 is "eenie", element 1 is "meenie", element 2 is "miney", and element 3 is "mo".

The split() method simplifies the URL example in Figure 11-7 to this:

```
var the_url = "http://www.webmonkey.com/javascript/";
var the_array = the_url.split("/");
var the_domain = the_array[2];
```

split() creates an array in which element 0 is "http:", element 1 is null (nothing at all), element 2 is "www.webmonkey.com", and element 3 is "javascript". Though split() can't always simplify string handling, it does come in handy when you have a character that breaks up a string, such as the slash (/) in the URL example or the comma (,) in the example before that. Figure 11-8 shows you a function that uses split() to make sure a date is formatted as mm/dd/yy (12/05/68 for December 5, 1968, for example).

```
function checkDate(the_date)
{
❶  var date_array = the_date.split("/");
❷  if ((date_array.length == 3) &&
❸     (date_array[0] > 0) && (date_array[0] < 13) &&
       (date_array[1] > 0) && (date_array[1] < 32) &&
       (date_array[2] >= 0) && (date_array[1] < 100))
    {
       return true;
    } else {
       alert("Please type the date in a mm/dd/yy format.");
       return false;
    }
}
```

Figure 11-8: Checking a date's format

This simple function splits a string into pieces along the slash character in ❶. The first check, in ❷, makes sure there are three pieces of information in the array (for month, day, and year). Line ❸ makes sure the first number, which should represent the month, is between 0 and 13 (noninclusive). The next two lines perform analogous checks for the day and year. If the tests in all three of these lines are true, the date is formatted correctly.

NOTE   *This code doesn't make sure the date is valid. The date 2/31/99 would pass the test, even though there are only 28 days in February. Browse to http://www.bookofjavascript.com/ Libraries/Form_validators for a complete set of date validation functions you can use to make sure an entered date is real.*

Matching String Patterns with Regular Expressions

Using indexOf(), substring(), charAt(), and split() to decide whether a string follows a specific format can get a little tedious. Regular expressions, which are patterns that a tested string needs to match, can make the process a little easier. The ability to deal with regular expressions has been built into all the major browsers, starting with Netscape Navigator 4.0 and Internet Explorer 4.0.

Regular expressions are string patterns. A very basic string pattern could be defined like this:

```
var my_first_expression = /yellow/;
```

First, notice that a regular expression is stored in a variable, just like numbers and strings. Second, notice that a regular expression begins and ends with slash characters. These act like the quotation characters used to define a string.

You can also define a regular expression like this:

```
var my_first_expression = new RegExp("yellow");
```

Now that you have a regular expression, what do you do with it? The most basic thing you can do is test to see whether a string contains your regular expression. To do this, use the test() method, as shown in Figure 11-9.

```
❶ var my_regexp = /yellow/;
  var my_string = "They call me mellow yellow.";
❷ if (my_regexp.test(my_string) == true) {
      alert("String contains yellow.");
  } else {
      alert("Nothing yellow here!");
  }
```

Figure 11-9: Using the test() method of a regular expression

Line ❶ defines the regular expression, and ❷ checks to see whether the string my_string contains the characters yellow. In this case it does, so the test is true, and the appropriate alert pops up.

So far, there's nothing very interesting about regular expressions. You could do the same thing using indexOf(). The excitement starts when we begin using the full powers of regular expressions.

In Figure 11-9, we were just checking to see whether a string had exactly the letters yellow. But a pattern can be much more complex than just a literal string. More realistically, a regular expression will contain a combination of literal characters, placeholders, and possibly operators.

You can use a dot (.) to match any character. For example, a regular expression like

```
/r.n/
```

would match any string containing r, then any character, then n; for example: "he ran home", "see dick run ", "I don't know what r^n means", and "hair net". Notice that last one—because a space is a character, the "r n" in "hair net" will match r space n. Because the dot (.) matches any character, it is often called a *wildcard*.

If you didn't want to match any character, but instead wanted to match only lowercase letters, you could use a regular expression like this:

```
/r[a..z]n/
```

This matches the letter r, then any letter a through z, and then n. This would rule out "hair net" and "r^n" but allow "ran" and "run".

Sometimes you want to match the dot (.) character itself. How do you instruct JavaScript to read the dot (.) character literally instead of as a wildcard? To match the character specifically, you need to escape it in the regular expression using a backslash:

```
/a \. marks the end of a sentence/
```

Here the backslash before the period tells JavaScript to consider that character (.) as text rather than as a wildcard.

Repeating Items

What if you wanted to wildcard two characters? You could use two dots. The regular expression

```
/ye..ow/
```

would match any string containing ye, then any two characters, and then ow, such as "yellow", "yeayow", or "ye3%ow". But what if you wanted to match any number of characters? You couldn't just list any number of dots. Instead, you can use one of the operators *, +, or ?. The * character means "zero or more of the previous item," the + matches one or more of the previous item, and ? matches either zero or one of the previous item.

Figure 11-10 shows how to do a simple check for email addresses.

```
❶ var mail_checker = /.+@.+\..+/;
❷ var the_email = prompt("What's your email address?","");
❸ if (my_regexp.test(the_email) == true) {
      alert("Nice address!");
  } else {
      alert("That's not legal!");
  }
```

Figure 11-10: Very basic email tester

The first line in Figure 11-10 defines the regular expression. It looks crazy, but it's actually easy to decipher. The expression consists of a space, followed by one or more of any character, followed by an @ sign, followed by one or more of any character, followed by a dot, and then any number of characters, followed by a space. This isn't the best email tester—it will match things like "!8675@309......foofoofoo". But it's a start.

The *, +, and ? characters can follow any character, not just the wildcard. If, for some reason, you wanted to check for zero or more Xs, you could use a regular expression /X*/. You can also specify precisely how many repeated characters you want by putting the number in curly brackets after the match character. For example, you could check for three Xs like this: /X{3}/. If you wanted 3, 4, or 5 Xs, you could write /X{3,5}/. Here the minimum is followed by a comma and the maximum.

Beginnings and Endings

In the examples we've seen so far, the regular expressions could match anywhere in the string. Remember that the regular expression /r.n/ matched not just strings starting with r, but also strings such as "hair net" where the pattern starts in the middle. Regular expressions have special characters to mark the beginning and ending of a pattern: ^ marks the beginning, and $ marks the end.

To match a string that starts with r, ends with n, and has zero or more letters in between, you could use the regular expression

```
/^r.*n$/
```

Notice the .* in the middle, which will match any character zero or more times.

Grouping

The last type of regular expression characters you should know about for validating form input are the grouping characters. Let's say you wanted to match a string that ended in com, org, edu, or net. You could define four different regular expressions—one for each of the substrings—and then check to see whether the input string matches any of them, using a long if then-else statement. You can, however, also define one regular expression that tests whether any of these are in the string. To do that, you use a | character when describing your regular expression:

```
var good_domains = /com|org|edu|net/;
```

This statement will be true if any of the four items appear in the string. If you further want to state that the item must appear at the end of the string, you need to add the $ and put the items in parentheses:

```
var good_domains = /(com|org|edu|net)$/;
```

If you just wrote

```
/com|org|edu|net$/
```

the regular expression would think the end character $ only belonged to the net substring, so it would match com, org, or edu anywhere, but net only at the end of the string.

I've only talked about those few regular expression characters most commonly used in form input validation; many more are available. A larger list is in Appendix C of this book.

The match() Method

Regular expressions can do more than just check to see whether a string contains a pattern of characters. They can also be used to tell you what the matching characters were, and they can replace the matching part of a string with something else.

To see whether the characters in a string match a certain regular expression, use the match() method of the String object. For reasons I'll explain shortly, match() returns values in an array.

For example,

```
var matches = "hokey pokey".match(/.ok/);
```

will result in an array called matches, which has only one item: the string "hok". In other words, matches[0] will equal "hok". Now, notice that there are actually two things in the string that could match the regular expression /.ok/: the hok in hokey, and the pok in pokey. To use the match() method to find both of these characters, stick a g at the end of the regular expression, after the final slash. This stands for *global* and means that the regular expression should look at the whole string when matching, not simply return the first match. In this case

```
var matches = "hokey pokey".match(/.ok/g);
```

will return an array with two values: matches[0] = "hok" and matches[1] = "pok".

There is one more little twist on match(). Sometimes a regular expression will match two parts of a string, and you want to see what both those parts are. Consider the email regular expression from Figure 11-10:

```
/.+@.+\..+/
```

If the string is "dave_thau@hotmail.com", your script may want to remember that the first part of the regular expression matched "dave_thau", the second matched "hotmail", and the third matched "com". To store these values separately, use parentheses to mark which parts of the regular expression you want to remember:

```
var matches = "dave_thau@hotmail.com".match(/(.+)@(.+)\.(.+)/);
```

See how the parentheses mark out the things you might want to remember? When you use parentheses in a match, the first item in the array is the entire string to be matched. In this case matches[0] would be dave_thau@hotmail.com. The next items in the array will be the substrings that match: matches[1] = "dave_thau", matches[2] = "hotmail", and matches[3] = "com".

How Dictionary.com's Form Validators Work

As usual, there are many ways to write any bit of JavaScript. Figure 11-11 shows the code that Dictionary.com uses to validate its forms (also see Figure 11-1). This is only part of Dictionary.com's form validating script, and it's still pretty long. Don't let the code's length intimidate you—after all, you know 90 percent of it already.

Because you should understand most of it, I'll just cover the broad strokes and then point out a few details I haven't covered yet.

```
<body>
<script language="JavaScript" type="text/javascript">
<!-- hide me from older browsers
❶ var error = new createerror();
var errors = new Array();
errors[31]="Illegal character in a numeric input";
errors[64]="The field is empty.";
errors[131]="Illegal character. You can only enter letters and blank spaces.";
❷ var alphachars = "abcdefghijklmnopqrstuvwxyzABCDEFGHIJKLMNOPQRSTUVWXYZ";
❸ function createerror() {
    this.val = 0;
    return this;
}
function validateForm() {
    var correct;
    correct = checkblank(document.frmMain.FirstName.value, error);
    if (!correct) {
        alert('First Name: ' + errors[error.val]);
        document.frmMain.FirstName.focus();
        return false;
    }
    correct = checkalpha(document.frmMain.FirstName.value, error);
```

```
        if (!correct){
            alert('Name: ' + errors[error.val]);
            document.frmMain.FirstName.focus();
            return false;
        }
        correct = checkblank(document.frmMain.DateOfBirth.value, error);
        if (!correct) {
            alert('Year of birth: ' + errors[error.val]);
            document.frmMain.DateOfBirth.focus();
            return false;
        }
        correct =
          checkrangenumeric(document.frmMain.DateOfBirth.value, error,1900,2006);
        if (!correct) {
            alert('Year of Birth: ' + errors[error.val]);
            document.frmMain.DateOfBirth.focus();
            return false;
        }
        return true;
    }

    function checkblank(fieldValue,error)
    {
        if (fieldValue.length == 0)     {
            error.val=64;
            return false;
        }
        for (var i=0; i<fieldValue.length; i++)     {
            if (fieldValue.charAt(i)!=' ' && fieldValue.charAt(i)!='\t') {
                return true;
            }
        }
        error.val=64;
        return false;
    }
    function isalpha(sChar){return (alphachars.indexOf(sChar)>=0)}

    function checkalpha(fieldValue,error)
    {
        for (var i=0; i<fieldValue.length;i++)
        {
            if (!isalpha(fieldValue.charAt(i))){
                error.val=131;
                return false;
            }
        }
        return true;
    }
    function checkrangenumeric(fieldValue, error, nMin, nMax)
    {
        errors[35]="The number must be bigger than ";
        errors[36]="The number must be lower than ";
        errors[37]="The number must be between ";
        if (fieldValue.length > 0)
        {
```

```
❹        if (isNaN(fieldValue) || fieldValue == "")
          {
              error.val=31;
              return false;
          }
          else
          {
              var sRange = '';
❺         if (typeof nMin!='undefined'){sRange='MIN';}
             if (typeof nMax!='undefined'){sRange=sRange+'MAX';}
❻         switch (sRange)
             {
❼         case "MIN":
                 if (fieldValue < nMin){
                     errors[35]=errors[35]+nMin;
                     error.val=35;
                     return false;
                 }else{return true;}
❽           break;
             case "MAX":
                 if (fieldValue > nMax){
                     errors[36]=errors[36]+nMax;
                     error.val=36;
                     return false;
                 } else { return true; }
                 break;
             case "MINMAX":
                 if (fieldValue < nMin||fieldValue > nMax) {
                     errors[37]=errors[37]+nMin + " and " + nMax;
                     error.val=37;
                     return false;
                 } else { return true; }
                 break;
             case "":
                 return true;
                 break;
             }
          }
      }
      else
      {
          return true;
      }
  }
  // show me -->
  </script>
  <form method="post" name="frmMain" >
  First Name <input name="FirstName" type="text"> <br>
  Year of Birth: <input name="DateOfBirth" type="text">
❾ <input value="Subscribe"
     onclick="javascript:return validateForm();" type="submit">
  </form>
  </body>
```

Figure 11-11: Dictionary.com's form validator

Line-by-Line Analysis of Figure 11-11

As I mentioned, this is only a small part of the Dictionary.com validation script. Browse to http://www.bookofjavascript.com/Websites/Chapter11 if you want to see the whole thing. Here I'll only highlight a few of the interesting things about the code in Figure 11-11.

The validator starts when a user clicks the submit button in ❾, calling the validateForm() function. Before this function is called, however, a couple of interesting global variables are created. Line ❶ introduces something new: the creation of a *custom object*. We've been dealing with built-in objects throughout this book. The window object, the form object, and the image object are just a few of the built-in objects we've encountered. JavaScript coders can, however, also create their own objects. This is an advanced JavaScript trick, and not one often used, but the Dictionary.com validation script will give you an idea about how to create your own custom objects. Line ❶ calls the function createerror(), which creates a new object and saves it to the variable error. The createerror() function returns an object with a property called val, and sets that property to 0. The val property of the object returned is just like any property of any object. For example, in "Image Preloading" on page 62 we saw the following lines:

```
var new_image = new Image();
new_image.src = "my_good_image.gif";
```

These lines created a new image object and set its src property to the name of a GIF file. The function in ❸ of Figure 11-11 creates a custom object and gives it a property named val. This property can be treated just like any property in JavaScript. Once the variable named error is created in ❶, the val property can be set like this:

```
error.val = 50;
```

And the property can be read like this:

```
var my_property_value = error.val;
```

If this doesn't quite make sense to you, don't worry; we'll see how they use the object in a couple of functions to come. If it still doesn't make sense, don't fear: Dictionary.com could easily have written their script without using this custom-made object—I think they were just trying to be fancy.

After creating the error variable and an array that contains some error messages, the Dictionary.com script creates a variable holding all the letters, upper- and lowercase. This long string will be used to see whether a user entered a letter where expected, or instead entered a number or some other character.

Now let's look at the `validateForm()` function, which is called when a user submits the form. This function first checks to see whether the `FirstName` field is blank, by calling the `checkBlank()` function. Notice that the `validateForm()` function sends the error variable to the `checkBlank()` function. Inside `checkBlank()`, if the user has done something improper, such leaving the form element blank, `error.val` is set to a number that represents the error that has occurred. When `checkBlank()` exits, it returns `true` if the form element was filled out and `false` if it wasn't. If `checkBlank()` returns `true`, `validateForm()` moves on to its next test, described below. If `checkBlank()` returns `false`, JavaScript displays an alert message describing the error, moves the cursor into the `FirstName` form element, and returns `false`, preventing the form from being submitted. There's a lot going on in just those few lines. Take it slowly and make sure you see how things are working.

If `validateForm()` has not exited, it then goes on to make sure that the user's input in the `FirstName` field is all letters. Study the `checkalpha()` and `isalpha()` functions to see how they use `charAt()`, `indexOf()`, and the variable created in ❷ to make sure that every character is a letter.

If `validateForm()` has not exited because of a nonalphabetic character in the `FirstName` field, it goes to make sure that the year entered in the `DateOfBirth` field makes sense. (In the real Dictionary.com code, there are also checks for valid email addresses and last names, but to save space I've left those out.) To ensure that the date is correct, Dictionary.com uses a very general function, `checkrangenumeric()`, which makes sure that a number is within a certain range. That function has several interesting and new JavaScript features.

The first new feature is the built-in `isNaN()` function. NaN stands for *Not a Number*. As you might expect, if the value passed to the function is not a number, the function returns `true`; otherwise it returns `false`.

The next interesting feature in the function is the built-in JavaScript operator `typeof`. This operator goes before a variable and returns the type of variable it is. Enter the following into your web browser to see the kind of results you get:

```
javascript:alert(typeof 12)
javascript:alert(typeof 'hi there')
javascript:var foo = 12; alert(typeof foo)
javascript:alert(typeof new Image())
```

You'll see that JavaScript will respond `number` if given a number or a variable containing a number, or `string` if given a string or a variable containing a string. It might also return the word `object` if given any sort of object, as seen in the last example. When given an undefined variable, `typeof` will return `undefined`. Try

```
javascript:alert(typeof my_purpose_in_life)
```

to see this work. The `typeof` operator will also return `undefined` if you try `typeof null`.

Line ❺ uses typeof to see what kinds of values were sent to the function checkrangenumeric(). The checkrangenumeric() function is called like this:

```
checkrangenumeric(fieldValue, error, nMin, nMax)
```

If you want to check whether a number is between two values, you could write this:

```
checkrangenumeric(100, error, 50, 150)
```

To make sure a number is over some value, you could write this:

```
checkrangenumeric(100, error, 50, null)
```

Similarly, if you want to see whether a number is under some value, you could write this:

```
checkrangenumeric(100, error, null, 500).
```

Line ❺ and the line following it create a variable called sRange. The value of this variable will be one of the following: 'MIN' if just the nMin value is given when the function is called; 'MAX' if just the nMax value is given when the function is called; 'MINMAX' if both values are given; or the empty string ' ' if neither has been given.

The next interesting line, ❻, is a switch statement. The switch statement is like a complicated if-else statement. It starts with the word switch, followed by some variable. The value of the variable determines which part of the switch statement will be executed. Line ❼ says "in case sRange is 'MIN', do everything from here down to either the first return, or the first break." A break is in line ❽. Below that, you'll see what the switch statement does if sRange is 'MAX', 'MINMAX', or ' '. This switch statement could easily have been written like this:

```
if (sRange == 'MIN') {
  // do the MIN stuff
} else if (sRange == 'MAX') {
  // do the MAX stuff
} else if (sRange == 'MINMAX') {
  // do the MINMAX stuff
} else if (sRange == '') {
  // do the empty string stuff
}
```

The if-else route is no better or worse than the switch statement, although the switch statement can be more efficient. People who try to write the fastest code possible will tend to use the switch statement. Here's another example of a switch statement.

```
var name = prompt("What is your name?","");
switch (name) {
  case "Dave":
  case "dave":
  case "Thau":
  case "thau":
    alert("Hello, Dave Thau!");
    break;
  default:
    alert("Howdy, stranger.");
}
```

In this example, any of the listed cases will trigger a *Hello, Dave Thau!* alert, because there were no break statements to cause the switch statement to stop. The term default in the final line means that anything should trigger this case unless a break or return has been reached first. The equivalent if-else statement looks like this:

```
var name = prompt("What is your name?","");
if (name == 'Dave' || name == 'dave' || name == 'Thau' || name == 'thau') {
    alert("Hello, Dave Thau!");
} else {
    alert("Howdy, stranger.");
}
```

The rest of the Dictionary.com script should be fairly straightforward. Take a close look and make sure you understand everything that's going on. For more good validation material, check out the scripts at http://www.bookofjavascript.com/Websites/Chapter11.

Summary

This chapter has covered the rest of what you need to know about forms, shown you how to use JavaScript to check a form before sending it to a server-side script, and demonstrated some of the string-handling methods that come in handy when checking forms for valid completion.

If you understood everything in this chapter, you should know how to:

- Make sure visitors have filled out all fields in a form
- Check an email address for valid formatting
- Submit a correctly filled-out form to a server-side script
- Use the most important string-handling methods to manipulate strings

The string-handling methods described here just scratch the surface. Check Appendix C to see what other tricks you can perform with strings; it provides a full list of string-handling instructions.

Assignment

The assignment in the last chapter was to make your own browser using frames. For this assignment, you will add code to your browser that makes sure the URLs entered in the browser's location bar are correct web addresses, meaning that the URL starts with http:// or https://, has no spaces, and has at least two words with a period between them. The following URLs are not valid:

- The URL www.nytimes.com is missing the http:// beginning.
- The URL http://nytimes needs the .com ending.
- The URL http://www..nytimes.com has two periods with nothing between them.

Enjoy!

12

SAVING VISITOR INFORMATION WITH COOKIES

It's often helpful to remember a little bit of information about a visitor after he or she has left your site: a login name, the last time the visitor visited, or any customization preferences a visitor has set while visiting your site. To remember this information, you'll have to save it somewhere.

Chapter 10 showed you how to use frames to a store a visitor's answers to quiz questions. Unfortunately, after the browser is closed, this method does not retain the information the visitor entered. Cookies provide a solution to this problem: They let you save information on your *visitor's* computer for a specified length of time.

Cookies aren't hard to use, but the code for saving and retrieving them can pose quite a challenge. You can use other people's code (I'll point out some good cookie libraries), but it's still a good idea to know how cookies work so that you can alter the code from libraries to suit your own needs.

In this chapter you'll learn:

- What cookies are
- What you can and can't do with cookies
- How to set a cookie
- How to read a cookie you've set
- How to remember names and dates with cookies
- Where to get good prewritten cookie code
- How to write cookie-based mini-applications

A Real-World Example of Cookies

Cookies are used in all sorts of applications. A common use is to determine whether a visitor has seen a page before. For example, at the bottom of the *Book of JavaScript* home page you'll find a link that brings you to a page which keeps track of how many times you've visited the *Book of JavaScript* home page (Figure 12-1). This information is stored using a cookie.

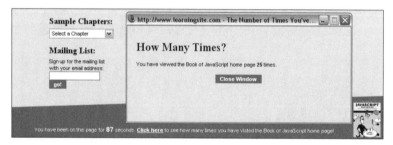

Figure 12-1: Tracking visits to the Book of JavaScript home page

For a more real-world example, the Google search engine uses cookies to store your preferences. By clicking the Preferences link to the right of Google's search box you can change the language of the Google user interface. Along with popular languages such as English, Chinese, and Spanish (the three most popular languages on the Internet), there are more esoteric ones such as Klingon, Pig Latin, and Bork, bork, bork! (the language of the Swedish Chef Muppet). A code for the selected language is stored in a cookie. Because the preference is in a cookie, the next time you visit Google, the interface will still be in that language. Figure 12-2 presents Google in my favorite language, Hacker. The cookie Google uses to store preference information appears at the bottom of the figure. The LD=xx-hacker in the middle of the cookie tells Google that I want the interface displayed in Hacker.

What Are Cookies?

Cookies are little bits of information a site leaves on the hard drive of visitors. Because the information ends up on the hard drive, it remains after the user leaves the current page and even after the computer is turned off. You'll find this feature extremely useful when you want to remember information about a user each time he or she visits your site.

Figure 12-2: Google's search window and its cookie

You can see the cookies saved on your computer by looking for the cookies.txt file for Netscape or the Cookies directory for Internet Explorer. In either case, you'll see a long list of site names, each with a string of text. The text might seem incomprehensible to you because most sites use packed and possibly encrypted formats for cookies for efficiency and security. But take a look to see who's left these little treats on your system—you'll find it very educational. You can also see whether a site you're viewing in your browser has stored any cookies on your computer, by typing the following into your browser:

```
javascript:alert(document.cookie)
```

If you try this, you'll soon see that almost every major site on the Internet uses cookies in one way or another.

What Cookies Can and Can't Do

Because cookies involve writing to and reading from your visitors' hard drives, cookie-friendly browsers deal with lots of security issues. As a result, using cookies has many limitations. The most important ones for the purposes of this chapter are these:

- Not everyone has a cookie-friendly browser.
- Not everyone who has a cookie-friendly browser chooses to accept cookies (but most people do).

- Each domain may have only 20 cookies (so use them sparingly).

- There is a 4KB limit on the amount of information one domain can store using cookies. That's just over 4,000 characters—actually quite a lot.

- A website can set and read only its own cookies (for example, Yahoo! can't read AOL's cookies).

Keep these limitations in mind when you consider using cookies on your site.

Working with Cookies

This section covers all the basic cookie operations: setting, reading, and resetting cookies, and setting expiration dates.

Setting Cookies

Setting a basic cookie is simple. Create a string in the form cookie_name = value and then set the document.cookie property to that string. The only trick is that cookie values can't include spaces, commas, or semicolons. Happily, the escape() and unescape() functions will code and decode cookies, so you don't have to worry about this restriction.

Figure 12-3 lists a simple example that stores a visitor's name in a cookie named username.

The first line of the function in Figure 12-3 (❶) asks for a visitor's name and saves it in the_name. Line ❷ creates the string to store in the cookie. The escape() function replaces characters that cookies can't handle with legal characters. For example, if I entered dave thau at the prompt, this line would create the string username=dave%20thau. The percent sign and 20 (%20) replace the space between dave and thau.

Line ❸ sets the cookie. To make sure you've set a cookie, type the cookie-viewing code into your browser's location bar:

```
javascript:alert(document.cookie)
function setCookie()
{
❶    var the_name = prompt("What's your name?","");
❷    var the_cookie = "username=" + escape(the_name);
❸    document.cookie = the_cookie;
     alert("Thanks!");
}
```

Figure 12-3: A cookie-setting function

Reading Cookies

It's pretty easy to read a cookie you've saved to someone's hard disk. Figure 12-4 shows you code that can read the cookie set in Figure 12-3.

```
function readCookie()
{
❶    var the_cookie = document.cookie;
❷    var broken_cookie = the_cookie.split("=");
❸    var the_name = broken_cookie[1];
❹    var the_name = unescape(the_name);
     alert("Your name is: " + the_name);
}
```

Figure 12-4: Reading a cookie

Line ❶ in Figure 12-4 is very important. Whenever your browser opens a web page, the browser reads whatever cookies that site has stored on your machine and loads them into the document.cookie property.

The tricky part about reading cookies is getting just the information you want from them. In Figure 12-4, all the instructions after the first line of the function are needed to pull the user's name out of the cookie. Once ❶ gets the cookie, ❷ breaks the cookie into a two-element array using the method we learned in "split()" on page 202. The first element in the array consists of everything in the cookie preceding the equal sign (=). In this case, it's username, so that is the first element in the array. The second element in the array consists of everything following the equal sign, which is dave%20. Line ❸ grabs this string from the array and stores it in the_name, and ❹ decodes the_name with the unescape() function by swapping %20 for a space.

NOTE   *If you get a JavaScript error while trying these examples, quit your browser after trying each example to erase the cookies you've set. Because cookies can store more than one value, the examples in this chapter would require additional—and complicated— code to separate the different cookie values. The section "Setting Multiple Cookies" on page 225 covers a more robust way of reading JavaScript cookies.*

Resetting Cookies

To reset (change the value of) a cookie, simply set its name to another value. For example, to keep track of the last time a visitor came to your site, set a cookie named date each time that person visits your site. Figure 12-5 is the code for a web page that keeps track of the last time a given visitor entered the web page.

Loading this page calls the JavaScript functions readCookie() (❷) and setCookie() (❸). The readCookie() function checks to see whether the site has set a cookie (❶). If the value between the parentheses of the if clause is false or the null string (""), the lines in the body of the if-then statement won't execute. If the string finds a cookie, document.cookie will return whatever that cookie is, so the lines in the body of the if-then statement will execute, extracting the date from the cookie and writing it to the web page using document.write().

After readCookie() does its thing, setCookie() sets a new cookie. This function gets the current date and sets a cookie named date to that date. Each time setCookie() is called, it replaces the last cookie named date with a new one. This is just like setting a variable.

```
<html><head><title>Date Cookie</title>
<script type = "text/javascript">
<!-- hide me from older browsers
function setCookie()
{
    var the_date = new Date();
    var the_cookie = "date=" + escape(the_date);
    document.cookie = the_cookie;
}

❶ function readCookie()
{
    if (document.cookie)
    {
        var the_cookie = document.cookie;
        var the_cookie_array = the_cookie.split("date=");
        var the_date = unescape(the_cookie_array[1]);
        document.write("The last time you visited here was: " + the_date);
        document.write("<br>");
    }
}
// show me -->
</script>
</head>
<body>
<h1>Welcome!</h1>
<script type = "text/javascript">
<!-- hide me from older browsers
❷ readCookie();
❸ setCookie();
// show me -->
</script>
</body>
</html>
```

Figure 12-5: Tracking a visitor's last visit to a web page

Setting More Than One Piece of Information

Adding more than one piece of information to a cookie is no problem. For example, to store a person's name, age, and phone number, you could set a cookie like this:

```
var the_cookie = "username:thau/age:just a tyke/phone:411";
document.cookie = "my_cookie=" + escape(the_cookie);
```

A slash separates properties (username, age, and phone), and a colon distinguishes the property names and values (username:thau and phone:411). The slash and colon are arbitrary; you can use any symbols—so long as you're consistent.

It's a bit harder to pull multiple pieces of information out of a cookie. Try using the method discussed in "Associative Arrays" on page 142 to store the information. For example, if you saved

```
my_cookie = username:thau/age:just a tyke/phone:411
```

to someone's hard drive, you could read the information into an associative array using the readTheCookie() function in Figure 12-6.

```
<html>
<head>
<title>Complex Cookie</title>
<script type = "text/javascript">
<!-- hide me from older browsers
function readTheCookie(the_info)
{
    // load the cookie into a variable and unescape it
    var the_cookie = document.cookie;
    var the_cookie = unescape(the_cookie);

    // separate the value pairs from the cookie name
    var broken_cookie = the_cookie.split("=");
❶  var the_values = broken_cookie[1];

    // break each name:value pair into an array
❷  var separated_values = the_values.split("/");

    // loop through the list of name:values and load
    // the associate array
    var property_value = "";
❸  for (loop = 0; loop < separated_values.length; loop++)
    {
        property_value = separated_values[loop];
        var broken_info = property_value.split(":");
        var the_property = broken_info[0];
        var the_value = broken_info[1];
❹      the_info[the_property] = the_value;
    }
}
function setCookie()
{
    var the_cookie = "my_cookie=name:thau/age:just a tyke/phone:411";
    document.cookie = escape(the_cookie);
}
❺ setCookie();
❻ var cookie_information = new Array();
❼ readTheCookie(cookie_information);

// show me -->
</script>
</head>
<body>
<h1>This Is What I Know About You</h1>
<script type = "text/javascript">
```

```
<!-- hide me from older browsers
❽ document.write("Name: " + cookie_information["name"] + "<br>");
   document.write("Age: " + cookie_information["age"] + "<br>");
   document.write("Phone: " + cookie_information["phone"] + "<br>");
   // show me -->
</script>
</body>
</html>
```

Figure 12-6: Loading a complex cookie into an associative array

When this page loads, ❺ sets a cookie, ❻ creates a new array, and ❼
sends the new, empty array to the readTheCookie() function. The function first
gets the cookie and splits off the cookie's name (my_cookie). After ❶, the_values
will equal "name:thau/age:just a tyke/phone:411" because that's how we set the
cookie in the setCookie() function.

Next, ❷ splits the_values into its component parts, loading "name:thau"
into separated_values[0], "age:just a tyke" into separated_values[1], and
"phone:411" into separated_values[2].

After the function breaks up the_values, ❸ loops through each of the
three elements (name, age, and phone) in separated_values. Each time through
the loop, the function breaks the element into two pieces along the colon. It
then loads the first part of the element into the_property and the second part
into the_value.

The first time through the loop, the_property is "name" and the_value
is "thau". Once the element is split like this, the associative array the_info
gets loaded in ❹. After the loop has occurred three times, you get these
results: the_info["name"] = "thau", the_info["age"] = "just a tyke", and
the_info["phone"] = "411".

With the associative array loaded properly, the three lines starting in ❽
retrieve the information and display it on a web page.

Setting the Duration of a Cookie

Until now, we've been creating cookies that disappear when a user exits the
browser. Sometimes this is for the best. Since each domain can have only 20
cookies on a user's machine, you don't want to waste space by saving unnecessary cookies between browser sessions. However, if you do want your cookies
to remain on a user's hard drive after he or she quits the browser, you have to
set an expiration date in UTC format. For example,

```
Sun, 12 Jan 1992 00:00:00 UTC
```

is the supposed birth date in of HAL 9000, the intelligent computer from
2001: A Space Odyssey, expressed in UTC. ("HAL? HAL? Are you out there?")

NOTE   *UTC time is the time at the Royal Observatory in Greenwich, England. Urbana,
Illinois, where HAL was built, is six hours west of Greenwich, so the date given
here is actually 6 PM local time on January 11.*

The UTC format can be sort of a pain, especially since you must figure out whether the day was a Monday, Friday, or whatever. Luckily, JavaScript's toUTCString() date method converts a date in a simpler format to a date in UTC format. Here's an easy way to set a date relatively far into the future:

```
var the_date = new Date("December 21, 2012");
var the_cookie_date = the_date.toUTCString();
```

NOTE   *JavaScript versions earlier than 1.3 used a date string format in which the day, month, and year were separated by hyphens instead of spaces, and the time was followed by the letters GMT to indicate that it was Greenwich Mean Time. This was therefore called GMT format, and JavaScript had a toGMTString() method instead of a toUTCString() method. The toGMTString() method is still provided, but UTC is the norm. For example, with Windows XP and Internet Explorer 6.0, toGMTString() returns a UTC string, and new Date() works when passed a UTC string but not when passed a GMT string.*

To set your cookie to expire, you have to add the expiration date to the cookie. Add expires = date to the string, and separate the cookie components with a semicolon:

```
cookie_name = whatever;expires = date
```

Figure 12-7 shows you how to build a cookie that will last until the end of the Mayan calendar:

```
function setCookie()
{
    // get the information
    //
    var the_name = prompt("What's your name?","");
    var the_date = new Date("December 21, 2012");
    var the_cookie_date = the_date.toUTCString();

    // build and save the cookie
    //
    var the_cookie = "my_cookie=" + escape(the_name);
    the_cookie = the_cookie + ";expires = " + the_cookie_date;
    document.cookie = the_cookie;
}
```

Figure 12-7: Setting a cookie that will expire far in the future

Before the_cookie in Figure 12-7 is escaped (using the escape() function), it will resemble the following line:

```
my_cookie = thau;expires = Fri, 21 Dec 2012 00:00:00 UTC
```

Once set, this cookie lives on your visitor's hard drive until the expiration date.

You can also use the expiration date to delete cookies. To do so, set the date to a time in the past. This can come in handy if you're using cookies to log people in and out of your site. When a visitor logs in, assign a cookie that shows that the visitor has done so. When the user wants to log out, delete the cookie.

Who Can Read the Cookie?

I've already mentioned that only the website that set a cookie can read it— McDonald's can't read Burger King's cookies, and vice versa. The full story is a little more complicated than that, however.

Letting One Page Read a Cookie Set on Another

By default, only the web page that set the cookie can read it. If one of your pages sets a cookie, to let other pages on your site read that cookie you must set its path. The cookie's path sets the top-level directory from which a cookie can be read. Setting the path of a cookie to the root-level directory of your site makes it possible for all your web pages to read the cookie.

To do this, add path=/; to your cookie. If you just want the cookie to be readable in a directory called food, add path=/food;.

Dealing with Multiple Domains

Some websites have lots of little domains. For example, the Yahoo! web portal has a main site (http://www.yahoo.com), a finance site (http://finance.yahoo.com), a personalized site (http://my.yahoo.com), and many others. By default, if a web page on the finance site sets a cookie, pages on the personalized site can't read that cookie. But if you add domain=*domain_name* to a cookie, all domains ending in *domain_name* can read the cookie. To allow all the web pages on any of the machines in the yahoo.com domain to read a cookie, Yahoo! has to add domain=yahoo.com to the cookie.

The Whole Cookie

Adding an expiration date, domain, and path to a cookie makes it pretty big. Figure 12-8 lists a function that sets all these variables so you can see the whole picture in one example.

```
function setCookie()
{
    var the_name = prompt("What's your name?","");
    var the_date = new Date("December 21, 2012");
    var the_cookie = escape(the_name) + ";";
    var the_cookie = the_cookie + "path=/;";
    var the_cookie = the_cookie + "domain=nostarch.com;";
    var the_cookie = the_cookie + "expires=" + the_date.toUTCString() + ";";
    document.cookie = "my_cookie=" + the_cookie;
}
```

Figure 12-8: Setting all the cookie properties

Figure 12-8 results in a cookie that looks like this (before escaping it):

```
my_cookie = thau;path=/;domain = nostarch.com;expires =
    Fri, 21 Dec 2012 00:00:00 UTC;
```

Of course, because I'm setting the domain to nostarch.com, only a web page from a No Starch Press computer can read this cookie.

Setting Multiple Cookies

Sometimes one cookie just isn't enough. For instance, if your website has two different JavaScript applications—one that uses cookies to store information about your visitors and one that uses cookies to keep track of their purchases—you'll probably want to store these two types of information in different cookies.

To save multiple cookies, just give each cookie a different name. Setting document.cookie to a cookie with a new name won't delete the cookies that are already there. Here's some code that sets two cookies:

```
var visitor_cookie = "this_person=" +
    escape("name:thau/occupation:slacker/phone:411");
document.cookie = visitor_cookie;
var purchase_cookie = "purchases=" + escape("tshirt:1/furbie:15/burrito:400");
document.cookie = purchase_cookie;
```

This code sets document.cookie twice. It looks as if the second document.cookie = statement should overwrite the information stored by the first one, as would happen if some other object were to the left of the equal sign. Assignment to document.cookie works differently, however. As long as the cookies have different names, you can store both in document.cookie. After running the lines above, document.cookie looks like this (except for the escaped characters):

```
this_person = name:thau/occupation:slacker/phone:411;purchases=tshirt:1/
furbie:15/burrito:400
```

In this example, storing two cookies in document.cookie works well because the JavaScript that looks at purchase information doesn't have to deal with the information in the other cookie. Unfortunately, it's a bit difficult to pull the contents of one cookie out of document.cookie because it contains multiple cookies. Here's where prewritten JavaScript libraries come in handy.

Cookie Libraries

You'll find many free cookie libraries on the Web. Just use any search engine, and search for *javascript cookie* to get a list. The functions in the libraries generally come ready to run, so you can just cut and paste them into your web pages. Webmonkey has exceptionally well-commented libraries, so we'll use its code here. You can find more of Webmonkey's free

JavaScript code at http://webmonkey.wired.com/webmonkey/reference/
javascript_code_library/wm_ckie_lib/?tw=reference&category=forms_data.

Figure 12-9 shows you Webmonkey's code for accessing one cookie when
document.cookie is storing multiple cookies.

```
function WM_readCookie(name) {
    if(document.cookie == '') { // there's no cookie, so return false
    return false;
    } else { // there is a cookie
    var firstChar, lastChar;
    var theBigCookie = document.cookie;
    firstChar = theBigCookie.indexOf(name);// find the start of 'name'
    var NN2Hack = firstChar + name.length;
    { // if you found the cookie
    if((firstChar != -1) && (theBigCookie.charAt(NN2Hack) == '='))
        firstChar += name.length + 1; // skip 'name' and '='
        // find the end of the value string (the next ';').
        lastChar = theBigCookie.indexOf(';', firstChar);
        if(lastChar == -1) lastChar = theBigCookie.length;
        return unescape(theBigCookie.substring(firstChar, lastChar));
    } else { // if there was no cookie of that name, return false
        return false;
    }
    }
} // WM_readCookie
```

Figure 12-9: Reading one cookie from document.cookie

To use these functions, cut and paste them into the page, and call the
functions appropriately. To retrieve a cookie named thisuser, call the function WM_readCookie("thisuser").

Webmonkey's well-commented functions speak for themselves. If you use
these, read them over first and make sure you understand how they work.

A Cookie-Based Shopping Cart

You can build fairly complicated applications using cookies. This section
discusses code that represents the start of a shopping cart script. You defi-
nitely do not want to use this code to run your own shopping cart—it's much
too simplistic. For example, you can't remove an item from the basket once
you've selected it.

However, this code should give you an idea of how to start building
complex applications using cookies. Figure 12-10 shows you the code for a
main page of a simple shopping cart (see Figure 12-11) with simple links to
pages that contain items to buy.

```
<html><head><title>Welcome to My Store</title>
</head>
<body>
<h1>Welcome to My Store!</h1>
Here you can buy:<br>
```

```
<a href = "parts.html">Computer parts!</a> and <br>
<a href = "clothes.html">Clothes!</a><br>
<p>
When you're done choosing items, you can
<form>
```
❶ ```
<input type = "button" value = "check out"
  onClick = "window.location='checkout.html';">
</form>
</body>
</html>
```

Figure 12-10: The shopping cart main page

Figure 12-11: What the shopping cart main page looks like

The only new and interesting feature in Figure 12-10 is ❶, which redirects visitors to the page checkout.html (listed in Figure 12-15 and discussed later in this section) when they click the check out button.

### Adding an Item to the Cart

Figure 12-12 shows you the code for one of the pages where you can buy a product.

```
<html><head><title>Clothes</title>
```
❶ ```
<script type = "text/javascript" src = "shopping.js"></script>
</head>
<body>
<h1>Buy these clothes!</h1>
<form name = "clothes">
T-shirt:
<input type = "text" name = "tshirt" size = "3" value = "1">
```
❷ ```
<input type = "button" value = "add"
  onClick = "addToCart(window.document.clothes.tshirt.value, 'tshirt',14);">
($14 each)
<p>
Jeans:
<input type = "text" name = "jeans" size = "3" value = "1">
<input type = "button" value = "add"
  onClick = "addToCart(window.document.clothes.jeans.value,'jeans',30);">
```
```

```
($30 each)
<p>
<a href = "main.html">Go back to main page</a>
or <br>
<form>
<input type = "button" value = "check out"
  onClick = "window.location='checkout.html';">
</form>
</body>
</html>
```

Figure 12-12: Code for a page where you can purchase goods

Most of this page describes the form that lists what visitors can buy. Each item has a button next to it that lets you buy the item (see Figure 12-13). Pushing that button (as in ❷) calls the function addToCart(), which takes three parameters: the quantity of the item to buy, what the item is, and how much it costs. The addToCart() function isn't stored on this web page but in a file called shopping.js (Figure 12-14), a normal text file that contains all the functions the shopping cart needs to work. The browser reads the shopping.js file into the page and interprets it in ❶. This technique is very handy when you have a set of functions that apply to many pages. In our example, all the shopping pages on the site will need the addToCart() function, so rather than cut and paste this function onto every page, we can use ❶ to call the functions from shopping.js. You'll also find this feature extremely useful when you want to change the function. Instead of having to track down every place you've cut and pasted it, you just need to change it once in the shopping.js file. Once you've changed it there, any page that uses the shopping.js file will load the changed version.

Figure 12-13: A shopping page

```
function addToCart(amount, item, price)
{
❶    var purch_string = escape(item + ":" + amount + ":" + price);
❷    var the_cookie = WM_readCookie("purchases");
❸    if (the_cookie)
```

```
      {
❹        purch_string = the_cookie + "/" + purch_string;
      }
❺      WM_setCookie("purchases",purch_string,0,"/");
    }
```

Figure 12-14: shopping.js

The `addToCart()` function in shopping.js creates a string to save into a cookie (❶) in the form `item:amount:price`. The function then uses the Webmonkey `WM_readCookie()` function to see whether the visitor has already received a cookie named `purchases` (❷ and ❸). If there is already a cookie, ❹ puts a forward slash (/) at its end and adds the string created in ❶. Each time a visitor buys an item, the cookie gets a slash followed by the item name. If you bought one T-shirt and one pair of jeans, the cookie would look like this:

```
purchases = tshirt:1:14/jeans:1:30
```

If you then bought another T-shirt, the cookie would look like this:

```
purchases = tshirt:1:14/jeans:1:30/tshirt:1:14
```

A more complete version of `addToCart()` would realize that you had already bought a T-shirt and, instead of tacking another `tshirt:1:14` to the end of the cookie, would add one to the T-shirt amount:

```
purchases = tshirt:2:14/jeans:1:30
```

However, since that "small" change involves a fair amount of code, I'm leaving it out.

After the new cookie string has been constructed, ❺ uses the Webmonkey library function `WM_setCookie()` to save the visitor's cookie information.

The Checkout Page

The final page to consider is the checkout page listing in Figure 12-15.

```
    <html><head><title>Checkout</title>
❶  <script type = "text/javascript" src = "shopping.js"></script>
    </head>
    <body>
    <h1>Here's Your Basket So Far</h1>
    <script type = "text/javascript">
❷  checkOut();
    </script>
    </body>
    </html>
```

Figure 12-15: Code for the checkout page

The checkout page loads in the shopping.js file in ❶ just as the product page does in Figure 12-12. Although there is a little HTML on this page, most of what you see when you visit this page (Figure 12-16 shows the page in IE) is generated by the checkOut() function, which is stored in the shopping.js file. Figure 12-17 lists the readTheCookie() function, which reads the cookie and formats it in a way that makes the checkOut() function's job easier. Figure 12-18 lists the checkOut() function itself.

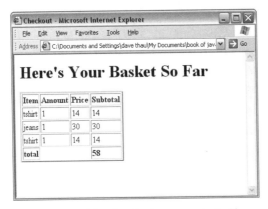

Figure 12-16: What the checkout page looks like

```
     function readTheCookie(the_info)
     {
         var split_stuff;
         // load the cookie into a variable and unescape it
❶       var the_cookie = WM_readCookie("purchases");
         if (the_cookie)
         {
❷           if (the_cookie.indexOf('/') != -1)
             {
                 split_stuff = the_cookie.split("/");
❸               for (var loop = 0; loop < split_stuff.length; loop++)
                 {
                     the_info[loop] = split_stuff[loop];
                 }
             } else {
❹               the_info[0] = the_cookie;
             }
         }
     }
```

Figure 12-17: Code for the readTheCookie() function

The readTheCookie() Function

The readTheCookie() function, which is called by the checkOut() function, breaks up the cookie into each item bought and loads the items into the array passed to it. As is shown in Figure 12-18, the array is new and empty when checkOut() calls readTheCookie(). Line ❶ reads the cookie using the WM_readCookie() function. If there is a purchases cookie (which the visitor would have set by adding an item—see Figure 12-13), ❷ determines whether the visitor bought more than one item. If he or she purchased only one item, that item gets loaded into the array in position 0 (❹). If he or she purchased two or more items, a forward slash appears between them and the cookie gets split into the split_stuff array. Then the loop in ❸ copies everything in the split_stuff array into the_info, the array sent into the readTheCookie() function. At the end of readTheCookie(), the_info contains all the items purchased.

```
     function checkOut()
     {
         var total = 0;
         var the_stuff = new Array();
❶       readTheCookie(the_stuff);
         document.writeln("<table border=2>");
         document.writeln("<th>Item</th><th>Amount</th><th>Price</th>
             <th>Subtotal</th>");
❷       for (var loop = 0; loop<the_stuff.length; loop++)
         {
❸           var this_item = the_stuff[loop].split(":");
❹           document.writeln("<tr>");
❺           for (var inloop = 0; inloop < this_item.length; inloop++)
             {
                 document.writeln("<td>");
                 document.writeln(this_item[inloop]);
                 document.writeln("</td>");
             }
❻           sub_total = this_item[1] * this_item[2];
❼           total += sub_total;
             document.writeln("<td>" + sub_total + "</td>");
             document.writeln("</tr>");
         }
         document.writeln("<tr>");
         document.writeln("<td><b>total</b></td>");
❽       document.writeln("<td></td><td></td><td><b>" + total + "</b></td>");
         document.writeln("</tr>");
         document.writeln("</table>");
     }
```

Figure 12-18: Code for the checkOut() function

The checkOut() Function

Once readTheCookie() loads the information from the cookie into the_stuff (❶), checkOut() writes the purchased items to the web page. Line ❷ loops through the_stuff, each element of which contains a purchased item. If the first item bought is one pair of jeans, for example, the first element in the array appears as jeans:1:14. Line ❸ then splits this element at the colons, loading the three resulting elements into the this_item array.

The rest of the code writes the table. Line ❹ begins a new row, and ❺ sandwiches each element in this_item between <td> and </td> tags.

Line ❻ calculates how much this_item costs by multiplying the price of the item (this_item[2]) by the quantity bought (this_item[1]). If the first element in the_info is jeans:1:14, then this_item[0] is jeans, this_item[1] is 1, and this_item[2] is 14 because of the split in ❸. Line ❹ then multiplies the quantity by the price to get the subtotal, and ❼ adds this subtotal to the total, written to the page in ❽. Figure 12-16 shows you what the checkout page looks like after someone buys a T-shirt, then a pair of jeans, and then another T-shirt.

Even though this shopping cart requires a lot of JavaScript, each of its functions is short and fairly easy to understand. Complicated applications such as shopping carts are usually just groups of smaller functions that work together.

Once you understand the basics of JavaScript, the hard part of writing an application is figuring out what functions you need and how they interrelate. This is the art of programming, and it comes only with a lot of practice. If you understand the shopping cart code in this example but don't think you could write it yourself, practice writing smaller scripts—you'll soon get the hang of it.

Summary

Cookies are an advanced JavaScript feature and can add a lot of functionality to your site. In addition to setting up a shopping cart, you can use cookies to keep track of when and how often a visitor comes to your site and to save customization preferences visitors might set. If you've thoroughly grasped this chapter, you now know:

- What cookies are
- How to set a basic cookie
- How to make a cookie last after the user has turned off the computer
- How to control which pages can read your cookie
- How to store more than one piece of information in a cookie
- How to set and read more than one cookie
- How to create a separate JavaScript file that other HTML files can include
- Where to find JavaScript cookie libraries
- How to build a complex application using cookies

Assignment

Write a page that greets new visitors with an alert box that says, *Welcome, new-timer!* This should only appear the first time a visitor sees the page— at the next visit, that alert box shouldn't appear.

13

DYNAMIC HTML

Dynamic HTML (DHTML) combines JavaScript, HTML, and Cascading Style Sheets (CSS) to give web page designers an incredible degree of freedom to animate their pages and add interactivity. If you've seen sites that have dynamic menus or images that dance all over the screen, you've seen DHTML in action. DHTML is also a key component of Asynchronous JavaScript and XML (Ajax), a technique used to create complete web-based applications. We'll talk more about Ajax in Chapters 14, 15, 16, and 17.

DHTML is an immense subject. This chapter will introduce DHTML and show you how what you've learned so far fits into the DHTML puzzle.[1]

---

[1] If you want to learn more about DHTML, I suggest you read *Dynamic HTML: The Definitive Reference* by Danny Goodman (O'Reilly, 2002).

This chapter covers the following topics:

- The CSS basics you need to know
- How JavaScript, HTML, and CSS work together to make objects move around your screen
- How to use fancy event handling to read the keyboard and discover the location of the user's mouse
- How to create dynamic drop-down menus

Real-World Examples of DHTML

DHTML can enhance your web pages in a variety of ways. There are entire sites devoted to DHTML examples and tutorials. A few good ones are:

- http://www.dhtmldrive.com
- http://www.dhtmlcentral.com
- http://www.dhtmlgoodies.com

Searching for *dynamic html* in any search engine will return dozens more choices.

DHTML is often used to create drop-down menus, examples of which can be seen on many websites, including the *Doctor Who* fan site, Outpost Gallifrey (http://www.gallifreyone.com), and *Fortune* magazine's website (http://www.fortune.com, shown in Figure 13-1). The code for these menus can be complicated, but by the end of this chapter, you should have a good sense of how it works.

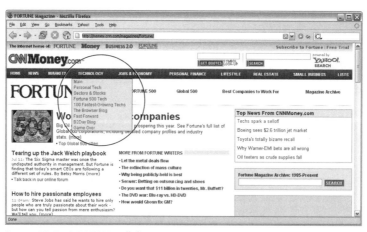

Figure 13-1: A DHTML pull-down menu

CSS Basics

As mentioned in the opening of the chapter, DHTML is a combination of JavaScript, HTML, and CSS. CSS enables you to position HTML precisely on your pages—no longer will you have to use bizarre tables and invisible GIFs to position elements. With a CSS you can easily place a GIF precisely in the center of your page, or position a block of text in the lower-right corner.

The <div> Tag

Before you can position any HTML, you have to use the <div> and </div> tags to tell your browser which displayed HTML you want to position. Figure 13-2 shows a simple use of <div> tags.

```
<html><head><title>Divide and Conquer</title></head>
<body>
<h1>Divide and Conquer</h1>
This text is not inside a div.
<p>
❶ <div id = "myFirstDiv">
But this text is.<br>
And so is this text.<br>
❷ </div>
<p>
But this text is not.
</body>
</html>
```

Figure 13-2: Basic div usage

The page displayed by this code (Figure 13-3) looks just like any other HTML page. However, ❶ and ❷ assign an id to a block of HTML by using a <div> tag with an id attribute of myFirstDiv. You can use any set of letters or numbers for a div's id, but it can't contain spaces or underscores, and the first character has to be a letter. Now that we've provided a way for code to refer to this block, we can use the div's id to position the block with CSS or to move it around dynamically with JavaScript.

Figure 13-3: An HTML page with divs

Positioning a div with CSS

You can position the contents of a <div> tag anywhere on a web page using the HTML style element. Replacing ❶ in Figure 13-2 with the following line moves the block of HTML called myFirstDiv into the lower middle of the page:

```
<div id = "myFirstDiv" style = "position:absolute; top:150; left:100;">
```

Figure 13-4 shows what this looks like.

As you can see, the style element goes inside the <div> tag and has three components separated by semicolons. The position component gives the div a reference point (with position:absolute, the reference point is the browser window's upper-left corner). The top component determines how many pixels down from the reference point the top-left corner of the div appears, and the left component determines how many pixels to the right of the reference point the top-left corner of the div appears.

Instead of positioning the div relative to the upper-left corner of the browser window, you can position it relative to where it would normally appear in the HTML. If you do not include any positioning information in the div, it would follow the line *This text is not inside a div*. However, if you use the style shown in Figure 13-4 but replace position:absolute with position:relative, the div appears 150 pixels below and 100 pixels to the right of the *This text is...* line. Figure 13-5 shows you what this would look like.

Figure 13-4: Moving a div into the lower middle of the page

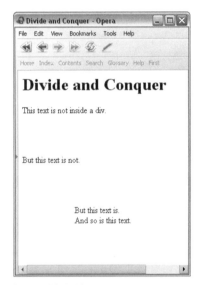

Figure 13-5: Using position:relative instead of position:absolute

Whether you use position:absolute or position:relative depends on what you're aiming for. If you want one block of HTML to appear directly to the right of another block, you might find it easier to use position:relative. But if you want to make sure an image appears in the center of the screen, you'll find position:absolute more useful.

Hiding a div

You can display or hide the contents of a div by setting its visibility to either visible or hidden. The style below puts the div in the lower center of the page and hides it.

```
<div id = "myFirstDiv" style =
  "position:absolute; top:150; left:100; visibility:hidden">
```

You can change the visibility of a div with JavaScript. Sometimes it makes sense to create a bunch of invisible divs on a page and then use JavaScript to make them appear when you need them. For example, you could make an entire section of HTML code blink on and off by alternately hiding and showing it. Later in the chapter, when we talk about drop-down menus, I'll show you how to use JavaScript to hide divs.

Layering divs

Another nice feature of divs is that you can layer them on top of each other. For example, you could put an image of a mouse in one div and an image of a maze in another div, then put the mouse in the maze by layering the mouse div on top of the maze div. Once you've done that, you can change the position of the mouse div to make it look like the mouse is exploring the maze.

To layer one div on top of another, set the div's z-index. A div with a higher z-index value appears on top of a div with a lower z-index. Figure 13-6 shows the code for a page with one GIF (a small white square) on top of another GIF (a bigger black square). The small white square has a higher z-index, giving the result shown in Figure 13-7. Figure 13-8 shows what would happen if the black square were given a higher z-index.

```
<html><head><title>Layering divs</title></head>
<body>
<div id = "whiteSquare" style =
  "position:absolute; top:100; left:100; z-index:2">
<img src = "white.gif">
</div>
<div id = "blackSquare" style = "position:absolute; top:0; left:0; z-index:1">
<img src = "black.gif">
</div>
</body>
</html>
```

Figure 13-6: Layering divs with z-index

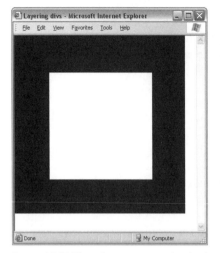 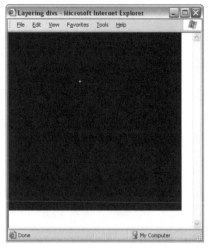

Figure 13-7: The white square with a higher
z-index than the black square

Figure 13-8: The black square with a higher
z-index than the white square

Normal HTML is at z-index 0. If you set the z-index of a div to a negative number, it appears behind the normal HTML, like a background image.

JavaScript and DHTML

DHTML becomes *dynamic* when you start using JavaScript to manipulate divs. For example, if you have a div named myFirstDiv (as in Figure 13-2), you could use this JavaScript to hide the div:

```
window.getElementById('myFirstDiv').style.visibility = "hidden";
```

This line gets the element whose id is myFirstDiv and then gets its CSS style object and changes the visibility value of that style object from visible to hidden.

Figure 13-9 shows how you can hide a div when the user clicks a link.

```
<html><head><title>Hiding a div</title></head>
<body>
<h1>Hide the Div</h1>
This text is not inside a div.
<p>
<div id = "myFirstDiv" style =
  "position:absolute; top:150; left:100; visibility:visible">
But this text is.<br>
And so is this text.<br>
</div>
<p>
But this text is not.
<br>
```

```
<a href = "#"
  onClick = "document.getElementById('myFirstDiv').style.visibility="hidden";
    return false;">Hide the div.</a>
</body>
</html>
```

Figure 13-9: Hiding a div

Making divs Move

The `top` property of a `div`'s style dictates the vertical position of the `div`, and the `left` property determines the horizontal position. You can use these properties to move a `div` around the screen. For example, to position a `div` 500 pixels from the left border of the browser window, do this:

```
document.getElementById('myDiv').style.left = 500;
```

Adding an amount to the `top` or `left` attribute of a `div`'s style will move it vertically or horizontally. If a `div` is 500 pixels from the left border of the window, and you add 5 to the `left` property, you will move the `div` to a position 505 pixels from the border. Unfortunately, adding numbers to the `left` and `top` properties is not straightforward, because most browsers will stick a *px* at the end of the `left` and `top` properties. For example, if you load Figure 13-9 into a browser, and then type

```
javascript:alert(document.getElementById('myFirstDiv').style.top)
```

the response will be 150px, and not the number 150. To get rid of the *px*, use the `parseInt()` method that you learned about way back in Chapter 3.

Here is an example:

```
document.getElementById('myDiv').style.left =
    parseInt(document.getElementById('myDiv').style.left) + 5;
```

To move a `div` 5 pixels to the left, subtract 5 from the value of the `left` property as follows:

```
document.getElementById('myDiv').style.left =
    parseInt(document.getElementById('myDiv').style.left) - 5;
```

Using setTimeout() and clearTimeout() to Animate a Page

The code described above makes a `div` jump across the screen. If you want the `div` to drift more slowly across the screen or to move along a specific path, you can use timing loops (discussed in Chapter 9) to animate your `div`.

To make a `div` move smoothly across the screen, write a function that moves the `div` a little bit, then uses `setTimeout()` to call itself in a few milliseconds. Figure 13-10 contains code that causes an image of the number 1 to roam randomly around the screen.

```
<html><head><title>The Wandering One</title>
<script type = "text/javascript">
<!-- hide me from older browsers
var the_timeout;
function moveNumber()
{
  var the_div, move_amount;
❶  the_div = window.document.all.numberOne.style;
❷  move_amount = parseInt(Math.random() * 10);
❸  if (parseInt(Math.random()*10) < 5)    {
    the_div.left = parseInt(the_div.left) + move_amount;
  } else {
    the_div.left = parseInt(the_div.left) - move_amount;
  }
❹  random_number = parseInt(Math.random() * 10);
❺  if (parseInt(Math.random()*10) < 5)
  {
    the_div.top = parseInt(the_div.top) + move_amount;
  } else {
    the_div.top = parseInt(the_div.top) - move_amount;
  }
❻  the_timeout = setTimeout("moveNumber();", 100);
}
// show me -->
</script>
</head>
<body>
<h1>The Wandering One</h1>
<div id = "numberOne" style =
  "position:absolute; top:150; left:100; z-index:-1">
<img src = "one.jpg">
</div>
<br>
❼ <a href = "#" onClick =
    "the_timeout=setTimeout('moveNumber();',100);
     return false;">Start wandering</a> <br>
❽ <a href = "#" onClick =
    "clearTimeout(the_timeout);
     return false;">Stop wandering</a>
</body>
</html>
```

Figure 13-10: The Wandering One

Line-by-Line Analysis of Figure 13-10

In Figure 13-10, the image of the number 1 starts wandering when a visitor clicks the link in ❼, calling the moveNumber() function. The moveNumber() function sets the_div to point to the div we want to move (❶) and then determines how far the div moves.

Generating Random Numbers

Line ❷ moves the div by a random amount between 0 and 9 pixels. It chooses this amount by generating a random number between 0 and 0.999... (that is,

0.9 repeating, a fraction with a decimal point followed by an infinite number of nines after it), using the `Math.random()` method, and then multiplying this number by 10. This yields a number between 0 and 9.999… The `parseInt()` function then drops the digits to the right of the decimal point. If `Math.random()` generates 0.543, then multiplying by 10 gives you 5.43, and `parseInt()` turns that into 5.

Determining the Direction of an Image's Motion

The `if-then` statement starting in ❸ generates another number between 0 and 9. If the number is below 5 (which happens exactly half the time), the amount generated in ❷ is added to the `left` property, moving the number 1 on the screen a little to the right. If the number is 5 or above, the amount is subtracted from the `left` property, moving the 1 to the left. Lines ❹ and ❺ act similarly, moving the 1 up or down.

After the 1 has moved a little horizontally and a little vertically, ❻ calls `setTimeout()` to call the function again in a tenth of a second (remember, there are 1,000 milliseconds in a second, so 100 milliseconds is one-tenth of a second). After 100 milliseconds pass, the `moveNumber()` function is called again, moving the number a little more and again setting `setTimeout()`. The 1 keeps wandering until the visitor clicks the link in ❽, clearing the last timeout set and ending the cycle.

Changing the Contents of a div

The contents of a `div` can be changed by setting the `div`'s `innerHTML` property. As the name of the property implies, `innerHTML` is the HTML inside a `div`. For example, Figure 13-11 shows a web page with a brainteaser—find all the Fs in the text.

In the HTML, the block of text is contained in a `div`. Clicking on the link makes the Fs bigger by replacing the contents of the div with a string of HTML that displays the same text, but with larger Fs. Figure 13-12 shows the code.

The JavaScript in Figure 13-12 should look very familiar to you by now. Line ❸ creates a div called `myDiv`, ❶ sets the variable `theDiv` to point to `myDiv`, and ❷ changes the `innerHTML` of that div to a new string containing a block of HTML. Changing the `innerHTML` of the div changes its contents, replacing the original HTML with the HTML in the string.

Figure 13-11: Find all the Fs in this text.

```
<html><head><title>How Many Fs Are There?</title>
<script type = "text/javascript">
<!-- hide me from older browsers
function swapText() {
①    var theDiv = document.getElementById("myDiv");
②    theDiv.innerHTML = "<font size='+3'>F</font>INISHED <font size='+3'>F</
font>ILES ARE THE RESULT O<font size='+3'>F</font> YEARS O<font size='+3'>F</
font> SCIENTI<font size='+3'>F</font>IC STUDY COMBINED WITH THE EXPERIENCE
O<font size='+3'>F</font> YEARS.";
}
// show me -->
</script>
<body>
③ <div id = "myDiv" style = "width:200;height:100">
FINISHED FILES ARE THE RESULT OF YEARS OF SCIENTIFIC STUDY COMBINED WITH
THE EXPERIENCE OF YEARS.
</div>
<a href = "#" onClick = "swapText(); return false;">Show me the Fs!</a>
</body>
</html>
```

Figure 13-12: Changing the innerHTML property of a div

spans and getElementsByTagName()

If each F were in a div of its own, this JavaScript could be rewritten so that
clicking an individual F would make it bigger. Unfortunately, browsers insert
line breaks before and after each
div, so the text would look like
Figure 13-13. To mark a bit of
HTML without introducing line
breaks, use the <span> tag. A span
is an HTML element that differs
from a div only in that it doesn't
create line breaks.

Figure 13-14 shows how
to use spans. It also introduces
the built-in JavaScript method
document.getElementsByTagName(),
which returns an array of all the
HTML elements of a given kind
on the web page.

Figure 13-13: Putting Fs inside
<div> tags

```
<html><head><title>How Many Fs Are There?</title>
<script type = "text/javascript">
<!-- hide me from older browsers
❶ function makeBig(theSpan) {
     var spanText = theSpan.innerHTML;
     var newText = "<font size='+3'>" + spanText + "</font>";
     theSpan.innerHTML = newText;
   }
   function countBig(correctNumber) {
❷   var theSpans = document.getElementsByTagName("span");
     var count = 0;
     for (var loop = 0; loop < theSpans.length; loop++) {
❹     if ((theSpans[loop].innerHTML.indexOf("FONT") != -1) ||
          (theSpans[loop].innerHTML.indexOf("font") != -1)) {
❺       count++;
        }
      }
❻   if (count == correctNumber) {
        alert("Congratulations! You got all " + correctNumber + " of them!");
      } else {
        var missed = correctNumber - count;
        alert("Not yet...there are still " + missed + " left.");
      }
   }
   // show me -->
   </script>
   <body>
   <h1>Click every F you see below.</h1>
   <div style = "width:200;height:100">
❼ <span onClick = "makeBig(this); return false;">F</span>INISHED <span
     onClick = "makeBig(this); return false;">F</span>ILES ARE THE RESULT O<span
     onClick = "makeBig(this); return false;">F</span> YEARS O<span
     onClick = "makeBig(this); return false;">F</span> SCIENTI<span
     onClick = "makeBig(this); return false;">F</span>IC STUDY COMBINED WITH THE
        EXPERIENCE O<span onClick = "makeBig(this); return false;">F</span> YEARS.
   </div>
❽ <a href = "#" onClick = "countBig(6); return false;">I'm done!</a>
   </body>
   </html>
```

Figure 13-14: Using <span> tags and getElementsByTagName()

The script in Figure 13-14 combines much of what has been covered in this book up until now. Line ❼ shows how onClick can be used inside a <span> tag to call some JavaScript. Notice that the built-in JavaScript variable this is passed into the makeBig() function. Recall from the chapter on forms and form elements that the word this stands for the element in which it occurs. In ❼, this means *this* <span> *tag*.

Clicking the F inside the span calls the makeBig() function, which starts in ❶. The makeBig() function loads the innerHTML of the span into a variable called spanText. The function then creates a new string called newText, which is the old text surrounded by beginning and ending <font> tags. Next, the function sets the span's innerHTML to this new text. The body of the function makeBig() could have been written as just one line like this:

```
theSpan.innerHTML = "<font size='+3'"> + theSpan.innerHTML + "</font>";
```

but breaking it up into three lines makes the function easier to understand.

The tricky part of the JavaScript comes when the user thinks all the Fs have been found and clicks the link in ❸. This calls the countBig() function, which takes the correct answer as a parameter.

The first line in the body of countBig() calls the built-in JavaScript method document.getElementsByTagName() to get an array containing all the span elements on the page (❷). Line ❸ loops over this array. For each span in the array, ❹ checks to see if the innerHTML of the span includes a <font> tag. Notice that ❹ checks for both the word font and its capitalized version, FONT. This is because some browsers, like Internet Explorer, automatically capitalize all HTML tags when they are accessed using innerHTML, whereas other browsers, like Firefox, automatically lowercase HTML tag elements. I'll talk more about cross-browser issues in the next section.

Getting back to the code, if the innerHTML of the <span> tag being considered does have a <font> tag, the count variable is increased by one. After the loop has inspected all the <span> tags, ❻ checks to see if the number of spans containing tags is correct. If so, the user gets a congratulatory message. If not, an alert comes up telling the user how many more Fs need to be found.

This script employs many of the techniques and features we've discussed in this book. Pat yourself on the back if you've understood the whole thing.

Advanced DOM Techniques

So far we've seen how to use JavaScript to change the HTML in a div and a span, and how to hide, show, and move HTML elements by changing various attributes of their style objects. We've also seen how to get access to HTML elements using getElementById() and getElementsByTagName(). All of these techniques make a web page dynamic by altering HTML elements that are already on the page. This section discusses a few ways to dynamically add new HTML elements to a web page.

Actually, we've already added new HTML elements to a web page by putting them in the innerHTML property of a span or div. The makeBig() function in Figure 13-14, for example, added a new <font> tag to the page. Often, injecting HTML into your web pages using innerHTML is the easiest and fastest way to add new HTML tags to your page.

Because it's quick and easy, most people use innerHTML when manipulating the contents of their web pages. However, innerHTML is not actually part of the official World Wide Web Consortium (W3C) standard for manipulating

HTML documents, so different browsers tend to support it slightly differently. We've already seen one inconsistency—some browsers capitalize HTML element names, and others lowercase the HTML element names. Another inconsistency occurs when a user types contents into the text element of a form. If the innerHTML of the form element is checked, Microsoft browsers will include the text typed by the users, but Firefox, Opera, and other non-Microsoft browsers will not include that text.

The standard, W3C-compliant way to add and delete HTML elements from a web page uses DOM methods. These methods work not only in JavaScript, but in other programming languages as well. This will become important when you're working in Ajax, as you'll see in the chapters that follow. If you're not planning on doing anything with Ajax and innerHTML does everything you want, you can comfortably skip to the section on drop-down menus. If you're ready to embrace the world of the W3C DOM, read on.

W3C DOM Overview

As you learned in Chapter 4, the W3C DOM defines the hierarchical structure of a web page. According to this model, a web page is a constructed from nodes, which are organized into a tree. Some of the nodes contain HTML elements, like <br> and <div>; others contain text. The top node contains the top-level HTML element, HTML. The HTML element node has two child nodes—the node containing the HEAD element and the node containing the BODY element. The BODY node might have several child nodes, some of which represent HTML tags on your page, such as <img> tags or hyperlinks. Some of these tag nodes will have children of their own. For example, a form element might have two text input nodes, each of which would be a child of the form node.

Creating and Adding Elements Using the W3C DOM

Creating a new HTML element node with the W3C DOM is pretty simple:

```
var newDiv = document.createElement("div");
```

This line creates a new div, but it doesn't put it into a web page. Note that this new div also lacks an id. If we were to stick it into a web page, there would be no way to refer to it. Before putting it into the web page, we should give our new div an id:

```
newDiv.setAttribute("id","newDiv");
```

Finally, it's time to stick the div into the web page. Let's put the div at the end of the web page using the DOM's appendChild() method. To use this method, you first have to figure out which node you want your new node to have as a parent. If we want the node to go at the end of the page, the parent will be the body of the document. The appendChild() method will add our new node to the end of the list of the parent's children. If our parent is the body of the document, that puts the div at the end of the document. First we have to get the <body> tag.

```
var bodyTags = document.getElementsByTagName("body");
var thisBody = bodyTags[0];
```

Remember that getElementsByTagName() returns a list of elements. That's why you need the second line to pull the <body> tag out of the list.

Once you've set a variable to point to the <body> tag, add the new div to the list of the <body> tag's children using appendChild():

```
thisBody.appendChild(newDiv);
```

Now we have a new div inserted at the end of the web page.

Adding Text to an Element

The above lines will add the following HTML to the end of a web page: <div id = "newDiv"></div>. You could use the new div's innerHTML property to put some text in there, but that would not be the W3C-compliant way. The standard says that you must first create a text node, and then make that text node a child of the div. Here's how to do it:

```
var textNode = document.createTextNode("I'm your new div.");
newDiv.appendChild(textNode);
```

Figure 13-15 presents a JavaScript that inserts a new div containing the text *I'm your new div* at the end of a web page.

```
<html><head><title>Inserting a div</title>
<script type = "text/javascript">
function addDiv() {
  var newDiv = document.createElement("div");
  newDiv.setAttribute("id","newDiv");
  var bodyTags = document.getElementsByTagName("body");
  var thisBody = bodyTags[0];
  thisBody.appendChild(newDiv);
  var textNode = document.createTextNode("I'm your new div.");
  newDiv.appendChild(textNode);
}
</script>
</head>
<body>
<a href = "#" onClick = "addDiv(); return false;">Add the new div.</a>
</body>
</html>
```

Figure 13-15: Adding a div to the end of a page

Adding Elements in the Middle of a Page and Removing Elements

In the last example, the div was added to the end of the web page, because the appendChild() method makes whatever is being inserted into the page the last child of the parent. The insertBefore() method is used when you want to insert a new element into the middle of a set of elements. Figure 13-16 shows a web page that asks for some standard information about a person. As seen at the right of the figure, clicking the Married radio button inserts a new text element into the middle of the form, which asks for the spouse's name.

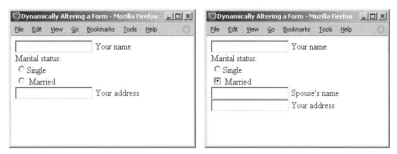

Figure 13-16: Clicking a radio button (left) makes a new form element appear (right).

The JavaScript in Figure 13-17 shows how you might create this page using DOM methods.

```
<html><head><title>Dynamically Altering a Form</title>
<script type = "text/javascript">
<!-- hide me from older browsers
function addSpouse(theRadio) {
❶   if (document.getElementById("newDiv") == null) {
❷       var newDiv = document.createElement("div");
        newDiv.setAttribute("id","newDiv");

❸       var newInput = document.createElement("input");
        newInput.setAttribute("type","text");
        newInput.setAttribute("id","spouseText");

❹       var nameText = document.createTextNode(" Spouse's name");

❺       newDiv.appendChild(newInput);
        newDiv.appendChild(nameText);
        newDiv.appendChild(document.createElement("br"));

        var theForm = document.getElementById("myForm");
        var theAddress = document.getElementById("address");

❻       theForm.insertBefore(newDiv, theAddress);
    }
}

function removeSpouse(theRadio) {
❼   if (document.getElementById("newDiv") != null) {
        var newDiv = document.getElementById("newDiv");
```

```
                var theForm = document.getElementById("myForm");
    ⑧          myForm.removeChild(newDiv);
        }
    }

    // show me -->
    </script>
    </head>
    <body>

    <form id = "myForm">
    <input type = "text" id = "name"> Your name<br>
    Marital status:<br>
⑨  <input type = "radio" onClick = "removeSpouse(this);" name = "ms">Single <br>
⑩  <input type = "radio" onClick = "addSpouse(this);" name = "ms"> Married<br>
    <input type = "text" id = "address"> Your address <br>

    </form>
    </body>
    </html>
```

Figure 13-17: Adding and removing elements with removeChild() and insertBefore()

In this script, the new form element appears just before the form element that asks for an address. Clicking the Single radio button removes that form element. Because the new form element also has a text string that says Spouse's name, we're going to put the form element and the text into a div. That will make it easier to remove both of them if the user clicks Single.

The fun begins in ⑩, which calls the addSpouse() function. This function first checks to see if there's already something on the page with an id of newDiv (❶). If there is, we don't want to add another one. If there isn't something on the page with an id of newDiv, looking for the element will return the JavaScript built-in term null. If that is the case, ❷ creates a new div and the next line sets its id to newDiv. Then ❸ creates a new text input field, and ❹ creates a new text node. The three lines starting in ❺ insert the new text input field, the new text node, and a <br> tag into the div. After setting the variable theForm to point to the form, and the variable theAddress to point to the form element that asks for an address, ❻ inserts the new div into the form before the address element. Notice that the insertBefore() method takes two parameters: the new element to insert and the element before which to insert it. Note also that these two elements need to have the same parent, which in this case is theForm.

Removing the div when a user clicks Single (⑨) is much easier. The removeSpouse() function first makes sure there's something to remove (❼). If there is something with an id of newDiv, the function sets newDiv to point to the div and theForm to point to the form, and then it removes the div from the form using the removeChild() method (⑧).

Additional DOM Details

You now know most of what you'll need to manipulate the DOM in the official way. There are a few additional details you may find helpful.

Node Properties

DOM nodes have many interesting properties. Each of the properties listed below can be accessed with this syntax: node.propertyName.

Table 13-1 provides a list of node properties.

Table 13-1: Node Properties

Node	Description
parentNode	Parent node of the node
childNodes	List of the children of the node
firstChild	First child of the node
lastchild	Last child of the node
nextSibling	Next node, which is a child of this node's parent
previousSibling	Previous node, which is a child of this node's parent
nodeValue	Text of the node if it's a text node, null otherwise
nodeType	Elements are type 1, attributes are type 2, text nodes are type 3
nodeName	Name of the attribute or node (h1, br, or form, for example); some browsers capitalize these names (BR, H1)
attributes	Array of attributes of this node

Many of these properties will be discussed in Chapter 14.

Looping Through Lists

In Figure 13-14 we used getElementsByTagName() to get an array of all the spans, and then we used normal array indexing to access each span (e.g., theSpans[0]). With getElementsByTagName() you can also loop through the elements using the item() method. Here is an example:

```
var myElements = document.getElementsByTagName("span");
var firstElement = myElements.item(0);
```

As with arrays, the first item in the list of elements is numbered 0. You may also use the item() method with the list returned by the childNodes attribute described above.

Cloning and Replacing Nodes

Sometimes you want to change many children of a node, but you don't want the changes to be observable. For example, you might want to rearrange the order of rows in a table, but only show users the rearranged table, and not the rows as they are moving around. A good way to do this is to clone the node that represents the table, make the changes on the clone, and then replace the original table with the cloned one.

To clone a node, use the cloneNode() method:

```
var myTable = document.getElementById("myTable");
var cloneTable = myTable.cloneNode(true);
```

The word true inside the cloneNode() method means that you want to clone the node and all its children. In this case it would be the table and all the contents of the table. If for some reason you didn't want to make a copy of the children, you'd put false there.

Once you've made your changes, you can replace the original table with the new one using the replaceNode() method. Like insertBefore() and removeChild(), this method is called by the parent of the nodes to be replaced. Given the myTable and cloneTable variables defined above, you could do this:

```
var tableParent = myTable.parentNode;
tableParent.replaceChild(cloneTable, myTable);
```

Manipulating a Page Using the DOM

As mentioned earlier, you could do most of the things described in this section with creative use of innerHTML. However, sometimes dealing with the complex strings needed to get innerHTML to be what you want can be difficult. In these cases, the DOM techniques are very helpful. When we get to the chapters on Ajax, you'll see even more applications of the DOM manipulation techniques.

Fancy Event Handling

Dynamic web pages call for dynamic reactions to user actions. We've discussed how to write JavaScript that reacts when users click links, buttons, and form elements. Now it's time to learn about more complicated event handling: how to accurately read the keyboard and the mouse.

The event Object

Whenever an event occurs, an event object is generated. The nature of this object depends on the event which generated it. To access the event object, simply pass the keyword event to whichever function is handling the event:

```
<a href = "#" onClick = "handleClick(event); return false; ">Click me!</a>.
```

The event object is most frequently accessed when you want to know which key a user has pressed, or precisely where the mouse is.

Keyboard Events

There are two main keyboard event handlers, the functions of which are pretty obvious: onKeyDown and onKeyUp. Triggering either of these event handlers creates an event object that stores which key has been pressed (or unpressed) and whether or not any special keys (ALT, CTRL, or SHIFT) were pressed at the same time. The relevant properties of the event object appear in Table 13-2.

Table 13-2: Properties for Keyboard Events

Property	Type	Description
altKey	boolean	True if the ALT key was down when this key was pressed
ctrlKey	boolean	True if the CTRL key was down when this key was pressed
shiftKey	boolean	True if the SHIFT key was down when this key was pressed
keyCode	integer	The Unicode decimal value for the key that was pressed; use String.fromCharChode(keyCode) to convert this to a string
Type	string	The type of event—keyup or keydown, for example

Figure 13-18 is short script that demonstrates how to use the event object to determine which key a user has pressed while in a text input field.

```
<html><head><title>Demonstrating Keyboard Events</title>
<script type = "text/javascript">
<!-- hide me from older browsers
function displayEvent(evt) {
  var type = evt.type;
❶  var code = evt.keyCode;
❷  var theChar = String.fromCharCode(code);
  var alt = evt.altKey;
  var ctrl = evt.ctrlKey;
  var shift = evt.shiftKey;
❸  var displayString = "event type: " + type + "; key code: " + code +
    ", which is the character " + theChar +
    "; ALT, CTRL, and SHIFT were: " +
    alt + ", " + ctrl + ", and " + shift + "\n\n";
❹  if ((code >= 65) && (code <= 90)) {
    document.getElementById("showEvents").value += displayString;
  }
}
// show me -->
</script>
</head>
<body>
<form>
Type here: <input type = "text"
❺    onKeyDown = "displayEvent(event);" onKeyUp = "displayEvent(event);"><br>
See the events here: <textarea id = "showEvents" cols = "80" rows = "20">
</textarea>
</form>
</body>
</html>
```

Figure 13-18: Demonstrating keyboard events

Although the script in Figure 13-18 is simple, there are some subtleties. First, whenever a user types anything while in the text field, the act of pressing the key down creates one event, and the act of releasing the key creates another event. These events are captured by the event handlers in ❺. In either case, the displayEvent() function is called. This function creates variables for each of the event's properties, combines them into a string, and then puts the resulting string into the textarea with the `id` of showEvents. The most interesting lines in this function are ❶, which gets a number representing the character being pressed, and ❷, which converts that number into an actual character. After those lines are executed, ❸ creates a string representing what happened in the event and ❹ puts that string in the text area if the key being pressed is a letter (letters have character code numbers between 65 and 90).

Figure 13-19 shows what happens when *a* and then *A* are typed into the text field. Notice that in both cases, the characterCode is 65, and the resulting character is *A*. In order to determine whether the user has entered a capital or lowercase letter, the shiftKey property of the event must be examined.

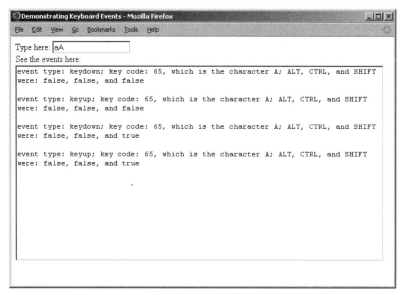

Figure 13-19: Typing a and A into the Figure 13-18 script

Mouse Events

Mouse events have their own properties. Unfortunately, some cross-browser differences complicate accessing the position of the mouse and determining which mouse button was clicked. Table 13-3 shows the properties of mouse events, and it gives some details about how to deal with cross-browser differences.

Table 13-3: Properties of Mouse Events

Property	Description
button	Equals 2 if it's a right-click—otherwise, it depends on the browser
clientX	Internet Explorer's X position for the mouse
clientY	Internet Explorer's Y position for the mouse
pageX	Most other browsers' X position for the mouse
pageY	Most other browsers' Y position for the mouse

As you can see from Table 13-3, all the properties of mouse events are browser dependent. The button property, for example, describes which button was clicked when an onMouseDown or onMouseUp event happened. However, the meaning of the numbers provided by the button property depend on the browser being used. In Internet Explorer, 1 means the left button was clicked, 2 means the right button, and 4 means the middle button. In most other browsers, 0 means the left button, 1 means the middle button, and 2 means the right button. Because 2 means the right button was clicked in both cases and many people don't have a middle button on their mouse, it is often safe to see if the button property of the event was 2 and call it a left-click if it was not.

The position of the mouse is a bit trickier. Browsers other than Internet Explorer generally use an event's pageX and pageY properties to give a number representing the X and Y positions (in pixels) of the event relative to the top-left corner of the browser window. These two properties take into consideration scrolling a window. If a window is 10,000 pixels long and the user has scrolled down to the very bottom, the pageY property will be around 10,000 at the bottom of the window. Internet Explorer, on the other hand, uses properties named clientX and clientY. These properties do not take scrolling into consideration, so to use them, you should add numbers representing how far down and to the left the browser has been scrolled. Those numbers are available as document.body.scrollTop and document.body.scrollLeft.

Figure 13-20 presents a script that determines the X and Y positions of a mouse and puts the results in a textarea.

```
<html><head><title>Checking Mouse Position</title>
<script type = "text/javascript">
<!-- hide me from older browsers
function displayEvent(evt)
{
  var x = 0;
  var y = 0;
❶ if (evt.pageX) {
❷   x = evt.pageX;
    y = evt.pageY;
❸ } else if (evt.clientX) {
❹   x = evt.clientX + document.body.scrollLeft;
    y = evt.clientY + document.body.scrollTop;
  }
❺ document.getElementById("results").value += x + " " + y + "\n";
}
// show me -->
</script>
</head>
<body>
<div id = "box" style = "height:100px;width:100px;border:1px black solid;"
❻ onMouseMove = "displayEvent(event);"
❼ onMouseOver = "document.getElementById('results').value='';"></div>
<form><textarea id = "results" cols = "80" rows = "20"></textarea></form>
</body>
</html>
```

Figure 13-20: Detecting the position of the mouse

In Figure 13-20, moving inside the div calls the `displayEvent()` function (❻), and moving the mouse onto the div clears the textarea that stores all the mouse information collected (❼). The `displayEvent()` function first checks to see if the browser knows about the `pageX` property of the event (❶). If so it uses `pageX` to get the *x* coordinate of the mouse, relative to the top-left corner of the browser window (❷) and `pageY` to get the *y* coordinate. If the browser does not know about the `pageX` property but does know about the `clientX` property (❸), it uses `clientX` and `clientY`. Notice in ❹ that the amount that the browser has been scrolled to the right or down must be added to the `clientX` and `clientY` property to account for scrolled windows. The last line in the function (❺) adds the appropriate information to the textarea with the `id` of `results`.

Adding Event Handlers Using JavaScript

Throughout this book, whenever we have wanted to trigger an event based on a user's behavior, we have put an event handler inside the triggering element. For example, in Chapter 4, when we wanted an alert box to pop up when a user clicked a link, we put an `onClick` event inside the link:

```
<a href = "#" onClick = "alert('Thanks!');">Click me</a>
```

Putting event handlers inside the elements that trigger the events can cause some problems:

- Doing so puts JavaScript inside your HTML elements rather than inside `<script>` tags. This means that someone trying to understand your JavaScript (and that person may be you) will have to hunt around in the HTML to find all the various bits of JavaScript on the page.

- Sometimes you want a JavaScript function to be triggered by many elements. For example, if you have 20 checkboxes, each of which has an `onClick`, you will need to stick the same code (`onClick = "doFunction();"`) in 20 different places. If the function's name changes, or if you decide to add a parameter to the function, you will need to change the page in 20 different places.

- You may want an event handler to be invoked in some cases, but not in others. In the case of writing drag-and-drop code, a given object, such as a div, should only be moved if the mouse has been clicked while on that object. In this case, the object's `onMouseMove` event should only trigger a function when the appropriate object has been clicked.

For these reasons, modern browsers provide ways for JavaScript to attach functions to the event handlers of objects. The template for this is:

```
element.handler = function;
```

For example, to call a function named doAlert() whenever a div with the id of myDiv is clicked, use the following line:

```
document.getElementById("myDiv").onclick = doAlert;
```

This line is unusual for two reasons. First, the event handler (onClick) is all lowercase. This is a requirement when assigning a function to a handler in this way. Second, notice that the function does not have parentheses after it. This means that no parameters may be passed to this function. However, a function called in this way does have access to the event that called the function, and it turns out that the event is almost always the only parameter you need.

As with all things related to events, there are some browser incompatibilities involved with getting access to the event object. In Internet Explorer, the event is automatically stored in a variable named event. To access the event, just use the event variable:

```
function doAlert() {
  myEvent = event;
  // do something with the myEvent variable
  alert("Got the event!");
}
```

In most other browsers, the event is automatically passed as a parameter to the function being called. This means that the function being called, doAlert() in the example given, needs to have a parameter in its definition:

```
function doAlert(myEvent) {
  // do something with the myEvent variable
  alert("Got the event!");
}
```

Once the event object has been accessed inside a function, it is sometimes helpful to retrieve information about the object that created the event. To do this, Internet Explorer uses an event object property called srcElement. Most other browsers use a property named target.

Figure 13-21 puts all this information together in a cross-browser script for assigning functions to events using JavaScript.

```
<html><head><title>Cross-Browser Event Handling</title>
<script type = "text/javascript">
<!-- hide me from older browsers
function attachHandlers() {
❶  var theElements = document.getElementById("myForm").childNodes;
   for (var loop = 0; loop < theElements.length; loop++) {
❷    if ((theElements[loop].nodeName == "input") ||
             (theElements[loop].nodeName == "INPUT")) {
❸      theElements[loop].onclick = doAlert;
     }
   }
}
```

```
      }
❹ function doAlert(evt) {
      var thisBox;
❺   if (!evt) {
        evt = event;
        thisBox = evt.srcElement;
❻   } else {
        thisBox = evt.target;
      }
      alert('You clicked on '  + thisBox.name);
    }

    // show me -->
    </script>
    </head>
❼ <body onLoad = "attachHandlers();">
    <form id = "myForm">
❽ <input type = "checkbox" name = "1"><input type = "checkbox" name = "2">
    <input type = "checkbox" name = "3"><br>
    <input type = "checkbox" name = "4"><input type = "checkbox" name = "5">
    <input type = "checkbox" name = "6"><br>
    </form>
    </body>
    </html>
```

Figure 13-21: Cross-browser script for attaching functions to event handlers

The script in Figure 13-21 creates a set of six checkboxes, each with a different name. Clicking any of these checkboxes results in an alert box providing the name of the checkbox that was just clicked. Notice that the HTML describing the checkboxes contains no onClick handlers (❽). This is because the handlers are assigned using JavaScript. The onLoad handler inside the <body> tag (❼) triggers the function which assigns the handlers. The function is called by the onLoad handler because an HTML element cannot have a function attached to its handler until the web browser knows about the element. If a piece of JavaScript tries to attach a handler to a form element that has not yet been processed by the browser, an error will result. For this reason, it's best to wait until all the elements have been loaded before assigning functions to their handlers.

The attachHandlers() function has several interesting aspects. First, it uses the DOM methods covered earlier in the chapter to access the checkboxes. These checkboxes are child elements of the form element, and so they are accessible as the childNodes of the form (❶). The childNodes property returns an array, which is then looped through. Each time through the loop, the JavaScript checks the next element in the array to see if it is an input element. Notice that both the strings INPUT and input are checked. This is because some browsers capitalize element names and other browsers don't. For each input element found, ❸ attaches the doAlert() function to the element's onclick handler.

Once the handlers have been attached, the page waits until a checkbox is clicked. When that happens, the onclick event is triggered, and the doAlert() function is called. Notice that the definition of doAlert() contains a parameter (❹). In Firefox and most other browsers, this parameter will be filled with an event object that contains information about the event that caused the doAlert() function to be called. If that parameter is not filled in, it means the user is most likely using Internet Explorer. In this case, ❺ is true. The evt variable is set to the Internet Explorer variable event, and thisBox is set to the checkbox that was clicked using Internet Explorer's srcElement property. If Firefox, or some other browser was used instead, the function's evt parameter would already contain the event object, and we'd only need to set thisBox to the checkbox that was clicked by accessing the target property (❻).

One final note about assigning functions to event handlers using JavaScript: If for some reason you want to remove an event handler from an object, simply set the handler's value to null. Here's an example:

```
document.getElementById("myDiv").onclick = null;
```

Drop-Down Menus

I'll close this chapter by showing how to build a basic drop-down menu with DHTML. The menu shown in Figure 13-22 has three links: Dogs, Cats, and Birds. Mousing over Cats causes a submenu to drop down with the names of several cat breeds. Clicking one of those links sends the browser to a web page about that kind of cat.

Figure 13-23 shows the code that drives this drop-down menu. I've already covered everything you must know to understand this code, so take a look at it, and see if you can figure out how it works before reading my explanation.

Figure 13-22: A drop-down menu

```
<html><head><title>Drop-Down Menus</title>
<script type = "text/javascript">
<!-- hide me from older browsers
❶ var div_array = new Array("divOne", "divTwo", "divThree");
function changeDiv(the_div, the_change)
{
❷   document.getElementById(the_div).style.visibility = the_change;
```

```
        }
        function closeAll()
        {
❸      for (var loop = 0; loop < div_array.length; loop++)
          {
              changeDiv(div_array[loop], "hidden");
          }
        }
        // show me -->
        </script>
        </head>
        <body>
        <div id = "top1" style = "position:absolute; top:20; left:0; z-index:1">
❹      <a href = "#"
          onMouseOver = "closeAll(); changeDiv('divOne','visible');">Dogs</a>
        </div>
        <div id = "top2" style = "position:absolute; top:20; left:40; z-index:1">
        <a href = "#"
          onMouseOver = "closeAll(); changeDiv('divTwo','visible');">Cats</a>
        </div>
        <div id = "top3" style = "position:absolute; top:20; left:80; z-index:1">
        <a href = "#"
          onMouseOver = "closeAll(); changeDiv('divThree','visible');">Birds</a>
        </div>
        <div id = "rightBorder" style = "position:absolute; top:20; left:50;">
        <a href = "#"
          onMouseOver = "closeAll();"><img src = "long_spacer.gif" border = 0></a>
        </div>
        <div id = "bottomBorder" style = "position:absolute; top:80; left:0;">
❺      <a href = "#"
          onMouseOver = "closeAll();"><img src = "long_spacer.gif" border = 0></a>
        </div>
❻      <div id = "divOne" style =
            "position:absolute; top:40; left:0; visibility:hidden;">
        <a href = "#">Collie</a><br>
        <a href = "#">Puli</a><br>
        <a href = "#">Corgie</a><br>
        </div>
        <div id = "divTwo" style =
            "position:absolute; top:40; left:80; visibility:hidden">
        <a href = "#">Siamese</a><br>
        <a href = "#">Manx</a><br>
        <a href = "#">Calico</a><br>
        </div>
        <div id = "divThree" style =
            "position:absolute; top:60; left:80; visibility:hidden">
        <a href = "#">Parakeet</a><br>
        <a href = "#">Finch</a><br>
        <a href = "#">Canary</a><br>
        </div>
        </body>
        </html>
```

Figure 13-23: A basic hierarchical menu

Line-by-Line Analysis of Figure 13-23

A drop-down menu has a div for each menu option. The nine divs in Figure 13-23 include one div for each top-level menu element (❹), one for each submenu (❻), one for the bottom border, and one for the right border. Each time a visitor mouses over one of the main menu options, only the submenu matching the link most recently moused over is shown. If the visitor mouses over Cats, making the list of cat breeds visible, and then mouses over Dogs, the closeAll() function hides the Cats submenu and changeDiv() displays the Dogs submenu. Mousing over the bottom or right border closes all the submenus.

The closeAll() Function

The closeAll() function loops through the array of divs defined in ❶. Each time through the loop in ❸, closeAll() calls the changeDiv() function to hide one of the divs.

The changeDiv() Function

The changeDiv() function takes two parameters: the name of a div to change, and whether to make the div hidden or visible. Line ❷ changes the visibility of the specified div to visible or hidden, depending on the value of the second parameter of changeDiv().

The Borders

The menu's bottom border is a long transparent (and therefore invisible) GIF (❺). The code in ❺ dictates that mousing over this invisible GIF hides all submenus. This GIF and the blank GIFs on the right of the menus make sure the submenu vanishes if the visitor's mouse leaves the menu area completely.

Figure 13-23 offers a basic example of how you might implement a hierarchical menu. For more complete versions, check out the menu and navigation section of Dynamic Drive's website. *Fortune* magazine's website used this one: http://www.dynamicdrive.com/dynamicindex1/dropmenuindex.htm.

Summary

DHTML is the topic of several excellent books—what we've discussed here should just whet your appetite. But you have learned a few DHTML basics, including the following:

- How to use divs to create blocks of HTML
- How to add styles to divs
- How to make divs, along with the HTML they contain, visible or invisible
- How to move divs

- How to animate divs with timed loops
- How to use DOM methods to alter HTML documents
- How to read keyboard and mouse events
- How to create a basic hierarchical menu

If you understood all that, you shouldn't have any problem with the assignment.

Assignment

Create a DHTML screensaver like the one shown in Figure 13-24. The smiley face in the figure continually bounces around the screen. When it hits one of the walls, it bounces off at a random angle. To make the smiley face move diagonally, change its top and left positions in a timing loop. To get it to bounce off a wall, make it change directions when it hits one side of the screen. Remember, to make the smiley move right, you would add to its left property, and to make it move left, you would subtract from its left property.

Figure 13-24: A screensaver created with JavaScript

14

AJAX BASICS

Ajax (Asynchronous JavaScript and XML) helps create web pages that act like desktop applications. By combining DHTML with the ability to download and display information from a webserver while a user is still interacting with a web page, Ajax puts an end to the old submit-and-wait cycle common to most interactive websites.

If you've used Google Maps (http://maps.google.com), you've seen Ajax in action. There are also Ajax versions of word processors, spreadsheets, and other common applications. Like DHTML, Ajax is a complex topic and is the focus of a number of books. However, with the JavaScript you've learned so far, and a few other details, you will be well on your way to becoming a master of Ajax.

This chapter introduces Ajax, including:

- An overview of Ajax and the technologies it encompasses
- The *A* in Ajax—*Asynchronicity*—and why you need it
- The basic JavaScript you'll need for Ajax

- Browser compatibility issues

- Potential pitfalls when using Ajax

- When to use Ajax and when to avoid it

- How to set up a webserver and write server-side programs that communicate with Ajax

This chapter tells only part of the Ajax story. In Chapter 15 you'll learn about the *X* in Ajax (which stands for the data transfer standard *XML*), and how to read and navigate XML documents in JavaScript and use them in Ajax applications.

A Real-World Example of Ajax

The best-known example of Ajax may be Google Maps (maps.google.com). Figure 14-1 shows you the map which results from searching for the office of No Starch Press. The map is very interactive; you can zoom in, zoom out, and pan around without having to reload the page. A smaller map in the bottom-right corner of the main map shows you the larger context of the map you're viewing. A blue box in the smaller map moves around as you pan across the large map.

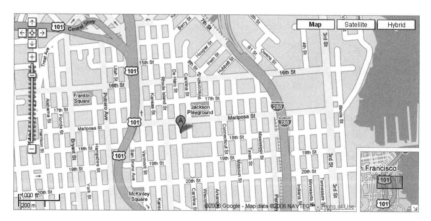

Figure 14-1: Google Maps

The map's interface can mark places you ask about, such as No Starch Press in Figure 14-1, and show directions between two points. For example, Figure 14-2 shows the route between the office and El Metate, one of my favorite Mexican restaurants in San Francisco. All of this interactivity involves frequent trips to Google's webservers without the user seeing the page reload.

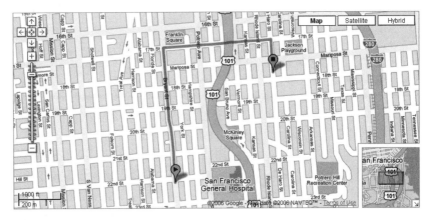

Figure 14-2: Getting directions with Google Maps

Introduction to Ajax

The term Ajax was coined by Jesse James Garrett[1] to describe a general approach to creating web applications. This approach involves the following steps:

1. An event, such as a user moving the mouse or typing into an input field, triggers one or more simultaneous requests to a webserver for more information.

2. While the webserver is processing the requests, the web browser goes about its business as usual, allowing the user to continue interacting with the web page.

3. The result from each request appears once the webserver has processed that request, and it is used to update the web page using the DHTML techniques you learned in Chapter 13.

Figure 14-3 shows how Ajax works and how it differs from the traditional style of communication between web browsers and webservers.

In the traditional style of browser-server communication, a user clicks a link or submits a form in a web browser. This causes the browser to send a request for information to a webserver: either the web page named in the href attribute of the link, or the results of a program or script named in the action attribute of the <form> tag. Once the request is sent, the browser sits idly, usually animating an icon in the upper-right corner of the window, and the user waits for the webserver to respond to the request. Eventually the server responds, and the web page reloads, presenting new information.

---

[1] For Garrett's original essay on Ajax, see http://adaptivepath.com/publications/essays/archives/000385.php.

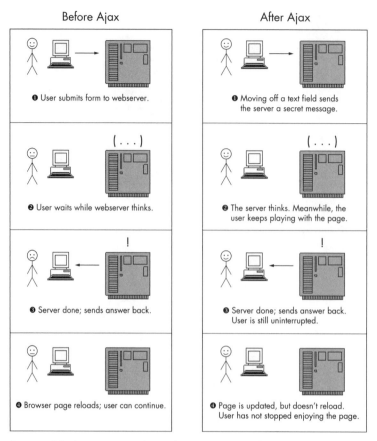

Before Ajax	After Ajax
❶ User submits form to webserver.	❶ Moving off a text field sends the server a secret message.
❷ User waits while webserver thinks.	❷ The server thinks. Meanwhile, the user keeps playing with the page.
❸ Server done; sends answer back.	❸ Server done; sends answer back. User is still uninterrupted.
❹ Browser page reloads; user can continue.	❹ Page is updated, but doesn't reload. User has not stopped enjoying the page.

Figure 14-3: Ajax versus traditional communications between a web browser and a webserver

In the Ajax style, on the other hand, the browser makes a request from the webserver without the user knowing about the request. The icon in the browser's corner doesn't spin, and the browser can still be used. When the response comes back from the webserver, the information displayed in the web browser is updated without reloading the page. The entire process occurs without causing a pause in the user's interactions with the web page.

Asynchronicity—The A in Ajax

The *A* in Ajax stands for *asynchronous*, which in this context means something like *non-waiting*. In asynchronous communication (the *After Ajax* part of Figure 14-3), the browser sends a request to a webserver and does not wait for the reply. Many asynchronous requests can be made simultaneously, and the browser deals with the responses as they come from the webserver. In contrast, the traditional style of browser-server communication described in the *Before Ajax* part of Figure 14-3 is synchronous; that is, the browser submits a request to a webserver and then waits for a reply, unable to send any other requests until the server responds.

An example of asynchronicity can be seen when you download a web page and watch images appearing on the page at different times. The images are requested simultaneously, and the browser displays them as it receives them. While this sort of asynchronicity is built in to all but the oldest web browsers, until recently JavaScript programmers couldn't control asynchronous communications with webservers. This all changed with the addition of a new JavaScript object called the request object.

XML—The X in Ajax

The *X* in Ajax stands for *XML*. Since the publication of the XML standard in 1998, XML has become *the* format for sharing structured text-based information between computers. As we will see, browsers have built-in ways for dealing with information that has been formatted as XML documents. This, and the ubiquity of XML documents, makes XML a great format for sharing information between web browsers and webservers.

JavaScript—The J in Ajax

Ajax uses JavaScript to create requests, send them to webservers, parse the XML results, and update web pages accordingly. The rest of the chapter describes how to use JavaScript to create and send requests, and deal with the asynchronous nature of the requests.

Creating and Sending Requests

The key to implementing the Ajax-style communication described above is the JavaScript *request object*, which is built into Internet Explorer 6.0 and later, Firefox 0.8 and later, Opera 7.54 and later, and Safari 1.2.2 and later. Your JavaScript can use this request object to query a webserver for information, store the returned information, and update the page when the server has provided the information.

There are four steps involved in using JavaScript to make an Ajax request:

1. Creating a request object
2. Telling the request object where to send the request
3. Telling the object what to do when the request is answered
4. Telling the object to make the request

Creating a Request Object

The first step in making an Ajax request is to create a request object. Sadly, there is a little bit of browser incompatibility involved in creating this object. In Internet Explorer,[2] a request object is created like this:

```
var request = new ActiveXObject("Microsoft.XMLHTTP");
```

---

[2] It's possible to get slightly different versions of the request object from different versions of IE. You only need to do this for fancy Ajax tricks that are beyond the scope of this discussion.

In browsers other than Internet Explorer, do this:

```
var request = new XMLHttpRequest();
```

Putting these together gives this:

```
var request = null;
if (window.XMLHttpRequest) {
    request = new XMLHttpRequest();
} else if (window.ActiveXObject) {
    request = new ActiveXObject("Microsoft.XMLHTTP");
}
```

Once this block of JavaScript has executed, the request variable will contain a request object.

Telling the Object Where to Send the Request

The request object will request information from some resource. Usually, that resource will be the webserver that served up the web page containing the JavaScript making the request. In this case, the request object needs to know the URL of a program or script that lives on the webserver (known as a *server-side program*). This server-side program will process the request and respond with the requested information. (Chapter 16 will focus more on server-side Ajax.)

If you don't have access to a webserver, you can instead ask the request object to request a file that lives in the same directory as the file containing the JavaScript making the call. To request a file, the request object simply needs to know the file's name, such as my_file.txt. Here's how to tell a request object to request the file named my_file.txt:

```
request.open("GET", "my_file.txt");
```

The open method of the request object takes two parameters. The first parameter is the type of request you want to make (GET, POST, HEAD, and so on). I'll discuss the difference between these in Chapter 16; for now, we'll only use GET.

The second parameter is a string that tells the object where to send the request. If the resource is password protected, the username and password can be provided as two additional (optional) parameters, like so:

```
request.open("GET", "my_file.txt", username, password);
```

What to Do When the Request Is Answered

As described in the introduction, a key feature of Ajax is asynchronicity. After a request object makes a request, the web browser is free to do whatever it wants, which may involve creating more request objects to make additional requests. Each request object is responsible for tracking the process of making its request, waiting for a reply, and realizing when all the information provided in response to the request has been completely downloaded. Your task as a JavaScript coder is to tell each request object what it should do when the requested resource has been completely downloaded, using a special property of the request object called its readyState.

As the request object moves through its stages, from creation, to being told about where to send the request, to sending the request, and so on, the value of the readyState property changes. The property is called readyState because each stage of a request object is called its *state*. Table 14-1 lists the values the readyState property can take and what they mean.

Table 14-1: Values of a Request Object's readyState Property

Property Value	State Name	Description
0	Uninitialized	The object has been created but not told about the request: open( ) has not been called.
1	Loading	The object knows about the request but has not sent it yet: send( ) has not been called.
2	Loaded	The request has been sent, and basic information about the response is available.
3	Interactive	The response is being loaded into the request object.
4	Completed	The entire response has been loaded into the request object and is now available.

The main trick in Ajax is to write a special function that is called whenever the readyState property changes value. To define this function and make sure it is called when the request object's readyState property changes, do something like this:

```
request.onreadystatechange = function() {
  alert("the state has changed!");
}
```

There's actually a lot happening in the code fragment above, so let's go slowly. The part of this JavaScript before the period refers to the request object we've created. The part following the period, onreadystatechange, is an event handler of the object.

We've seen plenty of event handlers before: onClick, onMouseOver, and so on. These handlers are part of the objects. For example, a form button (<input type = "button">) will have an onClick handler, which is triggered whenever a user clicks the button. We've used these handlers by referring to them inside the HTML tag. For example, the tag <input type = "button" onClick = "myFunction();"> will attach the function myFunction() to the button's onClick event handler.

Just as a button has an onClick handler, the request object has a handler called onreadystatechange, which is called automatically whenever the value of the request object's readyState property changes. And, just as we can attach a function to the button's onClick handler, we can attach a function to the onreadystatechange handler.

However, in contrast to the button's handler, we don't stick the function into an HTML tag. Instead, we set the onreadystatechange handler equal to something called an *anonymous function*. This function has no name; it is simply called function. By setting this handler equal to this anonymous function we ensure that whenever the request object's readyState property changes, the function—that is, the code in the braces—is called. It looks weird, but you'll get used to it.

Writing JavaScript That Is Called After the Request Has Been Answered

A request object begins life with a readyState of 0. Calling request.open() tells the request object where to send the request, and switches the object's readyState to 1. Because the readyState has changed, the anonymous function attached to the onreadystatechange handler is called.

Usually, you don't want your JavaScript to do anything special at this point, so the function should not do anything when the readyState has been changed to 1. In fact, the function usually does not do anything until the readyState has changed to 4, which, as you can see in Table 14-1, means that the request has been answered and that all the information sent by the server has been downloaded into the object. Once readyState 4 is reached, the function is ready to do something with the data.

Because JavaScripts usually don't do anything until the request object reaches a readyState of 4, the anonymous function often looks something like this:

```
request.onreadystatechange = function() {
  if (request.readyState == 4) {
    alert("Download complete! ");
  }
}
```

In the code above, the alert is called only after the request's readyState property changes to 4. The anonymous function is actually called when the property changes from 0 to 1, 1 to 2, and 2 to 3, but because of the if-then statement, the alert is called only when the readyState changes to 4. Although this code sample calls an alert, more typically the JavaScript inside the if-then statement will do something with the information that has been downloaded into the request object. We'll see examples of this soon.

Sending the Request

Once you've told the request object where to send the request and what to do when the request has been answered, it's time to tell the request object to send the request, like so:

```
request.send(null);
```

This command sends the request using the request object's send method. The single parameter of the send method contains information (for example, form information) to send to a webserver when making a POST request. Because the request we're making is of type GET (remember the first parameter of the request.open() method), the parameter of the send method is set to null, which is a predefined term meaning "no information."

Putting Everything Together

Figure 14-4 combines everything covered so far in one function, which includes creating the request object, telling it where to send the request, providing the anonymous function that is to be triggered when the request object changes state, and sending the request.

```html
<html><head><title>A Simple Ajax Script</title>
<script type = "text/javascript">
<!-- hide me from older browsers
❶ function doAjaxCall(the_request) {
     var request = null;
❷    if (window.XMLHttpRequest) {
        request = new XMLHttpRequest();
     } else if (window.ActiveXObject) {
        request = new ActiveXObject("Microsoft.XMLHTTP");
     }
❸    if (request) {
❹       request.open("GET", the_request);
❺       request.onreadystatechange = function() {
❻          if (request.readyState == 4) {
              document.getElementById("resultDiv").innerHTML =
                 "All done!";
           }
        }
❼       request.send(null);
     } else {
❽       alert("Sorry, you must update your browser before seeing Ajax in action.");
     }
  }
  // show me -->
  </script>
  </head>
  <body>
  <form>
❾ <input type = "button" value = "Make Ajax Request"
     onClick = "doAjaxCall('sample.txt'); return true;">
  </form>
❿ <div id = "resultDiv"></div>
  </body>
  </html>
```

Figure 14-4: A simple Ajax script

The action begins when the user clicks the button in ❾, which calls the doAjaxCall() function (❶) and sends it the name of a file to read.

NOTE *In general, a URL would go in here, but because I'm not assuming you have access to a webserver, we're just going to read a file that lives in the same directory as the file containing this JavaScript.*

The doAjaxCall() function creates a new request object (❷), which is either an XMLHttpRequest object or an ActiveXObject object. If the browser reading the JavaScript knows what the XMLHttpRequest object is, it will create a new object of this type; if instead it knows what the ActiveXObject is, it will create a new object of this type. If the browser doesn't know either of these objects, request will stay equal to null.

In ❸, we make sure that a request object was created. If not, ❽ lets the user know that he or she needs a browser upgrade.

If a request object was created, ❹ tells it where to send the request. The function to call when the readyState property of the request object changes is declared in ❺. This function says, "If the request is in state 4, the request object has sent the request and received an answer; put the *All done!* message into the div with the id of resultDiv (❻)."

Finally, the request object makes the request in ❼, which begins the process of downloading the requested text file. The request object then goes through its five states, and each state change triggers the anonymous function. Once the request object is in state 4, the anonymous function writes *All done!* into the div.

The magic in all of this is that while the request object is performing the query and getting the results, the browser does not freeze up and the page does not reload. And that is the beauty of Ajax.

Getting the Results

The code in Figure 14-4 performs the request, retrieves the results, and puts *All done!* into the div; it doesn't actually display the retrieved results. It's as if I asked you what you wanted for dinner and ignored what you said.

Usually, once the request object has entered state 4, you will want to look at the information the object has retrieved. This information is stored in one or two properties of the request object: The responseText property of the object always contains a text string with the results, and if the response is an XML document, the responseXML property of the request contains an XML object representing the results (more on this in Chapters 15 and 16). If the response is not an XML document, responseXML will contain the value null.

To put the results of the query into the div in ❿ in Figure 14-4, change the body of the if-then statement in ❻ to

```
document.getElementById("resultDiv").innerHTML = request.responseText;
```

Demonstrating Asynchronicity

Now it's time to have a deeper look at asynchronicity. Figure 14-5 demonstrates how two request objects can download files asynchronously. Here, clicking the Start Downloading button downloads two files, shortWait and longWait, which take different amounts of time for a webserver to process. The JavaScript behind this figure (shown in Figure 14-6) requests the file that takes the longest to process (longWait) first, and then requests the one that takes less time to process (shortWait).

Figure 14-5: Demonstrating asynchronicity

Were these files to be downloaded synchronously, the script would download the slowest file—longWait—first, and then the quickest file, shortWait (because that's the order in which they were requested). However, because these files are loaded asynchronously, all requests happen simultaneously. This means that shortWait will be downloaded before longWait.

Each line in the figure shows the name of the file being downloaded and the number of seconds it took to download. What you can't see in the figure is that each of the lines appeared on the web page as the file is downloaded: the first line 1.2 seconds after the button was clicked, and the next line about 4 seconds later.

Now let's have a look at the code behind Figure 14-5 to see how the magic works. Figure 14-6 reveals the trick.

NOTE *Before you can try out this example or most of the examples in Chapters 15, 16, and 17, you'll need to set up a webserver and PHP on your local computer. If you don't already have a webserver and PHP on your local machine, refer to "Setting Up a Webserver and PHP" on page 273. If you already have a webserver running on your machine, it has PHP installed, and you know where the webserver's top-level document directory is, you can try running the script in Figure 14-6. To do so, put the files longWait.php, shortWait.php, and Fig14-06.html in a directory named boj, and put that directory in the top-level directory of your webserver. Then browse to http://localhost/boj/Fig14-06.html. If that doesn't work, try http://127.0.0.1/boj/Fig14-06.html. If that doesn't work either, you should refer to your webserver's manual to determine how to connect with your webserver. The files longWait.php, shortWait.php, and Fig14-06.html are available at http://www.bookofjavascript.com/Chapter14.*

```
<html><head><title>Demonstrating Ansynchronicity</title>
<script type = "text/javascript">
<!-- hide me from older browsers
❶ function demoAsync() {
     var now = new Date();
     downloadFile("longWait", now );
     downloadFile("shortWait", now);
   }
❷ function downloadFile(the_request, start_time) {
     var request = null;
     if (window.XMLHttpRequest) {
       request = new XMLHttpRequest();
     } else if (window.ActiveXObject) {
       request = new ActiveXObject("Microsoft.XMLHTTP");
     }
     if (request) {
       request.open("GET", "http://localhost/boj/" + the_request +
         ".php");
❸     request.onreadystatechange =
         function() {
           if (request.readyState == 4) {
❹           document.getElementById("resultDiv").innerHTML +=
               "File " + the_request + " was downloaded in " +
❺           getExpiredTime(start_time) + " seconds <br>";
           }
         }
       request.send(null);
     } else {
       alert("Sorry, you must update your browser before seeing" +
         " Ajax in action.");
     }
   }
❻ function getExpiredTime(start_time) {
     var then = start_time.getTime();
     var now = new Date();
     var now_time = now.getTime();
     var diff = (now_time - then) / 1000;
     return diff
   }
   // show me -->
   </script>
   </head>
   <body>
❼ <form><input type = "button"
     onClick = "demoAsync(); return true;" value = "Start Downloading"></form>
   <div id = "resultDiv"></div>
   </body>
   </html>
```

Figure 14-6: Asynchronicity in Ajax

Line-by-Line Analysis of Figure 14-6

The action starts when a user clicks the button in ❼, which calls the demoAsync() function in ❶. This function creates a new Date object that tracks the time when the function was called, and then it calls the downloadFile() function twice (once for each file we want to download). Notice that the function asks for the largest file, longWait, first and the smallest file, shortWait, next.

The downloadFile() function that starts in ❷ looks like a typical Ajax function. It begins by trying to create a new request object, and if that succeeds, it tells the request which resource to access.

The anonymous function that is called when the request changes its state is defined in ❸. This function says that we should add some information to the contents of the div named resultDiv (❹) once the request has completed (that is, when the request object's readyState property equals 4). The information added is the name of the requested file and the time it took to download. Line ❺ calls getExpiredTime() to determine how long (in seconds) it took to download the file.

Next up, `getExpiredTime()` (⑥) is passed a `Date` object that represents the time when the `demoAsync()` function was called. The `getTime()` method of this `Date` object returns the number of milliseconds between January 1, 1970, and the time represented by the object (`getTime()` was described in Table 2-1). Next, a `Date` object that represents the current date and time is created, and `getTime()` calculates the number of milliseconds between the current time and January 1, 1970; the difference between these two numbers is the time (in milliseconds) that has passed since the `demoAsync()` function was called and the request object completed its download of the requested file. That number is divided by 1,000 (1,000 milliseconds in a second) to get a time in seconds.

Ajax and Usability

There are many good examples of Ajax (Google Maps, Flickr, and Google Suggest, to name a few), but it is very easy to create a confusing and difficult-to-use Ajax application. Below is a list of some roadblocks that you may encounter along your road to implementing excellent Ajax.

The Back Button

Web users are accustomed to using their browser's back button to return to pages they've just seen. Unfortunately, unless special care is taken, the back button does not work as expected in Ajax applications. For example, if you click the left side of a Google map and drag it to the right side of the screen, the map will change, but clicking the browser's back button won't return the map to its previous state. Instead, because all of an Ajax application happens on a single web page, clicking back will take you off that web page. In the case of Google Maps, this may take you out of Google Maps entirely. You can use many of the Ajax frameworks described in Appendix B to help make the browser's back button work in ways that will make more sense to your visitors. Dojo (http://www.dojotoolkit.org), Backbase (http://www.backbase.com), and RSH (http://codinginparadise.org/projects/dhtml_history/README.html) are three examples of such libraries.

URLs and Bookmarking

Web page URLs can be written down, sent to friends, and bookmarked. However, because the URL of a web page for an Ajax application does not change as the contents of the page change (all updates happen on the same page), special care must be taken to create URLs that can be bookmarked and emailed. Again, you'll find solutions to this problem in the Ajax frameworks in Appendix B.

Poor Design

People who have been browsing web pages for any length of time are probably all too familiar with the usual submit-wait-reload method of web interaction. In this style of communication, the entire web page updates when new information is returned from the server, which also signals to the visitor that the whole page is new. When using Ajax, on the other hand, the contents of a web page might change without the visitor noticing any signs of a change. As a web designer, you should be sure to signify important changes to web pages using design techniques, such as changing color or borders.

Ajax also offers new types of navigation to the web designer. Pre-Ajax, designers used links and images to help users navigate between web pages. Ajax and dynamic HTML offer much greater flexibility, but this flexibility can also create confusing means of navigation. For example, you *could* design a website with an interactive knob that visitors would turn to see different pages of your site. Although this interactive knob would be nifty, it might also confuse most web surfers, who are accustomed to navigating websites using hyperlinks. Adding a fancy new navigation style is probably not a good idea unless you are simply trying to show off your elite Ajax skills.

For more information about potential problems with Ajax, see Chris McEvoy's article "Ajax Sucks Most of the Time"[3] and Alex Bosworth's article "Ajax Mistakes."[4]

To Ajax, or Not to Ajax

Like all technologies, Ajax can be used for good or for evil. Opinions concerning the best times to use Ajax range from "never" to "whenever possible." I tread the middle ground by keeping in mind the following bad and good uses of Ajax:

Bad: Just Because You Can

No flashy web technique should be unleashed upon your visitors just because you think it's cool—unless, of course, your visitors are going to your site expressly to see cool web tricks.

Bad: It's the Hot New Thing

Similarly, just because Ajax is new doesn't mean it solves all problems, and as we've seen, it introduces new ones. Resist the urge to add Ajax to your site just because it is the hot new thing.

Bad: Replacing Something That Works with Something New and Confusing

Hyperlinks do a great job of leading people from one web page to another. Confusing your visitors with new and unnecessary forms of navigation will most likely result in fewer users.

---

[3] See http://www.usabilityviews.com/ajaxsucks.html. Note that this article is a rewriting of an older article by Jakob Neilsen titled "Why Frames Suck (Most of the Time)," which is available at http://www.useit.com/alertbox/9612.html.

[4] See http://sourcelabs.com/ajb/archives/2005/05/ajax_mistakes.html.

Good: In-Context Data Manipulation

Imagine you are the CEO of a big company, and you are presented with a table of information about your employees. This table may include the name, salary, and tenure of each employee. Now, imagine you want to sort that table by name, salary, or tenure. Without Ajax, you would click a button and wait for the whole page to reload. With Ajax, the table can stay on the screen while the data are being rearranged, which is far less disruptive.

In this example, the object you are manipulating stays in front of you while you are manipulating it. This is a good use of Ajax.

Another example of in-context data manipulation is Google Maps' use of Ajax. In Google Maps, you can move the map by dragging on it. The rest of the page does not change, and at no point is the screen blank. Mapping applications that do not use Ajax reload the entire web page each time you want to pan a map.

Good: Interactive Widgets

Interactive *widgets* are small components of a website that generally appear on the margins of a web page. Items such as news tickers, quick one-question polls ("Do you prefer cats or dogs?"), and login forms fall into this category. In each of these cases, interacting with the widget may produce results that do not require the entire web page to reload.

For example, if a visitor tries to log in with an invalid username or password, the error message might as well appear on the current web page, rather than bringing the visitor to an entirely new page that says nothing but *Invalid login*. Similarly, the current poll results might show up exactly where the poll the user just completed was placed.

Good: Saving State

Many word processors and other applications have an auto-save function, which stores a user's work from time to time. The same functionality can be added to a web application using Ajax's ability to send information to a webserver without alerting or disturbing the user. This kind of behind-the-scenes application of asynchronous behavior is a perfect context for Ajax.

Summary

This chapter has covered the basics of using Ajax, including:

- How client-server communication using Ajax differs from the traditional type of web-based client-server communication
- How to create a request object and send requests
- How to get results from a request object once the request has been fulfilled

- What asynchronicity means, and what it can do for you
- What problems may arise
- When to use Ajax

This is just the first of three chapters on Ajax. The next chapter deals with how to use XML to share information between a web browser and a webserver. Chapter 16 gets you started with writing programs that run on webservers and communicate with the Ajax you learned in this chapter and that you'll learn in Chapter 15.

Assignment

The JavaScript in Figure 14-4 used Ajax to read the contents of a file called sample.txt, but it did not display the contents of the file. Your assignment is to write a page that asks for a file to read in, and then displays the contents of that file in a div. Figure 14-7 depicts how a solution might look after a user entered sample.txt into the text field and clicked the Get the File button. Remember, the file that Ajax reads must live in the same directory as one that contains the Ajax code.

Figure 14-7: Displaying the contents of a file

15

XML IN JAVASCRIPT AND AJAX

Chapter 14 introduced Ajax and showed
how it works inside web browsers. Normally,
Ajax applications pass information back and
forth between a web browser and a webserver.
When a user drags a Google map, for example, the
browser sends information to the server about how the user is dragging
the map. The server then returns map-related information for the browser
to interpret and display.

Information passed back and forth between a web browser and a webserver can take many forms. This chapter discusses the form used by Ajax: XML.

In this chapter you will learn:

- What XML is and why it's useful
- How to format information using XML
- How to use JavaScript to read XML documents
- What browser-compatibility issues relate to processing XML
- How to use XML in Ajax communications

Once you've mastered the intricacies of XML, you'll be ready for Chapter 16, the final Ajax chapter. There you will learn how to write the server-side code for Ajax communications.

A Real-World Example of Ajax and XML

The photo-sharing community site Flickr (http://www.flickr.com) provides many fancy web-based tools for uploading, editing, and sharing your photos. Figure 15-1 shows how Flickr looks after I've logged in. At the top of the screen is a menu with an Organize button. Clicking that button brings you to a page like the one in Figure 15-2. Here, you can drag your pictures to the canvas, edit their descriptions, change their dates, and perform a variety of other image-organizing tasks. What you don't see is the behind-the-scenes communication Flickr uses to retrieve your images from its webserver. Using a handy debugging tool called the XmlHttpRequest debugger (which I'll describe in detail in Chapter 18), I was able to watch a bit of that communication. As the web page in Figure 15-2 opens, the browser sends an Ajax query to the Flickr server, and the server answers with a list of the images I have already uploaded. Figure 15-3 shows part of the webserver's response.

Figure 15-1: Flickr user home page

The gobbledygook you see in Figure 15-3 is XML, the standard way of communicating information in Ajax. If you look at it long enough, you'll see that the response describes three photos. Each photo has a title, a date it was uploaded, a date it was taken, and a bunch of other information. In addition to this information, you'll see lots of tags that look something like HTML tags. This information is processed by the JavaScript in Flickr's web page and turned into a nice interface like the one in Figure 15-2. The XML document is a bit hard to understand, but keep in mind that XML is meant for programs, not people. Normal humans are not supposed to see XML in the raw like this. Only programmers like us have that honor.

Figure 15-2: Flickr Organize page

Although Flickr is a great example of a site that uses XML in its client-server communications, the application is a bit too complicated to use as an instructional example. Instead, this chapter will show you how to use XML to create a application much like Google's enhanced search engine interface, Google Suggest.

```
<?xml version = "1.0" encoding = "utf-8" ?>
<rsp stat = "ok">
  <photos page = "1" pages = "1" perpage = "100" total = "32">
    <photo id = "51544990" owner = "76267260@N00" secret = "f69c737a26" server
= "27" title = "Strawberry Picking down the 1" ispublic = "1" isfriend = "0"
isfamily = "0" dateupload = "1129035992" datetaken = "2005-09-26 00:14:57"
datetakengranularity = "0" latitude = "0" longitude = "0" accuracy = "0"
ownername = "thau" iconserver = "0" />
    <photo id = "51544989" owner = "76267260@N00" secret = "e64704958b" server
= "33" title = "Fuel Cell Bus at Davis" ispublic = "1" isfriend = "0" isfamily
= "0" dateupload = "1129035992" datetaken = "2005-10-01 17:12:52"
datetakengranularity = "0" latitude = "0" longitude = "0" accuracy = "0"
ownername = "thau" iconserver = "0" />
    <photo id = "51542442" owner = "76267260@N00" secret = "6032d0feb8" server
= "27" title = "Grapes, ready for the crushing" ispublic = "1" isfriend = "0"
isfamily = "0" dateupload = "1129035221" datetaken = "2005-10-03 16:09:58"
datetakengranularity = "0" latitude = "0" longitude = "0" accuracy = "0"
ownername = "thau" iconserver = "0" />
  </photos>
</rsp>
```

Figure 15-3: Part of Flickr's webserver XML response (I removed 29 of the photos)

Google Suggest

Google Suggest (http://labs.google.com/suggest) is just like the usual Google search engine, but as you type a word into the search field, it presents a list of frequently searched-for terms beginning with the letters you have already typed, along with the number of results you'd get if you searched for each of those terms. For example, Figure 15-4 shows what happens when I commit the narcissistic act of typing my name into Google's search field. Each time I type a letter into the search field, Google Suggest gets information from Google's webserver and updates the page. In typical Ajax fashion, this trip to the server occurs invisibly.

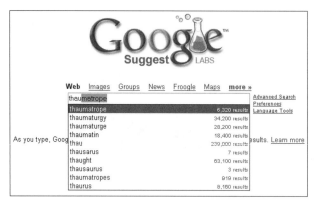

Figure 15-4: Finding myself in Google Suggest

In this chapter, we will use XML to create an Ajax application much like Google Suggest.

XML—the Extensible Markup Language

XML is a standard way of representing information that can be stored in a file or shared between machines. Computers have been storing and sharing information since they were first created. In the past, people who wrote software invented their own formats for sharing information. Imagine a language translation program that stores its dictionary in a file. The file will contain words in English and their translations into another language, say, Italian.

That file can be formatted any number of ways. For example, it might have each English word and its Italian translation on one line, separated by a colon:

```
a: un, uno, una
aardvark: oritteropo
```

Alternatively, the file could have an English word on one line, the Italian translation on the next line, and then a blank line before the next English word:

```
a
un, uno, una

aardvark
oritteropo
```

There are infinitely many ways to format a file for a computer. As long as the computer understands the format of the file, it will be able to do something with the information inside. Unfortunately, all these different file formats make it difficult to create tools that can work with arbitrary files. How can a program or a tool know that the first file uses one line for each English word and translation, while the second file uses two lines for the English word and its translation?

This is where XML comes in. XML is a standard file format ratified by the World Wide Web Consortium in 1998 (http://www.w3.org/XML). Since the standard's release, XML has become *the* way to store and share structured text documents.

A *structured document* is one that can be divided up into meaningful components. For example, *The Book of JavaScript* is structured. It has chapters, each of which has a title at the start and a summary near the end. Each chapter also has a number of large sections indicated by headers in large print, and these sections can be subdivided into shorter parts marked by smaller-print headers.

Most text documents designed to be read and processed by computers have some sort of structure; XML is a standard way to describe that structure to a computer. XML has become so popular that all modern web browsers come with built-in methods to read and process XML documents. Similarly, all major programming languages used by webservers also have XML-processing facilities. Because both web browsers and webservers under-stand XML, they can communicate with each other by sending messages that conform to the XML standard.

The Rules of XML

The rules for XML documents are simple and few. As another example of an XML document, consider the XML-style English-to-Italian dictionary in Figure 15-5.

```
❶ <?xml version = "1.0" ?>
❷ <dictionary>
    <word>
      <english>a</english>
      <translation>un, uno, una</translation>
    </word>
    <word>
❸     <english>aardvark</english>
      <translation>oritteropo</translation>
    </word>
  </dictionary>
```

Figure 15-5: A simple XML document

The XML Header

All XML documents start with an XML header like the one in Figure15-5. XML headers can also include an optional attribute called an *encoding*, as you can see in the first line of Figure 15-3. This encoding tells an XML processor what kind of characters to expect in the document.

XML Elements

XML elements are used to mark up information. For example, to indicate that something is an English word, we might define an XML element called english. Most XML elements have a start and end tag; in this case, the english element has a start tag, `<english>`, and an end tag `</english>`. To indicate that *aardvark* is an English word, we would use the following XML: `<english>aardvark</english>` (❸).

XML elements can nest inside each other. The nesting must be *proper*—that is, the inner XML element must be closed before the outer XML element is closed. Element names must begin with a letter and should not contain spaces or punctuation other than periods (.), hyphens (-), and underscores (_).

If there are no XML elements or text inside the open and close tags of an XML element, that element is called *empty*. An empty XML element can be shortened from `<emptyElement></emptyElement>` to `<emptyElement/>`. It does not have an end tag, but the closing bracket has a slash before it.

The document in Figure 15-5 has several XML elements: dictionary, word, english, and translation. A computer program that understands XML could read this document and know that aardvark and a are both considered english things, and that english things and translation things are parts of word things, which are parts of a dictionary thing. Because the document is in XML, we would not have to tell the program that the English and Italian words are separated by a colon or that each line represents an English/Italian pair.

XML Attributes

Elements can have *attributes*. An element with an attribute looks like this: `<a href = "http://www.nostarch.com">No Starch Press</a>` This is an XML element named a with an attribute named href. The value of the attribute is quoted. Attribute names follow the same rules as element names: They must begin with a letter and should not contain spaces or punctuation other than periods (.), hyphens (-), or underscores (_). Empty elements can still have attributes: `<person name = "thau!"/>`

NOTE *Did you notice that the XML above is also HTML? HTML is almost a type of XML. The main difference between it and XML is that HTML is more relaxed. For example, the element: `<img src = "hello.gif">` is valid HTML, but not valid XML. To be valid XML it would have to look like this: `<img src = "hello.gif"/>`. Notice the slash before the closing bracket.*

Illegal XML Characters

Certain special characters (', ", <, >, and &) are not allowed in an element name, an attribute name, attribute values, or text between the elements. If you need to use one of these characters you must use an encoding known as an *entity*, which is introduced by an ampersand (&) and terminated with a semicolon (;). Use the entities < and > to represent the angle brackets

< and >, and use &apos; and &quot; to represent apostrophe and quotation marks. Because it introduces entities, the ampersand itself is a special character. If you need to use an ampersand as itself, you must use the entity &amp;.

To ensure maximum cross-browser interoperability, all non-ASCII characters should be encoded using their Unicode decimal numbers. For example, the character á (a with an acute accent) should be encoded as &#225;. (See http://www.unicode.org/charts for the entire set of character entities and http://www.webmonkey.com/webmonkey/reference/special_characters for a less complete, but more usable, list.)

XML Documents Have a Single Root Element

An XML document must have only one *root element*. The root element is the first XML element in the document, and all the other elements of the XML document go between its open and close tags. For example, in Figure 15-5 the root element is dictionary (❷).

Final Comments About the XML Format

As already mentioned, XML has become an incredibly pervasive standard. One feature of XML that makes it particularly useful is that you can invent any element names you desire. This means that organizations can agree upon a set of XML elements that work for them and that can be used to structure all information within their organization or field. Varieties of XML, called *XML vocabularies* or *markup languages*, have been invented for many applications, such as SVG for describing two-dimensional graphics, GedML for genealogical information, GML for geographic information, VRML for describing objects in 3D, and SportsML, which the International Press Telecommunications Council uses to publish sports information. Each of these uses the rules of XML and a set of predefined element and attribute names. When using XML, you can either use existing vocabulary or create your own.

The format of an XML document is just the tip of the XML iceberg. There are many useful technologies built around XML, including standard ways to search XML documents, ways to convert XML documents into PDFs and HTML, and ways to ensure that XML documents conform to specific vocabularies (such as GML, VRML, and the others described above).

Processing XML

XML is so popular that web browsers have built-in mechanisms for dealing with XML documents. In fact, all of the methods used to process the DOM (discussed in Chapter 13) can also be used to process XML documents.

The script in Figure 15-6 shows how to use some of the methods that we used to process the DOM to create an application that looks up a word in three dictionary files (German, Portuguese, and Italian), which I downloaded from the Internet Dictionary Project (http://www.ilovelanguages.com/IDP).

```
    <html><head><title>Reading XML Documents</title>
    <script type = "text/javascript">
    <!-- hide me from older browsers
❶  function getTranslations(the_word) {
      var languages = new Array("german","italian","portuguese");
      for (var loop = 0; loop < languages.length; loop++) {
        getTranslationFromFile(languages[loop], the_word);
      }
    }
❷  function getTranslationFromFile(the_file, the_word) {
      var request = null;
      var xml_response = null;
      if (window.XMLHttpRequest) {
        request = new XMLHttpRequest();
      } else if (window.ActiveXObject) {
        request = new ActiveXObject("Microsoft.XMLHTTP");
      }

      if (request) {
❸      request.open("GET", the_file + ".xml");
        request.onreadystatechange =
          function() {
            if (request.readyState == 4) {
❹            xml_response = request.responseXML;
❺            document.getElementById(the_file).innerHTML =
                findTranslation(xml_response, the_word);
            } else {
❻            document.getElementById(the_file).innerHTML =
                "SEARCHING...";
            }
          }
        request.send(null);
      } else {
        alert("Sorry, you must update your browser before seeing" +
          " Ajax in action.");
      }
    }
❼  function findTranslation(xml_doc, the_word) {
      var the_translation = "unknown";
      var this_word = "";
      var this_english_element = null;
❽    var english_word_elements =
        xml_doc.getElementsByTagName("english");
      for (var loop = 0; loop < english_word_elements.length; loop++) {
        this_english_element = english_word_elements[loop];
❾      this_word = this_english_element.firstChild.nodeValue;
        if (this_word == the_word) {
❿          the_translation =
            this_english_element.nextSibling.firstChild.nodeValue;
        }
      }
      return the_translation;
    }
```

```
// show me -->
</script>
</head>
<body>
<form
  onSubmit = "getTranslations(document.getElementById('theText').value);
    return false;">
  <input type = "text" id = "theText">
  <input type = "button"
  onClick = "getTranslations(document.getElementById('theText').value);
    return false;" value = "Translate!">
</form>
<b>Portuguese:</b> <span id = "portuguese"></span><br>
<b>Italian:</b> <span id = "italian"></span ><br>
<b>German:</b> <span id = "german"></span ><br>
</body>
</html>
```

Figure 15-6: Reading an XML document

As you can see in Figure 15-7, entering aardvark into the text box and clicking the Translate! button translates the provided word into the three languages.

Figure 15-7: Translating aardvark

NOTE *Unless the XML dictionary files are served up using a webserver, the script in Figure 15-6 will not work in Internet Explorer. To understand why not, why it doesn't matter too much, and what you can do about it, see the section "Internet Explorer, responseXML, and Client-Side Ajax" on page 291.*

Line-by-Line Analysis of Figure 15-6

The script in Figure 15-6 begins when a user clicks the Translate! button or when the user presses ENTER while the cursor is in the text box (thereby submitting the form). In either case, the function getTranslations() is called with the contents of the text box. The getTranslations() function in ❶ simply calls getTranslationsFromFile() for each of the dictionary files.

NOTE *It's nice to use an array and a loop here, because if we want to add a new language file, we can just add it to the languages array.*

The getTranslationsFromFile() function in ❷ is called once for each language. It has two parameters: the name of a language and the word to translate. This function is the typical Ajax function we've seen, with a few twists. First, in ❸ notice that the request is getting a file whose name is the name of the language we want to translate, with the extension .xml. Once the request has been answered, ❹ retrieves the value of the request's responseXML property. Then ❺ calls the findTranslation() function and puts its results into an element with an id attribute set to the language.

NOTE   *Notice that the variable passed into the getTranslationsFromFile() function is used to name both the file being read and the element into which the answer should be placed. Using one variable in multiple contexts is a common trick. Also notice that ❻ puts the string "SEARCHING..." into the element, which will soon hold the result whenever the request object changes into any state other than 4. This is a good way to let your users know that your page is doing something and that there is more information to come.*

Visualizing the XML Document

All of the XML handling is done in the findTranslation() function (❼), which is called once the XML document has been fully loaded (after the equal sign in ❺). To understand better how findTranslation() works, see Figure 15-8, which represents part of the XML document in Figure 15-5 graphically. The root element of the XML document, dictionary, appears as a node at the top of Figure 15-8.

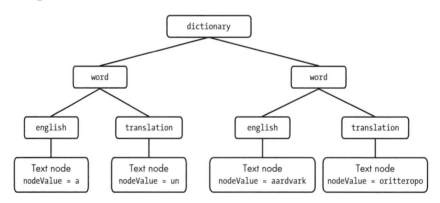

Figure 15-8: A graphical representation of part of the XML in Figure 15-5

The dictionary node has two child nodes, each named word, which represent the word elements in Figure 15-5. Each word node in Figure 15-8, in turn, has two children, named english and translation, representing the english and translation elements in Figure 15-5. These elements each have some text between their open and close tags: an English word and its translation. The text stored between the tags of an XML element is stored in a *text node* that is a child of that element. If the only thing between an element's open and close tags is text, the text node containing that text is the *first child* of the element. In order actually to get the text from the text node, the node's nodeValue property must be accessed. We'll see that working soon.

Navigating the XML Document

Now let's return to the findTranslation() function. The function first sets the translation to "unknown" and, if no other translation is found, this will be the result returned. The first sign of XML handling is in ❽, which uses the getElementsByTagName() method (discussed in Chapter 13) to return an array of all the elements of the XML document with the name "english". You can see these elements in the XML in Figure 15-5.

Once that array of elements is returned, the function loops through the array. Each time through the loop, the variable this_english_element is set to the next english element in the array, and ❾ extracts the English word between the open and close tags of the element. Line ❿ then extracts the translation of that english element.

Extracting Information from XML Elements

Lines ❾ and ❿ are complicated enough to deserve their own figure. Figure 15-9 is a graphic representation of the process of translating the word *aardvark*. Assume that we've retrieved the list of elements named english and have looped past the first english element. We're now looking at the second english element in the list, which is labeled in the figure with the box containing the words this_english_element. The this_english_element element has a child element that is a text node with a nodeValue of aardvark.

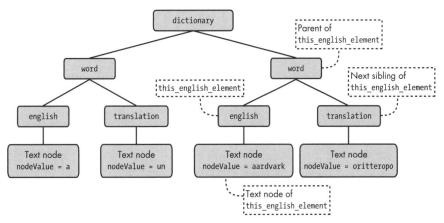

Figure 15-9: A graphical representation of getting a word's translation

Line ❾ extracts the value "aardvark" from this_english_element. Here's ❾ again:

```
this_word = this_english_element.firstChild.nodeValue
```

This line looks at the built-in firstChild property of the XML element stored in this_english_element, which is a text node, and then it retrieves the nodeValue of that text node. The line following ❾ checks to see whether this word is the word we want to translate. If it is, ❿ retrieves the translation of the word.

To understand ⑩, look back at Figure 15-9. Notice that the parent of the node labeled this_english_element is a word node and that it has been labeled *Parent of* this_english_element. This word node has two children: this_english_element and a translation node. As is true of people, any two XML nodes that share a parent are called *siblings*. The sibling that comes right after an XML node is called that node's *next sibling*. The sibling next to this_english_element is the node labeled *Next Sibling of* this_english_element. This next sibling can be accessed using the built-in property nextSibling. Now look at ⑩:

```
the_translation = this_english_element.nextSibling.firstChild.nodeValue
```

The code in ⑩ gets the translation of this_english_element by looking at this_english_element, finding its next sibling (the translation node), getting that node's first child (the text node), and then retrieving the nodeValue of that text node.

Wrapping Up

Before wrapping up Figure 15-6, let's review. A visitor has entered a word into a text field and clicked the Translate! button. This calls getTranslations(), which loops through a list of languages into which the provided word should be translated. Each time through the loop, getTranslationFromFile() is passed the name of a language and the word to translate. The getTranslationFromFile() function performs an Ajax call that reads in an XML dictionary for that language and then calls findTranslation() to get the translation. The findTranslation() function does all the XML handling just covered and returns the found translation back to the getTranslationFromFile() function. Now we're ready to wrap up.

Once findTranslation() finds and returns the translation of the requested word, ⑤ in getTranslationFromFile() puts the translation into the span with an id equal to the name of the language being processed. This makes the translation appear on the web page and completes the Ajax request for this language.

As with all things Ajax, the calls in getTranslationsFromFile() all are satisfied asynchronously. Once the user clicks the Translate! button, the language files are all accessed simultaneously, the translations are retrieved, and the results are placed in the <span> tags at the bottom of the HTML.

NOTE *I've used spans instead of divs to avoid a line break between the text listing the language (e.g., Italian) and the returned translation.*

This example has shown you the fundamentals of processing XML documents in JavaScript. The rest of the chapter will cover a few niggling details and then take you through another example of using XML in Ajax.

Internet Explorer, responseXML, and Client-Side Ajax

I noted in the previous section that the script in Figure 15-6 will not work on Internet Explorer if the XML dictionary files are not served up by a webserver. This is because Internet Explorer fills the `responseXML` property only if the browser is told that the file being read is an XML file. If the file is being read straight off the hard drive (and not sent by a webserver), Internet Explorer won't know that this is an XML file rather than an ordinary text file.

In general, this is not really a problem. If you are developing a web page that will be available to anyone other than you, you will need to use a webserver to serve it and all the documents relating to it. Therefore, in practice, the XML files will be served by a webserver, and Figure 15-6 should work just as it is. The only time this Internet Explorer "feature" will cause problems is when testing and debugging your Ajax code without using a webserver. Fortunately, there is a simple fix: Replace ❹ in Figure 15-6 with this:

```
xml_response = new ActiveXObject("Microsoft.XMLDOM");
xml_response.loadXML(request.responseText);
```

These lines use a special Microsoft ActiveXObject to turn the contents of the request's `responseText` property into XML.

Problems with White Space in XML

Some browsers, such as Firefox, like to treat blank spaces in XML documents (including spaces used to indent tags) as text nodes. As you might imagine, these unexpected text nodes can cause problems when using JavaScript to navigate around an XML page.

To solve this problem, you can write some JavaScript to remove all text nodes in the XML with `nodeValues` that contain only spaces, or you can write your JavaScript to simply ignore these blank text nodes (which usually appear between XML elements).

For example, if Firefox reads this line of XML

```
<word><english>a</english> <translation>un</translation></word>
```

the XML document stored in `request.responseXML` will contain a word element with three children: an english element, a text node with the space between the english and translation elements, and the translation element. This means that the `nextSibling` property of the english element would point to the text node rather than to the translation element. This is bad news for the script in Figure 15-6, which assumes that each english element will be followed by a translation element rather than by a text node containing only a space.

A more flexible version of Figure 15-6 would do one of two things. First, the JavaScript could preprocess the XML document, deleting all the text nodes that contain only spaces. Alternatively, the code could leave the extra text nodes in place but just skip nodes that it doesn't care about. For example, when looking for the translation of an English word, the code in Figure 15-6 could loop through the children of the parent of the english element, checking the nodeName of each child and stopping when it finds an element named translation.

As it is now, the code in Figure 15-6 works fine because the XML files I created do not have a space between the english and translation elements. For our purposes, this works. In the real world, however, you would want to write code that would deal with the possibility that somebody writing an XML dictionary for your application would accidentally put a space between the english and translation elements.

Creating a Suggest Application for Translation

Let's apply what we've learned so far to another example of using XML with Ajax. Google Suggest is a very fancy web application, with many interesting features that help it react quickly to user queries. As shown in Figure 15-4, Google Suggest provides suggested searches as you type letters into the search box. Although the JavaScript I'll describe in this section is not nearly as advanced as what you see in Google Suggest, it should help to demonstrate how Google Suggest works.

Figure 15-10 shows a simplified suggest application that translates English words into Italian. The figure shows how things look in Internet Explorer after I type bo. On the left side you see a list of the first ten English words in the dictionary that start with the letters *bo*, and on the right side are their translations. After each keypress, the script reloads the italian.xml file and looks for words that begin with whatever letters are in the text box. As is typical with Ajax, there is no submit button to push; the JavaScript accesses the information it needs and updates the page as I type.

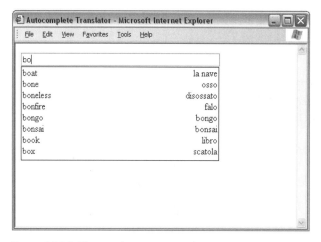

Figure 15-10: The translation script with suggestions

For a full description of how Google Suggest works, see Chris Justice's excellent analysis at http://serversideguy.blogspot.com/2004/12/google-suggest-dissected.html.

The code for this neat little application can be found in Appendix D and is available at http://www.bookofjavascript.com/Chapter15/translator.html. It is a bit long, so I will break it up a bit as I describe it here.

NOTE   *Remember, this code will not work if you are testing it in Internet Explorer unless you serve up the italian.xml file using a webserver. If you don't have access to a webserver and you want to test the script out, make sure to make the change described in the section "Internet Explorer, responseXML, and Client-Side Ajax" on page 291.*

Let's begin with the text entry form:

```
<form>
  <input type = "text" size = "55" id = "theText"
    onKeyUp = "getTranslations('italian', this.value);">
  <div id = "theResults" style = "width:22em; border:1px black solid;
    padding-left:2px;padding-right:2px">
  </div>
</form>
```

This form has one text input element and a div into which the results of the script will be placed. The ems you see in the style of the div set the width of the div equal to some multiple of the width of the letter *m* (em) in the font being used. The size of the em unit will vary with the font being used, in direct proportion to the width of the letter *m* in that font. As a result, if a user changes the font size on his or her browser, the script will automatically adjust the width of the div. The JavaScript code will automatically change the height of the div as the number of results to be shown changes.

Notice that the text input element has an onKeyUp event handler. When a letter is typed (that is, a key is pressed), and then released, the getTranslations() function is called upon the release of the key. This function is almost exactly like the getTranslationFromFile() function shown in Figure 15-6 except for the anonymous function defined after ❸, which has been changed to:

```
request.onreadystatechange =
  function() {
    if (request.readyState == 4) {
      xml_response = request.responseXML;
      displayResults(findTranslations(xml_response, the_word));
    }
  }
```

When the state of the request object changes to 4, it has completely downloaded the requested document. At this point it calls findTranslations() to get the relevant words and translations, and then it sends those results to the displayResults() function.

Finding the Translations

The findTranslations() function searches through the XML file for the correct words to display. Figure 15-11 is a slightly abridged version:

```
function findTranslations(xml_doc, the_word) {
    // obvious variable declarations and initializations (omitted)
    var these_translations = new Array();
    var english_word_elements = xml_doc.getElementsByTagName("english");
❶   var reg_exp = new RegExp("^" + the_word);
❷   while ((loop < english_word_elements.length) && (found == false)) {
❸     this_word = english_word_elements[loop].firstChild.nodeValue;
❹     if (reg_exp.test(this_word)) {
        the_translation =
          english_word_elements[loop].nextSibling.firstChild.nodeValue;
        found = true;
      }
      loop++;
    }
❺  if (found == true) {
❻    these_translations.push(this_word + "\t" + the_translation);
❼    for (var count = loop; count < (loop + 10); count++) {
❽      if (count < english_word_elements.length) {
        this_word = english_word_elements[count].firstChild.nodeValue;
        if (reg_exp.test(this_word)) {
          the_translation =
            english_word_elements[count].nextSibling.firstChild.nodeValue;
          these_translations.push(this_word + "\t" + the_translation);
        }
      }
    }
  }
  return these_translations;
}
```

Figure 15-11: Finding the translations

The findTranslations() function shown in Figure 15-11 is similar to the findTranslations() function shown in Figure 15-6, except that instead of getting just one translation for a word, it looks for up to ten words that begin with the letters in the text box, with their translations. If only seven words begin with the letters in the text box, only those seven words will be displayed.

The function uses regular expressions (discussed in Chapter 11) to determine whether a word starts with the letters in the box (❶). Next, it gets a list of all the XML elements named english and loops through that list until either it runs out of elements or it finds a word that matches the regular expression (❷). Each time through the loop, this_word is set to the English word (❸), and then ❹ checks to see whether this_word matches the regular expression. If it does, the translation of the word is retrieved from the english element's sibling, the found variable is set to true, and the loop ends.

At the end of the loop, ❺ checks to see whether a word has been found that matches the regular expression. If so, ❻ sticks the word, followed by a tab (\t) and the word's translation at the end of an array called these_translations. The these_translations array now has one word and its translation, and it will eventually contain all the words and translations to be displayed.

NOTE *The push() method (❻) is a handy way to add something to the end of an array; it pushes an element to the end.*

Once the retrieved word and translation have been added to the array, it's time to find other words that begin with the letters in the text field. The loop in ❼ begins by examining the items in the array of english elements, starting where the previous loop left off. It then looks at the next nine items. Each time through the loop, the code gets the next english element, checks to see whether it matches the regular expression, and if so, adds it and its translation to the these_translations array. The code in ❽ makes sure the loop ends if there are no more elements in the array of english elements to consider, which may happen, for example, if we are looking at words that begin with the letter *z*.

When the loop in ❼ ends, the function exits and returns the these_translations array, which is then fed into the displayResults() function.

Displaying the Results

The function displayResults(), which displays the results, is pretty straight-forward (as shown in Figure 15-12). The function first creates an HTML table and then inserts that table into the innerHTML of theResultsDiv. The only tricky thing about this script involves changing the size of the div so that its border expands and contracts as the table changes size.

```
    function displayResults(the_results) {
      var display_me = "";
      var splitter;
      var this_result = null;
❶    for (var loop = 0; loop < the_results.length; loop++) {
        this_result = the_results[loop];
        if (this_result != null) {
❷        splitter = this_result.split("\t");
❸        display_me += "<tr><td align='left'>" + splitter[0] +
            "</td><td align='right'>" + splitter[1] + "</td></tr>";
        }
      }
❹    document.getElementById("theResults").style.height =
        (the_results.length + parseInt(the_results.length / 5) + 1) + "em";
❺    document.getElementById("theResults").innerHTML =
        "<table width='100%' border='0' cellpadding='0' cellspacing='0'>" +
        display_me + "</table>";
    }
```

Figure 15-12: Displaying the results

The `displayResults()` function is passed an array of results to display. The code in ❶ loops through this array, setting `this_result` to the next result each time it goes through the loop.

NOTE   *Remember that each result is an English word, followed by a tab and the word's translation in Italian (see ❺ in Figure 15-11).*

The `split()` method in ❷ is a built-in method of `String` objects. Given a character, or a set of characters, the `split()` method divides a string into parts and stores those parts in an array. For example, the instance of `split()` in ❷ takes the string in `the_result` and divides it into two parts: the part before the tab (`\t`) and the part after the tab. These pieces are stored in an array called `splitter`; `splitter[0]` contains the part before the tab, and `splitter[1]` contains the part after the tab. The code in ❸ then takes these parts, creates a string representing a row in an HTML table, and adds this string to the `display_me` variable, which will contain all the rows of the table.

Once the loop completes, ❹ changes the `height` property of the div's style property, making it roughly as tall as the table that it will contain. The formula in ❹ gives an approximation of the div's height; it says that the div's height should equal the number of rows in the table plus a little bit for the space between the rows. The number of rows in the table, in turn, equals the number of items in the `the_results` array. Finally, ❺ puts the beginning and ending table tags on the table and puts the table into the `innerHTML` of the div.

There's a great deal more to Google Suggest, including choosing an element from the suggestion box, caching results to make the page react more quickly, and filling in a few letters in the text box. With the JavaScript you know now, and a little expertise with cascading style sheets, you should be able to add those features to your own applications.

Summary

This chapter has covered the basics of using XML with JavaScript and Ajax:

- What XML is used for
- How to format XML documents
- How Ajax applications use XML to share data
- How to process XML with JavaScript
- How to deal with cross-browser XML issues

The chapter has also given you more details about some objects you've already encountered:

- How to use the `split()` method to divide a string into parts
- How to use the `push()` method to add an element to the end of an array
- How to use `em` in a cascading style sheet to make the size of something proportional to the font being used

Now that you know how to perform Ajax calls from the browser, and how to format XML documents and process them with JavaScript, it's time to complete the Ajax cycle and learn about server-side programs. First, however, you should practice your Ajax skills with the following assignment.

Assignment

Write an Ajax address book like the one shown in Figure 15-13. First, create an XML file that is to be your address book. Each person should have a name, a home address, a phone number, and an email address. When the web page opens, it should get the names of the people in the XML file and then put them into the select field. When a user clicks a name in the select field, Ajax should look up that person in the phone book and display the results in the spans below the select box.

Figure 15-13: An Ajax-enabled address book

16

SERVER-SIDE AJAX

In Chapter 15 we saw how Ajax can enhance your user's experience by making asynchronous requests for information. In that chapter we focused entirely on client-side Ajax. In this chapter we'll focus on using Ajax to communicate with programs on webservers, which I will also call *server-side programs*.

This chapter explains:

- What server-side programs can do for you
- Different types of requests
- The basics of PHP, a server-side programming language
- How to use PHP to read and save files on webservers
- What to do if the webserver you are contacting doesn't respond
- How to update the contents of a web browser automatically when a server-side file changes

Real-World Examples of Server-Side Ajax

Almost all examples of Ajax on the Web involve communications between a web browser and a program running on a webserver. For example, when you search for a restaurant using Google Maps, Google's webservers provide the maps and determine where the icon showing the restaurant's location should go. The Ajax-driven To Do list site, http://www.tadalist.com, lets you create To Do lists and then share them so that others (whether in your household or organization) can add tasks, mark completed tasks, and so on.

Figure 16-1 shows my *Book of JavaScript* To Do list. At the top are uncompleted items (don't tell my publisher!), and below those are finished items. (I'm still waiting to celebrate; any day now, for sure.)

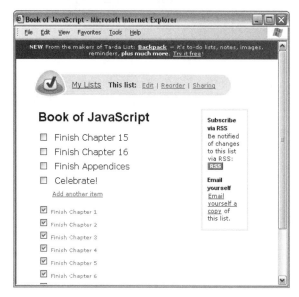

Figure 16-1: A Ta-da List To Do list

Figure 16-2 shows the screen after I click the Add Another Item link. As you can see, a text field and an Add This Item button appear. When I click the button, the new item appears on the bottom of the To Do list and is saved on the Ta-da List webserver. When I exit the browser and then return to the site, the saved To Do list is read from the Ta-da List webserver and displayed in my browser.

When we covered cookies in Chapter 12, we saw examples of how to store a user's information. For example, when a visitor bought clothing using the shopping cart, the items the visitor bought were stored on the visitor's hard drive. Then, when it was time to purchase the selected items, the checkout page retrieved this stored information and told the visitor how much was owed. The difference in the To Do list example is that rather than saving the information on the computer of the person using the web page, the application saves the information on the Ta-da List webserver. As you may recall, browsers limit the amount of information you can save in a cookie on a visitor's hard drive to about 80 kilobytes. In contrast, the amount of information stored on a webserver's hard drive is limited only by the amount of space on the hard drive. Another difference between saving information in a cookie on a user's hard drive and saving it on a webserver's hard drive is that information on a webserver can be shared by anybody who accesses that server with his or her web browser.

Figure 16-2: Adding a new item to the To Do list

Notice the Sharing link at the right end of the navigation bar at the top of the list in Figures 16-1 and 16-2. When the link is clicked, it brings up a page that allows you to input an email address for the person you want to set up as a sharer. Ta-da List then emails a code to that address that lets the recipient modify the list you've shared. Sharing is made possible because both you (the list owner) and the list sharer are using web browsers to alter information that is shared on a single, remote webserver that anyone with the correct code can access.

In this chapter I'll teach you what you need to know to build your own collaborative To Do list Ajax application. However, since such an application is complex and involves a fair amount of code (which pulls together elements from every chapter of this book), I will cover the application in depth only in Chapter 17.

The Power of Webservers

Until now, we have focused on JavaScript programs, which run in a web browser. These programs can save information on the local computer and rely on the local computer for their system resources. This chapter will focus on programs that run on webservers—programs that save information to a remote server and rely on that webserver for much of the heavy lifting.

We touched briefly on webserver-based programs in Chapter 7 when we discussed submitting forms to webservers. However, in that chapter, once the information was sent from the web browser to the webserver, we didn't worry about it. Now we do; it's time to dig into the details of webserver programs.

You can use programs that run on webservers to enhance your JavaScript in two ways. First, when a JavaScript program interacts with a server-side program, every web browser running that JavaScript can access and interact with the same webserver. For example, if 100 (or 10,000) people use that JavaScript, then all can interact with the same webserver. As a result, everyone's information can be stored in one central spot: the server. In contrast, when we use cookies to store information, the information is stored only on the user's machine. Because cookies store information locally, we're prevented from doing useful things such as compiling answers to a survey taken by multiple users. On the other hand, when a server-side program is used to store those answers on a webserver, all of those answers can be collected and analyzed simply by accessing that webserver.

You can also use server-side programs to enhance your JavaScript by invoking the "magical" powers of the machines running webservers. For example, although you can't use JavaScript to send email via a web browser (the browser doesn't know how to send email), a computer running a webserver may be able to send email, so you may be able to use it to send an email with information submitted via a web browser form.

Because a webserver can communicate with other Internet-connected servers, you can also use a webserver to circumvent one of the limitations of the request object that we covered in Chapter 14. Specifically, for security reasons, many web browsers, such as Firefox, will not let JavaScript that comes from one webserver send an Ajax request to another webserver—a limitation that can be quite restrictive.

For example, imagine that you want to write some Ajax that requests information from Google Maps and combines the returned information with weather information from weather.com, perhaps marking spots on the map where temperature records have been broken that day. Although some browsers will stop an Ajax script from using a request object to get information directly from weather.com, you can write an Ajax script that contacts a webserver, have the webserver get the information from weather.com, and then send that information back to the browser.

Figure 16-3 illustrates this transaction nicely. On the left side of the figure, you see a browser requesting and receiving a page from the No Starch Press website. The returned page contains some Ajax code that tries to use a request object to get information from the weather.com server. (I don't know; they're really into the weather in San Francisco.) Unfortunately, this request is illegal, and it triggers a "Permission denied" error in Firefox and other browsers.

We circumvent this error by using the technique demonstrated at the right side of Figure 16-3. This time, when the web browser requests a page from NoStarch.com, the Ajax in that page makes another request to NoStarch.com asking a program running on the NoStarch.com webserver to request information from the weather.com server. When the weather.com server answers that request, the NoStarch.com server-side program passes the information back to the user's web browser. Because the web browser never directly requests information from the weather.com server, the action is allowed, and you don't see the "Permission denied" error. This style of communication is possible only with server-side programs.

Next, you'll learn some server-side programming basics.

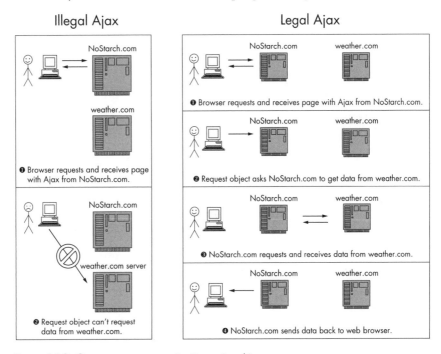

Figure 16-3: Cross-server communication using Ajax

A Server-Side Programming Language

Webservers can run programs written in many different programming languages, but JavaScript isn't one of them. Therefore, instead of JavaScript, we'll use PHP as our server-side programming language.

The acronym *PHP* stands for *PHP: Hypertext Preprocessor*. (This kind of self-referential naming passes for humor among computer programmers.) PHP is popular because its code can be incorporated directly into HTML pages, it's free, and it's cross-platform compatible.

NOTE   *In order to try the examples in this chapter, you'll need access to a webserver that runs PHP. See "Setting Up a Webserver and PHP" on page 273 for some resources describing how to set one up for Windows, Mac, and Linux computers.*

Popular alternatives to PHP include Perl, C++, C#, Python, Ruby, and Java (which is different from JavaScript; remember Chapter 1?). The language you use will largely be determined by the languages your webserver will run and what you're familiar with. (Don't worry too much about having to learn PHP in order to do Ajax. PHP and JavaScript are very similar in many ways.)

PHP Basics

PHP code can sit in its own text file, or it can be integrated into the HTML of a web page. The characters <?php mark the beginning of PHP code, and the characters ?> mark the end of the code. Names of files containing PHP code generally have the extension .php rather than .html.

Figure 16-4 shows the "Hello, world!" program, which tradition dictates should be your first program in any language.

```
<html><head><title>"Hello, world!" in PHP</title></head>
<body>
<h1>My First PHP Program</h1>
❶ <?php
❷   print "Hello, world!";
❸ ?>
</body>
</html>
```

Figure 16-4: A basic PHP program

If you copy the contents of Figure 16-4 into a file, name it something ending in *.php*, and put the file into a directory accessible by a webserver that understands PHP, you'll see something like Figure 16-5.

NOTE   *PHP programs must be run by a webserver. This means that you cannot simply "open" a PHP file using your browser. Instead, you need to enter the URL of the PHP program into your browser. If you put the PHP program in Figure 16-4 in the top-level directory of your webserver and name the file hello.php, you can access the file using this URL: http://localhost/hello.php. If that doesn't work, try http://127.0.0.1/hello.php. If that doesn't work, check your webserver's documentation to determine how to connect with your webserver.*

Figure 16-5: The web page resulting from Figure 16-4

That's it—your first PHP program. Now let's see what it does.

The code in Figure 16-4 is very simple. First, note that it's mostly HTML. The PHP starts with the opening characters in ❶ and ends with the closing characters in ❸. The only real line of PHP (❷) is the one that uses the PHP function print to put the string "Hello, world!" into the web page. This is like JavaScript's document.write() function.

As in JavaScript, strings in PHP are contained in quotation marks.

When a PHP-savvy webserver reads in a file with a name ending in *.php*, it looks for PHP statements between <?php and ?> characters and executes them. The result is a new web page that is sent to the web browser—in this case, a page with the string "Hello, world!" inside it. This transformation is similar to what happens when a web browser reads in a page with JavaScript. It looks for code between <script> and </script> tags, executes the code, and shows the user the result.

A web page can contain both PHP and JavaScript. If it does, the page is transformed twice: First, the page is read by the webserver, which executes the PHP code and sends the result to the web browser. Next, the browser executes the JavaScript code and displays the result to the user.

Sending Simple Input to PHP with a GET Request

Server-side programs generally take input from a web browser and use that input to determine what to send back to the browser. For example, with Google Maps, the input might be coordinates on a map, and the output of the server-side program would be a new map. With the Ta-da List To Do list, the input might be a new To Do item to save and the output might be a message saying whether or not the new item was successfully saved.

Input can be sent to a server-side program as part of a GET request or as part of a POST request. A GET request is used when the input you are sending to a server-side program is fairly short, such as sending a coordinate to Google Maps to be mapped. A POST request is typically used when the input is longer, such as the contents of a new To Do item. Let's start by focusing on GET requests.

Passing Input in a URL

We used GET requests when we requested a test file from our hard drive in Chapter 14. Here is an example:

```
request.open("GET", "my_file.txt");
```

This request has two parameters. The first indicates that we're making a GET request. The second tells JavaScript what we are requesting, in this case, the file named my_file.txt. However, rather than requesting a local file, a GET request usually goes to a webserver that is running a server-side program. Instead of the name of a file, the request is typically a specially formatted URL that has two parts: one part that indicates where a server-side program is running, and another part containing input to send to the program.

It's easiest to describe the format of this special URL with an example. Here's the URL used to ask Google Suggest to return a set of search terms that start with the string no starch:

```
http://www.google.com/complete/search?js=true&qu=no%20starch
```

Type that URL into your browser, and you'll get results from Google that
look like this:

```
sendRPCDone(frameElement, "no starch", new Array("no starch press", "no
starch", "no starch diet", "no starch recipes", "no starch publishing", "no
starch publisher", "no starch books", "no starch diets", "no starch
publications", "no starch vegetables"), new Array("512,000 results",
"1,150,000 results", "312,000 results", "162,000 results", "271,000 results",
" ", " ", " ", "401,000 results", "237,000 results"), new Array("")));
```

The results may look like nonsense right now, but we'll soon use them to
create a simplified version of Google Suggest.

There are a few interesting things about this URL. The part before the
question mark (`http://www.google.com/complete/search`) is just like a normal
URL; it points to where the resource lives on the Internet. The question mark
(?) indicates that the rest of the URL is input to be sent to the resource.

Input sent in a GET follows the form *key1=value1&key2=value2&key3=value3*
and so on. This example string is composed of three key-value pairs, joined
with ampersands (&). The three key-value pairs are *key1=value1*, *key2=value2*,
and *key3=value3*. A key-value pair is much like a variable and a value to store
in that variable. When this input is sent to the server-side program, the program will access the values *value1, value2,* and *value3* using the keys *key1, key2,*
and *key3*. We'll see how to do this in a moment.

NOTE   *Keys don't need to be named key1, key2 and key3. Like variables, they can be named
anything that begins with a letter or an underscore.*

Turning back to Google Suggest, the input js=true&qu=no%20starch contains
two key-value pairs: js=true and qu=no%20starch. The first of these key-value
pairs (js=true) tells Google that you want the reply to come back in a single
line of JavaScript. The second key-value pair (qu=no%starch) is the actual string
you want Google to search for. Notice the %20 in the value? Spaces are not
allowed in URLs, so we use the hexadecimal ASCII value for a space instead.

Different resources will require different inputs. There are three ways to
determine what form the input is supposed to take: One is to read the documentation provided by the resource (or someone else); the second is to code
the resource yourself (as we'll do in this chapter); and the third is to decon-
struct the JavaScript used by the resource by viewing the source on the web
page that calls the resource. How did I know that Google Suggest needs keys
named js and qu, and that the value for js needs to be true? I read it in a
good article (at http://serversideguy.blogspot.com/2004/12/google-suggest-
dissected.html). If you're writing your own server-side script, you'll go with
the second option—you'll be coding the resource yourself.

Using PHP to Read the Inputs of a GET Request

Consider the following URL:

```
http://localhost/myKeys.php?name=dave%20thau&job=slacker
```

This URL points to a PHP program called myKeys.php. The text file containing the program resides on a webserver running on my local computer, so I can reach it using the domain localhost instead of something like nostarch.com. This URL contains two input keys: name and job. Now the question is, how can the PHP program access and use this input? The answer lies in PHP's built-in $_REQUEST variable.

Figure 16-6 shows the results of running a simple PHP program that reads some keys from a URL like the one above and displays them in a web page. The code for this PHP program is shown in Figure 16-7.

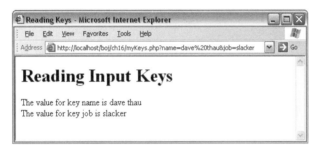

Figure 16-6: A web page displaying PHP parameters

```
<html><head><title>Reading Keys</title></head>
<body>
<h1>Reading Input Keys</h1>

<?php
❶   $name = $_REQUEST["name"];
    $job = $_REQUEST["job"];
?>

❷ The value for key name is <?php print $name; ?>  <br>

The value for key job is <?php print $job; ?> <br>

</body>
</html>
```

Figure 16-7: Accessing GET parameters in PHP

Like JavaScript, PHP has many built-in variables. One such variable is $_REQUEST, which contains all the keys sent to the PHP script using either GET or POST. To get the value of a GET key, just include that key's name in quotes between open and close brackets of the $_REQUEST variable. (In contrast to JavaScript, PHP variable names all begin with a $ sign, and they do not have to be declared with var.)

Now you should be able to understand the code in Figure 16-7. Line ❶ sets the $name variable to the value of the name key retrieved from the built-in PHP $_REQUEST variable. This value is then inserted into the web page in ❷.

Creating a Google Suggest Application with an Ajax GET Request

Let's take what we've covered so far and build a useful application with it. Figure 16-8 shows a homemade interface to the Google search engine that works much like Google Suggest. As you can see in the figure, I've typed the first few letters of the word *javascript*, and the application is showing how many results would be returned by searches starting with those letters.

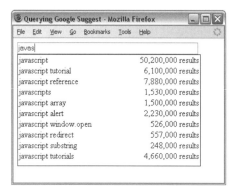

Figure 16-8: Searching for javascript in our version of Google Suggest

The page you see in Figure 16-8 is very similar to the translator example in Figure 15-10. In that example, we used Ajax to read a file containing English words and their Italian translations and then used the information in that file to show the words that matched specific user input. In Figure 16-8 the information we're showing comes from Google rather than from a file. In the following sections, I will modify the code in Figures 15-6, 15-11, and 15-12 to create a simple homemade version of Google Suggest that actually retrieves data from Google.

Contacting Third-Party Webservers with Ajax and PHP

The main challenge when modifying the code in Figures 15-6, 15-11, and 15-12 will be to retrieve information from Google instead of reading a file from the hard drive. Line ❸ in Figure 15-6 looked like this:

```
request.open("GET", the_file + ".xml");
```

This line tells JavaScript that we are requesting a file. In the section "Passing Input in a URL" on page 305, we saw how to format a URL with inputs that, when entered into a browser, get you some results from Google. It would be nice if we could simply put this URL in the second parameter of the open() method instead of a filename. Then, instead of requesting a file, we would be requesting information from Google. Unfortunately, because of the Ajax security limitation described by Figure 16-3, we can't use Ajax to query Google directly for results. Instead, we have to write a PHP script that queries Google for us.

Our solution will require two different files: a client-side file, which will contain the HTML, JavaScript, and Ajax calls, and a server-side PHP file, which will take user input from the web browser and use it to request information from Google. When Google responds to the server-side PHP program's request, the server-side PHP program sends the information back to the browser, which displays it.

This application is a bit complicated, so before getting into the nitty-gritty of the code, let me sketch out how the code will work. As usual, the action starts when a visitor types something into the text box in Figure 16-8. With each keystroke in that box, the following occurs:

1. A JavaScript function sends an Ajax request to a PHP program (which will be described shortly). The request includes as input the letters typed into the text box.

2. The PHP program sends a request to Google asking about the number of search results for words starting with those letters.

3. Google responds.

4. When the response is received, a JavaScript function called displayResults() parses Google's response and displays the answer.

Let's start by looking at the JavaScript side of this application.

The JavaScript for the Homemade Google Suggest Application

Figure 16-9 shows you the client-side code for Figure 16-8. Much of the code in Figure 16-9 is similar to the code in Figures 15-6, 15-11, and 15-12, so I'll just discuss the changes.

```
<html><head><title>Querying Google Suggest</title>
<script type = "text/javascript">
<!-- hide me from older browsers


function getSuggestions(the_word) {
  var request = null;
  var xml_response = null;
  if (window.XMLHttpRequest) {
    request = new XMLHttpRequest();
  } else {
    request = new ActiveXObject("Microsoft.XMLHTTP");
  }
  var escaped_word = escape(the_word);
❷  var the_URL = "http://localhost/boj/Fig16-10.php" + escaped_word;
  if (request) {
    request.open("GET", the_URL);
    request.onreadystatechange =
      function() {
        if (request.readyState == 4) {
```

```
❸           displayResults(request.responseText);
          }
        }
        request.send(null);
      } else {
         alert("Sorry, you must update your browser before seeing" +
            " Ajax in action.");
      }
    }

    function displayResults(the_response) {
❹     var the_results = eval(the_response);
      var display_me = "";
      var splitter;
      var this_result = null;
      for (var loop = 0; loop < the_results.length; loop++) {
        this_result = the_results[loop];
        if (this_result != null) {
          splitter = this_result.split("\t");
          display_me += "<tr><td align='left'>" + splitter[0] +
             "</td><td align='right'>" + splitter[1] + "</td></tr>";
        }
      }
      document.getElementById("theResults").style.height = (the_results.length +
          parseInt(the_results.length / 5) + 1) + "em";
      document.getElementById("theResults").innerHTML =
          "<table width='100%' border='0' cellpadding='0' cellspacing='0'>" +
          display_me + "</table>";
    }
❺   function sendRPCDone(ignore1, ignore2, word_array, count_array, ignore3) {
      var result_array = new Array();
      for (var loop = 0; loop < word_array.length; loop++) {
        result_array.push(word_array[loop] + "\t" + count_array[loop]);
      }
      return result_array;
    }

    // show me -->
    </script>

    </head>
    <body>
    <form>
❻    <input type = "text" size = "55" id = "theText"
       onKeyUp = "getSuggestions(this.value);">
       <div id = "theResults" style =
           "width:22em;border:1px black solid;padding-left:2px;padding-right:2px">
       </div>
    </form>
    </body>
    </html>
```

Figure 16-9: The client-side Google Suggest code

As is typical of Ajax, most of the action occurs when the user does something. In this case, whenever a user types a character in the box, the code in ❻ calls getSuggestions() with the box's contents. This function is much like the typical Ajax functions you've seen many times now (e.g., doAjaxCall() in Figure 14-4). It gets a request object, tells the object what request to make and what to do when the response is received, and then sends the request. For example, in Figure 16-9, the request object is told to request information from the URL described in ❶ and ❷.

Dealing with Spaces in URLs

When getSuggestions() is called in ❻, it is passed the string of characters that appear in the text box. This string may contain spaces or other characters that are not allowed in URLs.

Now recall the built-in JavaScript function escape() from Chapter 12. This function converts a string into something that can be legally saved in a cookie, and it encodes strings so that they may be sent in a URL (turning each space into %20, for example). Once the escape() function does its magic, ❷ creates the full URL of the PHP program used to query Google. This URL points to a document called Fig16-10.php, which is served up by my local webserver. At the end of the URL we see a question mark, the key name word, an equal sign, and then the URL-legal value of the characters the user entered in the text box.

Next the request object contacts the PHP program named in the URL and sets as input the letters typed into the text box. The PHP program (which we'll see in Figure 16-10) uses that input to request information from Google. When the request is sent, and the answer received, the code in ❸ executes, calling the function displayResults() and sending it whatever text the PHP program returned.

The Response from Google

The rest of the script displays the information that our PHP program received from Google and passed back to our JavaScript. To make sense of it, let's first see what Google actually sends. Because the PHP program asks Google to send the information back in a JavaScript-friendly form, Google's response looks like this:

```
sendRPCDone(frameElement, "javascript", new Array("javascript", "javascript
tutorial", "javascript reference", "javascripts", "javascript array",
"javascript alert", "javascript window.open", "javascript redirect",
"javascript substring", "javascript tutorials"), new Array("50,200,000
results", "6,100,000 results", "7,880,000 results", "1,530,000 results",
"1,500,000 results", "2,230,000 results", "526,000 results", "557,000
results", "248,000 results", "4,660,000 results"), new Array(""));
```

Although it may not seem obvious, this response is actually a call to a Google-created JavaScript function named sendRPCDone(), which is called with five parameters: frameElement, "javascript", two big arrays, and then an empty array.

The only things we care about are the two big arrays. The first array contains the words that match the input "javascript". The second array contains the numbers of results that each of those words would return if used in a Google search. For example, the first element in the first array, "javascript", will return the number of results stored in the first element of the second array, 50,2000,000 results.

The sendRPCDone() function is defined somewhere by Google. It probably does many interesting things with the function's five parameters and then displays the results on a Google-friendly web page. But we don't care how Google uses that function. We're going to define our own sendRPCDone() function that will do what we want it to do: format the contents of the function's second and third parameters and display the formatted information in our web page.

Processing the Google Results—The Magic of eval()

Recall that ❸ in Figure 16-9 sends the results returned by Google to a function called displayResults(). The first line of that function is very interesting because it uses a built-in JavaScript function called eval(). The eval() function takes a string and forces JavaScript to evaluate it. For example, if we run the following two lines, we'll end up with the_solution as 8:

```
var the_add_string = "3 + 5";
var the_solution = eval(the_add_string);
```

Notice that the_add_string is a string. If we printed the_add_string using document.write() or alert() statement, it would print out *3 + 5*. The eval() function, however, treats the string 3 + 5 as if it were a JavaScript statement and evaluates it.

As just discussed, that big string returned by Google is actually a sendRPCDone() function call with parameters that contain the information we requested. When the Ajax request has been completed, ❸ passes the string to the displayResults() function, at which point the eval() in ❹ evaluates and executes it.

Because we're writing the JavaScript, we can write the sendRPCDone() function so that it will transform the two big arrays sent by Google into something that our displayResults() function can handle.

Displaying the Results

Like the displayResults() function in Figure 15-12, this one displays an array of items in a div. In Figure 15-12, each item in the array was an English word, followed by a tab (\t), followed in turn by an Italian translation of that word. The displayResults() function formatted each item and then put the resulting lines into a div. The displayResults() function in this example does exactly the same thing: It too displays a group of items in an array, where each item is a search term, then a tab, and then the number of results that you'd get if you searched for the term in Google.

The sendRPCDone() function takes the results retrieved from Google and puts them into an array for displayResults() to process.

Take a look at sendRPCDone() in Figure 16-9. It takes the two big arrays, loops through them, creates a string of the form *search result, tab, number of results*, and adds that string to a new array. Finally, it sends that new array back to displayResults(), which puts it into our div, just as displayResults() did in Chapter 15.

Using PHP to Contact Other Webservers

That does it for the JavaScript side of this example. To recap, a user types something into the text box. Each key press calls the getSuggestions() function, which uses a request object to send a request to our PHP program. The PHP program then passes the request along to Google. Google answers the PHP program with that big sendRPCDone string, and the PHP program sends the string back to the request object. When the request object has received the string, the displayResults() function is called. This function calls eval() on the sendRPCDone string, and this evaluation results in a call to the sencdRPCDone() function we wrote. This function takes the response from Google and returns an array, which displayResults() then uses to update the web page.

The piece we need to add is the PHP program that takes the request from the JavaScript, sends it to Google, receives the answer from Google, and then passes the answer back to the JavaScript. You can see that PHP program listed in Figure 16-10.

```php
    <?php
❶  include "Snoopy.class.php";
❷  $snoopy = new Snoopy;
❸  $requestedWord = $_REQUEST["word"];
❹  $googleURL =
        "http://www.google.com/complete/search?js=true&qu=" .
            $requestedWord;
❺  $snoopy->fetchtext($googleURL);
❻  print $snoopy->results;
    ?>
```

Figure 16-10: The Google Suggest server-side program

When this PHP program is called, the value of the word key in the URL that is defined in ❷ in Figure 16-9 is automatically stored in the $_REQUEST["word"] PHP variable. The PHP program uses that value to create a Google URL with two keys, js and qu (as discussed in the section "Passing Input in a URL" on page 305). Setting the first key to true means we want our results to come back as JavaScript—that is, as that long string returned by Google, the one that starts with sendRPCDone. The second key identifies the phrase to search for.

Let's start at the top of the script. The first line (❶) provides access to a PHP library named Snoopy. Just as you can import external JavaScript files into your JavaScript code with a line like

```
<script type = "text/javascript" src = "blah.js"/>
```

you can include code from PHP libraries into your PHP code using the `include` command.

NOTE *Snoopy (available at http://snoopy.sourceforge.net) provides code that makes it very easy to send messages to other webservers. If you have a webserver running PHP, download Snoopy and follow the install instructions.*

Once Snoopy is included, we create a new Snoopy object in ❷. This object will send the request to Google and store the response. Lines ❸ and ❹ create the URL that will be used to contact Google. Line ❸ gets the value of the word key, which was set in the URL that was used to call the PHP program. Line ❹ puts that value at the end of the Google URL. (Notice here that PHP uses a period to connect two strings, as opposed to JavaScript, which uses a plus sign.)

Line ❺ in the PHP sends the request to Google and stores the response. Finally, ❻ prints the results and sends them to the JavaScript request object that requested the information. Once all the information has been loaded into that request object, ❸ in the JavaScript in Figure 16-10 calls the function `displayResults()` and the JavaScript proceeds as just discussed in the section "Displaying the Results" on page 312.

Snoopy handles much of the difficulty involved in sending the request to Google and receiving the results. (One of the great things about PHP is that there are many such libraries available.)

That about wraps up your first full Ajax client-server web application. We've covered many details in this example, but what's most important is that you understand how to write a web page with JavaScript that contacts a PHP program, how to use PHP to contact a different webserver in turn for information, and how to pass that information back to the JavaScript page.

Before you go on, make sure you understand how to use the GET method to pass input to the PHP program by appending key-value pairs to the end of the URL and how the PHP program can read those inputs. Finally, be sure that you know how to use eval() to execute a function returned by a webserver such as Google's. Other webservers, such as Yahoo!'s, also respond to Ajax requests by returning JavaScript that is meant to be evaluated.

Ajax and the POST Method

Passing information to PHP programs using a GET is useful for most situations in which you want to send information to a server-side program and when that information will easily fit in a URL. Sometimes, however, you want to send more information than can easily be put into a URL.

For those cases, it's best to use the POST method to send information to a server-side program.

The POST method is usually used in combination with an HTML form, such as the one shown in Figure 16-11.

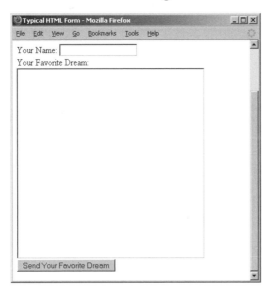

Figure 16-11: A typical HTML form

The code for the standard HTML form shown in Figure 16-11 might look like this:

```
<form method = "POST" action = "http://www.somesite.com/program_name">
Your Name: <input name = "personName" type = "text"><br>
Your Favorite Dream: <br>
<textarea name = "dream" rows = "20" cols = "40"><br>
<input type = "submit" value = "Send Your Favorite Dream">
</form>
```

In the non-Ajax style of web browser/webserver interaction, a user would fill out this form and click the submit button (labeled *Send Your Favorite Dream*). The web browser would package the information in the form and send it to the server-side program named in the action attribute of the <form> tag. That program would process the input and send a web page back to the browser, which would then reload to display the new web page.

Things are a bit different with Ajax. Instead of using the web browser's normal submission technique, a request object is used to send the form information. This means that the request can be sent to the webserver and the results can be displayed to the user without the page reloading.

Luckily for us, the PHP we covered in the previous section works exactly the same for the GET and POST methods. Only the JavaScript needs to change.

An Ajax-Friendly Form

Forms designed for Ajax are slightly different from normal HTML forms. The main differences are that you don't need to include an action in the ‹form› tag and you don't use a submit form element to submit the form. With these things in mind, here's an Ajax-friendly version of the form we just looked at:

```
<form>
Your Name: <input name = "personName" type = "text"><br>
Your Favorite Dream: <br>
<textarea name = "dream" rows = "20" cols = "40"><br>
<input type = "button" value = "Send Your Favorite Dream"
  onClick = "doSubmission(this.form)">
</form>
```

Notice that there are no action or method attributes in the ‹form› tag and that instead of an input of type submit at the end, an input of type button calls a JavaScript function when clicked. (An HTML link with an onClick in it would work just as well.)

POSTing with Ajax

Changing our now-familiar Ajax function from using a GET method to using a POST method requires only a few alterations.

First, the line that tells the request object about the resource to query needs to change from

```
request.open("GET", the_URL);
```

to

```
request.open("POST", the_URL);
```

Second, because the URL we'll be sending will not include any of the input that we sent with the GET method (the stuff after the question mark), we modify it for the POST method so that it indicates only where the server-side program resides.

Instead of putting the input at the end of the URL, we send it as a string with the request. Previously, the request object made the request using a line like this:

```
request.send(null);
```

Using the POST method, we replace null with a string containing the information we want to send to the server-side program:

```
request.send("personName=dave%20thau&dream=world%20peace");
```

The string looks exactly like the input string we sent using GET: It's a set of key-value pairs separated by ampersands (&).

Finally, we tell the server-side program that we'll be sending it POST-style information so that PHP will put this information into its $_REQUEST variable. To do so, use this line:

```
request.setRequestHeader("Content-Type","application/x-www-form-urlencoded;
charset = UTF-8");
```

This line says that we're sending a www-form-urlencoded request. The charset attribute specifies that the characters are encoded using Unicode, a standard for representing characters. You can use this line verbatim; just replace request with the name of the request object.

Figure 16-12 shows the JavaScript side of sending a POST message. Because the PHP code is almost exactly like the code in Figure 16-7, I won't discuss it.

```
<html><head><title>Typical HTML Form</title>
<script type = "text/javascript">
<!-- hide me from older browsers
function submitMe(my_form) {
   var request = null;
❶ var message = "personName=" + my_form.elements["personName"].value +
      "&dream=" + my_form.elements["dream"].value;
   if (window.XMLHttpRequest) {
     request = new XMLHttpRequest();
   } else {
     request = new ActiveXObject("Microsoft.XMLHTTP");
   }
❷ var the_URL = "http://localhost/boj/ch16/Figure16-12.php";
   if (request) {
❸    request.open("POST", the_URL);
❹    request.setRequestHeader("Content-Type",
        "application/x-www-form-urlencoded; charset=UTF-8");
     request.onreadystatechange =
        function() {
          if (request.readyState == 4) {
❺           document.getElementById("display").innerHTML =
               request.responseText;
          }
        }
❻    request.send(message);
   } else {
     alert("Sorry, you must update your browser before seeing" +
       " Ajax in action.");
   }
}
// show me -->
</script>
</head>
<body>
<h1>Make Your Dream Unchanging</h1>
❼ <div id = "display">
<form>
Your Name: <input name = "personName" type = "text"><br>
Your Favorite Dream: <br>
<textarea name = "dream" rows = "20" cols = "40"></textarea><br>
```

```
❽ <input type = "button" value = "Send Your Favorite Dream"
    onClick = "submitMe(this.form);">
</form>
</div>
</body>
</html>
```

Figure 16-12: Sending an Ajax POST

Clicking the button in ❽ calls the submitMe() function. This function is sent a pointer to the form, and ❶ reads the contents of the form and constructs the string that will be sent to the PHP program. The URL of that program is defined in ❷. Notice that the only information in the URL is the location of the program; there is no additional input.

In ❸ we tell the request object about this URL and that we're going to send a POST-style request. Line ❹ further specifies that the information we're sending the server-side program is coming from a form. Finally, ❻ sends the request and passes the string constructed in ❶.

The PHP program will process this message string and return some results. When the results are fully loaded into the request object, ❺ will place them into the div that initially contains the form (❼). Replacing the contents of the div will replace the form with whatever message has been sent back by the PHP program.

Sending XML Information from the Browser to a Webserver

Don't forget that the *X* in Ajax stands for *XML*. XML files can be sent to a PHP program just like any other contents. Because XML tends to be lengthy, it's generally best to send it by using the POST method and putting the XML into the request object's send() method.

HEAD Requests: Getting Information About a Server-Side File

The previous sections described how to use GET and POST methods to send information to a server-side program and retrieve the server-side program's response. Sometimes, in addition to the information returned by the webserver, a response can contain information about the response itself. This kind of information, sometimes called *metadata*, is stored in a normally invisible part of the response called the *response header*. A response can have many headers. Headers might include information such as the number of kilobytes in the response, when the response was sent, and when that file was last updated. Here are some of the headers returned by Flickr.com when it answers an Ajax request:

```
Date: Wed, 20 Dec 2006 21:11:46 GMT
Server: Apache/2.0.52
Content-Type: text/xml; charset = utf-8
```

These are just three of the headers Flickr sends back. The first one, named Date, sends back the time the response was sent. The header named Server describes the kind of webserver Flickr uses. The last header, Content-Type, gives you information about the format of the response (it's XML, sent using the UTF-8 character set).

These headers can be very useful. For example, in Chapter 17 we will discuss the details behind developing a multiuser To Do list application. In order to create a sharable To Do list, we will store the To Do list information in a file on a webserver so that it can be modified by many different users. When two people are working on a To Do list at the same time, one user should see the changes made by the other user soon after those changes have been made, without needing to reload the page.

In order to have our Ajax program always display the most up-to-date version of the To Do list, we might refresh the file every few seconds. However, if there are many items on the To Do list, the file containing the list might become very large. Rather than repeatedly download a very large file that may not have changed, we can simply look up the last time it was modified and use this information to see whether we need to get a newer version of the file.

When a webserver responds to any request, it can include response headers. When you are interested in a header but don't want to retrieve the entire response, you can use a HEAD request to retrieve just the response headers:

```
request.open("HEAD", the_URL);
```

When the request is answered and the response has been downloaded into the request object (the request object is in readyState 4) you can access the header information with the request object's getResponseHeader() method. The date and time a file was last modified is usually sent in a header named Last-Modified, which can be retrieved by calling the getResponseHeader() method with the string "Last-Modified":

```
var last_modified = request.getResponseHeader("Last-Modified");
```

Using the returned value to create a new Date() object makes it easy to access the information. Here is an example:

```
var last_modified_date = new Date(last_modified);
```

(In Figures 16-15 and 16-16 at the end of this chapter, you'll see an example of using a HEAD request to see whether a file has been updated.)

Adding Headers to Your Responses

Headers, such as the Last-Modified and Date header just described, are added to a response by the server-side program that sends the response. To add a header to a response sent by PHP, use PHP's header() function, which takes a string describing the header as a parameter. For example, to set a header named My-Header, use the following:

```
header('My-Header: I am a header');
```

The header information is sent as soon as PHP sees this line. The line should appear toward the top of your PHP program, before any print commands. If you try to set a header after using print, PHP will give an error. An example of setting headers will be shown soon in Figure 16-16.

Headers and XML

In Chapter 14 you saw two different ways to access the information stored in the request object: responseText and responseXML. A string version of all responses is stored in the request object's responseText property, and if the response is an XML document, an XML version of the response is accessible in the responseXML property. (The XML version is nice because it allows you to navigate the XML document using the XML-handling methods we discussed in Chapter 15.)

The request object needs to know that the response is an XML document before it will store the response in the responseXML property. To tell it that your response is XML, set the header information of the PHP response using the header() function. Simply placing the following line in your PHP program before using print to send a response should do the trick:

```
header("Content-Type: text/xml");
```

This will tell the request object that this response is an XML document.

The Caching Problem

We have now seen three different kinds of requests: GET, POST, and HEAD. Each of these requests requires a URL pointing to the resource being requested. In some situations, such as the interactive To Do list application we'll be discussing in Chapter 17, a file may be requested multiple times during the course of a user's interaction with the application. Although the contents of the file might change, the URL pointing to that file does not. This situation can cause problems for some browsers. Internet Explorer, for example, is notorious for not updating a web page even though the page's contents have changed.

Firefox and most other browsers generally behave as you would expect, updating the web page with the new information. Internet Explorer, however, decides whether or not to update the page based on the URL used in the request. If that URL looks familiar, IE assumes that the new page is just like the old one (it has the same URL after all), and it won't update. This is bad news for Ajax, because it means that the new information won't be shown.

Happily, there is an easy fix for this problem: Make each URL look different every time. Here is an example:

```
var the_URL = "http://mydomain.com?ignoreMe=" + new Date().getTime();
```

Recall from Chapter 2 that the getTime() method of a Date object returns the number of seconds between the time the method is called and January 1, 1970; a number that will differ every second. Setting a parameter such as ignoreMe equal to the results of getTime() makes the URL different every time the URL is used. This will trick Internet Explorer into thinking it's a new URL, inducing IE to update the page. We'll see an example of this trick in Figure 16-15.

File Handling in PHP

PHP programs can read and manipulate files that reside on webservers. With PHP, you can read a text file, create a new text file, and edit the text in a file on the server. Once a file is created on a webserver, it can be accessed by any web browser. When a webserver file is edited, those edits will be seen by anyone looking at the file.

Creating and Adding Contents to a Text File with PHP

To use PHP to create a new text file, or to change the contents of an existing text file, you must:

1. Open the file and signify that you want to write contents to the file
2. Write text to the file
3. Close the file

To open a file for writing, use PHP's fopen() function. This function takes two parameters: the name of the file you want to open and either a "w" if you want to replace the existing contents of that file with new text, or an "a" if you want to add text to the end of the file. The fopen() function returns a value, which you can use in your PHP program to refer to the file you've just opened. For example, to open myFile.txt for writing, use this line:

```
$myFile = fopen("myFile.txt", "w");
```

NOTE   *When you open a file with "w" as the second parameter, the old contents of the file are deleted. Therefore, if you want to edit the contents of a file, you should first read the contents of the file into a variable, then edit the contents of the variable, and then write the contents back to the file. We'll be doing this in Chapter 17.*

Once a file has been opened, use the PHP function fwrite() to write to it. This function takes the value returned by the fopen() function and the string you want to write to the file. The function returns either TRUE or FALSE, depending on whether or not it succeeded in writing to the file. (Writing may fail for several reasons: the hard drive might be full, or the webserver might not have permissions to write to the file.) For example, to write two lines to the file you opened above, use this line:

```
$success = fwrite($myFile, "line one\nline two");
```

The \n puts a line break into the file, which creates a two-line file in this case. If the write is successful, $success will contain the value TRUE; if not, it will contain the value FALSE.

Once you've written to a file, close it with fclose():

```
fclose($myFile);
```

Combining these lines gives you the PHP script below:

```php
<?php
  $myFile = fopen("myFile.txt", "w");
  $success = fwrite($myFile, "line one\nline two");
  fclose($myFile);
  if ($success == TRUE) {
    print "Write succeeded";
  } else {
    print "Write failed";
  }
?>
```

One of the more pernicious problems you'll encounter when dealing with server-side programming is that of ensuring that your webserver has permission to alter the files you want to alter. Sometimes a PHP program can fail to write to a file because the webserver running it does not have access to that particular file. If this happens, PHP will give an error like this:

```
Warning: fopen(yourFile.txt) [function fopen]: failed to open stream:
Permission denied.
```

File permissions work differently on different operating systems. If you get this kind of error, refer to your operating system's manuals to determine how to inspect and modify file permissions.

Reading Files in PHP

It's a bit trickier to read a file using PHP than it is to write to a file. The complication arises because the contents of a file are read line by line, and PHP needs to know when it has reached the end of a file so that it can stop reading. Luckily, the PHP function feof() will tell PHP when it has reached the end of a file. This function takes a variable that points to an open file (such as $myFile) and returns TRUE when the end of the file has been reached. Figure 16-13 shows an example of PHP reading a file.

```php
<?php
❶  $myFile = fopen("myFile.txt","r");
   $contents = "";
❷  while (feof($myFile) == FALSE) {
❸    $contents = $contents . fgets($myFile);
   }
```

```
❹   fclose($myFile);
    print "The file's contents are: " . $contents;
?>
```

Figure 16-13: Reading a file with PHP

In Figure 16-13, ❶ opens the file for reading and puts a pointer to the opened file into the variable $myFile. The most complicated line is ❷, which calls the feof() function on $myFile to see whether PHP has reached the end of the file. If not, feof() returns FALSE, and the line inside the while loop is executed. This line uses the function fgets() to read a line from $myFile. It takes that line and attaches it to the end of the $contents variable, so each time through the loop the next line of $myFile is appended to the end of $contents. Eventually, the last line of $myFile will be read and the feof() function will respond with TRUE. When that happens, the loop ends, and the program returns the contents of the file.

NOTE *Notice how similar PHP and JavaScript are. They have identically structured while loops, they both use two equal signs to see whether two things are the same, and they both use the values TRUE and FALSE (although in JavaScript these values are lowercase).*

When Communication Breaks Down

When a web browser contacts a webserver for information, many things can go wrong. Here are some examples:

- The page being requested may not actually be on the server.
- The user may not have permission to access the page.
- If a server-side program is being called, something might go wrong with that program.
- The server might take too long to get back to the web browser, and the browser might stop waiting.

When a request object sends a request and then says that the request has been fulfilled (its readyState is 4), all we really know is that the request has been answered in some way. Everything could have gone well, with the server sending the information requested, or something may have gone wrong.

To determine how the client-server communication went, we can check the status property of the request object for a status code, as listed in Table 16-1.

The most frequent numbers you'll see are 200, if everything went well; 404, if the URL provided to the request object does not exist on the server; and 500, if the request went to a server-side program, but something went wrong with the program. Somewhat less frequently you may see a 401 or 403 if the page or program you are trying to access is password-protected, 408 if the server took too long to respond, or 503 if the server exists but the server-side program you are sending the request to does not.

Table 16-1: Request Object Status Codes

Status Code	Meaning
200	OK
204	No Content
400	Bad Request
401	Unauthorized
403	Forbidden
404	Not Found
407	Proxy Authentication Required
408	Request Time-out
411	Length Required
413	Requested Data Entity Too Large
414	Requested URL Too Long
415	Unsupported Media Type
500	Internal Server Error
503	Service Unavailable
504	Gateway Time-out

Typically, you should make sure that the request was satisfied and everything went well (status code 200). To do so, add an if-then statement to JavaScript functions that make Ajax calls, as shown in Figure 16-14.

```
   request.open("GET", some_url);
   request.onreadystatechange = function() {
❶     if (request.readyState == 4) {
❷       if (request.status == 200) {
         doSomething();
       } else if (request.status == 404) {
❸       document.getElementById("errorDiv").innerHTML =
           'Sorry, the page you are accessing could not be found.';
       } else if (request.status == 500)
         document.getElementById("errorDiv").innerHTML =
           'Sorry, there was a problem with the server.';
       } else {
         document.getElementById("errorDiv").innerHTML =
           'Sorry, communication breakdown. Please try again.';
       }
     }
   }
```

Figure 16-14: Adding a status check to an Ajax call

In this code sample, once the request object has reached readyState == 4 (❶), we check its status. If the status is 200 (❷), then we do whatever it is that we want to do when the request has been answered. If not, then we want to tell the user that something went wrong—in this example, by putting a message into a div with the id of errorDiv (❸).

Automatically Updating a Web Page When a Server-Side File Changes

Figures 16-15 and 16-16 demonstrate how to use HEAD calls, server-side file reading, and the cache-tricking technique to read a file from a webserver, display its contents, and update the contents whenever the file on the server changes. This type of application is useful whenever more than one person can update a file on a webserver—for example, if two people have access to the same To Do list.

```
<html><head><title>Automatically Updating Display of a Changed File</title>
<script type = "text/javascript">
<!-- hide me from older browsers
var timeout;

function callReadFile(file_name) {
❶ readFileDoFunction(file_name, "GET",
❷    function() {
        if (request.readyState == 4) {
          if (request.status == 200) {
            var last_modified = request.getResponseHeader("Last-Modified");
            var last_modified_date = new Date(last_modified);
            displayResults(request.responseText, file_name,
              last_modified_date.getTime());
          }
        }
      }
    );
}

function readFileDoFunction(file_name, read_type, the_function) {
    if (window.XMLHttpRequest) {
      request = new XMLHttpRequest();
    } else {
      request = new ActiveXObject("Microsoft.XMLHTTP");
    }

❸    var the_url =
        "http://localhost/boj/ch16/readTextFile.php?fileName=" +
        file_name +
        "&t=" + new Date().getTime();

    var the_results;
    if (request) {
❹      request.open(read_type, the_url);
❺      request.onreadystatechange = the_function;
      request.send(null);
    } else {
      alert("Sorry, you must update your browser before seeing" +
        " Ajax in action.");
    }
}

function displayResults(the_results, file_name, last_modified) {
```

```
      document.getElementById("contents").innerHTML = the_results;
❻    timeout = setTimeout("callUpdateIfChanged(" + last_modified + ",'" +
      file_name + "')", 5000);

    }

    function callUpdateIfChanged(current_last_modified, file_name) {
      readFileDoFunction(file_name, "HEAD",
        function() {
          if (request.readyState == 4) {
            if (request.status == 200) {
              var last_modified =
                request.getResponseHeader("Last-Modified");
              var last_modified_date = new Date(last_modified).getTime();
              if (last_modified_date != current_last_modified) {
                callReadFile(file_name);
              }
              timeout = setTimeout("callUpdateIfChanged(" +
                last_modified_date + ",'" + file_name + "')", 5000);
            }
          }
        }
      );
    }

    function stopTimer() {
      clearTimeout(timeout);
    }

    // show me -->
    </script>
    </head>
    <body>

    <form>
    <input type = "button" value = "Read the File"
      onClick = "callReadFile('numbers.txt');">
    <input type = "button" value = "Stop Checking" onClick = "stopTimer();">
    </form>

    <div id = "contents">

    </div>

    </body>
    </html>
```

Figure 16-15: Client-side checking for updated server-side file

Figure 16-15 lists the client-side portion of the application. Clicking the Read the File button in the form at the bottom calls the callReadFile() function and sends it the name of a file to read. The callReadFile() function does only one thing—it calls a function named readFileDoFunction(), which does the actual work of getting the file. We'll take a look at readFileDoFunction() first and then turn back to callReadFile().

readFileDoFunction()

The `readFileDoFunction()` function is a very generic function that deals with situations where you want to use Ajax to read a file and then execute some function. In all the Ajax examples up until now, functions that made Ajax calls had a couple of lines like this:

```
request.open("GET", some_url);
request.onreadystatechange = function() {
    if (request.readyState == 4) {
        doSomething();
    }
}
```

As you know, this tells a request object where a request should be sent and what to do when the request has been satisfied.

The `readFileDoFunction()` function does the same thing, but it's a bit more flexible. The function is sent three parameters: the name of a file to read, the way to read it (use a `GET` or a `HEAD` call), and the function to execute when the `readyState` changes. Line ❸ in the function takes the first parameter, the name of the file, and creates a URL with it.

NOTE *Notice that the URL has "&t=" + new Date().getTime() at the end. This makes the URL look different every second and overcomes Internet Explorer's overzealous caching by tricking it into thinking that you're requesting something you haven't requested before.*

Lines ❹ and ❺ are the new versions of the typical Ajax lines mentioned above. Line ❹ tells the request object the kind of call to make (`GET` or `HEAD`) and where to send the request. Line ❺ assigns the function that should be called when the request object's `readyState` changes. Normally, an anonymous function would go after the equal sign, but in this case we put a variable which holds the anonymous function there.

callReadFile()

Now let's look back at the `callReadFile()` function to see what it's doing. Line ❶ calls the `readFileDoFunction()` function just described. This function takes three parameters, the first two of which are the name of the file, which was sent to `callReadFile()`, and the type of call we want to make, which is a `GET` call. The third parameter, which starts in ❷, is an entire anonymous function. We're taking the function that we normally would have put after the equal sign in ❺ and passing it as a parameter to `readFileDoFunction()`. This technique is nice because it means that we can use `readFileDoFunction()` whenever we want to use Ajax to read in some file and execute some function once the file is read.

In the case of `callReadFile()`, which is called when a user clicks the Read the File button, we want to read in the file whose name was passed into `callReadFile()`, numbers.txt; then, when the file has been completely read, we want to get the `Last-Modified` header of the file that was read and then call the `displayResults()` function, which will display what was retrieved from the file.

The `displayResults()` function takes three parameters: the contents of the file we have just read, the name of the file we've read, and the number of seconds between January 1, 1970 and the time the file was last modified (from now on, let's just call that the *last modified time*). The function first displays the contents of the file by putting them into the div with the id of `contents`. Then ❻ sets up a time-out that will call the `callUpdateIfChanged()` function in five seconds. Once five seconds have passed, this function does a `HEAD` call to read the `Last-Modified` header of the file. If at some point during the last five seconds the file has changed, the new `Last-Modified` header will differ from the one we retrieved when we first read the file. If the new `Last-Modified` value is different, the new version of the file will be read, the web page will be updated, and the last modified time will be updated to reflect the fact that the file changed.

callUpdateIfChanged()

Like `callReadFile()`, `callUpdateIfChanged()` does just one thing—it calls `readFileDoFunction()`. In this case, however, we're doing a `HEAD` call and sending a different anonymous function to be called when the request object's `readyState` changes. This anonymous function gets the value of the new `Last-Modified` header, checks to see whether the time is different from when we read the file the first time, and, if it is, makes another call to `callReadFile()`. Just as before, `callReadFile()` reads in the file and sets the last modified time. Lastly, `callUpdateIfChanged()` creates another time-out to call `callUpdateIfChanged()` again in five seconds.

stopTimer()

The only function left to describe is `stopTimer()`, which simply cancels the most recently set time-out. This function is called when the user clicks the Stop Checking button.

Recap and Breathe

Summarizing to this point, the interesting elements in Figure 16-15 include passing an anonymous function as a parameter to another function, using a `HEAD` call to retrieve the last modified time of a file, and attaching a `new Date().getTime()` to a URL to trick Internet Explorer into thinking you're making a request that is different from one you made earlier.

The Server-Side PHP Code

Now let's turn to Figure 16-16, which lists readTextFile.php, the server-side program called in ❸.

```php
<?php

   $fileName = $_REQUEST["fileName"];
❶ header('Last-Modified: '.
     gmdate('D, d M Y H:i:s', filemtime($fileName)) .
     ' GMT');

❷ if ($_SERVER["REQUEST_METHOD"] != "HEAD") {
     $myFile = fopen($fileName, "r");
     $contents = "";
     while (feof($myFile) == FALSE) {
       $contents = $contents . fgets($myFile);
     }
     fclose($myFile);
     print $contents;
   }
?>
```

Figure 16-16: The readTextFile.php called in ❸ of Figure 16-15

The PHP code in Figure 16-16 is fairly straightforward. After getting the name of the file to read from PHP's built-in $_REQUEST variable, the code in ❶ sends the Last-Modified header to the browser.

The tricky part of ❶ involves using built-in PHP functions to create a date and time that JavaScript can understand. The code uses two PHP functions: gmdate() formats the string, and filemtime() returns the time when the file named by $fileName was last modified.

Next, the code checks to see whether this is a HEAD request, using the code in ❷. This code looks at the built-in PHP variable $_SERVER["REQUEST_ METHOD"], which will store the value "GET", "POST", or "HEAD". If it is "HEAD", then all the PHP script should do is send the header information in ❶. If it is not a HEAD request, then the body of the if-then clause reads the contents of the file into the $contents variable, and ❸ sends that information to the browser.

Summary

Phew. Here's a rundown of everything covered in this chapter:

- How server-side programs let you store information from many users in one place and let you use facilities available to machines running webservers

- How the server-side language PHP uses variables, if-then clauses, and loops, much like JavaScript does

- How to use URLs and web forms to send information to server-side PHP programs

- How to send GET, POST, and HEAD requests to a server-side program

- How to use PHP and the Snoopy library to contact other webservers
- How to use PHP to save and read files on webservers
- How to trick Internet Explorer into not caching your web pages
- How to share XML information between client-side and server-side programs

Congratulations! You have now learned practically all the JavaScript this book has to teach. The next chapter contains only a small amount of new information; it mostly applies all the JavaScript you've learned so far to the task of creating a multiuser Ajax-driven To Do list application. So sit back, take a break, and bask in your new JavaScript knowledge.

Assignment

If you didn't complete the steps described in "Setting Up a Webserver and PHP" on page 273, do so now.

17

PUTTING IT ALL TOGETHER IN A SHARED TO DO LIST

This is it! The last big script of *The Book of JavaScript*! This is where we combine everything that we've learned so far to create a shared To Do list. This application draws from every chapter in this book. It uses the basic structure of JavaScript tags from Chapter 1, variables from Chapter 2, if-then clauses from Chapter 3, events from Chapter 4, window manipulation from Chapters 5 and 10, functions from Chapter 6, forms from Chapter 7, loops and arrays from Chapter 8, time-outs from Chapter 9, string handling from Chapter 11, cookies from Chapter 12, dynamic HTML from Chapter 13, client-side Ajax from Chapter 14, XML from Chapter 15, and server-side Ajax from Chapter 16.

I'll only cover part of the application here; your homework will be to complete it.

Features of the To Do List Application

Our shared To Do list application will have a membership base. New users can join the site, and once they've joined, can log in to and out of the site. When someone joins the site, that user starts with a blank To Do list, and I will call that user the *owner* of that list.

The owner of a list can add items to the list and mark items as completed or not. A list owner can also designate other users as *subscribers* to the list. Subscribers can modify the To Do list just as an owner can. I'll use the word *editor* to describe the list's owner or one of the list's subscribers.

To review, the application will provide the following features:

- New users will be able to sign up and create their own To Do lists
- Current users can log in to and out of the site
- Someone who has created a To Do list can allow other users to edit her list
- List editors can add new items to a To Do list
- List editors can mark items as completed
- List editors can mark completed items as uncompleted

In the scenarios that follow, two people, Nestor and Odysseus, have signed up for the To Do list service. Each has built his own To Do list and added items to it. Nestor has allowed Odysseus to see and modify his list, but Odysseus is keeping his own list private. Figures 17-1 through 17-6 show you the major features of the partial application. But first, a caveat. Although the design and user interface of this application are functional, they are also hideous. Apologies to those with delicate design sensibilities.

Figures 17-1 through 17-3 show the process of clicking the login button and logging in. Notice at the bottom of Figure 17-3 that Odysseus can choose to see either his own list or Nestor's list. If Nestor had logged in, he would see only his own list because Odysseus hasn't shared his list with Nestor. Notice also that Odysseus can log out.

Figure 17-4 shows the screen after Odysseus has chosen to see his own list. He has two uncompleted tasks on his To Do list.

Figure 17-1: The view when first coming to the site

Figure 17-2: After clicking the login link

Figure 17-3: After Odysseus logs in

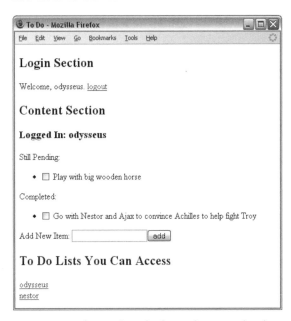

Figure 17-4: Viewing Odysseus's list

Figure 17-5 shows the screen after he clicks the checkbox next to the first task in the Still Pending list, signaling that he has completed it. If Odysseus has made a mistake and didn't really finish that task, he can click the checkbox next to the task in the Completed list and move it back to the Still Pending section. Finally, Figure 17-6 shows the screen after Odysseus has added a new item to his list.

Figure 17-5: After marking the first task as completed

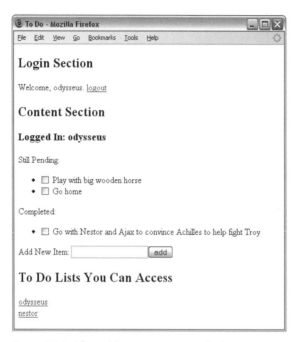

Figure 17-6: After adding a new item to the list

The application uses the automatic updating trick from Chapter 16. If Nestor is looking at his To Do list, and Odysseus adds something to Nestor's list, Nestor will automatically see his list update.

The same is true for the To Do lists each person can see. If someone new, say Achilles, decides to let Odysseus have access to his list, and Odysseus is logged in, Odysseus's page will automatically update to let him know that he now has access to Achilles's list.

There are three different types of files that make this application work: an HTML file with some JavaScript in it, which works in the browser; a server-side program, which runs on the webserver (a PHP program in this case); and some data files (XML), which store the information used by the application. Let's turn first to the data files.

To Do List Data Files

The To Do list application uses two different types of XML files: One file, userInfo.xml, describes all users with access to the application. The second type of file represents a To Do list. Each user will have one To Do list file.

userInfo.xml

userInfo.xml contains the name, password, and profiles of all the users who have signed up to use the To Do list application. It also contains information about who can edit which lists. Figure 17-7 shows an example of userInfo.xml.

```
❶ <?xml version = "1.0" ?>
❷ <users>
    <user>
❸   <name>nestor</name>
      <password>cup</password>
      <profile>King of Pylos, fought the centaurs</profile>
      <lists>
        <list>nestor</list>
      </lists>
    </user>
    <user>
❸   <name>odysseus</name>
      <password>horsie</password>
      <profile>Hero of the Iliad and Odyssey</profile>
      <lists>
        <list>odysseus</list>
        <list>nestor</list>
      </lists>
    </user>
</users>
```

Figure 17-7: XML representing information about users

Let's walk through this file. As with all valid XML files, the first line (❶) declares that this is an XML file. Line ❷ declares the one root element in the file, users.

The usernames odysseus and nestor follow in ❸, inside the beginning and ending <users> tags; these are the two users who have signed up for our application so far. Each username is followed with some specific information about that user including (but not limited to) a name, a password, a profile, and the lists to which that user has access.

This XML file is updated whenever the user information changes; for example, if a new user joins, or if one user permits another to see his or her list.

NOTE   *This partial version of the application does not have a "join" feature; adding one will be part of your homework. If it had such a feature, the file would update with information related to new users when they create an account in our application.*

To Do List File

The second type of XML file contains information about a user's To Do list. Each user owns one file, the name of which is based on the username. For example, Figure 17-8 shows the contents of odysseus.xml, which contains all the To Do list information shown in Figure 17-4.

```
<?xml version = "1.0" ?>
<list>
  <name>odysseus</name>
  <openitems>
❶   <item>
```

```
❷        <number>1</number>
❸        <contents>Go with Nestor and Ajax to convince....</contents>
       </item>
❹      <item>
          <number>2</number>
          <contents>Play with big wooden horse</contents>
       </item>
     </openitems>
❺    <doneitems>
     </doneitems>
   </list>
```

Figure 17-8: XML representing Odysseus's To Do list, stored in odysseus.xml

The root element in this XML file, list, contains three elements: the name of the list, a list of pending items (openitems), and a list of completed items (doneitems).

As you can see in Figure 17-8, Odysseus has two tasks to complete (❶ and ❹), and has no completed tasks (there's nothing between the <doneitems> tags in ❺). Each task in the list has two elements: a number (❷), which makes it easy to identify the item, and the item itself (❸). When Odysseus adds or changes an item's status, the XML file odysseus.xml is updated.

NOTE   *I invented the XML tags for both userInfo.xml and the To Do list file. If there was some generally accepted XML standard for To Do lists, I could have used that instead.*

To Do List Server Side

This example uses only two straightforward PHP programs. The first, readXMLFile.php, reads in an XML file; it is almost a copy of the code in Figure 16-16. If a HEAD request was sent, readXMLFile.php returns only the last-modified date of the file. If a GET request is sent, readXMLFile.php reads the requested file from the webserver and passes it to the browser. The only difference between Figure 16-16 and readXMLFile.php is that readXMLFile.php sends an additional header when responding to a GET request:

```
header("Content-Type: text/xml");
```

The second server-side program, saveXMLFile.php, saves an XML file. Figure 17-9 shows the PHP code. As I hope you'll see, it's very similar to the program we used to write out a text file in "Creating and Adding Contents to a Text File with PHP" on page 321.

```
<?php

❶ $fileName = $_REQUEST["fileName"];
❷ $contents = $_REQUEST["contents"];

❸ $myFile = fopen($fileName, "w");
❹ $success = fwrite($myFile, stripslashes($contents));
```

```
    fclose($myFile);

    if ($success == TRUE) {
        print "success";
    } else {
        print "failure";
    }

?>
```

Figure 17-9: PHP program for saving a string to a file

Let's take this program apart. This program receives a POST from the browser whenever a file needs to be saved. It is passed two keys: the name of the file to be saved and the contents of the file. These keys are accessed in PHP using ❶ and ❷. Line ❸ opens the file for writing, and ❹ writes the contents to the file.

Before actually writing the contents to the file, ❹ calls the built-in PHP function stripslashes(). This function is particularly important because some versions of PHP add backslashes to quotes inside text sent for parsing, and we want to remove those backslashes. For example, because we're sending XML information, the first line of the file we want to save is

```
<?xml version = "1.0" ?>
```

But when this is sent to some versions of PHP, it will be turned into

```
<?xml version = \"1.0\" ?>
```

The stripslashes() function removes those inserted backslashes.

The To Do List Client Side, Part 1: The HTML

Most of the power of our To Do list application is in the client-side code. The client-side code is quite long, so I'll describe it section by section. For a listing of the entire client side, see Appendix D.

Let's first look at the body of the HTML file as shown in Figure 17-10.

```
❶ <body onLoad = "checkIfLoggedIn()";>

❷ <div id = "errorDiv" style = "color:red">
  </div>

  <h2>Login Section</h2>
❸ <div id = "loginArea">
  <a href = "#" onClick = "displayLogin(); return false;">login</a>
  </div>

  <h2>Content Section</h2>
❹ <div id = "contentArea">
  Welcome! Please sign in to see your To Do lists.
```

```
      </div>

      <h2>To Do Lists You Can Access</h2>
❺   <div id = "listArea">
      </div>
      </body>
```

Figure 17-10: The application's HTML

The body of the page is divided into four sections. The first section (❷) is reserved for error messages. Whenever anything goes wrong in the application (for example, if someone logs in with an incorrect password or if something goes wrong with the server when trying to read a file), a message is put into the innerHTML of the div with the id of errorDiv. The error message will be displayed in red because of the style attribute inside the div.

Below that section, in ❸, is a div with the id of loginArea. When the page is first read in, this div will contain the login link. When that link is clicked, the contents of this area are replaced by a form that lets a user enter a username and password. Once the user logs in, the form is replaced with a greeting and the ability to log out.

The div in ❹ is reserved for displaying the contents of the list being viewed. It initially holds a greeting message.

Finally, ❺ marks the div that will contain information about which To Do lists a person can view. By keeping the contents of the list being viewed in a div that is separate from all other lists, we make it easy to update one list without updating any others.

Finally, notice that ❶ the <body> tag calls the checkIfLoggedIn() function when the page is loaded. This function ensures that if a logged-in user reloads the web page, or visits another page and returns to this one, the page recognizes that the user has already logged in and shows the user the appropriate information.

The To Do List Client Side, Part 2: The JavaScript

Now let's turn to the JavaScript code. Imagine you are assigned the task of developing the JavaScript for this To Do list application. Where would you start? Even though this application is simple when compared to something like Google Maps, it is still complicated enough to make the task of writing the code seem overwhelming.

When faced with a large problem, it is often helpful to apply a problem solving technique called *divide and conquer*. To solve a large problem, divide the large task into smaller ones, and then conquer the smaller projects one at a time.

For example, the code in the To Do list application can be divided into several different feature sets:

- Logging in and out
- Displaying available lists
- Displaying a specific list
- Processing changes to a list

Applying the divide and conquer technique means that you write the JavaScript to deal with all the features for logging in and out, then you write the JavaScript for displaying available lists, and so on. If any of these smaller tasks still seems overwhelming, apply divide and conquer again to break it up into smaller tasks that are easier to tackle.

The rest of the chapter will describe the code for each of the feature sets just listed. As usual, we will write our own functions to complete the tasks. Although there are only four general feature sets, each will require many functions. But before getting into the code itself, let's look at a road map for how the functions I will describe relate to each other.

The Function Road Map

Figure 17-11 shows each of the 27 functions I will describe. An arrow leading from one function to another means the first function calls the second function. The functions at the top of the figure are called by a user interacting with the web page in some way. As you can see, almost every function calls at least two other functions.

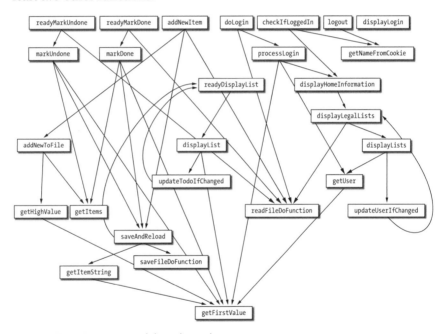

Figure 17-11: Functions and their dependencies

Functions with many arrows going into them are used by many others. For example, the getFirstValue() function is called by seven other functions, and the readFileDoFunction() function is called by six others. Putting the code of getFirstValue() in its own function means that the code can live in one place, rather than being repeated seven different times. If you had not yet been convinced of the magic of functions before seeing this application, you should be by now. (Don't let the complexity of this diagram bother you; the descriptions in this chapter should make everything crystal clear.)

Let's now turn to the first set of features: those that involve logging in to and logging out of the application.

Logging In and Out

The login process begins when a user clicks the link in the `loginArea` div (❸ in Figure 17-10), which calls the `displayLogin()` function shown here:

```
function displayLogin() {

  var theForm = "<form>Name: <input type='text' name='name'><br> " +
    "Password: <input type='password' name='password'> " +
    "<input type='button' value='submit' " +
    "onClick='doLogin(this.form);'><br>"

  document.getElementById("loginArea").innerHTML = theForm;


}
```

This function simply puts a form into the `innerHTML` of the `loginArea` div. When the user fills out the form and clicks the submit button, the JavaScript calls the `doLogin()` function.

The `doLogin()` function contains our first bit of Ajax. The form completed by the user is sent to it, and it calls the `readFileDoFunction()`, shown next.

```
function doLogin(my_form) {

 readFileDoFunction("userInfo.xml", "GET",
   function() {
     if (request.readyState == 4) {
       if (request.status == 200) {
         processLogin(request.responseXML, my_form);
       } else {
         document.getElementById("errorDiv").innerHTML =
           "Sorry, there was a problem with the server.";
       }
     }
   }
 );
}
```

Notice that `readFileDoFunction()` is sent `"userInfo.xml"` as the name of the file to read, and `processLogin()` is the function to call once the file has been read. Notice too that if something goes wrong with reading the file, an error is put into the div with the id of `errorDiv`.

The `readFileDoFunction()` function performs the Ajax call. This function is shown next, and, as you can see, it looks very much like the function described in Figure 16-15.

```
function readFileDoFunction(file_name, request_type, the_function) {

  if (window.XMLHttpRequest) {
    request = new XMLHttpRequest();
  } else {
    request = new ActiveXObject("Microsoft.XMLHTTP");
  }

  var theURL = "http://localhost/boj/ch17/readXMLFile.php?fileName=" +
    file_name + "&t=" + new Date().getTime();

  if (request) {
    request.open(request_type, theURL);
    request.onreadystatechange = the_function;
    request.send(null);
  } else {
    document.getElementById("errorDiv").innerHTML =
      "Sorry, you must update your browser before seeing Ajax in " +
      " action.";
  }
}
```

However, unlike the function in Figure 16-15, which called the server-side program readTextFile.php, this function calls a server-side program called readXMLFile.php. If the browser doesn't understand Ajax, readFileDoFunction() puts the error message in the errorDiv div.

As before, readFileDoFunction() executes the passed-in function whenever the readyState of the request object changes. In this case, when the readyState of the request object is 4, and the request is satisfied correctly (status is 200), the passed-in function calls processLogin(), which does the actual work of logging in.

Functions Related to Logging In

Figure 17-12 lists processLogin() and some of the helper functions it calls.

```
function processLogin(user_info, my_form) {

❶   var user_name = my_form.elements["name"].value;
    var user_password = my_form.elements["password"].value;
    var success = true;
    var this_password_node;
    var this_password;

❷   var this_user = getUser(user_info, user_name);
    if (this_user != null) {
❸     this_password = getFirstValue(this_user, "password");
      if (user_password == this_password) {
        success = true;
      }
    }
```

```
      if (success == true) {
❹      document.cookie = "user=" + user_name;
        displayHomeInformation(user_name);
        document.getElementById("contentArea").innerHTML = "";
      } else {
        document.getElementById("errorDiv").innerHTML +=
          "<span style='color:red'><br>Login error; please try again.</span>";
      }
    }


❺ function getUser(user_info, user_name) {

    var users = user_info.getElementsByTagName("user");
    var count = 0;
    var found_user = null;
    var this_user;
    while ((count < users.length) && (found_user == null)) {
      this_user = users[count];
      this_name = getFirstValue(this_user, "name");
      if (this_name == user_name) {
        found_user = this_user;
      }
      count++;
    }
    return found_user;
  }

❻ function getFirstValue(my_element, child) {
❼   return my_element.getElementsByTagName(child)[0].firstChild.nodeValue;
  }

❽ function displayHomeInformation(user_name) {
    document.getElementById("loginArea").innerHTML =
      "Welcome " + user_name + ".  " +
      " <a href='#' onClick='logout(); return false'>logout</a> ";

    displayLegalLists(user_name);
  }
```

Figure 17-12: Functions related to logging in

The processLogin() function is passed two files, the first of which is the XML document retrieved by readFileDoFunction(). This is the userInfo.xml file described in the section "To Do List Data Files" on page 334. The processLogin() function is also passed in the form that was filled out by the user. The processLogin() function first extracts the values submitted with the form (starting in ❶). Then, after declaring some variables, in ❷ the function calls getUser() which takes the XML document and the username entered into the form and returns a pointer to the XML element that represents that user. More on getUser() will be found in the next section.

Next, we want to see whether the password typed into the form is the same as the user's password stored in userInfo.xml. If you look at the userInfo.xml file, you'll see that each user element has four child elements: name, password, profile, and lists. Once getUser() returns a pointer to the correct user element, ❸ calls getFirstValue() to get the value of the user element's password child element. The getFirstValue() function (defined in ❻) takes as parameters a pointer to an element, and a string holding the name of the child of that element whose value you want to return. In this case, we want to return the value of the password child of the user element. (There are more details on getFirstValue() coming in the next section.)

If the user and password match, then the success variable will have been set to true, and three things will happen. First, a cookie is set with the username (❹), which will be used whenever the page is reloaded, to check whether a user has logged in. This cookie will be deleted either when the user logs out or when the user closes the browser.

Once the cookie is set, the function displayHomeInformation() is called (defined in ❽). This function updates the page to reflect that the user successfully logged in. Finally, the message currently in the contentArea div is erased. If something goes wrong with the login (the username doesn't exist, the password doesn't match, or there was a server error), a message is put into the errorDiv.

Helper Functions

Now let's turn to the helper functions just mentioned: getFirstValue(), getUser(), and displayHomeInformation(). Because getFirstValue() is used by many functions, we'll discuss it first.

getFirstValue()

The processLogin() function calls getFirstValue() in ❸ in order to get the password of a given user. The getFirstValue() function is passed a user element and the string "password". The single line of getFirstValue() in ❼ gets the password of that user.

The first part of ❼ calls the getElementsByTagName() function on the user element that is being passed in:

```
my_element.getElementsByTagName(child)
```

Because the child parameter is the string "password", this line returns an array of the password elements of the user element.

Because we control the XML stored in userInfo.xml, we know that each user element will have only one password. Therefore, we know that the array returned by getElementsByTagName() will have only one element. The [0] in ❼ refers to the first password element, which we know is the only password element.

Just as we can use my_array[0] to refer to the first element in my_array, we can use getElementsByTagName("password")[0] to refer to the first (and only) element in the array returned by getElementsByTagName().

We now have the user element's child password element thanks to my_element.getElementsByTagName(child)[0]. Because that password element has one child (which is the text node containing the password string), we can use the firstChild property to access that text node. Once we have accessed the text node, we can get its value from its nodeValue. To make getFirstValue() more clear, it could have been written like this:

```
function getFirstValue(my_element, child) {
  var child_array = my_element.getElementsByTagName(child);
  var first_child_element = child_array[0];
  var child_text_node = first_child_element.firstChild;
  var child_value = child_text_node.nodeValue;
  return child_value;
}
```

You can see that the longer version is easier to understand but takes up much more space.

getUser()

The getUser() function (defined in ❺) takes two parameters: the XML document representing the userInfo.xml file, which was read by readFileDoFunction(), and the username. getUser() returns a pointer to an XML user element that represents the user.

getUser() calls getElementsByTagName(), which returns an array of all the user elements of the XML document. It then loops through the array and uses getFirstValue() to determine the value of the name child of each user element. If the name child is the same as the name entered into the form, we have found the user element that matches that name, and this user element is returned.

displayHomeInformation()

The function displayHomeInformation() (defined in ❽) does two things. First, it changes the contents of the loginArea div so that it shows a welcome message and a logout link instead of the login form. Next, it calls displayLegalLists(), which determines which lists this user is allowed to see, and puts links to these lists into the listArea div.

Logging Out and Checking If Logged In

When displayHomeInformation() changes the contents of the loginArea div, it inserts a logout link into the web page. Logging out is handled by the function logout() and its helper function, getNameFromCookie(). The getNameFromCookie() function is also called by checkIfLoggedIn(), which is called whenever the To Do list application is visited (see ❶ in Figure 17-10). Each of these functions are shown in Figure 17-13. Let's see how they get the job done.

```
function logout() {
  var the_date = new Date("December 31, 1900");
  var the_cookie_date = the_date.toGMTString();
❶  var user_name = getNameFromCookie();
  document.cookie = "user=" + escape(user_name) +
    ";expires=" + the_cookie_date;

❷  clearTimeout(user_list_timeout);
  clearTimeout(current_list_timeout);
❸  window.location.reload();
```

```
    }
❹ function getNameFromCookie() {
       var cookieParts = null;
       var user_name = null;
       if (document.cookie != null) {
❺        user_name = document.cookie.split("=")[1];
       }
       return user_name;
    }

❻ function checkIfLoggedIn() {
       var user_name = getNameFromCookie();
       if (user_name != null) {
          displayHomeInformation(user_name);
       }
    }
```

Figure 17-13: Checking for logged-in user and logging out

logout()

The logout() function is called when a user clicks on the logout link shown in
Figure 17-3. The logout() function deletes the cookie that is storing the username, clears any time-outs that have been set, and resets the application to
the pre-logged-in state showing in Figure 17-1.

First, logout() deletes the cookie which is storing the username by
changing its date value to a prior date (as discussed in the section "Setting
the Duration of a Cookie" on page 222). It uses these two lines:

```
var the_date = new Date("December 31, 1900");
var the_cookie_date = the_date.toGMTString();
```

Next, ❶ calls getNameFromCookie(), which reads the cookie and returns a
string with the username. Then document.cookie is set with this expired cookie,
effectively deleting it.

A couple of time-outs are cleared in ❷ (more on these soon). Finally,
logout() calls the reload() method of the window's location object, which
reloads the page. Because the cookie has been deleted, the user is no longer
logged in, and when the page is reloaded it returns to its pre-logged-in state,
as shown in Figure 17-1.

getNameFromCookie()

getNameFromCookie() in ❹ retrieves the username from the cookie created upon
login by extracting it in ❺ with

```
user_name = document.cookie.split("=")[1];
```

This line splits whatever is stored in document.cookie into parts, using = as a
delimiter. Our To Do list application stores only one cookie, which, if the
user is logged in, will equal something like username=odysseus. The split()
method splits this string into two parts and puts those parts into an array;
[1] returns the second element of the array.

checkIfLoggedIn()

If a logged-in user clicks the reload button on his or her browser, the To Do list application should redisplay his or her information when the page is reloaded. The checkIfLoggedIn() function, defined in ❻, inspects the application's cookie, which contains a username, and displays the user's To Do list information using the displayHomeInformation() function.

Displaying Available Lists

Once a user has logged in, the line after ❹ in Figure 17-12 calls the displayHomeInformation() function (❽ in Figure 17-12).

This function updates the loginArea div with a welcome message and a logout link and then calls displayLegalLists(), which (together with the functions described below) determines which To Do lists a user can see and modify. The collection of available lists is placed inside listArea div.

If a second user decides to give the logged-in user access to his or her list, the available lists section for that logged-in user needs to be updated. We use a setTimeout to regularly check to see whether this kind of updating will be necessary.

Figure 17-14 lists the functions that display and update a user's list of available To Do lists.

```
function displayLegalLists(user_name) {

  readFileDoFunction("userInfo.xml", "GET",
    function() {
      if (request.readyState == 4) {
        if (request.status == 200) {
❶         var last_modified = request.getResponseHeader("Last-Modified");
          var last_modified_date = new Date(last_modified);
❷         displayLists(request.responseXML, user_name,
            last_modified_date.getTime());
        } else {
          document.getElementById("errorDiv").innerHTML =
            "Sorry, your lists could not be displayed due to a " +
            "problem with the server.";
        }
      }
    }
  );
}

function displayLists(user_info, user_name, last_modified_date) {
  var this_user = getUser(user_info, user_name);
  var display_info = "";
  var this_link;
  var this_list;
  if (this_user != null) {
❸   var lists_element = this_user.getElementsByTagName("lists")[0];
❹   var lists = lists_element.getElementsByTagName("list");
    for (var loop=0; loop < lists.length; loop++) {
❺     this_list = lists[loop].firstChild.nodeValue;
❻     this_link = "<a href=\"#\" onClick=\"readyDisplayList('" +
        this_list + "'); return false;\">" +
```

```
          this_list + "</a>";
        display_info += this_link + "<br>";
      }

      document.getElementById("listArea").innerHTML = display_info;
❼    user_list_timeout =
        setTimeout("updateUserIfChanged(" + last_modified_date + ",'" +
          user_name + "')", 60000);
    }
  }

❽ function updateUserIfChanged(current_last_modified, user_name) {

    readFileDoFunction("userInfo.xml", "HEAD",
      function() {
        if (request.readyState == 4) {
          if (request.status == 200) {
            var last_modified = request.getResponseHeader("Last-Modified");
            var last_modified_date = new Date(last_modified).getTime();
            if (last_modified_date != current_last_modified) {
❾            displayLegalLists(user_name);
            }
❿          user_list_timeout = setTimeout("updateUserIfChanged(" +
              last_modified_date + ",'" + user_name + "')",
              60000);
          } else {
            document.getElementById("errorDiv").innerHTML =
              "Problem updating user " + request.status;
          }
        }
      }
    );
  }
```

Figure 17-14: Functions to display and update a user's To Do list

The displayLegalLists() function starts by using readFileDoFunction() to
trigger an Ajax call.

```
readFileDoFunction("userInfo.xml", "GET", function() {...})
```

This call reads in the userInfo.xml file and executes the provided anonymous
function, function() {...}. Most of the anonymous function is executed when
the Ajax request object reaches readyState 4, and the server returns a 200
message, signifying that the request was properly satisfied. When these conditions are met, the anonymous function in ❶ reads the Last-Modified field
of the request object's response header and turns it into a Date object.

Next, the anonymous function calls displayLists() in ❷ and sends it
three parameters: the XML retrieved from the request, the name of the
logged-in user, and the time the userInfo.xml file was last updated.

NOTE   *The value passed to displayLists() is not the Date object itself. Instead, the Date's
getTime() method is called to return the number of seconds between the last time the
file was updated and January 1, 1970.*

displayLists()

The displayLists() function does most of the real work. It first calls getUser() to get the appropriate user element from the userInfo.xml file. Then, in ❸, it gets the first child element of the user element, named lists. Because there is only one element named lists for each user element, we know that we want the first one. Once we have the lists element, getElementsByTagName() is called again in ❹ to return an array filled with the set of list elements that are nested in the lists element.

Once we have our array, we loop through it to create a string to display each list element. The code in ❺ gets the name of the each list element in the loop. For example, the user Odysseus has two available lists: his and Nestor's. The array created in ❹ contains each of these lists. The first time through the loop, ❺ pulls out odysseus; the next time through, it pulls nestor.

Once ❺ determines the name of the list, ❻ creates the string to be displayed in the web browser, which will look something like this:

```
<a href="#" onClick="readyDisplayList('odysseus'); return false;">odysseus</a>
```

The body of the link is the name of the available list (shown here as odysseus). An onClick inside the link calls readyDisplayList() when clicked, which pulls the name of the list.

Once the loop completes, display_info will hold the string with all of the available To Do lists. This string is then put into the innerHTML of the listArea div. Finally, ❼ sets the time-out that will be used to check whether the userInfo.xml file has been changed. Line ❼ calls updateUserIfChanged() (defined in ❽) after one minute and passes it the date userInfo.xml was last modified and the name of the logged-in user.

THE IMPORTANCE OF FUNCTION PARAMETERS

Many functions in the To Do list application, including displayLists() and displayLegalLists(), take the name of the logged-in user as a parameter. Because the user is logged in, that name is also available by inspecting document.cookie. You may ask yourself, why bother passing the username as a parameter to a function if it's available in the cookie? For stylistic reasons, I like to pass in as parameters all the variables that impact the behavior of a function. This makes it easier to adapt the functions to new situations where, perhaps, the username is not stored in a cookie.

Think of a function as a black box. Input is sent into the box, something happens inside the box, and out comes some output. We know what goes into the function by looking at its parameters, and we know what comes out of the function by looking at the return values.

This style of coding makes it easier to see what a function does and to reuse functions in other scripts. If a function relies on values that are not passed into it as parameters, a person reading the function will have to read the whole thing to understand what information the function needs in order to work correctly.

updateUserIfChanged()

Now the updateUserIfChanged() function does a HEAD call to check whether the last modified date of the userInfo.xml file differs from the one that was passed into the function. If the last modified date of userInfo.xml is different, the file has been updated, and ❾ calls displayLegalLists() again to reload the user's legal list information. Finally, updateUserIfChanged() creates a new time-out to call updateUserIfChanged() again in one minute (❿). This time-out loop, in which updateUserIfChanged() is called and then a time-out is set to call updateUserIfChanged() again in a minute, keeps going until the user logs out, clearing the time-out.

Displaying a Specific List

Now the list of available To Do lists is displayed to the user with the name of each list as a link. Clicking on a link calls the function readyDisplayList(), which begins the process of displaying the contents of a given To Do list. Figure 17-15 lists readyDisplayList().

```
function readyDisplayList(list_name) {

❶ var file_name = list_name + ".xml";
❷ readFileDoFunction(file_name, "GET",
     function() {
        if (request.readyState == 4) {
          if (request.status == 200) {
            var last_modified = request.getResponseHeader("Last-Modified");
            var last_modified_date = new Date(last_modified);
❸          displayList(request.responseXML,
                last_modified_date.getTime());
          } else {
            document.getElementById("errorDiv").innerHTML =
              "Sorry, could not display To Do list " + list_name +
              " due to a problem with the server.";
          }
        }
      }
   );
}
```

Figure 17-15: Function to display a To Do list

Figure 17-16 lists the associated functions of readyDisplayList().

```
function displayList(the_list, last_modified_date) {
❶   var list_name = getFirstValue(the_list, "name");
    var intro_text = "<h3>Looking at list: " + list_name + "</h3>";
    var pending_display = "Still Pending:<br><ul>";
❷   var open_item_element =
      the_list.getElementsByTagName("openitems")[0];
```

```javascript
      var open_items = open_item_element.getElementsByTagName("item");
      for (var loop=0; loop < open_items.length; loop++) {
        this_item = open_items[loop];
        this_contents = getFirstValue(this_item, "contents");
        this_number = getFirstValue(this_item, "number");
❸      pending_display += "<li><input type='checkbox' " +
          "onClick=\"readyMarkDone('" + list_name +
          "'," + this_number + ");\"> " + this_contents;
      }
      pending_display += "</ul>";

      var done_display = "Completed:<br><ul>";
      var open_item_element =
        the_list.getElementsByTagName("doneitems")[0];
      var open_items = open_item_element.getElementsByTagName("item");
      for (var loop=0; loop < open_items.length; loop++) {
        this_item = open_items[loop];
        this_contents = getFirstValue(this_item, "contents");
        this_number = getFirstValue(this_item, "number");
        done_display += "<li><input type='checkbox' " +
          "onClick=\"readyMarkUndone('" + list_name + "'," +
          this_number + ");\"> " + this_contents;
      }
      done_display += "</ul>";


❹    document.getElementById("contentArea").innerHTML =
        intro_text + pending_display + done_display;

❺    document.getElementById("contentArea").innerHTML +=
        "<p> <form>Add New Item: <input type='text' name='newItem'>"+
        "<input type=\"button\" value=\"add\"  " +
        onClick=\"addNewItem(this.form, '" +
        list_name + "');\"></form>";

❻    todo_list_timeout =
        setTimeout("updateTodoIfChanged(" +
          last_modified_date + ",'" + list_name + "')",
          5000);
    }

    function updateTodoIfChanged(current_last_modified, list_name) {
❼    readFileDoFunction(list_name + ".xml", "HEAD",
        function() {
          if (request.readyState == 4) {
            if (request.status == 200) {
              var last_modified = request.getResponseHeader("Last-Modified");
              var last_modified_date = new Date(last_modified).getTime();
              if (last_modified_date != current_last_modified) {
❽              readyDisplayList(list_name);
              }
❾            todo_list_timeout = setTimeout("updateTodoIfChanged(" +
```

```
        last_modified_date + ",'" + list_name + "')",
        seconds_between_todo_list_update);
  } else {
    document.getElementById("errorDiv").innerHTML =
      "Problem updating To Do list " + request.status;
  }
    }
  }
);
}
```

Figure 17-16: The supporting functions for displaying a To Do list

readyDisplayList()

readyDisplayList()is very similar to displayLegalLists(), shown in Figure 17-14. Like displayLegalLists(), it takes the name of a list to read (for example, odysseus) and calls the Ajax function readFileDoFunction(), which reads the file containing the list and then calls another function.

The code in ❶ in Figure 17-15 sets the name of the file equal to the name of the list, concatenated with the string ".xml". If the user wants to see the odysseus list, the code in ❷ will read the file odysseus.xml. The anonymous function sent to readFileDoFunction() calls displayList() once the file has been completely loaded (❸). Finally, the displayList() function is sent an XML document read from the file and the file's last modification time.

displayList()

The displayList() function in Figure 17-16 does most of the work involved in displaying a To Do list. Its first line (❶) calls getFirstValue() to retrieve the name of the list from the XML document.

In Figure 17-8, you'll see that the name element is a child of the root of the XML file. The getFirstValue() function reads the string inside the first (and only) name element inside the list element. The next couple of lines start the strings that we will use to display the To Do list.

To Do List Strings

The To Do list is represented by two strings: one listing the set of items to complete (pending items), the other listing the set of items which have already been completed. These two strings are, in turn, constructed in two loops. The first loop adds the pending items to one string, and the second adds the completed items to the other string.

The first loop starts in ❷, where it accesses the first openitem element that is a child of the list element. This openitem element has a set of item elements inside. Each element is a task to complete. The loop iterates through each of these items, creating a string that is added to the pending_display string. (You should already be familiar will all the lines in that loop.) Each line in the loop gets a value of the item, either its contents or its identification number.

Line ❸ creates the string for each item, which looks like this:

```
<li><input type='checkbox' onClick="readyMarkDone('odysseus', 2);"> Beat Troy
```

As you can see, each item gets a checkbox that, when clicked, calls the function readyMarkDone(). This function marks an item completed, moving it from the pending to the completed list. The function has two parameters: the name of the list to update and the item to be updated.

Once the loop describing the pending items completes, the loop that lists the completed item kicks in. This loop is just like the previous one, except that it iterates through all the items inside the doneitems element and prints out a checkbox with an onClick that calls the function readyMarkUndone(), which moves an item from the completed list back to the pending list.

Adding the Content to the Web Page

Once both loops have run their course, ❹ puts the introductory text, the list of pending items, and the list of done items into the contentArea div. Line ❺ adds a form to that div (with an input box and a button) that calls addNewItem() to add new items to the To Do list once the add button has been clicked.

Finally, ❻ starts a time-out that works just like the time-out in ❿ of Figure 17-14, except that it calls updateTodoIfChanged() instead of updateUserIfChanged().

updateTodoIfChanged()

The updateTodoIfChanged() function is like updateUserIfChanged() (shown in ❽ in Figure 17-14). There are three key differences between these functions. First, updateTodoIfChanged() and updateUserIfChanged() read different XML files. updateUserIfChanged() reads the userInfo.xml file, and as you can see in ❼ of Figure 17-16, updateTodoIfChanged() reads in the XML file storing the requested To Do list (for example, odysseus.xml). Second, the functions updateTodoIfChanged() and updateUserIfChanged() call different functions after reading their requested files. The updateUserIfChanged() function calls displayLegalLists() to display the list of To Do lists a user may edit.

In contrast, the updateTodoIfChanged() function calls readyDisplayList() to display the requested To Do list once it has finished reading the requested To Do list file (❽). The final difference between updateTodoIfChanged() and updateUserIfChanged() is the time-out set in ❾, which sets a time-out to call updateTodoIfChanged() instead of calling updateUserIfChanged(), as occurs in updateUserIfChanged.

Processing Changes to a List

A user may change a To Do list by moving an item between the pending and completed lists or by adding a new item to the To Do list. Let's turn first to Figure 17-17, which covers the functions needed to change the status of an existing item.

```
❶ function readyMarkDone(list_name, the_item) {

     var file_name = list_name + ".xml";
❷  readFileDoFunction(file_name, "GET",
       function() {
         if (request.readyState == 4) {
           if (request.status == 200) {
❸            markDone(request.responseXML, the_item, list_name);
           } else {
             document.getElementById("errorDiv").innerHTML =
               "Sorry, this item could not be marked done due to a " +
               "problem with the server.";
           }
         }
       }
     );
   }

❹ function markDone(the_document, the_item, list_name, last_modified_date) {

❺    var open_items = getItems(the_document,"openitems");
     var done_items = getItems(the_document,"doneitems");
     var this_number;
     var found_item = null;
     var count = 0;
❻    while ((count < open_items.length) && (found_item == null)) {
       this_number = getFirstValue(open_items[count], "number");
       if (this_number == the_item) {
         found_item = open_items[count];
       } else {
         count++;
       }
     }
❼    if (found_item != null) {
❽      open_items.splice(count, 1);
❾      done_items.push(found_item);
❿      saveAndReload(open_items, done_items, list_name);
     }
   }
```

Figure 17-17: Changing the status of a task

Figure 17-17 shows the two main functions involved in changing an item
from pending to done: readyMarkDone() and markDone().

readyMarkDone()

The readyMarkDone() function in ❶ is called whenever someone clicks a
checkbox next to a pending item in the To Do list. This function is passed
the name of the list to edit and the number of the task to be moved from
pending to done. The function then calls readFileDoFunction() in ❷ and
passes it the name of the To Do list file to load, as well as an anonymous
function to execute when the request object changes its readyState.

The anonymous function executes the markDone() function once the To Do file has been completely loaded. The markDone() function takes four parameters: the name of the requested XML file, the identification number of the item that is changing its status, the name of the requested list, and the list's last modification date.

markDone()

When called, markDone() in ❹ creates two arrays: open_items (❺) contains all the pending tasks in the To Do list, and done_items contains all the done tasks. (These arrays are created by getItems(), which we'll discuss shortly.) Once these arrays have been created, ❻ loops through the open_items array, looking for the item identified by the number passed into markDone()'s second parameter. If it finds the item, three things happen, beginning in ❼:

1. markDone() removes the item from the open_items array using the built-in array method splice(). (This method takes two parameters: an item in the array to remove and the number of items to remove, including the one in the first parameter.)

2. The splice() method in ❽ removes just the found item from the open_items array, and the item is put at the end of the done_items array, using the array method push() in ❾.

3. In ❿ saveAndReload() turns the arrays into a new XML file, sends the XML back to the webserver for saving, and then updates the To Do list.

getItems() and saveAndReload()

The markDone() function in Figure 17-17 relied on some helper functions: getItems() and saveAndReload(). The getItems() function is passed an XML document and the name of an XML element, and it returns an array of all XML elements from the document with the given name. The saveAndReload() function saves an XML document to the webserver and updates the To Do list seen in the web browser. These helper functions are shown in Figure 17-18.

```
❶ function getItems(the_document, the_item_type) {
     var the_items_array = new Array();
     var item_elements = the_document.getElementsByTagName(the_item_type)[0];
     var items = item_elements.getElementsByTagName("item");
     for (var loop=0; loop < items.length; loop++) {
       the_items_array[loop] = items[loop];
     }
     return the_items_array;
   }


❷ function saveAndReload(open_items, done_items, list_name) {
❸   var the_string = "<?xml version='1.0' ?>";
     the_string += "<list>";
     the_string += "<name>" + list_name + "</name>";
❹   the_string += getItemString("openitems", open_items);
     the_string += getItemString("doneitems", done_items);
     the_string += "</list>";
```

```javascript
     var file_name = list_name + ".xml";
❺  saveFileDoFunction(file_name, the_string,
     function() {
       if (request.readyState == 4) {
         if ((request.responseText == "success") &&
           (request.status == 200)) {
           readyDisplayList(list_name);
         } else {
           document.getElementById("errorDiv").innerHTML =
             "Sorry, there was an error saving your list. ";
         }
       }
     }
   );
   }

❻ function getItemString(item_list_name, item_list) {
     var the_string = "<" + item_list_name + ">";
     for (var loop = 0; loop < item_list.length; loop++) {

       the_string += "<item>";
       the_string += "<number>" +
         getFirstValue(item_list[loop], "number") + "</number>";
       the_string += "<contents>" +
         getFirstValue(item_list[loop], "contents") + "</contents>";
       the_string += "</item>";
     }
     the_string += "</" + item_list_name + ">";

     return the_string;
   }

❼ function saveFileDoFunction(file_name, the_contents, the_function) {

   if (window.XMLHttpRequest) {
     request = new XMLHttpRequest();
   } else {
     request = new ActiveXObject("Microsoft.XMLHTTP");
   }

❽  var the_url = "http://localhost/boj/ch17/saveXMLFile.php?t=" +
     new Date().getTime();
❾  var the_message = "fileName=" + file_name + "&contents=" + the_contents;
   if (request) {
❿    request.open("POST", the_url);
     request.setRequestHeader("Content-type",
       "application/x-www-form-urlencoded; charset=UTF-8");
     request.onreadystatechange = the_function;
     request.send(the_message);
   } else {
     document.getElementById("errorDiv").innerHTML =
       "Sorry, you must update your browser before seeing Ajax in action.";

   }
   }
```

Figure 17-18: More functions involved in changing a task's status

getItems()

The function getItems() in Figure 17-18 (❶) retrieves an array of tasks that are either openitems or doneitems. The function getItems() is called with an XML document and a type of item to get: either items inside an openitems element or items inside a doneitems element. getItems() calls getElementsByTagName() to get an array of elements of the given type and then it loops through this array, loading each item into a new array called the_items_array.

Limitations on Manipulating XML Documents

Ordinarily, there's no reason to loop through one array just to add all of its elements to a new array as I'm doing in getItems(). But here's why I'm doing that.

When getItems() uses getElementsByTagName() to retrieve an array of elements, that array comes from the XML document. You may recall that the markDone() function alters the array returned by getItems(), calling splice() to remove elements from the array and push() to add elements. Unfortunately, most browsers won't allow changes to arrays retrieved from the XML document. Therefore, getItems() creates its own JavaScript array and copies the items out of the array returned by getElementsByTagName() into the new array called the_items_array.

saveAndReload()

The next helper function, saveAndReload(), is defined in ❷. It creates a string containing an XML document, which is based on the information in the open_items and done_items arrays created by markDone() and markUndone(), and then it sets up the Ajax call that saves this string to the webserver.

Line ❸ begins the creation of a string that holds the XML document. The next few lines add the name of the To Do list and the opening list element tag. The next two lines (starting with ❹) call getItemString() to create strings that contain the information stored in the open_items and done_items arrays.

getItemString()

The getItemString() function, declared in ❻, loops through the provided array and creates a string representing each item. (You should find the code in getItemString() easy to follow by now.)

The lines after ❹ add the closing list tag, then set up the Ajax call that will save the altered To Do list to the webserver and call the functions used to display the To Do list. This Ajax call, performed by saveFileDoFunction(), is similar to readFileDoFunction() (discussed in "Logging In and Out" on page 340), except that it saves a file instead of reading it.

saveAndReload()

The function saveAndReload() calls saveFileDoFunction() in ❺ and passes it the name of a file to save, the string to be saved into the file, and an anonymous function that is called when the Ajax request object changes its readyState.

In this case, once the file has been saved to the server, the anonymous function calls readyDisplayList(), which, if you remember from Figures 17-15 and 17-16, sets up an Ajax call that reads the file that was just saved and displays the results.

saveFileDoFunction()

The contents of saveFileDoFunction(), which start in ❼ in Figure 17-18, should look very familiar to you. Line ❽ defines the URL that points to the server-side program being called (saveXMLFile.php). Line ❾ creates the message to send with the POST, which includes the name of the file to be saved and the file's contents. (Because the contents are sent via POST, rather than GET, I don't need to use escape() here, as I did when sending information in a GET in Figure 16-9.)

Finally, ❿ and the subsequent lines send the POST request.

NOTE *It would be a good idea to remove all of the characters that are illegal XML, however, such as quotation marks and less than and greater than symbols. To do that, replace each with its HTML encoding: ", <, and >. For brevity's sake, I'll leave that as an exercise for the reader.*

Adding a New Item

The final section of code in the application adds a new item to a To Do list when a user fills in the Add New Item text box in Figure 17-4. Clicking the add button calls addNewItem() and sends it the form and the name of the list being edited.

Figure 17-19 shows you the addNewItem() function and the functions it relies on.

```
❶ function addNewItem(the_form, list_name) {

     var file_name = list_name + ".xml";
     readFileDoFunction(file_name, "GET",
       function() {
         if (request.readyState == 4) {
           if (request.status == 200) {
❷            addNewToFile(request.responseXML, the_form.newItem.value,
                 list_name);
           } else {
             document.getElementById("errorDiv").innerHTML =
               "Sorry, new item could not be added to To Do list for" + list_name +
               " due to a problem with the server.";
           }
         }
       }
     );
   }

❸ function addNewToFile(the_document, new_contents, list_name) {

❹   var open_items = getItems(the_document,"openitems");
     var done_items = getItems(the_document,"doneitems");
```

```
⑤  var high_number = getHighValue(the_document);
   var new_number = high_number + 1;
⑥  var new_item = document.createElement("item");
   var new_item_number = document.createElement("number");
   var new_item_content = document.createElement("contents");
   new_item_number.appendChild(document.createTextNode(new_number));
   new_item_content.appendChild(document.createTextNode(new_contents));
   new_item.appendChild(new_item_number);
   new_item.appendChild(new_item_content);
⑦  open_items.push(new_item);
⑧  saveAndReload(open_items, done_items, list_name);
   }


⑨ function getHighValue(the_document) {
   var high_number = 0;
   var this_number = 0;
   var items = the_document.getElementsByTagName("item");
   for (var loop=0; loop < items.length; loop++) {
     this_number = parseInt(getFirstValue(items[loop], "number"));
     if (this_number > high_number) {
       high_number = this_number;
     }
   }
   return high_number;
}
```

Figure 17-19: Adding new items

Function addNewItem() in ❶ is a now-familiar Ajax setup function. It calls readFileDoFunction(), tells it to read the appropriate To Do list, and defines an anonymous function that calls addNewToFile() in ❷, once the request list has been read.

The addNewToFile() function in ❸ is passed an XML document representing the To Do list, new information to add to that list, and the name of the list. Line ❹ uses the getItems() function described in Figure 17-18 to get all pending items in the To Do list, and the following line gets all the completed items.

The rest of addNewToFile() creates the item to add to the list, each of which has an identifier number, which the various functions use to refer to each item. These identifiers are assigned in order, so each new item gets a number one higher than the highest-numbered item in the To Do list.

Line ❺ calls getHighValue() to determine the highest numbered item on the To Do list; the following line adds one to that value to set a new identifier number. The lines beginning in ❻ and ending in ❼ use XML methods to create a new item. Once they complete, new_item will be an XML element that looks like this:

```
<item>
    <number>6</number>
    <contents>This is a new item</contents>
</item>
```

Line ❼ adds this new item to the array of open items retrieved in ❹. Finally, ❽ calls saveAndReload() (introduced in Figure 17-18) to save the two item arrays.

getHighValue()

Believe it or not, we are almost done. The only function left to describe, getHighValue() (❾), loops through all the items in a list, retrieves their identifier numbers, and returns the highest number among them.

And that, dear reader, is the entirety of the application so far.

A Few Closing Notes

This application combines elements from every chapter of this book. If you've understood everything here, you can consider yourself well versed in JavaScript lore. However, before closing, I have two final issues to raise about the application: how to decide whether code should run in the client side versus the server side, and considerations about the security of the application.

Client-Side or Server-Side Code?

Most of the code in this application was written in JavaScript and therefore appeared on the client side. I designed the application this way because this is *The Book of JavaScript*, not *The Book of PHP* (which may be in the works).

Nevertheless, some of the code would have been better placed on the server side. For example, displayLegalLists() in Figure 17-14 displays a user's list of available To Do lists. However, even though the application cares only about changes to the logged-in user's information, displayLegalLists() actually retrieves the entire userInfo.xml file. The entire file must be read, because all the code for extracting the information specific to the logged-in user from userInfo.xml appears in the JavaScript.

In contrast, when information about the user is extracted on the server side instead, the PHP can send only the part of userInfo.xml that we care about. This sends less information across the network and gives the JavaScript less to deal with. When one million people have signed up for your shared To Do list service, the difference between a few lines of XML and millions of lines of XML is enormous.

Sending information across the Internet is often the biggest bottleneck in any client-server application, so do what you can to minimize the amount of information that clients and servers pass back and forth.

Security Issues

When writing server-side applications, you must pay attention to security issues. Many servers are hacked because of poorly written server-side code.

The application described here is insecure in two ways. First, user passwords are sent from the web browser to the webserver without encryption. Second, the application does not do enough to ensure that a user has successfully logged in before giving the user access to To Do lists.

Password Encryption

Information does not pass directly from a web browser to a webserver; it is routed around the Internet, passing from one server to another until it reaches its destination. Any server along the way can spy on you, looking for passwords, and if those passwords are sent without encryption (also called a *cleartext*), the spy's job is made even easier.

One solution might be to write a JavaScript function to encrypt the password before it is sent to the webserver, and then decrypt it on the server side. This is a bad solution, because anyone can view the JavaScript on your web page and figure out how your encryption function works.

The solution is to use a secure webserver that understands the HTTPS protocol (that is, secure HTTP). HTTPS works just like HTTP except that it adds an additional encryption/authentication layer between HTTP and TCP. Okay, that's enough of that mumbo jumbo for now.

To send a message to a secure HTTPS server, use https:// instead of http:// at the beginning of your URL. When https:// is used, the web browser and webserver act together to encrypt and decrypt information securely.

To send information securely within your application (assuming that you have access to a secure server), use an https:// URL in your Ajax calls and the username and password parameters in the `request.open()` method (see "Telling the Object Where to Send the Request" on page 266).

NOTE *All commonly used brands of webservers have a secure mode, so if you are running your own webserver, check that server's documentation. If you are not running your own webserver, ask your server's system administrator whether your server supports secure transactions.*

Using Server-Side Sessions

Our application uses a cookie to determine if a user has logged in. This poses another security problem. Because cookies live on the client side of the application, they can be faked by clever users. A malicious user could create his own `username=odysseus` cookie, put it on his hard drive, and get access to Odysseus's account.

To avoid this potential problem, you should have your server track users who have logged in properly. When a user logs in properly with the login function, the server records that. Then, whenever a user wants to get information from the webserver, the server checks to see whether this user has properly logged in. If not, the server doesn't give the user access to restricted information or services.

The traditional way to track logged in users is with a *session*. When a user logs in, the server starts a session, which tracks the user. All server-side languages, including PHP, provide some way of creating sessions.

NOTE *To learn more about sessions in PHP, pick up a PHP book or search the Internet. In addition, many of the toolkits described in Appendix B, such as Sajax, help you handle sessions.*

Summary

The primary point of this chapter has been to show how you can integrate everything in this book to create a useful and practical web application. If you've lost track of how all the functions described work together, see the road map in Figure 17-11, and then check the JavaScript again to see where the dependencies arise.

Although most of the application used JavaScript learned earlier in the book, there were a few new tidbits of information. We discussed:

- Using splice() to delete elements from arrays (Figure 17-17)
- Dealing with browsers that won't let you edit XML documents (see "Limitations on Manipulating XML Documents" on page 356)
- Using https:// and the open() method of the request object to send information securely
- Applying the divide and conquer problem-solving technique when faced with an overwhelming task

Congratulations on making it this far! You are now ready to start writing very complex JavaScript applications. Be warned, however! As your JavaScript gets more complex, bugs get trickier to detect and weed out. The next chapter discusses the very important topic of debugging and introduces you to a number of tools and techniques that will help you find and stomp out those bothersome bugs.

Assignment

Your assignment is to add these critical features to the application discussed in this chapter:

- Allow new users to join the service
- Allow a user to permit another user to access his or her To Do list

How you add these features and what they look like is completely up to you. You're the expert now!

18

DEBUGGING JAVASCRIPT AND AJAX

Now that you've mastered the basics of JavaScript, it's time to start writing some complicated scripts of your own. This chapter will help you solve the problems that inevitably arise in writing even simple scripts. The key point is to think before you code. Having a clear idea of how your script will work before you write it will cut down tremendously on your rewriting and bug fixing.

Of course, you can't avoid bugs altogether, so you'll need to learn how to decrease the number of bugs in your scripts and figure out why a program isn't doing what you want. This chapter covers some common debugging tips and techniques, including how to:

- Write clear and relatively bug-free code
- Avoid common mistakes
- Print out variables and log messages in various ways
- Use and interpret your browser's JavaScript bug detector

- Use a more complete JavaScript debugger
- Debug Ajax
- Fix bugs without creating new ones

Good Coding Practices

Two keys to good programming are to *write programs for people, not for computers,* and to *think before you code.*

Writing programs for people means using comments to guide readers through your code, using meaningful variable names, and writing code that's easy to understand rather than clever. Clever coding is cute, but the clever coder gets the bug.

Sketching out your code using comments is a good way to wind up with commented and well thought-out code. Programmers often think that they will have time to "clean up" the code after they have everything working. Unfortunately, once one bit of code works, there will always be more to write, so people rarely have time to go back and comment their code. Commenting first ensures that the comments will be there when you are done. It also forces you to figure out how your JavaScript will work before you dive in and start coding. Thinking before you code means that you will be less likely to pursue a path that will not work. Writing comments first also means that you will have a feeling for how much work lies before you. As you write the JavaScript that performs the tasks described by your comments, you will be able to keep track of what you have accomplished and how much remains.

Starting with Comments

Here's an example of writing the comments for a function before writing the function itself:

```
//function beKind()
// beKind asks for a user's name, chooses a random affirmation,
// and returns an alert box with the name and the kind words
function beKind()
{
  // first construct a list of affirmations
  //

  // next get the user's name
  //

  // then choose a random affirmation
  //

  // finally return the personalized kindness
  //
}
```

Filling In the Code

Now that you have your JavaScript plotted out in comments, you can fill in the code itself, step by step.

```javascript
//function beKind()
// beKind asks for a user's name, chooses a random affirmation,
// and returns an alert box with the name and the affirmation
function beKind()
{
  // first construct a list of affirmations
  //
  var the_affirmation_list = new Array();
  the_affirmation_list[0] = "You are a great coder!";
  the_affirmation_list[1] = "Your JavaScript is powerful!";
  the_affirmation_list[2] = "You finished the whole book!";

  // next get the user's name
  //
  var the_name = prompt("What's your name?", "");

  // then choose a random affirmation
  //
  var the_number = Math.floor(Math.random() * 5);
  var the_affirmation = the_affirmation_list[the_number];

  // finally return the personalized kindness
  //
  alert("Congratulations, " + the_name + ". " + the_affirmation);
}
```

Commenting not only forces you to think before you code; it also makes the task of coding seem a lot easier. Instead of facing one huge task, you've already broken it down into easily coded sections.

Avoiding Common Mistakes

Most beginning programmers make simple syntactic mistakes. It takes a long time to stop forgetting to close quotes, curly brackets, and parentheses, but luckily modern browsers have JavaScript bug detectors that detect such errors for you. Those bug detectors will be described later in the chapter. This section covers techniques for avoiding a few common mistakes that many browser bug detectors won't catch.

Use a Consistent Naming Convention

The JavaScript bug detector often misses incorrect capitalization and pluralization of variable and function names, a common and annoying error. You'll greatly reduce the occurrence of such mistakes if you stick to one convention for naming variables and functions. For instance, I name my variables in all lowercase and with underscores replacing spaces (my_variable, the_date, an_example_variable, and so on), and I use in-caps notation for functions (addThreeNumbers(), writeError(), and so on). See the section "Naming Your Functions" on page 85 for more information. I avoid pluralizing anything because it's easy to forget which variables you've made plural.

Avoid Reserved Words

You can't use words reserved for JavaScript as variables. For example, you can't name a variable if, because JavaScript uses if. Though it's not likely you'd name a variable if, you might want to use a variable called, for example, document. Unfortunately, document is a JavaScript object, so using it as a variable would wreak all kinds of havoc.

Even more unfortunately, different browsers reserve different words, so there's no complete list of words to eschew. The safest course of action is to avoid words used in JavaScript and in HTML. If you're having problems with a variable and you can't figure out what's wrong, you may be running into such a problem—try renaming the variable.

Remember to Use Two Equal Signs in Logical Tests

Some browsers catch the equal-sign error; some don't. This very common mistake is extremely difficult to detect if the browser doesn't find it for you. Here's an example:

```
var the_name = prompt("What's your name?", "");
if (the_name = "thau")
{
  alert("Hello, thau!");
} else {
  alert("Hello, stranger.");
}
```

This code shows you the Hello, thau! alert box regardless of what you type in the prompt, because only one equal sign appears in the if-then statement. The equal sign sets the_name equal to "thau" and returns a value of true. This extremely insidious bug will drive you batty. For your own sanity's sake, concentrate on not making mistakes like this. Your psychiatrist will thank you.

I avoid this mistake by thinking about two equals signs as *is the same as*, and one equal sign as *equals*. When I code, I say to myself, "If the_name is the same as "thau", then. . . ." Thinking about the code this way helps me remember the difference between one and two equal signs.

Use Quotation Marks Correctly

This one gets me time and time again. The only way JavaScript knows the difference between a variable and a string is that strings have quotes around them and variables don't. Here's an obvious error:

```
var the_name = 'Ishmael';
alert("the_name is very happy");
```

The above code yields an alert box that says *the_name is very happy* even though the_name is a variable. Once JavaScript sees quotes around something, it simply treats it like a string. Putting the_name in quotes stops JavaScript from looking up the_name in its memory.

Here's a less obvious variation of this bug, which we saw in Chapter 9:

```
function wakeMeIn3()
{
  var the_message = "Wake up! Hey! Hey! WAKE UP!!!!";
  setTimeout("alert(the_message);", 3000);
}
```

The problem is that you're telling JavaScript to execute alert(the_message) in three seconds—but three seconds from now the_message won't exist because you've exited the wakeMeIn3() function (the function itself defines the_message variable). Here's the solution to this problem:

```
function wakeMeIn3()
{
    var the_message = "Wake up!";
    setTimeout("alert('" + the_message + "');", 3000);
}
```

When you pull the_message out of the quotes, the setTimeout() schedules the command alert("Wake up!");—which is the result you want.

Finding Bugs

Much of the debugging process involves discovering where the bug is in the first place. Unfortunately, finding the little pests isn't always easy.

You can look for bugs in lots of different ways. This section covers some of your major options, from writing alerts into your code to using your browser's bug detector and other debugging tools.

Printing Variables with alert() Statements

The most tried-and-true debugging method is to use alert() statements to print out what's going on in your script.

Figure 18-1 lists two functions. In one, if you enter random names in the prompt boxes, you'll see the greeting *Ahoy, polloi!* If you enter Dave in the first prompt box and Thau in the second one, you're supposed to get the message *Howdy, partner!* However, running the functions won't work because one of them contains an error.

Running theGreeting() doesn't result in any JavaScript syntax errors, but the function works incorrectly. In this simple example, you may discover the error easily just by looking at the JavaScript. However, as your scripts get more complicated, you'll find it harder to locate errors by eyeballing your code.

```
function getName()
{
    var first_name = prompt("What's your first name?","");
    var last_name = prompt("What's your last name?","");
    var the_name = first_name + " " + last_name;
}

function theGreeting()
{
    var the_name = getName();
    if (the_name == "Dave Thau")
    {
        alert("Howdy, partner!");
    } else {
        alert("Ahoy, polloi!");
    }
}
```

Figure 18-1: Find the error

If JavaScript doesn't catch your error and you can't figure it out by looking at the script, try printing out the variables. The easiest way to do this is to use an alert() to print out a variable, as in Figure 18-2:

```
function getName()
{
    var first_name = prompt("What's your first name?","");
    var last_name = prompt("What's your last name?","");
    var the_name = first_name + " " + last_name;
❶   alert("in getName, the_name is: " + the_name);
}
function theGreeting()
{
    var the_name = getName();
❷   alert("after getName, the_name = " + the_name);
    if (the_name == "Dave Thau")
    {
        alert("Howdy, partner!");
    } else {
        alert("Ahoy, polloi!");
    }
}
```

Figure 18-2: Using alert() to print out variables

After you enter the names Dave and Thau at the prompts in getName(), the alert in ❶ says "in getName, the_name is Dave Thau." That looks fine, so you can be pretty sure nothing's wrong up to the point of ❶. However, the alert in ❷ says "after getName, the_name = undefined." That means the script has a problem somewhere between ❶ and ❷—the_name is correct just before getName() exits, but it's wrong after theGreeting(). Because getName() gets the right answer but theGreeting() fails to receive that answer from getName(), the problem probably lies in the way the script passes the answer from getName() to theGreeting().

Sure enough, that's the problem. The `getName()` function figures out the name but never returns it. We need to put `return the_name` at the end of the function.

Debugging Beyond Alerts

Putting alert boxes in your code is a good debugging tool, but when you need to examine variables at many places in a JavaScript it can be annoying to have to press the OK button every other line.

One trick that can make your debugging experience more pleasant involves using a variable to set different levels of debugging, such as brief, extreme, and none. The brief level might use `alert()` statements to print a few debugging messages along the way, while the extreme level might print a ton of debugging messages into another window or a textarea inside a form. The third option, none, won't print any messages at all. Figure 18-3 lists some code that uses a variable to determine what kind of debugging you want to do.

```
❶ var debug = "none";
   function getName()
   {
     var first_name = prompt("What's your first name?","");
     var last_name = prompt("What's your last name?","");
     var the_name = first_name + " " + last_name;

❷   doError("in getName, the_name is: " + the_name);
   }
   function theGreeting()
   {
     var the_name = getName();
     doError("after getName, the_name = " + the_name);
     if (the_name == "Dave Thau")
     {
       alert("Howdy, partner!");
     } else {
       alert("Ahoy, polloi!");
     }
   }
   function doError(the_message)
   {
     if (debug == "brief")
     {
❸     alert(the_message);
     } else if (debug == "extreme") {
❹     window.document.the_form.the_text.value +=
          the_message + "\n";
     }
   }
```

Figure 18-3: Using a debug variable

Figure 18-3 uses a function called `doError()` to handle its debugging. For example, ❷ passes a debugging message to `doError()`; the `doError()` function then decides what to do with this message based on how ❶ sets the `debug` variable. If it sets `debug` to `"brief"`, ❸ puts the debugging message in an alert box. Using alerts is handy when you want to check variables in just a few places and you don't mind pressing OK in each alert box. However, if you want to look at a lot of debugging messages simultaneously, it's more helpful to set the `debug` variable to `"extreme"` (❹). Finally, when you're ready to show your code to the world, just set `debug` to `"none"` to prevent the debugging messages from appearing at all.

Setting a debug variable like the one in Figure 18-3 saves you the hassle of having to find and remove multiple debugging statements. Depending on how you set `debug`, you can even use `document.write()` to show or hide the textarea you're using to display the debug message. That way, you can show the textarea while debugging the script and then hide it when you're ready to let visitors see your JavaScript.

A number of people have written logging libraries that you can add to your JavaScripts if you don't feel like writing something like Figure 18-3. Two good examples are Andre's JSLog, available at http://earthcode.com/blog/2005/12/jslog.html, and Log4Ajax by Eric Spiegelberg, available at http://today.java.net/pub/a/today/2005/12/13/log4ajax.html.

Using Your Browser's Bug Detector

If you've been trying the examples and doing the assignments as we've gone along, you've no doubt encountered your browser's bug detector. When you've made a coding mistake, running your code in the browser often results in a window that describes the error. Some browsers, such as Internet Explorer 5.0 and up, warn you by putting an error icon at the bottom-left corner of the window. Clicking the error icon opens a window that describes the error. Other browsers, such as Firefox, may not show errors at all but instead have a console that displays errors. To see the console, type **javascript:** in the location box of your browser.

Sometimes you may find the JavaScript error messages helpful; other times they may seem confusing. For serious debugging, you may have to move up to a full-fledged JavaScript debugger.

Using JavaScript Debuggers

If you use Firefox or Mozilla, you can download the handy JavaScript debugger named Venkman at https://addons.mozilla.org/firefox/216. Once you have installed the extension, a new JavaScript Debugger option appears under Firefox's Tools menu, as shown in Figure 18-4. Selecting this option brings up the Venkman debugger, which looks like Figure 18-5. There are many little windows in Venkman, and like any debugger, Venkman is a complicated application. For our purposes, the most important window is the middle one on the left, named Local Variables.

Figure 18-4: Selecting the Venkman JavaScript debugger
extension in Firefox

As long as the debugging window is open, the debugger can be invoked
at any point in your JavaScript program by adding the line:

```
debugger;
```

at the point where you want the debugger to start.

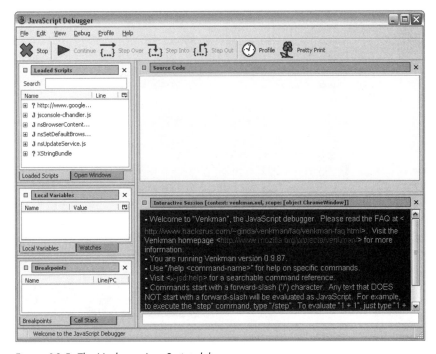

Figure 18-5: The Venkman JavaScript debugger

Consider the code in Figure 18-6.

```
function getName()
{
  var first_name = prompt("What's your first name?","");
  var last_name = prompt("What's your last name?","");
  var the_name = first_name + " " + last_name;
}

function theGreeting() {
❶   debugger;
  var the_name = getName();
  if (the_name == "Dave Thau")
  {
    alert("Howdy, partner!");
  } else {
    alert("Ahoy, polloi!");
  }
}
```

Figure 18-6: Starting the debugger

As before, we suspect that something funny is going on with getName().
In this case, rather than putting in an alert or using logging, we invoke the
JavaScript debugger in ❶. This stops the JavaScript program and makes
the JavaScript debugger window look like Figure 18-7. The debugger; line
appeared within theGreeting(), so the Local Variables section of the debugger
shows you what it knows about the function. Initially, it knows that there is
one variable, the_name, and that it has no value (the value is void).

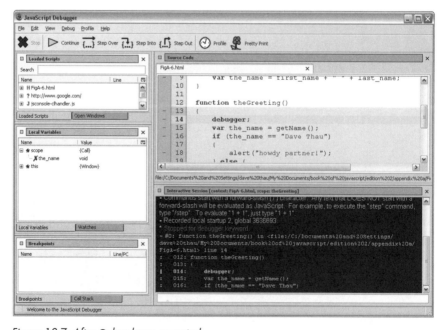

Figure 18-7: After ❶ has been executed

After I click the Step Into button a couple of times to get into getName(), then fill in some prompts, the debugger in Figure 18-8 shows that first_name and last_name are set correctly.

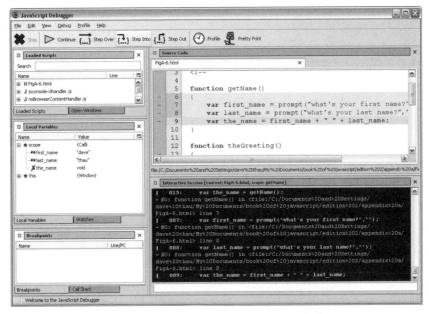

Figure 18-8: Examining variables; first_name and last_name look correct

I click the Step Into button a few more times until I've exited getName(), and I see in Figure 18-9 that for some reason the_name is still void. From this I can deduce that the value is not getting passed out of the getName() function.

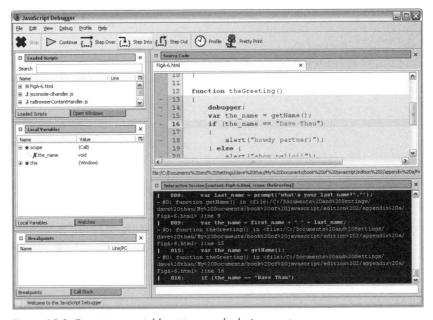

Figure 18-9: Examining variables; the_name looks incorrect

In this simple example, the complexity of a full-blown debugger such as Venkman is unnecessary. However, with complicated functions, being able to step through the JavaScript one line at a time, and see the values of the variables at every step, can cut down debugging time immensely. If you'd like to learn more about how to use Venkman, you can find an excellent tutorial at http://www.svendtofte.com/code/learning_venkman.

The Venkman debugger is by far the easiest JavaScript debugger to use and is itself a reason to download Firefox. If you are trying to debug a problem that occurs only in Internet Explorer, you will need a debugger that works for Internet Explorer. The best option here is the Microsoft Script Editor,[1] which comes packaged with Microsoft Office.

Debugging Ajax in Firefox 1.5 and 2.0

Debugging Ajax is much like debugging JavaScript. However, the client-server communication that goes on in debugging Ajax adds a bit of complexity. An extension for Firefox 1.5 and 2.0 called Greasemonkey,[2] combined with a script called the XMLHttpRequest Debugging Script,[3] can give you a window into how your web browser and a webserver are communicating.

Once you have downloaded and installed Greasemonkey and the XMLHttpRequest Debugging script, you can monitor requests sent and received by Firefox request objects. The XmlHttpRequestDebugging script maintains a list of JavaScripts that might have request objects that need to be monitored. To add JavaScripts that run on your desktop computer to that list, choose **Tools ▸ Manage User Scripts** from the Firefox menu, and add http://localhost/* to the Included Pages list, as seen in Figure 18-10.

Once you have done so, a div is added to any web page on this list that makes an Ajax-style request. For example, Figure 18-11 shows the debugging window after Odysseus has logged into the To Do list application from Chapter 17. The figure shows two Ajax calls. The first line of a call tells you the type of call it was, in this case a GET. The next line tells you where the request was sent. The third line lets you see what message was sent with the request when the request.send() method was invoked. In the case of a GET, the message is null. With POST, the message will be the string sent. On the third line is also an [edit&replay] button, which gives you a window like Figure 18-12. In this window you can change the message sent in the request and then resend the request to see what happens.

The fourth line of the window in Figure 18-11 gives you the status of the webserver's response. Clicking [export] opens a window with the complete response from the webserver (Figure 18-13). As you can gather, this tool is extremely useful for debugging client-server communications in Ajax.

---

[1] A good tutorial is available at http://www.jonathanboutelle.com/mt/archives/2006/01/howto_debug_jav.html.

[2] See http://greasemonkey.mozdev.org.

[3] See http://blog.monstuff.com/archives/images/XMLHttpRequestDebugging.v1.2.user.js.

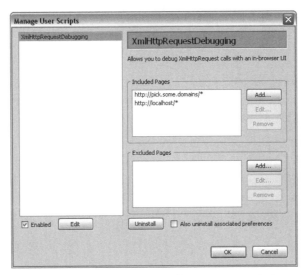

Figure 18-10: Adding JavaScripts that run on your desktop machine to the list of scripts to monitor

NOTE   *Only you (and other users who have added Greasemonkey and the XMLHttpRequest Debugging script and have added your web page to their watch list) will see the XmlHttpRequest debugging window. Don't worry about anyone else being affected by it.*

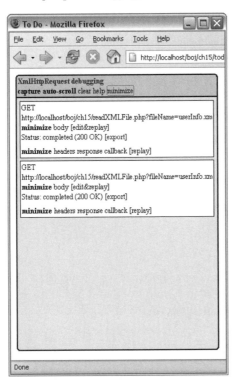

Figure 18-11: XmlHttpRequest debugger showing client-server traffic

Figure 18-12: Using the XmlHttpRequest debugger to examine and edit an Ajax message

Other Debugging Resources

Before closing this section on debugging, I should mention two other debugging tools. Firebug[4] is a relatively new and popular debugger for Firefox 1.5 that combines logging, a JavaScript debugger, and the ability to watch Ajax requests. Microsoft's Visual Web Developer Express Edition[5] is a free website development environment that includes a JavaScript debugger and can also watch Ajax requests.

Fixing Bugs

Once you've found where your bugs are, you need to fix them—and you have multiple options for this, both good and bad. This section covers a few things you should do when getting rid of bugs.

---

[4] See http://www.joehewitt.com/software/firebug.

[5] See http://msdn.microsoft.com/vstudio/express/vwd.

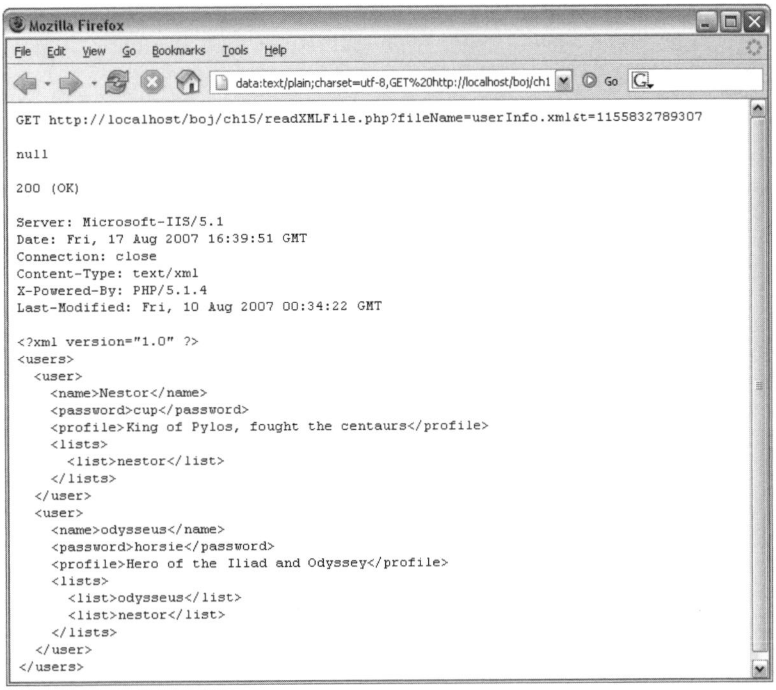
Mozilla Firefox
File Edit View Go Bookmarks Tools Help
data:text/plain;charset=utf-8,GET%20http://localhost/boj/ch1
Go
GET http://localhost/boj/ch15/readXMLFile.php?fileName=userInfo.xml&t=1155832789307
null
200 (OK)
Server: Microsoft-IIS/5.1
Date: Fri, 17 Aug 2007 16:39:51 GMT
Connection: close
Content-Type: text/xml
X-Powered-By: PHP/5.1.4
Last-Modified: Fri, 10 Aug 2007 00:34:22 GMT
<?xml version="1.0" ?>
<users>
<user>
<name>Nestor</name>
<password>cup</password>
<profile>King of Pylos, fought the centaurs</profile>
<lists>
<list>nestor</list>
</lists>
</user>
<user>
<name>odysseus</name>
<password>horsie</password>
<profile>Hero of the Iliad and Odyssey</profile>
<lists>
<list>odysseus</list>
<list>nestor</list>
</lists>
</user>
</users>

Figure 18-13: A detailed look at the client-server communication

Back Up Your Program

Some bugs are really hard to get rid of. In fact, sometimes in the process of eradicating a little bug that's driving you nuts, you end up destroying your entire program. This happens a lot, so saving a backup of your program before you start to debug is the best way to ensure that a bug doesn't get the best of you.

Fix One Bug at a Time

If you have multiple bugs, fix one and test your fix before moving to the next bug. Fixing a lot of bugs at once increases the risk of adding even more bugs.

Avoid Voodoo Coding

Sometimes you know a bug exists, but you don't really know why. Let's say you have a variable called `index` and for some reason `index` is always 1 less than you think it should be. At this point you can do two things. You can sit there for a while and figure out why `index` is 1 less than it should be, or you can just shrug, add 1 to index before using it, and move on. The latter method is called *voodoo programming*. When you start thinking, "What the hell? Why is index 2 instead of 3 here? Well . . . I'll just add 1 for now and fix it later," you're engaging in voodoo programming.

Voodoo programming may work in the short term, but eventually it will doom you. It's like sweeping dust under a rug. The problem resurfaces— either you get yet another weird error you can't figure out, or the next poor soul cursed to look at your code will find it extremely hard to understand.

Don't practice voodoo coding.

Look for Similar Bugs

In some ways, the ability to cut and paste code is the worst thing that ever happened to programmers. Often you'll write some JavaScript in one function, then cut and paste it into another function. If the first function had a problem, you have now created problems in two functions. I'm not saying you shouldn't cut and paste code—but keep in mind that bugs have a way of multiplying, so if you find one bug, look for similar bugs elsewhere in your code. One bug that typically crops up several times in every JavaScript is misspelled variable names. If you misspell the_name as teh_name in one place, chances are you've done it someplace else too.

Clear Your Head

You're sitting there staring at a bug, and you just can't figure out what's going on or how to fix it. Or maybe you can't even find the bug in the first place. The best thing to do is walk away from your computer. Go read a book and take a stroll around the corner. Get a tasty beverage. Do something— anything—but don't think about the program or the problem. This technique is called *incubation*, and it works amazingly well. After you've had a little break and relaxed a bit, try finding the bug again. Often you'll approach the problem in a new, more fruitful way. Incubation works because it breaks you out of a dysfunctional mindset.

Ask for Help

Sometimes you get stuck in your own contorted thought patterns, and you need someone who hasn't thought about the problem to find the hole in your logic. In structured coding environments, programmers periodically review each other's code. Code review not only helps iron out bugs but also results in better code. Don't be afraid to show other people your JavaScripts. You'll become a better JavaScripter.

Summary

Programming is a skill that improves dramatically over time, and learning how to debug efficiently is one of the biggest components of that process. Whenever you program, you will need to debug. A completely bug-free program is almost never written in one draft. The best you can do is to try to minimize the bugs and to write your programs in a way that makes it easy to detect and fix the bugs that slip in. The tools and techniques covered in this chapter should help make your debugging experience as pleasant as possible.

Congratulations! You now know everything you need to start a career as an official JavaScripter. All that remains is lots and lots of practice. View source on every page that catches your fancy, and check out the free JavaScript resources listed in Appendix B.

If you've made it this far, you've learned a lot of JavaScript, but this book hasn't by any means covered every detail of this huge subject—so leaf through Appendix C to get a feel for the other JavaScript functions and objects at your disposal. If you're going to do a lot of JavaScripting, get a good JavaScript reference book, like David Flanagan's *JavaScript: The Definitive Guide* (O'Reilly, 2006). But most importantly, experiment freely and push the boundaries of what you've learned here. Now go forth and code!

A

ANSWERS TO ASSIGNMENTS

 Here are solutions to the assignments I've given at the end of each chapter. The scripts and images used in the solutions may be found on this book's companion website (http://www .bookofjavascript.com). The JavaScript in this appendix contains comments where I think explanation is necessary. If your solution works and is not much longer than mine, you've done a good job. There is no assignment for Chapter 1, so we'll start with Chapter 2.

Chapter 2

The Chapter 2 assignment asks you to change Figure 2-12 so that seconds are displayed along with minutes and hours. Use the Date object's getSeconds() method to get the number of seconds and the fixTime() function to fix the formatting of the seconds.

```
<html>
<head>
<title>Chapter 2 Assignment</title>
<script type = "text/javascript">
<!-- hide me from older browsers
// get the date information
//
var today = new Date();
var the_day = today.getDate();
var the_month = today.getMonth();
var the_hour = today.getHours();
var the_minutes = today.getMinutes();
var the_seconds = today.getSeconds();

// correct for the month starting from zero
//
the_month = the_month + 1;

// add leading zeros if necessary
the_day = fixTime(the_day);
the_minutes = fixTime(the_minutes);
the_seconds = fixTime(the_seconds);

// create the string you want to print
//
var the_whole_date = the_month + "/" + the_day + " ";
var the_whole_time = the_hour + ":" + the_minutes + ":" + the_seconds;

// This is the time fixer function--don't worry about how this works either.
function fixTime(number) {
  if (number < 10) {
    number = "0" + number;
  }
  return number;
}

// show me -->
</script>
</head>
<body>
Right now it's:

<script type = "text/javascript">
<!-- hide me from older browsers

// write the date
//
document.write(the_whole_date);
document.write(the_whole_time);

// show me -->
</script>
</body>
</html>
```

Chapter 3

In this assignment, you are asked to send people you like to one page, people you don't like to another page, and everyone else to a third page. This should exercise your new understanding of if-then-else-if statements.

```
<html><head><title>Chapter 3 Assignment</title></head>
<body>
<script type = "text/javascript">
<!-- hide me from older browsers
// get the visitor's name
//
var the_name = prompt("What's your name?", "");

// If the name is thau, dave, pugsly, or gomez,
// send the visitor to Sesame Street.
// If it's darth vader, the evil emperor, or jar jar binks,
// send the visitor to the American Psychological Association
// for some therapy.
// If it's none of the above, send him or her to the New York Times.
if ((the_name == "thau") || (the_name == "dave") ||
    (the_name == "pugsly") || (the_name=="gomez"))
{
   window.location = "http://www.sesamestreet.com/";
} else if ((the_name == "darth vader") || (the_name == "the evil emperor") ||
    (the_name == "jar jar binks"))
{
    window.location = "http://www.apa.org/";
}
else
{
    window.location = "http://www.nytimes.com/";
}
// show me -->
</script>
</body>
</html>
```

Chapter 4

This assignment asks you to create an image swap that changes two images at once. Do this by putting two image swap statements inside the event handlers.

```
<html>
<head>
<title>Chapter 4 Assignment</title>
</head>
<body>
<h1>Welcome to the Book of JavaScript Website!</h1>
<p>
<img src = "front_cover.gif" name = "cover">
</p>
<p>
<a href = "#"
```

```
  onMouseOver = "window.document.cover.src='back_cover.gif';
      window.document.turn.src='turn_back.gif';"
  onMouseOut = "window.document.cover.src='front_cover.gif';
      window.document.turn.src='turn_over.gif';">
<img src = "turn_over.gif" border = "0" name = "turn">
</a>
</p>
</body>
</html>
```

Chapter 5

This assignment asks you to write a web page that contains two links. When the web page opens, it should also open a little window containing an image. When clicked, the two links on the main page should swap different images into the little window. Make sure that index.html and image_page.html are in the same directory.

index.html

The index.html file opens the little window.

```
<html>
<head>
<title>Chapter 5 Assignment</title>
<script type = "text/javascript">
<!-- hide me from older browsers
// open the little window with the page image_page.html and call the
// little window the_window
//
var the_window =
      window.open("image_page.html","the_window","width=100,height=100");
// show me -->
</script>
</head>
<body>
<h1>Play with a little window</h1>
<a href = "#"
  onClick = "the_window.document.the_image.src='sad_face.gif';">Make him
sad</a><br>
<a href = "#"
  onClick = "the_window.document.the_image.src='happy_face.gif';">Make him
happy</a><br>
</body>
</html>
```

image_page.html

The image_page.html file specifies the content of the little window.

```
<html><head><title>Little Window</title></head>
<body>
```

```
<img name = "the_image" src = "happy.gif">
</body>
</html>
```

Chapter 6

This assignment asks you to create a function that swaps one image with another and opens a new window to a given URL. The function takes three parameters: the name of an image to swap, the URL of a new image to put in its place, and a URL to open in the new window.

```
<html><head><title>Chapter 6 Assignment</title>
<script type = "text/javascript">
<!-- hide me from older browsers
// function fancySwap() takes three parameters:
// 1. the web page image that's getting swapped out
// 2. the filename of an image to swap into the web page image
// 3. a URL to open into a new window
//
function fancySwap(the_image, new_image, the_url)
{
    the_image.src = new_image;
    var my_window = window.open(the_url, my_window, "height=300,width=150");
}
// show me -->
</script>
</head>
<body>
<a href = "#"
onMouseOver = "fancySwap(window.document.apple,'hilight_apple.gif',
'http://www.apple.com/'); "
    onMouseOut = "window.document.apple.src='normal_apple.gif';">
  <img src = "normal_apple.gif" name = "apple" border = "0">
</a>
<a href = "#"   onMouseOver =
"fancySwap(window.document.sun,'hilight_sun.gif','http://www.sun.com/');"
    onMouseOut = "window.document.sun.src='normal_sun.gif';">
  <img src = "normal_sun.gif" name = "sun" border = "0">
</a>
<a href = "#" onMouseOver =
"fancySwap(window.document.monkey,'hilight_monkey.gif',
'http://www.webmonkey.com/');"
    onMouseOut = "window.document.monkey.src='normal_monkey.gif';">
  <img src = "normal_monkey.gif" name = "monkey" border = "0">
</a>
</body>
</html>
```

Chapter 7

This assignment asks you to write a script for a clock that tells the time in San Francisco, New York, London, and Tokyo. The clock should have a text field for the time, a button to update the clock, and four radio buttons, one for each of those time zones. When you click on one of the radio buttons, the correct time should appear in the text field. When you click on the update button, the clock should update with the time from the zone you've selected with the radio buttons.

This solution has two main functions: updateClock() is called when the update button is clicked, and updateReadout() is called when one of the time zone radio buttons is clicked.

```
<html><head><title>Chapter 7 Assignment</title>
<script type = "text/javascript">
<!-- hide me from older browsers
// Function updateReadout() takes one parameter, the time zone to
// convert the time to. The parameter can be either newyork, sanfran or
// tokyo.
// The function determines the time for that time zone and then sets the
// value of a text field to that time.
function updateReadout(the_zone)
{
    // get the current UTC time
    //
    var now = new Date();
    var the_hours = now.getUTCHours();
    var the_minutes = now.getUTCMinutes();
    var the_seconds = now.getUTCSeconds();

    // adjust for selected time zone
    //
    if (the_zone == "newyork")
    {
        the_hours = the_hours - 4;
    } else if (the_zone == "sanfran") {
        the_hours = the_hours - 7;
    } else if (the_zone == "tokyo") {
        the_hours = the_hours + 9;
    }

    // now fix the hours if over 24 or under 0
    //
    if (the_hours < 0)
    {
        the_hours = the_hours + 24;
    } else if (the_hours > 24) {
        the_hours = the_hours - 24;
    }

    // put zeros in front of minutes and seconds if necessary
    the_minutes = formatTime(the_minutes);
    the_seconds = formatTime(the_seconds);

    // now put the time in the text box
    var the_time = the_hours + ":" + the_minutes + ":" + the_seconds;

    window.document.clock_form.readout.value = the_time;
}
```

```
// function formatTime() takes a number as a parameter.
// If that number is less than 10, it puts a 0 in front
// of it for formatting purposes.
//
function formatTime(the_time)
{
    if (the_time < 10) {
        the_time = "0" + the_time;
    }


    return the_time;
}
// By looping through a set of radio buttons, function updateClock()
// checks to see which time zone has been selected by the viewer. Once
// it determines the selected time zone, it calls updateReadout().
//
function updateClock()
{
    var selected_zone = "";
    for (var loop = 0; loop < window.document.clock_form.zones.length; loop++)
    {
        if (window.document.clock_form.zones[loop].checked == true)
        {
            selected_zone = window.document.clock_form.zones[loop].value;
        }
    }
    updateReadout(selected_zone);
}

// show me -->
</script>
</head>
<body>
<form name = "clock_form">
<input type = "text" name = "readout">
<input type = "button" value = "update" onClick = "updateClock();"><br>
San Francisco <input type = "radio" name = "zones" value = "sanfran"
    onClick = "updateReadout('sanfran');" checked><br>
New York <input type = "radio" name = "zones" value = "newyork"
    onClick = "updateReadout('newyork');"><br>
London <input type = "radio" name = "zones" value = "london"
    onClick = "updateReadout('london');"><br>
Tokyo <input type = "radio" name = "zones" value = "tokyo"
    onClick = "updateReadout('tokyo');"><br>
</form>
</body>
</html>
```

Chapter 8

This assignment uses arrays and loops to draw a chart based on user input.
One function, getNumbers(), creates an array that stores the values to the
chart. After collecting these values from the user, getNumbers() then loops
through the array, calling drawSquares() to draw each line of the chart.

```html
<html><head><title>Chapter 8 Assignment</title>
<script type = "text/javascript">
<!-- hide me from older browsers
// function getNumbers() gets a number of bars to draw
// and the length of those bars. It calls the drawSquares()
// function to actually draw the bars to the web page.
//
function getNumbers()
{
  // create a new array
  //
  var the_values = new Array();

  // find out how many bars the person wants
  //
  var how_many = prompt("How many bars?","");

  // now loop that many times, asking for a value
  // each time and loading that value into the array
  //
  for (var loop = 0; loop < how_many; loop++)
  {
    var value = prompt("How long is this bar? (1-10)","");
    the_values[loop] = value;
  }

  // now loop through the array and print out the bars
  //
  for (var loop = 0; loop < how_many; loop++)
  {
    drawSquares(the_values[loop]);
  }
}

// function drawSquares()
// takes a number of squares to draw, and then draws them to
// the web page
//
function drawSquares(the_number)
{
    for (var loop = 0; loop < the_number; loop++)
    {
        window.document.write("<img src='square.gif'>");
    }
    window.document.write("<br>");
}

// show me -->
</script>
</head>
<body>
<a href = "#" onClick = "getNumbers(); return false;">Draw the histogram</a>
</body>
</html>
```

Chapter 9

This assignment asks you to alter Figure 9-11 so that mousing over the image stops the slide show, and mousing off the image starts it again. The solution is very much like Figure 9-11. The only addition is the link around the image that clears the time-out when it is moused over and restarts the slideshow when the mouse moves off of it.

```html
<html>
<head>
<title>Chapter 9 Assignment</title>
<script type = "text/javascript">
<!-- hide me from older browsers

// preload the images
var the_images = new Array();
the_images[0] = new Image();
the_images[0].src = "one.jpg";
the_images[1] = new Image();
the_images[1].src = "two.jpg";
the_images[2] = new Image();
the_images[2].src = "three.jpg";
var the_timeout;
var index = 0;
// function rotateImage() swaps in the next image in the_images
// array and increases the index by 1. If the index exceeds the
// number of images in the array, index is set back to zero.
// setTimeout is used to call the function again in one second.
function rotateImage()
{
    window.document.my_image.src = the_images[index].src;
    index++;
    if (index >= the_images.length)
    {
        index = 0;
    }
    the_timeout = setTimeout("rotateImage();", 1000);
}
// show me -->
</script>
</head>
<body>
<a href = "#"
    onMouseOver = "clearTimeout(the_timeout);"
    onMouseOut = "rotateImage();">
<img name = "my_image" src = "one.jpg"></a>
<form>
<input type = "button" value = "Start the show"
        onClick = "clearTimeout(the_timeout); rotateImage();">
<input type = "button" value = "Stop the show"
        onClick = "clearTimeout(the_timeout);">
</form>
</body>
</html>
```

Chapter 10

This assignment asks you to create a page with at least two frames. The first frame should contain a submit button and a text box into which a visitor should type a URL. After the submit button is clicked, the second frame shows the web page called by the URL in the text box. In addition to providing a location box, the browser page in the solution uses *Salon*'s image map to show various URLs in the display frame.

Because it uses frames, this assignment requires three HTML files: index.html, assignment-nav.html, and blank.html.

index.html

The first page, index.html, lays out the frameset.

```
<html><head><title>Chapter 10 Assignment</title></head>
<frameset rows = "50%,*">
<frame src = "assignment-nav.html" name = "nav">
<frame src = "blank.html" name = "contents">
</frameset>
</html>
```

assignment-nav.html

The second page, assignment-nav.html, contains the image map and the form. Clicking on an area in the image map or submitting the form loads a URL into the lower frame. Notice the use of this in the form's onSubmit.

```
<html><head><title>nav</title></head>
<body>
<table border = 0>
<tr><td>
Type a URL below, or
<br>
click on an area of the map.
<form onSubmit = "parent.contents.location=this.the_url.value; return false;">
<input type = "text" name = "the_url">
</form>
</td>
<td>
<img src = "src/left.gif" name = "left" isMap useMap = "#left">
</td>
</tr>
</table>
<MAP name = "left">
<AREA coords = "9,23,41,42" shape = "RECT" href = "#"
  target = "thePicture"
  onClick = "parent.contents.location = 'http://www.whitehouse.gov/'; return
false;"
  onmouseOver = "window.document.left.src='src/us.gif';"
  onMouseOut = "window.document.left.src='src/left.gif';">
```

```
<AREA coords = "26,42,75,64" shape = "RECT" href = "#"
  target = "thePicture"
  onClick = "parent.contents.location = 'http://www.whitehouse.gov/'; return
false;"
  onmouseOver = "window.document.left.src='src/us.gif';"
  onMouseOut = "window.document.left.src='src/left.gif';">
<AREA coords = "28,65,55,78" shape = "RECT" href = "#"
  target = "thePicture"
  onClick = "parent.contents.location = 'http://www.gob.mx/wb/'; return
false;"
  onmouseOver = "window.document.left.src='src/mexico.gif';"
  onMouseOut = "window.document.left.src='src/left.gif';">
</MAP>
</body>
</html>
```

blank.html

The third page, blank.html, is just a blank page which appears in the lower
frame.

```
<html><head><title>blank</title></head>
<body>
</body>
</html>
```

Chapter 11

This assignment extends Chapter 10's assignment by adding string validation
to make sure the URLs entered in the browser's location bar are valid web
addresses. This means the URL should start with *http://* or *https://*, have no
spaces, and have at least two words with a period between them.

The solution begins with the code from Chapter 10's assignment and
adds a function named domainCheckAndGo() that performs the string validation.
Like the Chapter 10 assignment, this assignment requires three HTML files
because it uses frames.

index.html

The first page, index.html, lays out the frameset.

```
<html><head><title>Chapter 11 Assignment</title></head>
<frameset rows = "50%,*">
<frame src = "assignment-nav.html" name = "nav">
<frame src = "blank.html" name = "contents">
</frameset>
</html>
```

assignment-nav.html

The second page, assignment-nav.html, contains the contents of the top frame, including the JavaScript.

```
<html><head><title>nav</title>
<script type = "text/javascript">
<!-- hide me from older browsers
// function domainCheckAndGo()
// This function makes sure a URL is legal. If it is, it
// sends the visitor to that URL.
function domainCheckAndGo(the_url)
{
  // split the URL into two parts, along the //
  // there should be two parts to it, the protocol (for example, http:)
  // and the address
  var first_split = the_url.split('//');
  if (first_split.length != 2)
  {
    alert("Sorry, there must be one // in a domain name");
    return false;
  }
  // Now check to see if the URL is legal--see the alerts in the
  // if-then statement to see what the if-then statement is checking.
  // If any of the conditions are violated, the script calls up an
  // alert box explaining the error and then uses return to exit
  // the function without changing the URL in the bottom frame.
  if ((first_split[0] != 'http:') && (first_split[0] != 'https:'))
  {
    alert("Sorry, the domain must start with http:// or https://");
    return false;
  }
  if (the_url.indexOf(' ') != -1)
  {
    alert("Sorry, domains can't have spaces");
    return false;
  }
  // get everything after the http://
  //
  var two_slashes = the_url.indexOf('//');
  var all_but_lead = the_url.substring(two_slashes + 2, the_url.length);
  var domain_parts = all_but_lead.split('.');
  if (domain_parts.length < 2)
  {
    alert("Sorry, there must be at least two parts to a domain name");
    return false;
  }
  // Loop through all the parts of the domain, making
  // sure there's actually something there--for example,
  // http://i.am.happy...com is not legal because there
  // are three dots in a row.
```

```
  for (var loop = 0; loop < domain_parts.length; loop++)
  {
    if (domain_parts[loop] == '')
    {
        alert("Sorry, there must be some text after each .");
        return false;
    }
  }
  // If we've made it this far, the URL must be legal,
  // so load the URL into the frame.
  parent.contents.location = the_url;
}

// show me -->
</script>
</head>
<body>
<table border = 0>
<tr><td>
Type a URL below, or
<br>
click on an area of the map.
<form onSubmit = "domainCheckAndGo(this.the_url.value); return false;">
<input type = "text" name = "the_url">
</form>
</td>
<td>
 <img src = "src/left.gif" name = "left" isMap useMap = "#left">
</td>
</tr>
</table>
<MAP name = "left">
<AREA coords = "9,23,41,42" shape = "RECT" href = "#"
target = "thePicture"
onClick = "parent.contents.location = 'http://www.whitehouse.gov/'; return
false;"
onmouseOver = "window.document.left.src='src/us.gif';"
onMouseOut = "window.document.left.src='src/left.gif';">
<AREA coords = "26,42,75,64" shape = "RECT" href = "#"
target = "thePicture"
onClick = "parent.contents.location = 'http://www.whitehouse.gov/'; return
false;"
onmouseOver = "window.document.left.src='src/us.gif';"
onMouseOut = "window.document.left.src='src/left.gif';">
<AREA coords = "28,65,55,78" shape = "RECT" href = "#"
target = "thePicture"
onClick = "parent.contents.location = 'http://www.mexico.gov/'; return false;"
onmouseOver = "window.document.left.src='src/mexico.gif';"
onMouseOut = "window.document.left.src='src/left.gif';">
</MAP>
</body>
</html>
```

blank.html

The third page, blank.html, is just a blank page which appears in the lower frame.

```
<html><head><title>blank</title></head>
<body>
</body>
</html>
```

Chapter 12

This assignment asks you to use cookies to keep track of whether or not a user has visited a web page. The solution below uses Webmonkey's cookie library to set and read a cookie named was_here.

```
<html><head><title>Chapter 12 Assignment</title>
<script type = "text/javascript">
<!-- hide me from older browsers
// this is from the webmonkey cookie library at http://www.webmonkey.com/
//
function WM_readCookie(name) {
    if(document.cookie == '') {
    // there's no cookie, so go no further
     return false;
    } else {
    // there is a cookie
     var firstChar, lastChar;
     var theBigCookie = document.cookie;
     firstChar = theBigCookie.indexOf(name);
     // find the start of 'name'
     var NN2Hack = firstChar + name.length;
     if((firstChar != -1) && (theBigCookie.charAt(NN2Hack) == '=')) {
         firstChar += name.length + 1; // skip 'name' and '='
         lastChar = theBigCookie.indexOf(';', firstChar); //
         if(lastChar == -1) lastChar = theBigCookie.length;
         return unescape(theBigCookie.substring(firstChar, lastChar));
     } else {
     // If there was no cookie of that name, return false.
         return false;
     }
    }
}
// WM_readCookie

// Function setCookie() sets a cookie named was_here to expire far
// in the future.
//
function setCookie()
{
    var the_future = new Date("December 31, 2023");
    var the_cookie_date = the_future.toGMTString();

    var the_cookie = "was_here=yes;expires=" + the_cookie_date;
    document.cookie = the_cookie;
```

```
}

// Function checkFirst() checks if the was_here cookie
// has been set. If it hasn't, the alert pops up and the
// cookie is set using setCookie();.
//
function checkFirstTime()
{
    var the_date = WM_readCookie("was_here");
    if(the_date == false)
    {
        alert("Welcome, newtimer!");
        setCookie();
    }
}
// show me -->
</script></head>
<body>
<h1>My Page</h1>
<script type = "text/javascript">
<!-- hide me from older browsers
checkFirstTime();
// show me -->
</script>
Don't you just love this page?
</body>
</html>
```

Chapter 13

This assignment asks you to create a bouncing smiley face screen saver using Dynamic HTML. The script below uses two variables, x_motion and y_motion, to keep track of the horizontal and vertical directions in which the smiley face is moving. These variables will either hold the value "plus" or "minus". A "plus" value calls for a number to be added to the current position. If the variable is x_motion, adding a value will move the smiley face to the right. If the variable is y_motion, adding a value will move the smiley face down.

```
<html>
<head>
<title>Chapter 13 Assignment</title>
<script type = "text/javascript">
<!-- hide me from older browsers
// set the direction
//
var x_motion = "plus";
var y_motion = "plus";

// set the borders
//
var top_border = 100;
var bottom_border = 200;
var left_border = 100;
var right_border = 300;
```

```
// This function moves the face 5 pixels in the vertical dimension
// and 5 pixels in the horizontal dimension. It uses two variables,
// x_motion and y_motion, to determine the direction left versus
// right and up versus down. When the face reaches a horizontal or
// vertical border, the x_motion or y_motion variable changes, so that
// the next time the face moves, it moves in the opposite direction.
function moveSmile()
{
    var the_smile = document.getElementById("smile").style;
    if (x_motion == "plus")
    {
      the_smile.left = parseInt(the_smile.left) + 5;
    } else {
      the_smile.left = parseInt(the_smile.left) - 5;
    }

    if (y_motion == "plus")
    {
      the_smile.top = parseInt(the_smile.top) + 5;
    } else {
      the_smile.top = parseInt(the_smile.top) - 5;
    }

    if (parseInt(the_smile.left) > right_border)
    {
      x_motion = "minus";
    } else if (parseInt(the_smile.left) < left_border) {
      x_motion = "plus";
    }

    if (parseInt(the_smile.top) > bottom_border)
    {
      y_motion = "minus";
    } else if (parseInt(the_smile.top) < top_border) {
      y_motion = "plus";
    }

    theTimeOut = setTimeout('moveSmile()', 100);
}

// show me -->
</script>
</head>
<body>
<form>
<input type = "button" value = "Make happiness bounce"
    onClick = "moveSmile();">
<input type = "button" value = "Stop that smiley!"
onClick = "clearTimeout(theTimeOut);">
</form>
<div id = "smile" style = "position:absolute; left:100; top:100;">
<img src = "happy_face.gif" width = "130" height = "75">
</div>
</body>
</html>
```

Chapter 14

This assignment asks you to create an address book using Ajax. The address information should be stored in an XML file. Each entry should have a name, a home address, a phone number, and an email address. The solution requires two files: addressBook.xml, which stores the address information, and index.html, which contains the Ajax code.

addressBook.xml

The first file is an XML file storing information in the address book.

```
<?xml version = "1.0"?>
<addressBook>
  <person>
    <name>Herman Munster</name>
    <address>1313 Mockingbird Lane, Transylvania</address>
    <phone>(415) 555-1212</phone>
    <email>herman@munster.com</email>
  </person>
  <person>
    <name>Nicholas Nickleby</name>
  </person>
</addressBook>
```

index.html

The second file is the HTML page that contains the JavaScript and Ajax calls to read in and display the file.

```
<html><head><title>Chapter 14 Assignment</title>
<script type="text/javascript">
<!-- hide me from older browsers
// gets the names from addressBook.xml and puts them into the select box
function populatePullDown() {
  if (window.XMLHttpRequest) {
    request = new XMLHttpRequest();
  } else if (window.ActiveXObject) {
    request = new ActiveXObject("Microsoft.XMLHTTP");
  }
  if (request) {
    request.open("GET", "addressBook.xml");
    request.onreadystatechange =
      function() {
        var name_array = new Array();
        if (request.readyState == 4) {
          xml_response = request.responseXML;
          elements = xml_response.getElementsByTagName("name");
          for (var loop = 0; loop < elements.length; loop++) {
            if (elements[loop].firstChild != null) {
              name_array.push(elements[loop].firstChild.nodeValue);
            } else {
              name_array.push(" ");
```

```
            }
          }
            writeSelect(name_array);
        }
      }
    }
    request.send(null);
}
// takes an array and writes the contents to theSelect
function writeSelect(the_array) {
  var this_option;
  var this_select = document.getElementById("theSelect");
  for (var loop = 0; loop < the_array.length; loop++) {
    this_option = new Option();
    this_option.value = the_array[loop];
    this_option.text = the_array[loop];
    this_select.options[loop] = this_option;
  }
}
// takes a name, gets the information about that person from
// addressBook.xml and writes it to the correct divs
function loadInfo(the_name) {
  if (window.XMLHttpRequest) {
    request = new XMLHttpRequest();
  } else if (window.ActiveXObject) {
    request = new ActiveXObject("Microsoft.XMLHTTP");
  }
  if (request) {
    request.open("GET", "addressBook.xml");
    request.onreadystatechange =
      function() {
        if (request.readyState == 4) {
          xml_response = request.responseXML;
          elements = xml_response.getElementsByTagName("name");
          for (var loop = 0; loop < elements.length; loop++) {
            if ((elements[loop].firstChild != null) &&
              (elements[loop].firstChild.nodeValue == the_name)) {
              parent = elements[loop].parentNode;
              children = parent.childNodes;
              var address_node;
              var phone_node;
              var email_node;
              for (var inner = 0; inner < children.length; inner++) {
                if (children[inner].nodeName == "address") {
                  address_node = children[inner];
                } else if (children[inner].nodeName == "phone") {
                  phone_node = children[inner];
                } else if (children[inner].nodeName == "email") {
                  email_node = children[inner];
                }
              }
              insertValue(document.getElementById("theName"),
                elements[loop]);
              insertValue(document.getElementById("theAddress"),
                address_node);
              insertValue(document.getElementById("thePhone"), phone_node);
              insertValue(document.getElementById("theEmail"), email_node);
```

```
                    }
                  }
                }
              }
            }
        request.send(null);
      }
      // writes the text value of an XML element (the_node) to a div (the_element)
      function insertValue(the_element, the_node) {
        if (the_node.firstChild != null) {
          the_element.innerHTML = the_node.firstChild.nodeValue;
        }
      }
      // show me -->
    </script>
  </head>
  <body onLoad = "populatePullDown()";>
  <form>
  <select id = "theSelect" size = "8" onChange = "loadInfo(this.value);"></select>
  </form>
  <b>Name:</b> <span id = "theName"></span><br>
  <b>Address:</b> <span id = "theAddress"></span><br>
  <b>Phone:</b> <span id = "thePhone"></span><br>
  <b>Email:</b> <span id = "theEmail"></span><br>
  </body>
  </html>
```

Chapter 17

This is your final exam. If you got this working, take yourself out to dinner. If you gave it a good shot, take yourself out to dinner. Heck, if you've read to this point in the book, take yourself out to dinner.

The assignment was to add these critical features to the To Do list application described in the chapter:

- Allow new users to join the service
- Allow a user to permit another user to access his or her To Do list

Only the HTML file containing the JavaScript needs to be changed here. First, you needed to make a change to the HTML at the bottom of the page to add the "join" link to the login section:

```
<h2>Login Section</h2>
<div id = "loginArea">
<a href = "#" onClick = "displayLogin(); return false;">login</a> or
<a href = "#" onClick = "displayJoin(); return false;">join</a>
</div>
```

Then there are a number of new functions. First, I'll cover the functions necessary to provide the ability to join, then the functions necessary to allow someone to give another user access to his or her list.

Join Functions

Seven functions work together to create a new user:

displayJoin()   Displays the form that will collect new user information

doJoin()   Called when the join link is clicked; reads in userInfo.xml and calls processJoin()

processJoin()   Creates a new user and adds it to userInfo.xml

createUserFileAndLogin()   Creates an empty To Do list for a new user

addUser()   Actually creates a new userInfo.xml file

makeNewUser()   Makes a new user element

makeUserInfoDoc()   Converts the userInfo.xml file into a string to save to a file

```
// puts a join form into the loginArea
function displayJoin() {
  var theForm = "<form>Name: <input type='text' name='name'><br> " +
    "Password: <input type='password' name='password'><br> " +
    "Password again: <input type='password' name='password2'><br> " +
    "Profile: <input type='text' name='profile'><br> " +
    "<input type='button' value='submit'   " +
    "onClick='doJoin(this.form);'></form>";
  document.getElementById("loginArea").innerHTML = theForm;
}
// reads in the userInfo.xml file and calls processJoin
function doJoin(my_form) {
 readFileDoFunction("userInfo.xml", "GET",
    function() {
      if (request.readyState == 4) {
        if (request.status == 200) {
          processJoin(request.responseXML, my_form);
        } else {
          document.getElementById("errorDiv").innerHTML =
            "Sorry, there was a problem with the server.";
        }
      }
    }
  );
}
// creates a new user and adds it to the userInfo.xml file
function processJoin(user_info, my_form) {
  var user_name = my_form.elements["name"].value;
  var user_password = my_form.elements["password"].value;
  var user_password_2 = my_form.elements["password2"].value;
  var profile = my_form.elements["profile"].value;
  var error = "no error";
  var this_user = getUser(user_info, user_name);
  if (this_user != null) {
      error = "A user with this name already exists.";
  } else if (user_password != user_password_2) {
      error = "The two provided passwords don't match.";
  }
if (error == "no error") {
    var new_user_doc = addUser(user_name, user_password, profile, user_info);
```

```
        saveFileDoFunction("userInfo.xml", new_user_doc,
          function() {
            if (request.readyState == 4) {
              if ((request.responseText == "success")&&(request.status == 200)) {
                createUserFileAndLogin(user_name);
              } else {
                document.getElementById("errorDiv").innerHTML =
                  "Sorry, there was an error saving the user information. ";
              }
            }
          }
        );
    } else {
      document.getElementById("errorDiv").innerHTML +=
        "<font color='red'><br>Sorry, " + error + "</font>";
    }
  }


  // creates an empty To Do list for a new user and then logs the user in
  function createUserFileAndLogin(the_user) {
   var the_file = "<?xml version='1.0'?><list>" +
      "<name>" + the_user + "</name>" +
      "<openitems></openitems><doneitems></doneitems></list>";
    saveFileDoFunction(the_user + ".xml", the_file,
      function() {
        if (request.readyState == 4) {
          if (request.status == 200) {
            document.cookie = "user="+the_user;
            displayHomeInformation(the_user);
            document.getElementById("contentArea").innerHTML = "";
          } else {
            document.getElementById("errorDiv").innerHTML =
              "Sorry, there was a problem saving the To Do list for " +
                the_user;
          }
        }
      }
    );
  }
  // creates a new userInfo.xml document with the new user
  function addUser(the_name, the_password, profile, user_info) {
    var users_array = user_info.getElementsByTagName("user");
    var new_users_array = new Array();
    for (var loop = 0; loop < users_array.length; loop++) {
      new_users_array[loop] = users_array[loop];
    }
    new_users_array[loop] = makeNewUser(the_name, the_password, profile,
        new Array(the_name));
    var new_document = makeUserInfoDoc(new_users_array);
    return new_document;
  }
  // makes a new user element
  function makeNewUser(the_name, the_password, profile, list_array) {
    var new_user = document.createElement("user");
    var new_name = document.createElement("name");
    new_name.appendChild(document.createTextNode(the_name));
    var new_password = document.createElement("password");
```

```
new_password.appendChild(document.createTextNode(the_password));
var new_profile = document.createElement("profile");
new_profile.appendChild(document.createTextNode(profile));
var new_lists = document.createElement("lists");
var new_list;
for (var loop = 0; loop < list_array.length; loop++) {
  new_list = document.createElement("list");
  new_list.appendChild(document.createTextNode(list_array[loop]));
  new_lists.appendChild(new_list);
}
new_user.appendChild(new_name);
new_user.appendChild(new_password);
new_user.appendChild(new_profile);
new_user.appendChild(new_lists);
return new_user;
}
// builds the new XML string for the userInfo.xml file
function makeUserInfoDoc(user_array) {
  var the_doc = "<?xml version='1.0' ?>";
  var this_user;
  the_doc += "<users>";
  for (var loop = 0; loop < user_array.length; loop++) {
    this_user = user_array[loop];
    the_doc += "<user>";
    the_doc += "<name>" + getFirstValue(this_user, "name") + "</name>";
    the_doc += "<password>" + getFirstValue(this_user, "password") +
      "</password>";
    the_doc += "<profile>" + getFirstValue(this_user, "profile") +
      "</profile>";
    the_doc += "<lists>";
    this_lists = this_user.getElementsByTagName("lists")[0];
    var these_lists = this_lists.getElementsByTagName("list");
    for (var list_loop = 0; list_loop < these_lists.length; list_loop++) {
      the_doc += "<list>" + these_lists[list_loop].firstChild.nodeValue +
        "</list>";
    }
    the_doc += "</lists>";
    the_doc += "</user>";
  }
  the_doc += "</users>";
  return the_doc;
}
```

Giving a User Access to Your To Do List

These seven functions allow a user to share his or her To Do list with another user. I'll use the word *owner* to refer to the user who owns the To Do list, and the word *collaborator* to refer to the user being given access to the owner's To Do list.

displayHomeInformation()   Just like the one in Chapter 16, but adds an additional link that calls giveAccess()

giveAccess()   Reads in all the system's users and calls listAllUsers()

listAllUsers()   Creates a form with a radio button for each potential collaborator, so one may be chosen

readyAddAvailableUser()   Reads in the userInfo.xml list and calls addAvailableUser()

addAvailableUser()   Adds the newly chosen collaborator to the owner's lists section in the userInfo.xml file

addNewAvailableToUserElement()   Returns a new user element with the collaborator's name added to the owner's lists element

```
// add a "Give another user access" link to the loginArea after a person has
// logged in by changing displayHomeInformation()
function displayHomeInformation(user_name) {
    document.getElementById("loginArea").innerHTML =
        "Welcome " + user_name + ".  " +
        " <a href = '#' onClick = 'logout(); return false;'>logout</a> " +
        " <a href = '#' onClick = 'giveAccess(\"" + user_name +
        "\"); return false;'>give another user access</a> ";
    displayLegalLists(user_name);
}
// get userInfo.xml and list all the users
function giveAccess(the_user) {
    readFileDoFunction("userInfo.xml", "GET",
    function() {
      if (request.readyState == 4) {
        if (request.status == 200) {
          listAllUsers(request.responseXML, the_user);
        } else {
          document.getElementById("errorDiv").innerHTML =
            "Sorry, could not get a list of the users.";
        }
      }
    }
  );
}
// create the form showing all the users
function listAllUsers(user_info, current_user) {
  var display = "<form>";
  var all_users = user_info.getElementsByTagName("user");
  var this_user;
  var this_name;
  for (var loop = 0; loop < all_users.length; loop++) {
    this_user = all_users[loop];
    this_name = getFirstValue(this_user,"name");
    if (this_name != current_user) {
      display += "<input type='radio' onClick='readyAddAvailableUser(\"" +
        this_name + "\",\"" + current_user + "\");'>" + this_name + "<br>";
    }
  }
  display += "</form>";
  document.getElementById("contentArea").innerHTML = display;
}
// get userInfo.xml and add a new available user
function readyAddAvailableUser(user_to_add, this_user) {
    readFileDoFunction("userInfo.xml", "GET",
    function() {
      if (request.readyState == 4) {
        if (request.status == 200) {
```

```
            addAvailableUser(request.responseXML, user_to_add, this_user);
          } else {
            document.getElementById("errorDiv").innerHTML =
              "Sorry, there was a problem getting the list of users.";
          }
        }
      }
    );
}
// add the new user to the user's available list, then
// create a new userInfo.xml document and save it
function addAvailableUser(user_info, user_to_add, current_user) {
  var new_user_array = new Array();
  var curr_user_array = user_info.getElementsByTagName("user");
  var count = 0;
  for (var loop = 0; loop < curr_user_array.length; loop++) {
    this_user = curr_user_array[loop];
    this_name = getFirstValue(this_user, "name");
    if (this_name == current_user) {
      add_to_array = addNewAvailableToUserElement(this_user, user_to_add);
    } else {
      add_to_array = this_user;
    }
    new_user_array[loop] = add_to_array;
  }
  var new_user_doc = makeUserInfoDoc(new_user_array);
  saveFileDoFunction("userInfo.xml", new_user_doc,
    function() {
      if (request.readyState == 4) {
        if ((request.responseText == "success")&&(request.status == 200)) {
          document.getElementById("contentArea").innerHTML = "";
          displayLegalLists(current_user);
        } else {
          document.getElementById("errorDiv").innerHTML =
            "Sorry, there was an error saving the user information. ";
        }
      }
    }
  );
}
// return a new user element with the new user added to the available list
function addNewAvailableToUserElement(this_user, user_to_add) {
  var lists = this_user.getElementsByTagName("lists")[0];
  var the_name = getFirstValue(this_user, "name");
  var profile = getFirstValue(this_user, "profile");
  var the_password = getFirstValue(this_user,"password");
  var lists_array = lists.getElementsByTagName("list");
  var new_lists_array = new Array();
  for (var loop = 0; loop < lists_array.length; loop++) {
    new_lists_array[loop] = lists_array[loop].firstChild.nodeValue;
  }
  new_lists_array[loop] = user_to_add;
  var new_user = makeNewUser(the_name, the_password, profile,
      new_lists_array);
  return new_user;
}
```

B

RESOURCES

You are not alone. There are plenty of JavaScript and Ajax resources to guide and support you along the path to JavaScript mastery. This book is just the beginning of your journey. In this appendix you'll find tutorials, libraries, frameworks, and blogs that will give you more information than you could possibly process.

Tutorials

This book covered all of the basics of JavaScript and Ajax, and many advanced topics as well. Here are tutorials that will help you fill in the details not covered in this book.

HTML Tutorials

HTML is the backbone of any web page. The following sites provide in-depth HTML details:

Webmonkey http://www.webmonkey.com/webmonkey/authoring

W3 Schools http://www.w3schools.com/html

Cascading Style Sheets Tutorials

Cascading Style Sheets (CSS) and the JavaScript style object were used throughout the book to add formatting to HTML elements. CSS is a big topic all on its own.

Webmonkey http://www.webmonkey.com/webmonkey/authoring/stylesheets

W3 Schools http://www.w3schools.com/css/default.asp

Westciv http://www.westciv.com/style_master/academy/css_tutorial

Advanced Topics in JavaScript

There aren't many aspects of JavaScript not covered in this book. You might want to learn even more about object-oriented programming in JavaScript, how events work in different browsers, and handling errors.

Object-Oriented Programming

Object-oriented programming (OOP) is a programming style that simplifies many aspects of programming. The following tutorials at WebReference.com describe OOP in detail and discuss how to use this style of coding with JavaScript:

http://www.webreference.com/js/column79

http://www.webreference.com/js/column80

Advanced Event Handling

Chapters 2 and 13 covered many details about how to handle events in JavaScript. Believe it or not, there is a bit more to learn on the topic. A series of articles at the bottom of this QuirksMode.org page give an excellent in-depth discussion of advanced event handling:

http://www.quirksmode.org/js/contents.html

Exception Handling

JavaScript has some fancy ways of responding to errors in your code. The following tutorial at Dev Shed discusses how to use the JavaScript commands try and catch to capture errors and respond to them.

http://www.devshed.com/c/a/JavaScript/JavaScript-Exception-Handling

Ajax Tutorials

Because Ajax is a complex topic, there are many tutorials about it. For tutorials that focus on Ajax frameworks, see "Ajax Frameworks" on page 408. For general Ajax tutorials, a regularly updated list of Ajax tutorials may be found at http://www.maxkiesler.com/index.php. Especially helpful will be the "Round-up of 30 AJAX Tutorials" (March 15, 2006) and "60 More AJAX Tutorials" (May 8, 2006).

Example JavaScript and Ajax Code

The following sites contain many examples of JavaScript and Ajax code that you can cut and paste into your web pages.

dhtmlgoodies.com   http://www.dhtmlgoodies.com
A nicely laid-out site from Alf Magne Kalleland

The JavaScript Source   http://javascript.internet.com
EarthWeb's JavaScript resource, with over two thousand scripts and counting

Dynamic Drive   http://www.dynamicdrive.com
Another very nicely laid-out site, with a CSS library as well

JS Made Easy.com   http://www.jsmadeeasy.com
Code examples, tutorials, and JavaScript cheat sheets

Webmonkey   http://www.webmonkey.com/webmonkey/reference/javascript_code_library
An oldie but a goodie, close to my heart

Good Ajax Websites

These sites provide news and tips for Ajax programmers.

ajaxian   http://ajaxian.com
My favorite site for Ajax news

Ajax Goals   http://ajaxgoals.com
Another good Ajax news site

AjaxPatterns   http://ajaxpatterns.org
An Ajax wiki with a great deal of information about advanced Ajax topics

AJAX Magazine   http://ajax.phpmagazine.net
Not updated as frequently as the rest, but that can be a good thing

Ajax Frameworks

As you've seen, the code for Ajax applications can get complicated and long. However, there is a fair amount of code that is common to many Ajax applications. Creating a request object, for example, occurs in every Ajax application.

Ajax frameworks do a great deal of the work for you. Frameworks exist for handling XML, achieving common interface effects such as drag and drop, and working with numerous server-side languages. Here is a list of some of the most commonly used frameworks, separated into categories based on the server-side languages they work with. All the frameworks are free, or have a free version, unless otherwise specified. This is just a sample of available frameworks. See http://ajaxpatterns.org/Ajax_Frameworks for a more exhaustive list.

JavaScript

The following sites provide numerous JavaScript widgets and libraries used by many professional sites to ease their JavaScript coding.

Dojo   http://dojotoolkit.org
Lots of navigation and page layout tools, such as drag and drop, slide shows, collapsible trees, rich text editors, and more

Lightbox   http://www.huddletogether.com/projects/lightbox2
Nice library for displaying and managing images using Prototype and Scriptaculous, which are available from sites in this list

Mochikit   http://mochikit.com
Hundreds of JavaScript functions, covering areas including string formatting, date and time handling, logging, CSS manipulation, and all sorts of visual effects

Prototype   http://prototype.conio.net
A JavaScript programming framework that promotes good object-oriented programming and includes Ajax support, higher-order programming constructs, and easy DOM manipulation (lots of other toolkits use this, so most likely you will too)

Rico   http://openrico.org
A very popular user interface client that uses Prototype

Simple Ajax Code Kit (SACK)   http://twilightuniverse.com/resources/code/sack
Gives you a fancy way to deal with the standard request object

Sarissa   http://sarissa.sf.net
An excellent toolkit to support XML manipulation, including good ways to query XML documents and easy calls to turn XML documents into strings

Scriptaculous   http://script.aculo.us
This very popular framework gives you lots of visual effects, using Prototype

Spry   http://labs.adobe.com/technologies/spry
A framework from Adobe intended to give web designers access to the powers of Ajax without having to know very much JavaScript

PHP

The following sites provide tools for developing Ajax applications using PHP.

CakePHP   http://cakephp.org
A popular rapid development framework for PHP that integrates well with the Prototype JavaScript library

Ajax Task List   http://grahambird.co.uk/cake/tutorials/ajax.php
A good tutorial for CakePHP, also based on a To Do list application

Simple Ajax Toolkit (Sajax)   http://www.modernmethod.com/sajax
Lets you call PHP code from within your JavaScript and makes it easier to do PHP calls without having to bother with sending information to the webserver via a request object

Java

Fans of the Java programming language can find useful tools for Ajax programming in the following list.

AjaxTags   http://ajaxtags.sourceforge.net
Tags for Java Server Pages to provide common Ajax techniques such as form validation, text box auto-complete, and content highlighting

Direct Web Remoting (DWR)   http://getahead.ltd.uk/dwr
A very popular framework that allows you to embed Java calls inside your JavaScript, much like the PHP framework Sajax

Echo2   http://www.nextapp.com/platform/echo2/echo
A Java servlet that generates the JavaScript for you to create and run an entire Ajax application in Java

Google Web Toolkit (GWT)   http://code.google.com/webtoolkit
A Java-to-JavaScript translator that enables you to code your Ajax in Java, then convert it to JavaScript; similar to Echo2, except in GWT all the code runs on the client side

Comparing the Google Web Toolkit to Echo2
http://www.theserverside.com/news/thread.tss?thread_id=40804
A thorough comparison of Echo2 and GWT (written by the author of Echo2)

.NET

Coders who prefer to use Microsoft's .NET technology will find Ajax support at the following sites.

Atlas   http://atlas.asp.net
Free web development framework from Microsoft, marketed as integrating "cross-browser client script libraries with the ASP.NET 2.0 server-based development framework"

ComfortASP.NET   http://www.comfortasp.de
A framework that enables you to add many Ajax features to sites in the Active Server Pages (ASP) environment without needing to know how to program; features include timers, prevention of multiple form submits, and handling the Ajax calls

Ruby

Ruby is not a new programming language, but it has recently become very popular among web developers.

Ruby on Rails   http://www.rubyonrails.org
A framework for developing database-backed web applications that has Ajax support and a cultlike following (some of my friends swear by it)

C

REFERENCE TO JAVASCRIPT OBJECTS AND FUNCTIONS

 This reference covers all objects and functions currently part of JavaScript in Firefox and various versions of Internet Explorer. Each entry appears with the earliest version of Internet Explorer that supports it and whether or not Firefox supports it. For example, an entry listed with *FF, IE 5* will work in Firefox 1.0, Internet Explorer 5, and later versions of those browsers.

In the summer of 2006, according to a variety of sites (including W3 Schools,[1] Counter.com,[2] and the Browser News[3]), approximately 70 percent of users were using some version of Internet Explorer (mostly IE 6), and

---

[1] See http://www.w3schools.com/browsers/browsers_stats.asp.

[2] See http://www.thecounter.com/stats/2006/August/browser.php.

[3] See http://www.upsdell.com/BrowserNews/stat.htm.

18 percent of users were using some version of Firefox. An additional 4 percent were using a browser that executes JavaScript much as Firefox does (such as Netscape, Opera, or Safari). The remaining 8 percent represent a hodge-podge of earlier browsers, Internet spiders (like Google's) that crawl around the Internet adding websites to their databases, and later browsers that may or may not support JavaScript but, if they do, probably support the same objects and methods as Firefox. If you want the flashiest web pages, writing JavaScript for IE 5.5 and Firefox will allow at least 92 percent of web browsers to see your pages. To expand that by another 1 percent or so, you could go through the extra effort of writing special code for IE 4 and Netscape 4 browsers. In that case, I recommend you buy the latest version of *The JavaScript Bible* by Danny Goodman (Wiley, 2004).

If I have used an entry in this book or consider it an important function, I define it here and illustrate it with an example. For the less common JavaScript functions and objects, I provide brief descriptions and list the browsers that support them. This reference capitalizes object entries and lists them with their methods, properties, and handlers (properties come first, in alphabetical order, followed by methods, and then handlers). Because certain browsers support some but not all of an object's properties, methods, and handlers, I list each item with the earliest browser versions that support it. Object properties can be read-only or read-write. If a property is read-write, JavaScript can look up and change its value. However, JavaScript can't change a read-only property—JavaScript can only look up the value of that property. For example, JavaScript changes (writes to) the src property of an image in an image swap:

```
window.document.my_image.src = "happy.gif";
```

JavaScript can also look it up (read it):

```
var the_gif_showing = window.document.my_image.src;
```

On the other hand, JavaScript can only look up the firstChild property of a DOM node:

```
var my_child = window.document.getElementById('something').firstChild;
```

In Firefox and other similar browsers, some properties can be written to only if the script is "signed." See http://www.mozilla.org/projects/security/components/signed-scripts.html for more information on signed scripts.

Unless stated otherwise, the properties in this appendix are read-write.

Although this reference tries to cover all the objects and methods you are likely to need when writing JavaScript, browsers have literally hundreds of browser-specific methods and properties, and new ones are added with each new browser version. Get the most complete references straight from the horses' mouths:

Internet Explorer   http://www.microsoft.com/technet/prodtechnol/IE

Firefox   http://developer.mozilla.org

alert() [FF, IE 3]

Displays a dialog box with one button labeled OK and a message specified by the function's parameter.

For example:

```
alert("Hello, world!");
```

creates a dialog box with the words *Hello, world!* and an OK button. The browser window is frozen until the user clicks the OK button.

Anchor

All anchors on a page are stored in the document's anchor array: `window.document.anchors[]`.

Example:

```
<a name = "some_name"></a>
```

Properties

hash	FF, IE 3	Contents of an anchor after the # character
host	FF, IE 3	Hostname and the port of a link
hostname	FF, IE 3	Hostname of an anchor
href	FF, IE 3	href of the anchor
name	FF, IE 4	Anchor tag's name
pathname	FF, IE 3	Part of an anchor after the host
port	FF, IE 3	Port of an anchor (usually null)
protocol	FF, IE 3	Protocol of an anchor (http and ftp are the most common)
rel, rev	FF, IE 3	Additional attribute, called rel or rev, used in some anchors to add more information about the link
search	FF, IE 3	Part of an anchor following the ? character
target	FF, IE 3	HTML target of an anchor

Applet

Refers to a Java applet. All applets on a page are stored in the JavaScript array `window.document.applets[]`.

Properties

code	FF, IE 4	Read-only: URL string of the applet's Java class file
codeBase	FF, IE 4	Read-only: Path to the applet, not including the class file name
height, width	FF, IE 4	Size of the applet display section
hspace, vspace	FF, IE 4	Padding around the applet display, in pixels
name	FF, IE 4	Read-only: Applet's name

Methods

start()	FF, IE 3	Starts a Java applet
stop()	FF, IE 3	Stops a Java applet

For example:

```
window.document.applets[0].start();
```

tells the first Java applet on a web page to start, while

```
window.document.applets[0].stop();
```

tells the first Java applet on a web page to stop.

Area   [FF, IE 3]

An HTML tag that describes a clickable region inside a client-side image map. Area tags are stored in the JavaScript array window.document.links[]; an area is treated just like a link object (see "Link" on page 431 for more information).

Array   [FF, IE 3]

A list of information. There are two ways to create an array:

```
var the_array = new Array();
var the_array = new Array(element_one, element_two, element_three...);
```

You can look up or change elements in an array using their position numbers (numbering starts with 0):

```
the_array[0] = "thau!";
window.document.writeln(the_array[0] + " wrote this book.");
```

Properties

length	FF, IE 3	Number of elements in an array

Example:

```
var my_array = new Array("eenie", "meenie", "miney", "moe");
var number_of_things = my_array.length;
```

The variable number_of_things holds the value 4, because there are four elements in the array.

prototype	FF, IE3	Adds properties and methods to all objects of an array. See the tutorials in "Object-Oriented Programming" on page 406.

Methods

join()   FF, IE 3   Creates a string from an array. Each element in the array will be listed in the string and separated by a space from the previous and following elements, unless some other delimiter is listed as a parameter to join().

Example:

```
var my_array = new Array("eenie", "meenie", "miney", "moe");
var my_string = my_array.join(":");
```

The variable my_string contains eenie:meenie:miney:moe.

reverse()   FF, IE 3   Returns a copy of an array with the elements reversed

Example:

```
var my_array = new Array("eenie", "meenie", "miney", "moe");
var new_array = my_array.reverse();
```

The variable new_array contains an array with the elements moe, miney, meenie, and eenie, in that order.

sort()   FF, IE 4   Returns an array with the elements of another array sorted in alphabetical order. If the name of a function is listed as a parameter to sort(), that function will define the order of two elements passed to it as follows:

- If the function returns a value less than 0, the first element is smaller than the second.
- If the function returns a value greater than 0, the second element is smaller than the first.
- If the function returns 0, do not change the order of the elements.

Examples:

```
var my_array = new Array("eenie", "moe", "miney", "meenie");
var sorted_array = my_array.sort();
```

The variable sorted_array contains the elements eenie, meenie, miney, and moe in that order.

```
var my_array = new Array(1, 12, 2);
var sorted_array = my_array.sort(numericalSorter);
function numericalSorter(element_one, element_two)
{
    return element_one - element_two;
}
```

The variable sorted_array contains the elements 1, 2, and 12, in that order.

Less Common Methods

concat()	FF, IE 4	Concatenates many elements into one array
pop()	FF, IE 5.5	Returns the last element of an array and deletes that element from the array
push()	FF, IE 5.5	Appends a value to the end of an array
shift()	FF, IE 5.5	Returns the first element of an array and shifts the other elements to replace it
slice()	FF, IE 4	Creates a new array by taking a piece out of this array
splice()	FF, IE 5.5	Replaces or deletes parts of an array or puts something in the middle
toString()	FF, IE 3	Converts an array into a comma-separated string
unShift()	FF, IE 5.5	Appends a value to the start of an array

Button (Including Submit and Reset Buttons)

The button, submit, and reset form elements.

Properties

form	FF, IE 3	Read-only: Form containing the button
name	FF, IE 3	Name of a button. Note that name is not the text that shows up in the button on the web page (see the value property).
type	FF, IE 3	Read-only: Type of button: button, submit, or reset
value	FF, IE 3	String shown on the button

Handlers

onClick	FF, IE 3	Triggered when a visitor clicks on the button
onMouseDown	FF, IE 4	Triggered when the mouse is clicked on the button
onMouseUp	FF, IE 4	Triggered when the mouse is released after clicking

Example:

```
<input type = "button" value = "Click me" onClick = "this.value='Stop
clicking me!';">
```

When the user clicks this button, the words on the button change from *Click me* to *Stop clicking me!*

Methods

click()	FF, IE 3	Simulates the act of clicking the button

Checkbox

The checkbox form element.

Properties

checked	FF, IE 3	true if a visitor has selected the checkbox, false otherwise. Setting the property to true will cause the checkbox to act as if a visitor had selected the box.
form	FF, IE 3	Read-only: Form containing the checkbox
name	FF, IE 3	Name of a checkbox
type	FF, IE 3	Read-only: Set to 'checkbox'
value	FF, IE 3	Value of the checkbox

Example:

```
if (window.document.my_form.the_checkbox.checked == true)
{
    alert("Thanks for clicking the checkbox!");
}
```

Handlers

onClick	FF, IE 3	Triggered when a visitor clicks the checkbox

Methods

click()	FF, IE 3	Simulates the act of clicking the checkbox

clearInterval()   [FF, IE 4]

Cancels an interval set by setInterval(). JavaScript commands may execute repeatedly every *n* milliseconds. See "setInterval()" on page 440 for more information.

clearTimeout()   [FF, IE 3]

Cancels a time-out set by setTimeout(). See "setTimeout()" on page 441 and Chapter 9 for more information on time-outs.
For example:

```
clearTimeout(my_timeout);
```

cancels a time-out named my_timeout.

confirm()   [FF, IE 3]

Creates a dialog box with two buttons, OK and Cancel, and text specified by the function's parameter. Clicking OK results in the function returning a value of true, and clicking Cancel results in a false value.

Example:

```
if (confirm("Are you feeling happy?"))
{
    alert("Clap your hands!");
} else {
    alert("Don't worry!");
}
```

This example calls up a dialog box with the text *Are you feeling happy?* along with an OK button and a Cancel button. Clicking the OK button causes the function to return true, executing the first part of the if-then-else statement with an alert box showing the words *Clap your hands!* Clicking Cancel causes the function to return false, triggering the else clause of the if-then-else statement and calling an alert box showing the words *Don't worry!*

Date

This object represents dates; you can create it in several ways:

```
var the_date = new Date();
var the_date = new Date("month dd, yyyy");
var the_date = new Date("month dd, yyyy hh:mm:ss");
var the_date = new Date(yy, mm, dd);
var the_date = new Date(milliseconds);
```

Here *month* is the name of the month (January, February, and so on), *dd* is a two-digit day (01 to 31), *yyyy* is a four-digit year (0000 to 9999), and so on. If you create a Date object without anything in the parentheses, JavaScript will assume you mean the current date and time according to the computer that's running the JavaScript.

The Date object has numerous methods for getting and setting the date. Except where noted, the methods work for all JavaScript-enabled browsers.

Methods for Getting the Date and Time

Supported by FF and IE 3 except where noted.

getDate()	Returns the day of the month as an integer from 1 to 31
getDay()	Returns the day of the week as an integer, where 0 is Sunday and 1 is Monday
getFullYear()	Returns the year as a four-digit number (only in FF, IE 4)
getHours()	Returns the hour as an integer between 0 and 23
getMinutes()	Returns the minutes as an integer between 0 and 59

getMonth()	Returns the month as an integer between 0 and 11, where 0 is January and 11 is December
getSeconds()	Returns the seconds as an integer between 0 and 59
getTime()	Returns the current time in milliseconds, where 0 is January 1, 1970, 00:00:00

Example:

```
var the_date = new Date();
var the_hours = the_date.getHours();
```

If the clock on the computer running the JavaScript thinks it's 8 PM, the_hours contains the number 20.

Methods for Getting the UTC Date and Time

The following methods (FF, IE 4) return dates and times in UTC time (Coordinated Universal Time, measured somewhat differently from Greenwich Mean Time, which it replaced as the world standard).

getUTCDate()	Returns the day of the month as an integer from 1 to 31
getUTCDay()	Returns the day of the week as an integer, where 0 is Sunday and 1 is Monday
getUTCFullYear()	Returns the year as a four-digit number
getUTCHours()	Returns the hour as an integer between 0 and 23
getUTCMinutes()	Returns the minutes as an integer between 0 and 59
getUTCMonth()	Returns the month as an integer between 0 and 11, where 0 is January and 11 is December
getUTCSeconds()	Returns the seconds as an integer between 0 and 59

The Problematic getYear() Method

The getYear() method should return the number of years since 1900, but its behavior differs from browser to browser. Some browsers perform as advertised—for example, returning 110 if the year is 2010. Others, however, equate getYear() with getFullYear(), returning 2010 if the year is 2010. Because of these cross-browser discrepancies, it's best to adjust the date provided by getYear() as follows:

```
var the_date = new Date();
var the_year = the_date.getYear();
if (the_year < 1000)
{
    the_year = the_year + 1900;
}
```

This code always results in the_year containing the correct four-digit year.

Methods for Setting the Date and Time

The following methods change the contents of a Date object (FF, IE 3, except where noted):

setDate()	Sets the day of the month as an integer from 1 to 31
setFullYear()	Sets the year as a four-digit number (only in FF and IE 4)
setHours()	Sets the hour as an integer between 0 and 23
setMinutes()	Sets the minutes as an integer between 0 and 59
setMonth()	Sets the month as an integer between 0 and 11, where 0 is January and 11 is December
setSeconds()	Sets the seconds as an integer between 0 and 59
setTime()	Sets the current time in milliseconds, where 0 is January 1, 1970, 00:00:00
setYear()	Sets the year—uses two digits if the year is between 1900 and 1999, four digits otherwise

Example:

```
var the_date = new Date();
the_date.setHours(22);
the_date.setYear(2012);
```

The Date object called the_date thinks it's 10 PM in the year 2012.

Methods for Setting the UTC Date and Time

The following methods (FF, IE 4) are like the ones just described, except the dates and times set by the methods are adjusted to reflect UTC time, the replacement for Greenwich Mean Time.

setUTCDate()	Sets day of the month as an integer from 1 to 31
setUTCFullYear()	Sets the year as a four-digit number
setUTCHours()	Sets the hour as an integer between 0 and 23
setUTCMinutes()	Sets the minutes as an integer between 0 and 59
setUTCMonth()	Sets the month as an integer between 0 and 11, where 0 is January and 11 is December
setUTCSeconds()	Sets the seconds as an integer between 0 and 59

Example:

```
var the_date = new Date();
the_date.setUTCHours(10);
```

If the computer is one time zone to the west of Greenwich, England, the_date will now think it's 9 AM UTC.

Methods for Converting Dates to Strings

These methods turn the date stored in a Date object into a string.

toGMTString()	FF, IE3	Returns the date adjusted to reflect Greenwich Mean Time, the former world standard
toUTCString()	FF, IE4	Suggested method for later browsers

Document

The document of a window holds all the HTML elements of the web page in that window.

Properties

alinkColor	FF, IE 3	Color of a link when you click it
anchors[]	FF, IE 3	Read-only: Array of anchor objects. See "Anchor" on page 413 for more information.
applets[]	FF, IE 3	Read-only: Array storing the applets in the document. See "Applet" on page 413 for more information.
bgColor	FF, IE 3	Background color of a page. The value can be the name of a color or a hexadecimal triplet.

Example:

```
window.document.bgColor = "#000000";
```

This line makes the background of a page black.

body	FF, IE 4	Body element of a web page
cookie	FF, IE 3	HTML cookie associated with this document. See Chapter 12 for more information on cookies.
documentElement	FF, IE 5	Read-only: Root element of an XML file
domain	FF, IE 4	Domain of a web page (e.g., nostarch.com)
embeds[]	FF, IE 4	Read-only: Array of embeds[]
fgColor	FF, IE 3	Default font color
forms[]	FF, IE 3	Array that stores all of a document's forms. See "Form" on page 424 for more information.
images[]	FF, IE 3	Array that stores all of a document's images. See "Image" on page 429 for more information.
lastModified	FF, IE 3	Read-only string that stores the date on which a user most recently changed the document

Example:

```
window.document.writeln("last changed on: " + window.document.lastModified);
```

This line writes the date of the last time the page was modified.

linkColor	FF, IE 3	Default color of a link
links[]	FF, IE 3	Array storing all of a document's hyperlinks. See "Link" on page 431 for more information.
referrer	FF, IE 3	Read-only string containing the domain name of the hyperlink that led to this page

For example:

```
window.document.writeln("Thanks for coming from " + window.document.referrer);
```

writes *Thanks for coming from www.nostarch.com* if a hyperlink from the No Starch Press website led to the page.

styleSheets[]	FF, IE 4	Read-only: Array of all style elements
title	FF, IE 3	Contains the document's title

For example:

```
window.document.title = "Presto Chango";
```

changes the title of the page to *Presto Chango*.

URL	FF, IE 4	URL of the document
vlinkColor	FF, IE 3	Color of visited links; can't be changed once you write the link

Methods

close()	FF, IE 3	Use close() when you've finished writing to the document (optional). Sometimes, because of browser bugs, writing to a web page using document.write() won't actually complete that action unless you execute document.close() after executing document.write().
createAttribute()	FF, IE 6	Given a string, creates an XML attribute named that string
createElement()	FF, IE 4	Given a string, creates an XML element named that string
createTextNode()	FF, IE 5	Given a string, creates a text node with a nodeValue equal to the string
getElementById()	FF, IE 5	Returns the element in a document that has the id equal to a provided string
getElementsByName()	FF, IE 5	Returns an array of elements that have a name attribute set to a given string
getElementsByTagName()	FF, IE 5	Returns an array of elements which have a given name, such as or <person>
open()	FF, IE 3	Use open() if you want to clear the contents of a web page before writing to it using write() or writeln(). If you use document.open(), use document.close() when you're done writing to the page.
write(), writeln()	FF, IE 3	Writes to a web page. The only difference between these two methods is that writeln() appends a line break at the end of whatever is written.

elements[] [FF, IE 3]

An array in the form object that stores all the elements (buttons, check-boxes, radio buttons, and so on) of a form. See "Form" on page 424 for more information.

escape() [FF, IE 3]

Formats a string so that it conforms to URL encoding. Generally used for setting cookies (Chapter 12) and sending information to servers (Chapters 15 and 16).

Example:

```
var encoded_string = escape("a string safe for cookies");
```

The variable encoded_string now holds a%20string%20safe%20for%20cookies because the escape function replaces spaces with %20. See "unescape()" on page 448 for more information.

eval() [FF, IE 3]

Evaluates a string. Example:

```
var the_sum = eval("2 + 3");
```

The variable the_sum will equal 5 because eval() forces JavaScript to evaluate the string "2 + 3".

Event

The event object describes an event that just happened: a mouse click, a cursor movement, and so on. See Chapter 13 for more details.

Properties

altKey	FF, IE 4	true if the ALT key is held down
button	FF, IE 4	If the event involves a click, this says what kind. A 2 means the right button was clicked. Some other number probably means the left button. See Chapter 13 for more information.
clientX	IE 4	x coordinate of an event in a window
clientY	IE 4	y coordinate of an event in a window
ctrlKey	FF, IE 4	true if the CTRL key is held down
keyCode	FF, IE 4	ASCII value of the key that was pressed
pageX	FF	x coordinate of an event in a window
pageY	FF	y coordinate of an event in a window
screenX	FF, IE 4	x coordinate of an event on the screen
screenY	FF, IE 4	y coordinate of an event on the screen
shiftKey	FF, IE 4	true if the SHIFT key is held down
srcElement	IE 4	Element that received the event

target	FF	Element that received the event
type	FF, IE 4	Type of event

FileUpload

The FileUpload form element lets a visitor choose a file on the computer to submit to a CGI script along with the form. Use the syntax <input type = "file">.

Properties

name	FF, IE 3	Name of the FileUpload field
value	FF, IE 4	Read-only: Filename selected

Methods

blur()	FF, IE 3	Removes the cursor from the FileUpload element
focus()	FF, IE 3	Moves the cursor to the FileUpload element
select()	FF, IE 3	Selects the text inside the FileUpload element

Handlers

onBlur	FF, IE 3	Called when the user removes the cursor from the field
onChange	FF, IE 3	Triggered when a visitor changes the contents of the field
onFocus	FF, IE 3	Called when the user puts the cursor into the field

Form

Every form on a web page has a form object. The window.document.forms[] array stores all of a web page's form objects.

Properties

Each type of Form element—button, checkbox, FileUpload, hidden, password, radio, reset, select, submit, text, and textarea—has its own object listing in this appendix. See each individual object for more information.

action	FF, IE 4; read-only in IE 3	Triggers a specified CGI script when a user submits the form

Example:

```
if (user == "expert")
{
    window.document.the_form.action = "expert_script.cgi";
} else {
    window.document.the_form.action = "basic_script.cgi";
}
```

If the user is considered an expert, the form is set to run expert_script.cgi when the user submits the form.

elements[]   FF, IE 3   Array of the elements of this form

For example:

```
window.document.form_name.elements[0].checked = true;
```

will set the checked value of the first element of the form named form_name to true.

encoding	FF, IE 4; read-only in IE 3	How the information in the form is encoded when it's sent to a CGI script. It's almost always "application/x-www-form-urlencoded" and there's almost never a reason to change it.
length	FF, IE 3	Number of elements in a form

Example:

```
var number_elements = window.document.the_form.length;
```

method	FF, IE 4; read-only in IE 3	Specifies how a form sends information (via either POST or GET) to the CGI script listed in the action tag

Example:

```
window.document.the_form.method = "GET";
```

name   FF, IE 3   Looks for a form by name if you need to locate it

For example:

```
window.document.form_name
```

indicates the form named form_name.

target	FF, IE 3; read-only in IE 3	Window in which the form is to write the results of the form's CGI script. If the target specifies a window that does not exist, a new window opens.

Example:

```
var target_window = window.open("blank.html","my_target");
window.document.the_form.target = "my_target";
```

The first line opens a window with the name my_target. The second line tells the form named the_form that the CGI script it runs should return its results to the window named my_target.

Methods

reset()	FF, IE 4	Resets the elements of a form, as if a visitor clicked a reset button

Example:

```
window.document.the_form.reset();
```

submit()	FF, IE 3	Submits the form, as if a visitor clicked a submit button, except that the onSubmit handler is not called when the submit() method is invoked

Handlers

onReset	FF, IE 3	Triggered when a form is reset
onSubmit	FF, IE 3	Triggered when a form is submitted. Executing return false inside a submit handler stops submission of the form to the CGI script.

Example:

```
<FORM onSubmit = "if (formNotDone(this)) {return false;})">
```

This calls the function formNotDone() on the form. If the function returns true, the if-then statement returns false and the form is not submitted. Note that formNotDone() is not a built-in JavaScript function. See Chapter 11 for more information on form validation.

Hidden

An invisible form element that can store values on a web page without the visitor seeing them; useful for sending secret information to a CGI script.

Properties

name	FF, IE 3	Name of a hidden element
value	FF, IE 3	Value of a hidden element

For example:

```
window.document.the_form.my_hidden.value = "a nice person";
```

will set the value of the hidden element named my_hidden to a nice person. If the form is subsequently sent to a CGI script, the value will be passed along.

History

The history of URLs visited by the visitor's browser.

Properties

length	FF, IE 4	Number of URLs in the history list

Methods

back()	FF, IE 3	Returns to the previous page (like clicking the browser's back button)

Example:

```
history.back();
```

forward()	FF, IE 3	Advances to the next page (like clicking the browser's forward button)

Example:

```
history.forward();
```

go()	FF, IE 3	Takes one parameter: the number of URLs to advance (positive values) or go back (negative values). In IE 3, the parameter can be only –1, 0, or 1.

Example:

```
history.go(-2);
```

HTMLElement   [FF, IE 4]

All HTML elements (images, links, forms, and form elements) are considered objects.

Properties

all[]	FF, IE 4	Read-only: Array holding all the elements the element contains
attributes[]	FF, IE 5	Read-only: Array holding all the attributes of an element
childNodes[]	FF, IE 4	Read-only: Array of child nodes
className	FF, IE 4	CSS identifier for the element
dir	FF, IE 5	Contents of an HTML element's dir attribute
disabled	FF, IE 4	If set to true, dims the element so that it looks inactive
document	FF, IE 4	Read-only: Reference to the element's document
firstChild, lastChild	FF, IE 5	Read-only: First or last child node of an element
height, width	FF, IE 5	Height and width of an element
id	FF, IE 4	id attribute of an element
innerHTML	FF, IE 4	HTML text inside the element, not including the start and end tags
lang	FF, IE 4	Element's lang attribute, used by Internet Explorer to determine how to display language-specific characters

nextSibling, previousSibling	FF, IE 5	Read-only: Next or previous sibling of an element or node. See Chapter 14 for details.
nodeName	FF, IE 5	Read only: Name of a node or element
nodeType	FF, IE 5	Read only: Type of node or element. 1 = element, 2 = attribute, 3 = text node, 8 = comment, 9 = document node
nodeValue	FF, IE 5	Value of a textNode, or null
offsetHeight, offsetWidth	FF, IE 4	Read-only: Element's height and width
offsetLeft, offsetTop	FF, IE 4	Read-only: Horizontal or vertical position of the element in pixels, relative to the containing element
offsetParent	FF, IE 4	Read-only: Reference to the element that contains this element
parentNode	FF, IE 5	Read-only: Parent node of this node or element
scrollHeight, scrollWidth	FF, IE 4	Read-only: Measurements of an element regardless of how much is visible
scrollLeft, scrollTop	FF, IE 4	Read-only: Amount an object is scrolled, in pixels
style	FF, IE 4	Element's CSS style information
tabIndex	FF, IE 4	Position of this element in the traversal order (the order in which elements are selected successively by pressing the TAB key)
tagName	FF, IE 4	HTML tag name of the element

Methods

addEventListener(), removeEventListener()	FF	Advanced event handling for Firefox. See "Advanced Event Handling" on page 406.
appendChild()	FF, IE 5	Append a node to the end of another node's array of child elements
attachEvent(), detatchEvent()	IE 5	Advanced event handling for Internet Explorer. See "Advanced Event Handling" on page 406.
blur()	FF, IE 3	Moves focus off an element
click()	FF, IE 3	Simulates a click on an element
cloneNode()	FF, IE 5	Makes a copy of a node. If true is passed as a parameter, the node and all its children (and their children . . .) are also copied.
dispatchEvent()	FF	Advanced event handling for Firefox. See "Advanced Event Handling" on page 406.
fireEvent()	IE 5.5	Advanced event handling for Internet Explorer. See "Advanced Event Handling" on page 406.
getAttribute()	FF, IE 4	Given a string with an attribute name, returns the value of the attribute of this element
focus()	FF, IE 3	Moves focus onto an element
getAttributeNode()	FF, IE 6	Given a string with an attribute name, gets a node representing the attribute of this element
getElementsByTagName()	FF, IE 5	Given a string with the name of an HTML or XML element, returns an array with all the elements with that tag name
hasChildNodes()	FF, IE 5	Returns true if this element has child elements

insertBefore()	FF, IE 5	Given a new child node and a reference child node, inserts the new child node into this element's list of children before the reference child node
item()	FF, IE 5	Given a number, returns the child of this node with that index number (the first child is item 0)
releaseCapture(), setCapture()	IE 5	Advanced event handling for Internet Explorer. See "Advanced Event Handling" on page 406.
removeAttribute()	FF, IE 4	Given the name of an attribute, removes it from this element
removeAttributeNode()	FF, IE 6	Given an attribute node, removes it from this element
removeChild()	FF, IE 5	Given a node, removes it from the children list of this element
replaceChild()	FF, IE 5	Given a new child node and an old child node, replaces the old child node with the new one
setAttribute()	FF, IE 6	Adds an attribute node to this element

Handlers   [FF, IE 4]

onBlur	onDblclick	onHelp	onKeyPress	onMouseDown	onMouseOut	onMouseUp
onClick	onFocus	onKeyDown	onKeyUp	onMouseOver	onMouseOver	onResize

Image

JavaScript stores images in the images array of the document object. A user may create a new image object as follows:

```
var new_image = new Image();
```

This statement creates a new image and sets its src property to a GIF or JPEG, then preloads that file. See Chapter 4 for more information about images and preloading.

Properties

align	FF, IE 4	Orientation of an image relative to the surrounding text. Values can be: absbottom, absmiddle, baseline, bottom, left, middle, right, texttop, top
alt	FF, IE 4	alt text of an image
border	FF, IE 4	Size of the border around the image

Example:

```
var the_border_size = window.document.my_image.border;
```

complete	FF, IE 4	Read-only: true if the image has completely downloaded and false otherwise

Example:

```
if (window.document.pretty_bird.complete)
{
    alert("you should now see a pretty bird");
}
```

height, width	FF, IE 4	Height of an image in pixels
hspace, vspace	FF, IE 4	Number of transparent pixels around an image
isMap	FF, IE 4	If set to true, the x and y coordinate of the image is sent to whatever server-side program appears in an anchor link around the image
lowsrc	FF, IE 4	Image to show on a low-resolution monitor

Example:

```
window.document.the_image.lowsrc = "small_image.gif";
```

name	FF, IE 4	Name of an image; JavaScript can use this to identify the image

Example:

```
<img src = "sad.gif" name = "my_image">
```

If this appears on your web page, the following JavaScript swaps sad.gif with happy.gif:

```
window.document.my_image.src = "happy.gif";
```

The name of the image, my_image, identifies which image to swap.

src	FF, IE 4	Name of the file containing the image to show

For example:

```
window.document.my_image.src = "happy.gif";
```

swaps the image contained in the file happy.gif into the image named my_image.

isNaN() [FF, IE 4]

Returns true if the parameter is not a number, false otherwise. Example:

```
var zip_code = "none of your business";
if (isNaN(zip_code))
{
    alert("Please provide something that at least looks like a zip code!");
}
```

Since zip_code contains a string, isNaN() returns true, triggering the alert.

Link

The hypertext link object: `<a href = "">`</A>. See "Anchor" on page 413 for more information.

Location

The `location` object controls the URL shown in the browser window.

Properties

hash	FF, IE 3	Part of the URL following a hash mark

Example:

```
window.location.hash = "where_to_go";
```

This will cause the browser to jump to the position of the current page that has the anchor `<a name = "where_to_go">`</a>.

host	FF, IE 3	Hostname and port of a URL

For example, if the URL is http://www.feedmag.com:80/index.html, the host is www.feedmag.com:80.

hostname	FF, IE 3	Domain of the URL shown in the browser

Example:

```
if (window.location.hostname == "www.nostarch.com")
{
    alert("welcome to No Starch Press");
}
```

href	FF, IE 3	Full path of the page shown. Changing href causes the browser to load the specified page.

For example:

```
window.location.href = "http://www.nostarch.com/index.html";
```

loads the page index.html from the No Starch Press website.

pathname	FF, IE 3	Path and filename shown in the browser window (the URL minus the domain information)

Example:

```
var the_path = window.location.pathname;
```

The variable the_path will hold `"index.html"` if the window is currently showing http://www.nostarch.com/index.html.

port	FF, IE 3	URL's port

If the URL is http://www.feedmag.com:80/index.html, the `port` will be 80.

protocol	FF, IE 3	URL's protocol

If the URL is http://www.feedmag.com:80/index.html, the `protocol` will be "http".

search	FF, IE 3	Part of a URL following a question mark

If the URL is http://www.webmonkey.com/index.html?hello_there,

```
var the_search = window.location.search;
```

the variable `the_search` will contain "hello_there".

Methods

reload()	FF, IE 4	Reloads the page

For example:

```
window.location.reload();
```

will act as if a visitor clicked the reload or refresh button in the browser.

replace()	FF, IE 4	Loads the page specified by the URL passed as a parameter into the browser window. The page shown when `replace()` is called is removed from the browser's history and replaced with the new page. This means that clicking the back button after the new page has replaced the currently shown page won't result in revisiting the current page. It's as if you're telling the browser to forget the currently shown page.

Example:

```
window.location.replace("http://www.npr.org"); 0
```

Math [FF, IE 3]

The `math` object contains numerous properties and methods. Except where noted, all of these properties and methods work in Firefox, IE 3, and more recent browsers, and all the properties are read-only. Because most of the methods and properties are self-explanatory, I will give few examples. I'll round all numbers to the sixth decimal point.

Properties

E	e, Euler's constant, the base of natural logarithms (2.718282)
LN2	Natural log of 2 (0.693147)
LN10	Natural log of 10 (2.302585)
LOG2E	Base 2 log of e (1.442695)
LOG10E	Base 10 log of e (0.434294)
PI	Pi (3.141593)
SQRT2	Square root of 2 (1.414214)

Methods

`abs()`	Absolute value of the argument, for example, `var ab_value = Math.abs(-10);` sets `ab_value` to 10
`acos()`	Arc cosine of the argument in radians
`asin()`	Arc sine of the argument in radians
`atan()`	Arc tangent of the argument in radians
`ceil()`	Integer greater than or equal to the number passed, for example, `var the_ceiling = Math.ceil(9.5);` sets `the_ceiling` to 10
`cos()`	Cosine of the number of radians passed as the argument
`exp()`	Value of e raised to the power passed as the argument
`floor()`	Integer lower than or equal to the number passed as the argument
`log()`	Natural log of the argument
`max()`	Higher of the two numbers passed as arguments, for example, `var the_higher = Math.max(10,11);` sets `the_higher` to 11
`min()`	Lower of the two numbers passed as arguments
`pow()`	First argument raised to the power passed as the second argument, for example, `two_cubed = Math.pow(2,3);` sets `two_cubed` to 8 (2 to the third power)
`random()`	Random number between 0 and 1
`round()`	Argument rounded up if its decimal value is greater than or equal to 0.5 and rounded down otherwise
`sin()`	Sine of the number of radians passed as the argument
`sqrt()`	Square root of the argument
`tan()`	Tangent of the number of radians passed as the argument

Navigator

The navigator object lets JavaScript know what type of web browser your visitor is using.

Properties

appName	FF, IE 3	Manufacturer of the browser (Netscape, Internet Explorer, Opera, and so on)

Example:

```
if (navigator.appName == "Netscape")
{
    window.location = "netscape_index.html";
}
```

This code sends a visitor to a page called netscape_index.html if the visitor is using Netscape.

| appVersion | FF, IE 3 | String representing the version of the browser. It's not useful unless interpreted with the parseFloat() function. |

Example:

```
if (parseFloat(navigator.appVersion) < 2)
{
    alert("Isn't it time to upgrade?");
}
```

Less Common Properties

appCodeName	FF, IE 3	Read-only: Browser's code name
browserLanguage	IE 4	Read-only: Language in which the browser's interface is displayed, for example, "en-us" for U.S. English or "ar-iq" for Iraqi Arabic
cookieEnabled	FF, IE 4	Read-only: true if the browser can take cookies
language	FF	Read-only: Language of the browser
online	FF, IE 4	Read-only: true if the browser is online
platform	FF, IE 4	Read-only: Browser's operating system
systemLanguage	IE 4	Language in which the operating system's interface is displayed
userAgent	FF, IE 3	Generally a string composed of appCodeName and appVersion

Methods

| javaEnabled | FF, IE 4 | Read-only: true if Java is on |

Number

The Number object has some helpful read-only properties.

Properties

MAX_VALUE	FF, IE 4	Read-only: Highest integer possible given the configuration of the browser and the computer it's on
MIN_VALUE	FF, IE 4	Read-only: Lowest integer possible given the configuration of the browser and the computer it's on
NaN	FF, IE 4	Read-only: Not a number, the result if a mathematical operation fails (Math.sqrt(-1), for example); can be tested with the isNaN() function

Example:

```
if (isNaN(Math.sqrt(-1)))
{
    alert("Get real! You can't take the square root of -1!");
}
```

NEGATIVE_INFINITY	FF, IE 4	Read-only: Value smaller than `Number.MIN_VALUE`. You know no number will ever be less than this value.
POSITIVE_INFINITY	FF, IE 4	Read-only: Value bigger than `Number.MAX_VALUE`. No number will ever exceed this value.

Methods

toExponential()	FF, IE 5.5	Displays the number in exponential notation. An integer parameter specifies the number of digits to the right of the decimal point.

Example:

```
var the_answer = 4321;
alert(the_answer.exponential(2));
```

The alert contains the string 4.32e+3.

toFixed()	FF, IE 5.5	Sets the number of digits following a decimal point. The number is rounded up if it has more trailing digits than n, and "0"s are used after the decimal point if needed to create the desired decimal length.
toPrecision()	FF, IE 5.5	Formats any number so it is of length n, where n is an integer passed as a parameter. Also called significant digits. A decimal point and "0"s are used if needed to create the desired length.
toString()	FF, IE 3	Turns a number into a string

Option

The option object refers to an option in a select element of a form—either a pull-down menu or scrollable list. All the options of a select element are stored in the options[] array of that element.

Properties

Form	FF, IE 3	Form containing the option
selected	FF, IE 3	true if the option has been selected and false otherwise

Example:

```
if (window.document.the_form.the_pulldown.options[0].selected == true)
{
    var the_option_text =
        window.document.the_form.the_pulldown.option[0].text;
    alert("thanks for picking " + the_option_text);
}
```

text	FF, IE 3	Text associated with an option (see the preceding example)
value	FF, IE 3	Value of the option

parseInt() [FF, IE 3]

Converts a string to an integer as long as the first character is a number. If the first character is not a number, parseInt() returns NaN (not a number). If the string is a number followed by letters, parseInt() grabs the first set of digits in the string.

Example:

```
var the_string = "123abc456";
var the_numbers = parseInt(the_string);
```

The variable the_numbers contains 123.

parseFloat() [FF, IE 3]

Converts a string to a floating-point number as long as the first character is a number. If the first character is not a number, parseFloat() returns NaN (not a number). If the string is a number followed by letters, parseFloat() grabs the first set of numbers in the string.

Example:

```
var the_string = "3.14etc";
var the_numbers = parseFloat(the_string);
```

The variable the_numbers contains 3.14.

Password

The password form element, like the text form element, allows a visitor to type a line of text into a form. In a password element, however, asterisks or bullets replace the letters to hide the contents from view. The element is represented like this in HTML: <input type = "password">.

Properties

defaultValue	FF, IE 3	Read-only: Browser-set default value for the element
Form	FF, IE 3	Read-only: Form containing the element
maxLength	FF, IE 4	Maximum number of characters allowed in the field
name	FF, IE 3	Name of the password field
readOnly	FF, IE 4	true if users can't enter data into the field
size	FF, IE 4	Width of the field
type	FF, IE 4	Read-only: Set to 'PASSWORD'
value	FF, IE 3	Text that appears in the password field

Example:

```
<input type = "password" onChange = "alert(this.value);">
```

When a visitor enters a password into this field and presses ENTER, whatever the visitor typed gets sent to the alert() function.

Methods

blur()   FF, IE 3   Removes the cursor from the password element

Example:

```
window.document.my_form.the_password.blur();
```

focus()   FF, IE 3   Moves the cursor to the password element

Example:

```
window.document.my_form.the_password.focus();
```

This line puts the cursor inside the password element named the_password. Unless the focus is changed, the next characters typed go into the_password.

select()   FF, IE 3   Selects the text inside the password element

Example:

```
window.document.my_form.the_password.select();
```

Handlers

onBlur   FF, IE 3   Called when a visitor removes the cursor from the password element

Example:

```
<input type = "password" onBlur = "alert('Don\'t forget your password!');">
```

onChange   FF, IE 3   Triggered when a visitor changes the contents of the field and then clicks out of the field or presses ENTER

Example:

```
<input type = "password" onChange = "Thanks for the password!">
```

onFocus	FF, IE 3	Called when the cursor is put into the password field

Example:

```
<input type = "password" onFocus = "window.open('instruct.html','inst')";>
```

This method opens a window when a visitor clicks inside the password field.

prompt()

A dialog box that has OK and Cancel buttons, a place for a message to the visitor, and a box into which the visitor may type a reply. The prompt() function returns the visitor's reply and takes two parameters: a message that appears above the input area and a default value to put in the input area. If the visitor clicks Cancel, prompt() returns the value null.

Example:

```
var the_name = prompt("What's your name?", "your name here");
if (the_name == null)
{
    the_name = prompt("Come on! What's your name?","Please...");
}
```

This calls up a prompt box asking visitors for their names. The words *your name here* appear as default text in the input area. If a visitor clicks Cancel, the if-then statement asks for the name one more time.

Radio

The radio button form element. Radio buttons given the same name are considered a set and are stored in an array with the set's name. A visitor can select only one radio button of the set at any given time. If a web page has five radio buttons named favorite_color, the second radio button in the set is referred to as:

```
window.document.the_form.favorite_color[1]
```

Properties

checked	FF, IE 3	true if a visitor has selected the radio button and false otherwise. Setting the property to true causes the radio button to act as if a visitor selected the button.

Example:

```
if (window.document.the_form.favorite_color[3].checked == true)
{
    alert("I like that color too!");
}
```

This `if-then` statement calls an alert box if a visitor selects the fourth radio button named `favorite_color`.

defaultValue	FF, IE 3	Read-only: Browser-set default value for the element
length	FF, IE 3	Read-only: Number of elements in a group of radio buttons with the same name
name	FF, IE 3	Radio button's name
type	FF, IE 3	Read-only: Identifies element as a radio button
value	FF, IE 3	Value of a radio button

Methods

click()	FF, IE 3	Simulates a click on the element

Handlers

onClick	FF, IE 3	Triggered when a visitor clicks the radio button

Reset

See "Button (Including Submit and Reset Buttons)" on page 416.

Screen

The screen object contains a number of read-only properties that provide information about the computer screen used to view a web page.

Properties

availHeight, availWidth	FF, IE 4	Read-only: Available height and width of the screen, in pixels. Excludes the taskbar in Windows systems and any other permanent screen elements.

Example:

```
var screen_height = screen.availHeight;
```

height, width	FF, IE 4	Read-only: Height and width of the screen in pixels
colorDepth	FF, IE 4	Read-only: Number of colors on the screen (bits per pixel in IE, natural log in FF)
pixelDepth	FF, IE 4	Read-only: Bits per pixel

Select

The select form element can either be a pull-down menu or a scrollable list. The items in it are called the options of the select and are stored in the select element's `options[]` array.

Properties

length	FF, IE 3	Number of options in the select
multiple	FF, IE 4	If true, accept multiple selections in select box
name	FF, IE 3	select object's name
options[]	FF, IE 3	Read-only: Array containing the select's options. See "Option" on page 435 for more information.
selectedIndex	FF, IE 3	Contains the selected option's array position in a select element. If no item has been selected, selectedIndex is –1. If more than one option has been selected, selectedIndex contains the position of the first option. To determine all the options selected, use a loop to look at the selected property of each option object. See "Option" on page 435 for more information.

Example:

```
var option_number = window.document.the_form.the_select.selectedIndex;
if (selected_option_number != -1)
{
    var option_text =
window.document.the_form.the_select.options[option_number].text;
    alert("Thanks for choosing " + option_text);
}
```

This code determines which option (if any) has been selected, and it presents an alert box with the selected option's text.

Handlers

onChange	FF, IE 3	Triggered when a visitor selects or deselects an option

Example:

```
<select onChange = "alert(this.options[selectedIndex].text + ' is a good
choice');">
<option>Cat</option>
<option>Dog</option>
</select>
```

Selecting Cat or Dog triggers the select's onChange, resulting in an alert box commending the visitor on his or her choice.

setInterval() [FF, IE 4]

Executes JavaScript statements at repeated time intervals, given two parameters: the JavaScript statements to execute and the number of milliseconds between each execution. The function returns a reference to the interval so that clearInterval() may cancel it.

For example:

```
var the_interval = setInterval("alert('Stop procrastinating!');", 10000);
```

creates an interval that calls up an alert box every 10 seconds.

setTimeout()   [FF, IE 3]

Executes JavaScript statements once after a specified amount of time, given two parameters: the JavaScript statements to execute and the number of milliseconds in the future to execute the statements. The function returns a reference to the time-out so that `clearTimeout()` may cancel it.

For example:

```
var the_timeout = setTimeout("alert('Stop procrastinating!');", 10000);
```

creates a time-out that calls up an alert box in 10 seconds.

String

Strings are sets of characters between quotes. See Chapter 11 for more information on strings.

Properties

length	FF, IE 3	Read-only: Number of characters in a string

Example:

```
var the_string = "hello";
var the_length = the_string.length;
```

This code sets the_length to 5.

Methods

anchor()	FF, IE 3	Takes a name as a parameter and returns an anchor tag with the string as the text of the link

For example:

```
var the_string = "Information About Fish";
var the_anchor = the_string.anchor("fish_info");
window.document.writeln(the_anchor);
```

writes `<a name = "fish_info">Information About Fish</a>` to a web page.

big()	FF, IE 3	Puts the string between `<big>` and `</big>` tags

For example:

```
var the_string = "something really important";
window.document.writeln(the_string.big());
```

writes `<big>something really important</big>` to a web page.

bold()   FF, IE 3   Puts the string between `<b>` and `</b>` tags

For example:

```
var the_string = "something really important";
window.document.writeln(the_string.bold());
```

writes `<b>something really important</b>` to a web page.

charAt()   FF, IE 3   Takes a number as a parameter and returns the character in that position of the string. Returns null if there is no character.

For example:

```
var the_string = "rabbit";
var the_first_char = the_string.charAt(0);
```

sets the_first_char to r because r is in position 0 of the string.

charCodeAt()   FF, IE 4   Takes a number as a parameter and returns the ASCII code of the character in that position of the string. Returns null if there is no character.

concat()   FF, IE 4   Given a string, adds it to the end of this string

For example:

```
var the_string = "Hi";
window.document.writeln(the_string.concat(" there"));
```

writes "Hi there" to a web page.

fixed()   FF, IE 3   Puts the string between `<tt>` and `</tt>` tags

fontcolor()   FF, IE 3   Takes the name of a color or a hexadecimal triplet as a parameter and encloses the string between `<font color = "the_color">` and `</font>` tags

For example:

```
var the_string = "pretty";
window.document.writeln(the_string.fontcolor("pink"));
```

writes `<font color = "pink">pretty</font>` to a web page.

fontsize()   FF, IE 3   Takes an integer as a parameter and encloses the string between `<font size = "the_size">` and `</font>` tags

For example:

```
var the_string = "cheese";
window.document.writeln(the_string.fontsize(48));
```

writes `<font size = "48">cheese</font>` to a web page.

String.fromCharCode()   FF, IE 4   Constructs a string from ASCII codes

For example:

```
alert(String.fromCharCode(72, 73));
```

puts up an alert with the string "HI".

indexOf()   FF, IE 3   Searches within the string for the substring specified by the first parameter. The optional second parameter is an integer that dictates where in the string to start searching. If the string contains the substring, indexOf() returns the position of the substring within the string. If the string does not contain the substring, indexOf() returns −1.

For example:

```
var the_string = "The Waldorf Astoria";
var wheres = the_string.indexOf("Waldo");
```

sets wheres to 4 because the *W* in *Waldo* is in position 4 in the string.

italics()   FF, IE 3   Puts the string between <i> and </i> tags

For example:

```
var the_string = "tower";
window.document.writeln(the_string.italics());
```

writes <i>tower</i> to a web page.

lastIndexOf()   FF, IE 3   Returns the position of the last occurrence of a substring in a string. Like indexOf(), it can take one or two parameters. The first is the substring to search for, and the second is where in the string to start searching.

For example:

```
var the_string = "The last word.";
var last_space = the_string.lastIndexOf(" ");
```

sets last_space to 8.

link()   FF, IE 3   Takes a URL as a parameter and creates a hyperlink with the string as the text of the link and the URL as the contents of the href attribute

For example:

```
var the_string = "News for Geeks";
window.document.writeln(the_string.link("http://www.slashdot.org"));
```

writes <a href = "http://www.slashdot.org">News for Geeks</a> to a web page.

split()	FF, IE 4	Splits a string into an array along a substring passed as a parameter

Example:

```
var the_string = "Jan,Feb,Mar,Apr,May,Jun,Jul,Aug,Sep,Oct,Nov,Dec";
var the_months = the_string.split(",");
```

This code creates an array called the_months, which has "Jan" in position 0, "Feb" in position 1, and so on.

localeCompare()	FF, IE 5.5	Compares Unicode versions of this string and the string passed as a parameter. Returns zero if they are the same, 1 if this string sorts after the parameter, and –1 if this string sorts before the parameter.

For example:

```
the_string = "Apple"; alert(the_string.localeCompare("\u0041pple"))
```

returns zero.

match()	FF, IE 4	Takes a regular expression as the parameter. Returns true if the string matches the regular expression. See Chapter 11 for more information.
replace()	FF, IE 4	Takes a regular expression and a string as parameters. Replaces the match for the regular expression with the string.

Example:

```
var the_string = "Happy";
alert(the_string.replace(/p/, "r"));
alert(the_string.replace(/p/g, "r"));
```

The first alert will say *Harpy* and the second will say *Harry*.

search()	FF, IE 4	Takes a regular expression as a parameter and returns the position in the string that matches the expression, or –1 if the regular expression does not match
slice()	FF, IE 4	Returns a substring of a string. Takes a start position and an end position of the substring. If end position is not included, returns from start position to the end of the string.
small()	FF, IE 3	Puts the string between <small> and </small> tags
sub()	FF, IE 3	Puts the string between _{and} tags
substr()	FF, IE 4	Extracts a substring from a string. Takes two parameters: the position of the first character of the substring and the length of the substring. Similar to the substring() method.

Example:

```
var the_string = "core";
var the_extract = the_string.substr(1, 2);
```

This code sets the_extract to "or" because "o" is in position 1 in the string and is 2 letters long.

substring()	FF, IE 3	Extracts a substring from a string. Takes two parameters: the position of the first character of the substring and the position of the character after the last character in the substring. Similar to the substr() method, except it works in more browsers and takes a different second parameter.

Example:

```
var the_string = "core";
var the_extract = the_string.substr(1, 3);
```

This code example sets the_extract to "or" because "o" is in position 1 of the string and "e", the letter after the last character in "or", is in position 3.

sup()	FF, IE 3	Puts the string between ^{and} tags
toLocaleLowerCase(), toLocaleUpperCase()	FF, IE 5.5	Converts a string to lowercase or upper case. Can handle Unicode characters.

Example:

```
var the_string = "\u0041pple";
window.document.writeln(the_string.toLocaleLowerCase());
```

This code writes *apple* to a web page.

toLowerCase(), toUpperCase()	FF, IE 3	Converts a string to lowercase or uppercase. Doesn't know Unicode.

Style   [FF, IE 4]

The object that represents a Cascading Style Sheet (CSS). As discussed in Chapter 13, you can use CSS in combination with JavaScript to animate a web page in many ways. Style sheets are often attached to <div> HTML tags as follows:

```
<div id = "mystyle" STYLE = "position:absolute;top:100;left:100;">
Here's a style sheet!
</div>
```

This code gives div an id of "mystyle" and positions the text between the <div> and </div> tags 100 pixels from the left and 100 pixels from the top of the screen.

The style object is available for all HTML elements. The following line accesses the style object for the div in the preceding example:

```
var the_style = document.getElementById("mystyle").style;
```

All the properties of a style object are read-write. There are many, many properties for the style object. The ones compatible with both Firefox and Internet Explorer 5 and above are listed in the following table. For more information about those properties, pick up a good book on CSS or Dynamic HTML.

Properties   [FF, IE 5]

background	borderRightWidth	fontVarient	paddingTop
backgroundAttachment	borderStyle	fontWeight	pageBreakAfter
backgroundColor	borderTop	height	pageBreakBefore
backgroundImage	borderTopColor	left	position
backgroundPosition	borderTopStyle	letterSpacing	right
backgroundRepeat	borderTopWidth	lineHeight	tableLayout
border	borderWidth	listStyleImage	textAlign
borderBottom	bottom	listStylePosition	textDecoration
borderBottomColor	clear	listStyleType	textIndent
borderBottomStyle	clip	margin	textIndex
borderBottomWidth	color	marginBottom	textTransform
borderColor	cssText	marginLeft	top
borderLeft	cursor	marginRight	unicodeBidi
borderLeftColor	direction	marginTop	verticalAlign
borderLeftStyle	display	overflow	visibility
borderLeftWidth	font	padding	whiteSpace
borderRight	fontFamily	paddingBottom	width
borderRightColor	fontSize	paddingLeft	wordSpacing
borderRightStyle	fontStyle	paddingRight	zIndex

Submit

The submit button sends an onSubmit event to the form that contains it. See "Button (Including Submit and Reset Buttons)" on page 416 for more information.

Text

The text form element allows a visitor to type a line of text into a form. See "Password" on page 436 for more information.

Textarea

A textarea is a multiline box into which text can be typed. Its HTML looks like this:

```
<textarea rows = "10" cols = "40">some default text</textarea>.
```

Properties

cols	FF, IE 4	Number of columns of the textarea
defaultValue	FF, IE 3	Read-only: Browser-set default value for the element
form	FF, IE 3	Read-only: Form containing the element
maxLength	FF, IE 4	Maximum number of characters allowed in the field
name	FF, IE 3	Name of the textarea field
readOnly	FF, IE 4	true if users can't enter data into the field
rows	FF, IE 4	Number of rows of this textarea
type	FF, IE 4	Read-only: Set to "TEXTAREA"
value	FF, IE 3	Text that appears in the textarea

Methods

blur()	FF, IE 3	Removes the cursor from the textarea

Example:

```
window.document.my_form.the_area.blur();
```

focus()	FF, IE 3	Moves the cursor to the textarea

Example:

```
window.document.my_form.the_area.focus();
```

This line puts the cursor inside the password element named the_password. Unless the focus is changed, the next characters typed go into the_password.

select()	FF, IE 3	Selects the text inside the textarea

Example:

```
window.document.my_form.the_area.select();
```

Handlers

onBlur	FF, IE 3	Called when a visitor removes the cursor from the textarea
onChange	FF, IE 3	Triggered when a visitor changes the contents of the field and then clicks outside the field or presses ENTER
onFocus	FF, IE 3	Called when the cursor is put into the password field

this   [FF, IE 3]

A term that refers to the object in which it appears. Example:

```
<input type = "checkbox" name = "riddle_me" onClick = "alert(this.name)">
```

Here, this refers to the checkbox named riddle_me because that's where this appears. The alert box will have the text riddle_me inside.

unescape()   [FF, IE 3]

Decodes a string encoded with escape(). Example:

```
var decoded_string = unescape("a%20string%20safe%20for%20cookies");
```

The variable decoded_string now holds the string "safe for cookies" because the unescape function replaces each %20 with a space. See "escape()" on page 436 for more information.

var   [FF, IE 3]

A term used the first time a variable is named. Example:

```
var a_new_variable = "I feel good!";
```

window

The window object is either a browser window or a frame. Many methods of the window object have been listed in this appendix already. Those are left out of the description of the window object.

Properties

closed	FF, IE 4	Read-only: true if a window has been closed and false if it is still open. The window referenced is generally created using the window.open() method.

Example:

```
if (my_window.closed == false)
{
    my_window.location = "http://www.hits.org";
}
```

This example makes sure the window named my_window has not been closed before sending a visitor to http://www.hits.org.

defaultStatus	FF, IE 3	Read-only: Browser's default message in the status area of the window
document	FF, IE 3	Read-only: document object of the window. See "Document" on page 421 for more information.
frames[]	FF, IE 3	Read-only: Array of frames stored in a window. Each frame is considered another window object.

Example:

```
window.frames[0].document.writeln("Hello!");
```

This line writes the word *Hello!* into the document of the first frame in the window's frame set.

history	FF, IE 3	Read-only: History object of a window. See "History" on page 426 for more information.
innerHeight	FF	Height of the display area of the web page (only signed scripts can make this smaller than 100 pixels)
innerWidth	FF	Width of the display area of the web page (only signed scripts can make this smaller than 100 pixels)
name	FF, IE 3	Name of a frame or window. The frame set provides the name of a frame. The name of a window is the second parameter in the window.open() method.
navigator	FF, IE 4	Read-only: navigator object of the window

Example:

```
var first_frame_name = window.frames[0].name;
```

onerror	FF, IE 4	The name of a function to trigger when there's a JavaScript error. The function must take three parameters: the error message, the URL of the document in which the error occurred, and the line of the error.

Example:

```
function alertError(the_message, the_url, the_line)
{
    var the_string = "Warning, Will Robinson! " + the_message;
    the_string += " occurred on line " + the_line " of " + the_url;
}
window.onerror = window.alertError;
```

Now, whenever there is a JavaScript error, an alert will pop up with the contents of that error.

offscreenBuffering	IE 4	Setting this to true may reduce flicker in DHTML animations
opener	FF, IE 3	Reference back to the window or frame that opened the current window

Example:

```
window.opener.location = "http://www.nostarch.com";
```

This example changes the URL shown in the window that opened the current window.

outerHeight	FF	Height of the window (only signed scripts can make this smaller than 100 pixels)
outerWidth	FF	Width of the window (only signed scripts can make this smaller than 100 pixels)
pageXOffset	FF	Read-only: How far to the right the screen has scrolled in pixels
pageYOffset	FF	Read-only: How far down the screen has scrolled in pixels
parent	FF, IE 3	Read-only: Parent of this window (used in the context of frames)

Example:

```
parent.frames[1].location = "http://www.aclu.org";
```

This line changes the URL of the second frame in a frame set when called by another frame in the same frame set.

screen	FF, IE 4	Read-only: Window's screen object
screenLeft	IE 5	Read-only: Horizontal coordinate (in pixels) of the left border of the browser window's content area relative to the upper left corner of the screen. The content area is where the web page resides.
screenTop	IE 5	Read-only: Vertical coordinate (in pixels) of the top border of the browser window's content area relative to the upper left corner of the screen. The content area is where the web page resides.
screenX	FF	Horizontal coordinate of the left side of the window
screenY	FF	Vertical coordinate of the top of the window
scrollX	FF	Read-only: Horizontal scrolling of the browser window
scrollY	FF	Read-only: Vertical scrolling of the browser window
self	FF, IE 3	Read-only: Reference to the current window or frame, the same as window

Example:

```
self.location = "http://www.npr.org";
```

status	FF, IE 3	Contents of the window's status bar

Example:

```
window.status = "Don't forget to smile!";
```

top	FF, IE 3	Read-only: Topmost window in a window hierarchy. Helpful when your JavaScript is in a deeply nested frame and you want it to affect the whole web page.

Example:

```
window.location = "http://www.theonion.com";
top.location = "http://www.theonion.com";
```

When executed inside a frame, the first line changes the URL of the frame to www.theonion.com, and the second line changes the URL of the entire web page.

Methods

blur()	FF, IE 4	Sends a window behind all the other windows on the screen

Example:

```
window.blur();
```

close()	FF, IE 3	Closes a window
open()	FF, IE 3	Opens a new window and returns a reference to it. Takes three parameters: the URL of the window to open, the target name of the window, and a comma-delimited list of features the window should have. Some of the features, such as width and height, must have values assigned to them. If the third parameter is left out, the new window contains the same features as the window that opened it.

Example:

```
var little_window = window.open("http://www.ebay.com", "little_window",
"height=50,width=50,resizable");
```

The above code opens up a small resizable window holding eBay's website.

Features

The following list contains all the features a window may have and which browsers allow which features. The first list contains the window features that work in Netscape 2, Internet Explorer 3, and more recent versions of these browsers.

copyhistory	Copies the history of the current window to the window being opened (that is, it enables the use of the back button in the new window)
directories	Directory buttons
height	Height of the new window
location	Location bar (where URLs may be typed)

menubar	Menu bar (File, Edit, and so on); always present on a Macintosh
resizable	Makes the window resizable (Macintosh windows are always resizable)
scrollbars	Provides scrollbars when the content of the window exceeds the window size
status	Shows the status bar
toolbar	Toolbar (back, forward, and so on)
width	Width of the window

The following list contains features that only work in Firefox and similar browsers. Certain features, noted by an asterisk, require that Firefox sign your script.

alwaysLowered*	Always puts this window behind others on the screen
alwaysRaised*	Always puts this window above others on the screen
dependent	Closes the new window when the opening window closes
hotkeys	Disables keyboard shortcuts except Quit
innerHeight	Height of the window's content region
innerWidth	Width of the window's content region
outerHeight	Total height of the window
outerWidth	Total width of the window
screenX	How far from the left side of the screen the window appears
screenY	How far from the top of the screen the window appears
titlebar*	Set titlebar = no to hide the title bar
z-lock*	Puts the window below all other browser windows

Methods

scroll()	FF, IE 4	Takes two parameters: a number of pixels to scroll horizontally and a number to scroll vertically

Example:

```
window.scroll(100,500);
```

This line moves the scroll bars so that the part of the screen 100 pixels from the left border and 500 pixels from the top of the screen appears at the upper left corner of the screen.

scrollBy()	FF, IE 4	Takes two parameters: the number of pixels to scroll the window horizontally and vertically (use negative numbers to move the scroll bars to the left or up)

Example:

```
window.scrollBy(50,-100);
```

This line scrolls the window 50 pixels to right and 100 pixels up.

Less Common Methods

back()	FF	Goes back a page (like clicking the browser's back button)
find()	FF	Searches in the document for the string passed as the parameter
forward()	FF	Goes forward a page (like clicking the browser's forward button)
home()	FF	Goes to the home page (like clicking the browser's home button)
moveBy()	FF, IE 4	Moves the window a specified number of pixels horizontally and vertically. Firefox script must be signed to move the window off the screen.
moveTo()	FF, IE 4	Moves the window to a certain x, y position relative to the upper left corner of the browser window. Firefox script must be signed to move the window off the screen.
print()	FF, IE 5	Prints the current web page (like clicking the browser's print button)
resizeBy()	FF, IE 4	Takes two parameters: an amount in pixels to resize the window horizontally and an amount to resize it vertically
resizeTo()	FF, IE 4	Takes two parameters: a width in pixels and a height in pixels. Resizes the window to these dimensions.
scrollTo()	FF, IE 4	Just like window.scroll()
stop()	FF	Stops loading the web page (like clicking the browser's stop button)

Handlers

Window handlers go inside the <body> tag of the web page.

onBlur	FF, IE 4	Triggered when the window is no longer topmost on the screen

Example:

```
<body onBlur = "window.close();">
```

This window closes itself if the user selects another window.

onError	FF, IE 4	Triggered when a JavaScript error occurs

Example:

```
<body onError = "alert('Warning! JavaScript error!');">
```

onFocus	FF, IE 4	Triggered when the user selects the window

Example:

```
<body onFocus = "alert('Nice to see you again.');">
```

onLoad	FF, IE 3	Triggered when the page, including all its images, has completely loaded

For example:

```
<body onLoad = "startThauScript();">
```

calls the function startThauScript() when the page has fully loaded.

onResize	FF, IE 4	Triggered when the visitor has resized the page

Example:

```
<body onResize = "alert('Hey, that tickles.');">
```

onUnload	FF, IE 3	Triggered when a visitor is about to leave the page. This occurs even when the browser holding the page is closed, when the visitor clicks a link, or when the visitor reloads the page.

Example:

```
<body onUnload = "alert('Sorry to see you go!');">
```

XMLHttpRequest [FF] and ActiveXObject("Microsoft.XMLHTTP") [IE 5.5]

These objects are used extensively in Ajax, as described in Chapters 14, 15, 16, and 17.

Properties

readyState	State of the request
responseText	String containing the response to the request
responseXML	If the response is an XML document, it is stored here
status	Response status from the server

Methods

abort()	Cancels the request
open()	Tells the request object where the request should go and what kind of request it is. See Chapter 14 for more information.
send()	Sends the request. If this is a POST-type request, the information to send to the server is sent as a parameter. Otherwise, the parameter is null.

Handlers

onReadyStateChange	Triggered when the request object's readyState property changes

D

CHAPTER 15'S ITALIAN TRANSLATOR AND CHAPTER 17'S TO DO LIST APPLICATION

The examples given in this appendix were too long to list in their entirety in Chapters 15 and 17. For more information about how each works, please refer to the appropriate chapter.

Chapter 15's Italian Translator

```
<html><head><title>Translator Suggestion Script</title>
<script type = "text/javascript">
<!-- hide me from older browsers

function getTranslations(the_file, the_word) {
  var request = null;
  var xml_response = null;

  if (window.XMLHttpRequest) {
    request = new XMLHttpRequest();
  } else {
    request = new ActiveXObject("Microsoft.XMLHTTP");
```

```
        }

        if (request) {
          request.open("GET", the_file + ".xml");

          request.onreadystatechange =
            function() {
              if (request.readyState == 4) {
                xml_response = request.responseXML;
                displayResults(findTranslations(xml_response, the_word));
              }
            }

          request.send(null);
        } else {
          alert("Sorry, you must update your browser before seeing" +
            " Ajax in action.");
        }

}

function findTranslations(xml_doc, the_word) {
  var these_translations = new Array();
  var this_word = "", this_result = "";
  var found = false;
  var loop = 0;
  var reg_exp = new RegExp("^" + the_word);
  var the_translation = null;

  if (the_word.length == 0) {
    return these_translations;
  }
  var english_word_elements = xml_doc.getElementsByTagName("english");

  while ((loop < english_word_elements.length) && (found == false)) {
    this_word = english_word_elements[loop].firstChild.nodeValue;
    if (reg_exp.test(this_word)) {

      the_translation =
          english_word_elements[loop].nextSibling.firstChild.nodeValue;
      found = true;
    }
    loop++;
  }
  if (found == true) {
    this_result = this_word + "\t" + the_translation;
    these_translations.push(this_result);

    for (var count = loop; count < (loop + 10); count++) {
      if (count < english_word_elements.length) {
        this_word = english_word_elements[count].firstChild.nodeValue;
        if (reg_exp.test(this_word)) {
          the_translation =
              english_word_elements[count].nextSibling.firstChild.nodeValue;
          this_result = this_word + "\t" + the_translation;
          these_translations.push(this_result);
        }
```

```
          }
        }
      }
      return these_translations;
    }

    function displayResults(the_results) {
      var display_me = "";
      var splitter;
      var this_result = null;
      for (var loop = 0; loop < the_results.length; loop++) {
        this_result = the_results[loop];
        if (this_result != null) {
          splitter = this_result.split("\t");
          display_me += "<tr><td align='left'>" + splitter[0] +
            "</td><td align='right'>" + splitter[1] + "</td></tr>";
        }
      }
      document.getElementById("theResults").style.height =
        (the_results.length + parseInt(the_results.length / 5) + 1) + "em";
      document.getElementById("theResults").innerHTML =
        "<table width='100%' border='0' cellpadding='0' cellspacing='0'>" +
        display_me + "</table>";
    }
    // show me -->
    </script>

    </head>
    <body>
    <form>
      <input type = "text" size = "55" id = "theText"
        onKeyUp = "getTranslations('italian', this.value);">
      <div id = "theResults"
        style = "width:22em;border:1px black solid;padding-left:2px;padding-right:2px">

      </div>
    </form>

    </body>
    </html>
```

Chapter 17's To Do List Application

The To Do list application used one HTML file and two PHP files.

todo.html

```
<html><head><title>To Do</title>
<script type = "text/javascript">
<!-- hide me from older browsers

var user_list_timeout;
var current_list_timeout;
var seconds_between_user_list_update = 60000;
```

```
var seconds_between_todo_list_update = 5000;
var request;

function displayLogin() {

  var theForm = "<form>Name: <input type='text' name='name'><br> " +
    "Password: <input type='password' name='password'> " +
    "<input type='button' value='submit' onClick='doLogin(this.form);'><br>"

  document.getElementById("loginArea").innerHTML = theForm;

}

function doLogin(my_form) {
 readFileDoFunction("userInfo.xml", "GET",
   function() {
     if (request.readyState == 4) {
       if (request.status == 200) {
         processLogin(request.responseXML, my_form);
       } else {
         document.getElementById("errorDiv").innerHTML =
           "Sorry, there was a problem with the server.";
       }
     }
   }
 );
}

function getUser(user_info, user_name) {
  var users = user_info.getElementsByTagName("user");
  var count = 0;
  var found_user = null;
  var this_user;
  while ((count < users.length) && (found_user == null)) {
    this_user = users[count];
    this_name = getFirstValue(this_user, "name");
    //this_user.getElementsByTagName("name")[0].firstChild.nodeValue;
    if (this_name == user_name) {
      found_user = this_user;
    }
    count++;
  }
  return found_user;
}


function processLogin(user_info, my_form) {
  var user_name = my_form.elements["name"].value;
  var user_password = my_form.elements["password"].value;
  var this_password_node;
  var success = false;
  var this_password;

  var this_user = getUser(user_info, user_name);
  if (this_user != null) {
    this_password = getFirstValue(this_user, "password");
    if (user_password == this_password) {
```

```
        success = true;
      }
  }

  if (success == true) {
    document.cookie = "user=" + user_name;
    displayHomeInformation(user_name);
    document.getElementById("contentArea").innerHTML = "";

  } else {

    document.getElementById("errorDiv").innerHTML +=
      "<font color='red'><br>Login error; please try again.</font>";
  }
}

function displayHomeInformation(user_name) {
    document.getElementById("loginArea").innerHTML =
      "Welcome, " + user_name + ".  " +
      "<a href='#' onClick='logout(); return false'>logout</a> ";

    displayLegalLists(user_name);
}

function readFileDoFunction(file_name, request_type, the_function) {

  if (window.XMLHttpRequest) {
    request = new XMLHttpRequest();
  } else {
    request = new ActiveXObject("Microsoft.XMLHTTP");
  }

  var theURL = "http://localhost/boj/ch17/readXMLFile.php?fileName=" +
    file_name + "&t=" + new Date().getTime();

  if (request) {
    request.open(request_type, theURL);
    request.onreadystatechange = the_function;
    request.send(null);
  } else {
     document.getElementById("errorDiv").innerHTML =
       "Sorry, you must update your browser before seeing Ajax in action.";
  }
}

function saveFileDoFunction(file_name, the_contents, the_function) {

  if (window.XMLHttpRequest) {
    request = new XMLHttpRequest();
  } else {
    request = new ActiveXObject("Microsoft.XMLHTTP");
  }

  var the_url = "http://localhost/boj/ch17/saveXMLFile.php?t=" +
    new Date().getTime();
  var the_message = "fileName=" + file_name + "&contents=" + the_contents;
```

```
      if (request) {
        request.open("POST", the_url);
        request.setRequestHeader("Content-type",
          "application/x-www-form-urlencoded; charset=UTF-8");
        request.onreadystatechange = the_function;
        request.send(the_message);
      } else {
        document.getElementById("errorDiv").innerHTML =
          "Sorry, you must update your browser before seeing Ajax in action.";

    }
  }

  function displayLegalLists(user_name) {
   readFileDoFunction("userInfo.xml", "GET",
     function() {
        if (request.readyState == 4) {
          if (request.status == 200) {
          var last_modified = request.getResponseHeader("Last-Modified");
          var last_modified_date = new Date(last_modified);
            displayLists(request.responseXML, user_name,
              last_modified_date.getTime());
          } else {
            document.getElementById("errorDiv").innerHTML =
              "Sorry, your lists could not be displayed due to a problem with " +
              "the server.";
          }

        }
      }
    );
  }


  function displayLists(user_info, user_name, last_modified_date) {
    var this_user = getUser(user_info, user_name);
    var display_info = "";
    var this_link;
    var this_list;
    if (this_user != null) {
      var lists_element = this_user.getElementsByTagName("lists")[0];
      var lists = lists_element.getElementsByTagName("list");
      for (var loop = 0; loop < lists.length; loop++) {
        this_list = lists[loop].firstChild.nodeValue;
        this_link = "<a href=\"#\" onClick=\"readyDisplayList('" +
          this_list + "'); return false;\">" + this_list + "</a>";
        display_info += this_link + "<br>";
      }

      document.getElementById("listArea").innerHTML = display_info;
      user_list_timeout =
        setTimeout("updateUserIfChanged(" + last_modified_date + ",'" +
          user_name + "')", seconds_between_user_list_update);
    }
  }

  function updateUserIfChanged(current_last_modified, user_name) {
```

```
readFileDoFunction("userInfo.xml", "HEAD",
  function() {
    if (request.readyState == 4) {
      if (request.status == 200) {
        var last_modified = request.getResponseHeader("Last-Modified");
        var last_modified_date = new Date(last_modified).getTime();
        if (last_modified_date != current_last_modified) {
          displayLegalLists(user_name);
        }
        user_list_timeout = setTimeout("updateUserIfChanged(" +
          last_modified_date + ",'" + user_name +
          "')",seconds_between_user_list_update);
      } else {
        document.getElementById("errorDiv").innerHTML =
          "Problem updating user " + request.status;
      }
    }
  }
);
}


function updateTodoIfChanged(current_last_modified, list_name) {
  readFileDoFunction(list_name + ".xml", "HEAD",
    function() {
      if (request.readyState == 4) {
        if (request.status == 200) {
          var last_modified = request.getResponseHeader("Last-Modified");
          var last_modified_date = new Date(last_modified).getTime();
          if (last_modified_date != current_last_modified) {
            readyDisplayList(list_name);
          }
          todo_list_timeout = setTimeout("updateTodoIfChanged(" +
            last_modified_date + ",'" + list_name + "')",
            seconds_between_todo_list_update);
        } else {
          document.getElementById("errorDiv").innerHTML =
            "Problem updating To Do list " + request.status;
        }
      }
    }
  );
}

function addNewItem(the_form, list_name) {
  var file_name = list_name + ".xml";
  readFileDoFunction(file_name, "GET",
    function() {
      if (request.readyState == 4) {
        if (request.status == 200) {
          addNewToFile(request.responseXML, the_form.newItem.value,
            list_name);
        } else {
          document.getElementById("errorDiv").innerHTML =
            "Sorry, new item could not be added to To Do list for" + list_name +
            " due to a problem with the server.";
        }
```

```
        }
      }
    );
  }

  function addNewToFile(the_document, new_contents, list_name) {
    var open_items = getItems(the_document,"openitems");
    var done_items = getItems(the_document,"doneitems");
    var high_number = getHighValue(the_document);
    var new_number = high_number + 1;
    var new_item = document.createElement("item");
    var new_item_number = document.createElement("number");
    var new_item_content = document.createElement("contents");
    new_item_number.appendChild(document.createTextNode(new_number));
    new_item_content.appendChild(document.createTextNode(new_contents));
    new_item.appendChild(new_item_number);
    new_item.appendChild(new_item_content);
    open_items.push(new_item);
    saveAndReload(open_items, done_items, list_name);
  }


  function getHighValue(the_document) {
    var high_number = 0;
    var this_number = 0;
    var items = the_document.getElementsByTagName("item");
    for (var loop = 0; loop < items.length; loop++) {
      this_number = parseInt(getFirstValue(items[loop], "number"));
      if (this_number > high_number) {
        high_number = this_number;
      }
    }
    return high_number;
  }

  function readyDisplayList(list_name) {
   var file_name = list_name + ".xml";
   readFileDoFunction(file_name, "GET",
     function() {
       if (request.readyState == 4) {
         if (request.status == 200) {
           var last_modified = request.getResponseHeader("Last-Modified");
           var last_modified_date = new Date(last_modified);
           displayList(request.responseXML, last_modified_date.getTime());
         } else {
           document.getElementById("errorDiv").innerHTML =
             "Sorry, could not display To Do list " + list_name +
             " due to a problem with the server.";
         }
       }
     }
   );
  }


  function displayList(the_list, last_modified_date) {
    var list_name = getFirstValue(the_list, "name");
```

```javascript
var intro_text = "<h3>Looking at list: " + list_name + "</h3>";
var pending_display = "Still Pending:<br><ul>";
var open_item_element = the_list.getElementsByTagName("openitems")[0];
var open_items = open_item_element.getElementsByTagName("item");
for (var loop = 0; loop < open_items.length; loop++) {
  this_item = open_items[loop];
  this_contents = getFirstValue(this_item, "contents");
  this_number = getFirstValue(this_item, "number");
  pending_display += "<li><input type='checkbox' " +
    "onClick=\"readyMarkDone('" + list_name + "'," +
    this_number + ");\"> " + this_contents;
}
pending_display += "</ul>";

var done_display = "Completed:<br><ul>";
var open_item_element = the_list.getElementsByTagName("doneitems")[0];
var open_items = open_item_element.getElementsByTagName("item");
for (var loop = 0; loop < open_items.length; loop++) {
  this_item = open_items[loop];
  this_contents = getFirstValue(this_item, "contents");
  this_number = getFirstValue(this_item, "number");
  done_display += "<li><input type='checkbox' " +
    "onClick=\"readyMarkUndone('" + list_name + "'," + this_number +
    ");\"> " + this_contents;
}
done_display += "</ul>";
document.getElementById("contentArea").innerHTML = intro_text +
  pending_display + done_display;

document.getElementById("contentArea").innerHTML +=
  "<p> <form>Add New Item: <input type='text' name='newItem'>" +
  "<input type=\"button\" value=\"add\"  " +
  "onClick=\"addNewItem(this.form, '" + list_name + "');\"></form>";

todo_list_timeout =
    setTimeout("updateTodoIfChanged(" + last_modified_date + ",'" +
      list_name + "')", seconds_between_todo_list_update);
}

function getFirstValue(my_element, child) {
  return my_element.getElementsByTagName(child)[0].firstChild.nodeValue;
}

function readyMarkDone(list_name, the_item) {
 var file_name = list_name + ".xml";
 readFileDoFunction(file_name, "GET",
   function() {
     if (request.readyState == 4) {
       if (request.status == 200) {
         markDone(request.responseXML, the_item, list_name);
       } else {
         document.getElementById("errorDiv").innerHTML =
           "Sorry, this item could not be marked done due to a problem " +
           "with the server.";
       }
     }
   }
```

```
      );
    }


    function readyMarkUndone(list_name, the_item) {
     var file_name = list_name + ".xml";
     readFileDoFunction(file_name, "GET",
       function() {
          if (request.readyState == 4) {
            if (request.status == 200) {
              markUndone(request.responseXML, the_item, list_name);
            } else {
              document.getElementById("errorDiv").innerHTML =
                "Sorry, this item could not be marked undone due to a problem " +
                "with the server.";
            }
          }
        }
      );
    }

    function markDone(the_document, the_item, list_name, last_modified_date)  {
      var open_items = getItems(the_document,"openitems");
      var done_items = getItems(the_document,"doneitems");
      var this_number;
      var found_item = null;
      var count = 0;
      while ((count < open_items.length) && (found_item == null)) {
        this_number = getFirstValue(open_items[count], "number");
        if (this_number == the_item) {
          found_item = open_items[count];
        } else {
          count++;
        }
      }
      if (found_item != null) {
          open_items.splice(count, 1);
          done_items.push(found_item);
          saveAndReload(open_items, done_items, list_name);
      }
    }


    function markUndone(the_document, the_item, list_name)  {
      var open_items = getItems(the_document,"openitems");
      var done_items = getItems(the_document,"doneitems");
      var this_number;
      var found_item = null;
      var count = 0;
      while ((count < done_items.length) && (found_item == null)) {
        this_number = getFirstValue(done_items[count], "number");
        if (this_number == the_item) {
          found_item = done_items[count];
        } else {
          count++;
        }
      }
```

```
    if (found_item != null) {
        done_items.splice(count, 1);
        open_items.push(found_item);
        saveAndReload(open_items, done_items, list_name);
    }
}

function getItems(the_document, the_item_type) {
    var the_items_array = new Array();
    var item_elements = the_document.getElementsByTagName(the_item_type)[0];
    var items = item_elements.getElementsByTagName("item");
    for (var loop = 0; loop < items.length; loop++) {
        the_items_array[loop] = items[loop];
    }
    return the_items_array;
}

function saveAndReload(open_items, done_items, list_name) {
    var the_string = "<?xml version='1.0' ?>";
    the_string += "<list>";
    the_string += "<name>" + list_name + "</name>";
    the_string += getItemString("openitems", open_items);
    the_string += getItemString("doneitems", done_items);
    the_string += "</list>";

    var file_name = list_name + ".xml";
    saveFileDoFunction(file_name, the_string,
        function() {
            if (request.readyState == 4) {
                if ((request.responseText == "success") && (request.status == 200)) {
                    readyDisplayList(list_name);
                } else {
                    document.getElementById("errorDiv").innerHTML =
                        "Sorry, there was an error saving your list. " +
                        request.responseText;
                }
            }
        }
    );
}


function getItemString(item_list_name, item_list) {
    var the_string = "<" + item_list_name + ">";
    for (var loop = 0; loop < item_list.length; loop++) {

        the_string += "<item>";
        the_string += "<number>" + getFirstValue(item_list[loop], "number") +
            "</number>";
        the_string += "<contents>" +
            getFirstValue(item_list[loop], "contents") + "</contents>";
        the_string += "</item>";
    }
    the_string += "</" + item_list_name + ">";
    return the_string;
}

function logout() {
    var the_date = new Date("December 31, 1900");
```

```
        var the_cookie_date = the_date.toGMTString();
        var user_name = getNameFromCookie();
        document.cookie = "user=" + escape(user_name) +
          ";expires=" + the_cookie_date;

        clearTimeout(user_list_timeout);
        clearTimeout(current_list_timeout);
        window.location.reload();

    }

    function getNameFromCookie() {
      var cookieParts = null;
      var user_name = null;
      if (document.cookie != null) {
        user_name = document.cookie.split("=")[1];
      }
      return user_name;

    }

    function checkIfLoggedIn() {
      var user_name = getNameFromCookie();
      if (user_name != null) {
        displayHomeInformation(user_name);
      }
    }

    // show me -->
    </script>

    </head>
    <body onLoad = "checkIfLoggedIn()";>

    <div id = "errorDiv" style = "color:red">
    </div>

    <h2>Login Section</h2>
    <div id = "loginArea">
    <a href = "#" onClick = "displayLogin(); return false;">login</a>
    </div>

    <h2>Content Section</h2>
    <div id = "contentArea">
    Welcome! Please sign in to see your To Do lists.
    </div>

    <h2>To Do Lists You Can Access</h2>
    <div id = "listArea">

    </div>


    </body>
    </html>
```

readXMLFile.php

```php
<?php

  $fileName = $_REQUEST["fileName"];

  header('Last-Modified: '.
    gmdate('D, d M Y H:i:s', filemtime($fileName)).' GMT');

  if ($_SERVER["REQUEST_METHOD"] != "HEAD") {
    header('Content-Type: text/xml');

    $myFile = fopen($fileName, "r");
    $contents = "";
    while (feof($myFile) == FALSE) {
      $contents = $contents . fgets($myFile);
    }
    fclose($myFile);

    print $contents;
  }
?>
```

saveXMLFile.php

```php
<?php

  $fileName = $_REQUEST["fileName"];
  $contents = $_REQUEST["contents"];

  $myFile = fopen($fileName, "w");
  $success = fwrite($myFile, stripslashes($contents));
  fclose($myFile);

  if ($success == TRUE) {
    print "success";
  } else {
    print "$success";
  }

?>
```

INDEX

Ajax, *continued*
	client-side, 291
	code examples, 407
	for contacting third-party webserver,
		308–309
	creating and sending requests,
		265–270
	cross-server communication
		using, 303
	debugging in Firefox, 374
	decision to use, 275–276
	forms for, 316
	frameworks, 408
	in-context data manipulation, 276
	introduction, 263–265
	and POST method, 314–318
	reading file, 327
	real-world examples, 262, 280–281
	script example, 269
	tutorials, 407
	and usability, 274–275
	web resources, 407
alarm
	canceling, 149–150
	setting, 148
alert box, 22
	line break in, 195
alert() method, 22–23, 84, 413
	for printing variables, 367–369
	timer to display, 148
alerts, link to call, 54
align property, of image object, 429
alinkColor property, of document
		object, 421
all array, of HTMLElement object, 427
alt attribute, of <img> tag, 64
alt property, of image object, 429
altKey property
	of event object, 423
	of keyboard event, 251
alwaysLowered feature, for window, 452
alwaysRaised feature, for window, 452
ampersand (&), in XML entities, 284
ampersands (&&), for AND operator, 198
	in if-then statements, 44–45
anchor element, 413
	target attribute of, 70
anchor() method, of string, 441
anchors array, of document object, 421
AND (&&) operator, 198
	in if-then statements, 44–45
Andre's JSLog, 370

animation, timing loops for, 239–241
anonymous function, 268, 272, 327, 347
AntWeb page, process for checking off
		checkboxes, 133–134
Apache webserver, 272
apostrophe (')
	entities in XML for, 285
	escaping, 56
appCodeName property, of navigator
		object, 434
appendChild() method, 245–246, 428
applet element, 413–414
applets array, of document object, 421
appName property, of navigator object, 433
appVersion property, of navigator
		object, 434
appVersion variable, 48
area element, 414
arithmetic, with variables, 18
array element, 414–416
array.length in loops, 131
Array object, 135
arrays, 36
	associative, 142–144
	checking last element in, 137
	code for going through elements,
		126–127
	creating, 134–135
	creating empty, 140
	determining number of items in, 126
	examples, 123–124
	of HTML elements, returning, 243
	JavaScript built-in, 124–126
	loading values into, 141
	reading cookie information into, 221
	testing limits, 137–138
	for tip box on website, 136–139
	and while loops, 129–130
asin() method, of math object, 433
Ask.com, 136
associative arrays, 142–144
asterisk (*)
	for multiplication, 18
	in regular expressions, 204–205
asynchronicity, 264–265, 271–274
Asynchronous JavaScript and XML. *See*
		Ajax (Asynchronous JavaScript
		and XML)
atan() method, of math object, 433
attachEvent() method, of HTMLElement
		object, 428

attributes array, of `HTMLElement` object, 427

attributes property, of nodes, 249

`availHeight` property, of `screen` object, 78, 439

`availWidth` property, of `screen` object, 78, 439

B

back button, in Ajax applications, 274

`back()` method
  of `history` element, 427
  of `window` object, 453

Backbase, 274

background color, event handler to customize, 57–58

backslash (\)
  for escaping apostrophe, 56
  for escaping in regular expressions, 204

backup, before fixing bug, 377

bars (||), for `OR` operator, 44

BBEdit, 8

`bgColor` property, of `document` object, 421

`big()` method, of string, 441

blank statements, checking for, 137

blocked pop-ups, 76

`blur()` method, 74
  of `FileUpload` element, 424
  of `HTMLElement` object, 428
  of `password` element, 437
  of `textarea` element, 447
  of `window` object, 451

BODY node, in W3C DOM, 245

body of HTML page, JavaScript tags in, 10

body property, of `document` object, 421

`<body>` tag, for status bar content, 74

`bold()` method, of string, 442

bookmarks, for Ajax application, 274

Book of JavaScript website, 16
  About the Author link, 68
  array use, 124
  pull-down menu, 101
  rollovers, 52, 54
  timer, 148, 155–157
  tip box, 136–139
  tracking visits, 216

Boole, George, 38

Boolean expressions, 38–40
  details, 47–48

OR (||) in if-then statements, 43–44

AND (&&) in if-then statements, 44–45

border property, of `image` object, 429

borders, for drop-down menus, 259

Bosworth, Alex, 275

branching, 38. *See also* if-then statements

browser. *See* web browsers
  -server communications
    Ajax style, 264
    problems, 323–324
    synchronous, requests in, 264
    traditional style, 263–264
  sniffers, 36, 50
  -specific content, provided by Netscape, 48–50

`browser_info` variable, 36

`browserLanguage` property, of `navigator` object, 434

bug-eating script, in *Salon*, 186–189

bugs. *See* debugging

button
  element, 416
  property
    for event object, 423
    for mouse events, 252

buttons
  for closing windows, 73
  on forms, 103, 104

C

cache of browser, preloading images to, 63

calculator, from form elements, 109–110

camel-caps notation, 85

canceling alarm, 149–150

caret (^), for beginning of regular expression pattern, 205

Cascading Style Sheets (CSS), 234–237
  to position div element, 235–237
  tutorials, 406

case, of HTML tags, 244

case sensitivity
  of function names, 85
  of variable names, 18, 23

`ceil()` method, of math object, 433

center of screen for window placement, 78–80
  function for, 86

CGI (Common Gateway Interface) scripting, 5–7

characters
  checking email for illegal, 199
  illegal XML, 284–285, 357
charAt() method, 198–199
  of string, 442
charCodeAt() method, of string, 442
checkalpha() function, 211
checkBlank() function, 211
checkbox element, 417
checkboxes, 112–114
  AntWeb's process for checking,
    133–134
  array for storing, 124
  checked Boolean attribute of, 112
  on forms, 103
checked property
  of checkbox element, 417
  of radio element, 438
checkrangenumeric() function, 211, 212
child nodes
  in W3C DOM, 245
  in XML, 288
childNodes array, of HTMLElement
    object, 427
childNodes property, of nodes, 249
className property, of HTMLElement
    object, 427
clearing time-outs, 153
clearInterval() function, 417
cleartext, 360
clearTimeout() function, 149–150,
    151, 417
  for animation, 239–241
click() method
  of button element, 416
  of checkbox element, 417
  of HTMLElement object, 428
  of radio element, 439
clicking link, to hide div element,
    238–239
client-server applications, Internet as
    bottleneck, 359
client-side
  Ajax, 291
  programs
    JavaScript for Google Suggest
      application, 309–313
    vs. server-side, 359
clientX property
  of event object, 253, 254, 423
  of mouse event, 252

clientY property
  of event object, 253, 254, 423
  of mouse event, 252
clock
  checking local time on, 26
  with timing loops, 154–155
cloneNode() method, 249–250
  of HTMLElement object, 428
cloning nodes, 249
close() method, 72–73
  of document object, 422
  of window object, 451
closed property, of window object, 448
closing windows, 72–73
codeBase property, of applet element, 413
code property, of applet element, 413
color, background, event handler to
    customize, 57–58
colorDepth property, of screen object, 439
cols
  element, 172
  property, of textarea element,
    106, 447
comments in code, 364–365
  in HTML, 11
  in JavaScript, slashes for, 10
Common Gateway Interface (CGI)
    scripting, 5–7
communication between browser and
    server
  Ajax style, 264
  CGI requirements for, 5
  problems, 323–324
  traditional style, 263–264
companion website
  brwsniff.js file, 36
  credit card script, 196
  date validation functions, 203
  isValidUrl(), 202
  substring() for checking credit card
    numbers, 202
complete property, of image object, 429
concat() method
  of array element, 416
  of string, 442
confirm() method, 418
constants, 161
cookieEnabled property, of navigator
    object, 434
cookie property, of document object, 218,
    219, 421

errors. *See also* debugging
  from global variables, 161
  from undefined values, 130
escape() function, 218, 311, 423
European Computer Manufacturers
        Association (ECMA), 8
European Space Agency (ESA), 15, 116
  date on website, 30–31
eval() function, 312, 423
event handler, 54, 406
  adding with JavaScript, 254–257
  attaching function to, 254–255
  to customize background color, 57–58
event object, 250–254, 423–424
events
  for Ajax, 263
  as function parameter, 255
  triggering, 53–58
  types, 53–55
  variables for storing, 255
exception handling, tutorials, 406
exp() method, of math object, 433
expiration date for cookie, 222–223
  and deleting cookie, 224
Extensible Markup Language. *See* XML
        (Extensible Markup Language)

F

false value, storing in variable, 47
fclose() function (PHP), 322
features parameter, of open() method,
        70–72
feof() function (PHP), 322
fgColor property, of document object, 421
fgets() function (PHP), 323
file handling (PHP), 321–323
filemtime() function (PHP), 329
FileUpload form element, 424
find() method, of window object, 453
Firebug, 376
fireEvent() method, of HTMLElement
        object, 428
Firefox
  case of HTML tags, 244
  -compatible web browser, 49
  console for error display, 370
  debugging Ajax in, 374
  ECMA standard compliance by, 8
  navigator.appName variable for, 35
  request object, 265
  treatment of XML document white
        space, 291
  updating web page, 320–321

user input to form text element, 245
users, 412
windows in, 72
firstChild property
  of HTMLElement object, 427
  of nodes, 249
fixed() method, of string, 442
Flanagan, David, 3, 379
Flash, 7
Flickr.com, 280, 281
  headers for, 318–319
floating-point number, for browser
        versions, 35
floor() method, of math object, 159, 433
focus() method, 74
  of FileUpload element, 424
  of HTMLElement object, 428
  of password element, 437
  of textarea element, 447
fontcolor() method, of string, 442
font size, and em unit, 293
fontsize() method, of string, 442
<font> tag, 244
fopen() function (PHP), 321
for loops, 132, 150
form
  object, 424–426
  property
    of button element, 416
    of checkbox element, 417
    of option object, 435
    of password element, 436
    of textarea element, 447
form elements
  array for, 125
  attaching handlers to, 256
  checking for completion, 192–196
  for event handling, 116–117
  id attribute for, 119
  names for, 107
  number on page, 131
  parseInt() function with, 152–153
  reading and setting, 109–116
  select element, 104–105
  textarea element, 106
forms
  adding and removing elements, 248
  for Ajax, 316
  basics, 101–106
    buttons, 103, 104
    checkboxes, 103
    radio buttons, 103, 104
    text fields, 102

forms, *continued*
    example, 100–101
    and JavaScript, 107–109
    and POST method, 315
    sending to server-side program, 195–196
forms array, of document object, 421
form validation, 191
    check for mandatory information, 192–196
    Dictionary.com, 207–213
    example, 192
Fortune magazine website, 259
forward() method
    of history element, 427
    of window object, 453
frameborder, 183
frames, 169
    basics, 170–172
    busting, 179–180
    changing contents of two at once, 176–177
    example, 170
    and image swapping, 174–175
    and JavaScript, 172–173
    nesting, 177–178, 188
    referring to, 173
        in JavaScript, 179
    storing information with, 181–184
frames array, of window object, 449
<frameset> tag, 178
<frame> tag, noresize attribute, 183
fromCharCode() method, of string, 443
functions, 21–25
    anonymous, 268, 272, 327, 347
    attaching to event handlers, 254–255
    basic structure, 84–85
    built-in date, 26
    called by frame when declared in another frame, 184
    declaring variables for time-outs outside, 153–154
    determining when to use, 96
    example, 85–86
    flexibility for, 86–91
    getting information from, 91–92
    hiding variables inside, 95
    for multiple pages, 228
    names for, 85, 365
    parameters for, 25–26
        adding, 87–89
        importance of, 348

road map for planning, 339
    as shortcuts, 84–86
    text file for, 228
fwrite() function (PHP), 321

G

Garrett, Jesse James, 263
GedML, 285
Geography Markup Language (GML), 285
GET request (Ajax), creating Google Suggest application with, 308–314
GET request (PHP)
    reading inputs of, 306–307
    to send simple input, 305–307
getAttribute() method, of HTMLElement object, 428
getAttributeNode() method, of HTMLElement object, 428
getDate() method, 27, 418
getDay() method, 27, 418
getElementById() method, 119, 238–239
    of document object, 422
getElementsByName() method, of document object, 422
getElementsByTagName() method, 243, 244, 246, 289, 343, 348, 422, 428
getFullYear() method, 418
getHours() method, 27, 31, 155, 418
getMinutes() method, 27, 155, 418
getMonth() method, 27, 29, 419
getResponseHeader() method, 319
getSeconds() method, 27, 155, 419
getTime() method, 27, 156–157, 159, 273, 419
getUTCDate() method, 419
getUTCDay() method, 419
getUTCFullYear() method, 419
getUTCHours() method, 419
getUTCMinutes() method, 419
getUTCMonth() method, 419
getUTCSeconds() method, 419
getYear() method, 26, 27, 93, 419
GIF, using invisible, 259
global match, for regular expression, 206
global variables, 160–161
    risks from, 163
gmdate() function (PHP), 329
GML (Geography Markup Language), 285
GoLive, 8

go() method, of history element, 427
Goodman, Danny (*The Javascript Bible*), 412
Google
    Maps, 261, 262, 274
        in-context data manipulation, 276
    Suggest, 281–282
        with Ajax GET request, 308–314
        creating application
            JavaScript for homemade application, 309–313
            processing results, 312
            for translation, 292–296
            URL to return set of search terms, 305–306
graphics
    JavaScript limitations, 8
    preloading, 62–64
    referring to by number, 126
    src property, 61
    swapping, 58–59
        and frames, 174–175
        between windows, 81
    working with multiple, 59–60
Greasemonkey, 374, 375
greater than (>) symbol, 39
grouping characters, in regular expressions, 205–206

H

hasChildNodes() method, of HTMLElement object, 428
hash mark (#), in href tag, 56
hash property
    of <a> tag, 413
    of location object, 431
HEAD element, in W3C DOM, 245
header() function (PHP), 319
head of HTML page
    declaring functions in, 86
    JavaScript tags in, 10
height of screen, determining, 78
height property, 451
    of applet element, 413
    of browser window, 72
    of HTMLElement object, 427
    of image object, 430
    of <img> tag, 64
    of screen object, 439
help windows, 68, 73
hidden form element, 426

hiding
    JavaScript from browsers without capability, 11
    variables inside functions, 95
history element, 426–427
history property, of window object, 449
home() method, of window object, 453
HomeSite, 8
hostname property
    of <a> tag, 413
    of location object, 431
host property
    of <a> tag, 413
    of location object, 431
hotkeys, for window, 452
href property
    of <a> tag, 413
    hash mark (#) in, 56
    of location object, 431
hspace property
    of applet element, 413
    of image object, 430
.htm file extension, saving documents with, 9
HTML (Hypertext Markup Language)
    <!-- and // --> for comments, 11
    and JavaScript, 30
    name parameter, for open() method, 70
    tags, case of, 244
    for To Do list application, 337–338
    tutorials, 406
    vs. XML, 284
HTML elements
    returning array of, 243
    vs. <script> tags, 254
    in W3C DOM, 245
.html file extension, saving documents with, 9
HTMLElement object, 427–429
HTTPS protocol, 360
Hypertext Markup Language. *See* HTML (Hypertext Markup Language)

I

IDP (Internet Dictionary Project), 285
id property
    assigning to HTML block, 235
    for elements in DOM, 245
    for form elements, 119
    for HTMLElement object, 427

and image maps, 186

limitations, 7–8

links for browsers with JavaScript turned off, 57

permissions, vs. CGI, 7

and PHP, 305

read-only vs. read-write properties, 412

slashes (/), for comments, 10

tutorials, 406

widgets and libraries, 408–409

The JavaScript Bible (Goodman), 412

JavaScript: The Definitive Guide (Flanagan), 3, 379

join() method, of array element, 415

Justice, Chris, 293

K

keyboard, event handlers, 250–252

keyCode property
  for event object, 423
  for keyboard event, 251

key-value pairs
  for GET, 306
  for POST, 316

L

lang property, of HTMLElement object, 427

language property, of navigator object, 434

lastChild property
  of HTMLElement object, 427
  of nodes, 249

lastIndexOf() method, 196, 443

Last-Modified header, 319

lastModified property, of document object, 421

layering <div> tags, 237–238

left
  component, 236
  property
    of browser window, 72
    of div element, 239

length property
  of array element, 126, 414
  of form object, 425
  of history element, 427
  of radio element, 439
  of select element, 440
  of string, 441

less than (<) symbol, 39

libraries, for cookies, 225–226

limits of arrays, testing, 137–138

line breaks
  in alert box, 195
  and <div> tag, 242

link
  object, 431
  property, for document object, 422

link events, 53

link() method, of string, 443

links array, for document object, 422

link tag. *See also* <a> tag
  to open and center window, 84
  status property for information about, 75
  target element of, 70
  var inside, 74

Linux, webserver and PHP for, 272

literal numbers, minimizing use, 131

LN2 property, of math object, 433

LN10 property, of math object, 433

localeCompare() method, of string, 444

Local Variables window in Venkman JavaScript debugger, 370, 371, 372

location
  in browser window, 71, 72
  for window, 451

location object, 431–432

LOG2E property, of math object, 433

Log4Ajax, 370

LOG10E property, of math object, 433

logging in and out, for To Do list application, 340–341

logging libraries, 370

logical tests, 38. *See also* if-then statements

log() method, of math object, 433

looping through lists, with DOM, 249

loops, 127
  array.length used in, 131
  for loops, 132
  incrementing in, 132, 138
  infinite, 131
  initializing, 132
  nesting, 140
  performance and, 134
  timing, for clock, 154–155
  while loops, 128–131

lowercase letters, in regular expressions, 204

lowsrc property, of image object, 430

M

Macintosh, windows in, 72
Macintosh OS X, webserver and PHP for, 272
Macromedia, 7
Mad Lib, 141–142
MAMP package, 272
mandatory information, checking for completion, 192–196
maps. *See* image maps
markup language, 285
match( ) method, 206, 444
math object, 432–433
    and floor( ) method, 159
    and random( ) method, 241
maxLength property
    of password element, 436
    of textarea element, 447
max( ) method, of math object, 433
MAX_VALUE property, of Number object, 434
McEvoy, Chris, 275
menubar for window, 71, 72, 452
menus. *See* pull-down (drop-down) menus
metadata, 318
method property, of form object, 425
methods, 26
Microsoft
    Internet Explorer. *See* Internet Explorer (IE)
    Script Editor, 374
    Visual Web Developer Express Edition, 376
    Word, 8
min( ) method, of math object, 433
minus sign (-), 18
MIN_VALUE property, of Number object, 434
MOD operator, 160
modulus, 160
mortgage calculator, 110–111
mouse
    detecting position, 253
    event trigger from moving, 54–55
mouse events, 252–254
moveBy( ) method, 78, 453
moveTo( ) method, 77–78, 80, 453
moving
    div elements, 239
    images, determining direction, 241
    windows, 77–80
        to front or back of screen, 74

Mozilla Firefox–compatible web browser, 49
    ECMA standard compliance by, 8
    windows in, 72
multiple domains, and cookies, 224
multiple property, of select element, 440
multiplication, asterisk (*) for, 18
MySQL database, 272

N

name property
    <a> tag, 413
    applet element, 413
    button element, 416
    checkbox element, 417
    FileUpload element, 424
    form object, 425
    hidden element, 426
    image object, 430
    password element, 436
    radio element, 104, 439
    select element, 440
    textarea element, 447
    window object, 449
names
    elements, vs. id attributes, 119–120
    form elements, 107
    functions, 85
    graphics, 58, 59
    <option> tag, 108–109
    radio buttons, 108
    variables, 17–18, 364
        date, 29
        vs. function name, 85
    windows, 69, 73
    XML elements, 284
naming convention, consistency in, 365–366
NaN (Not a Number), 153, 211
    property, of Number object, 434–435
navigation. *See also* pull-down (drop-down) menus
    in Ajax, 275
    forms for, 100
    in XML documents, 289
navigator
    object, 433–434
        appName variable, 35
        appVersion variable, 35
        userAgent variable, 36
    property, of window object, 449

triggering events, 53–58
  for form elements, 116
troubleshooting
  alert() method for, 22–23
  equality test, 39
  opening windows, 76
  window feature appearance, 71
true value, storing in variable, 47
tutorials, web resources, 405–406
typeof operator, 211
type property
  button element, 416
  checkbox element, 417
  event object, 424
  keyboard event, 251
  password element, 436
  radio element, 439
  textarea element, 447

U

undefined, 130
undefined variable, 23–24
unescape() function, 218, 448
unShift() method, of array element, 416
updating web page, after server-side file
        change, 325–329
URL
  parameter, for open() method, 70
  property, for document object, 422
URLs
  for Ajax application, 274
  avoiding spaces in, 306
  passing input in, 305–306
  in window status bar, 74
usability and Ajax, 274–275
useMap element, 185
userAgent property, of navigator
        object, 434
userAgent variable, 48
userInfo.xml file, 334–335, 342
users
  data entry and event creation, 251
  dynamic reactions to, 250
  getting information from, 99. *See also*
        forms
  information. *See* cookies
UTC (Coordinated Universal Time)
        date and time
  format for cookie expiration date,
        222–223
  methods for, 419

V

validateForm() function, 210
validation. *See* form validation
value property
  button element, 416
  checkbox element, 417
  FileUpload element, 424
  hidden element, 426
  option object, 436
  password element, 436
  pull-down menu or scrollable list, 115
  radio element, 108, 439
  textarea element, 447
values, loading into array, 141
var, 17, 95, 161, 448
  inside link, 74
  and timing loop, 163–164
variables, 16–18
  alert() method for printing, 367–369
  arithmetic with, 18
  assigning string to, 20
  built in to PHP, 307
  declaring, 45
    for time-outs outside functions,
        153–154
  defining, 94–96
  in different functions, 95
  frame referring to one stored in
        another frame, 184
  global, 160–161
  inside function parentheses, 89
  misspellings, 378
  names for, 17–18, 364, 365
    date, 29
    vs. function name, 85
  quotes and, 92
  risks from declaring outside
        function, 163
  for storing events, 255
  storing true or false in, 47
  syntax, 16–17
  value from function, 91–92
  for windows, 69
VBScript, 7
Venkman JavaScript debugger, 370–374
vertical bars (||), for OR operator, 44
visibility, of div element, 237
vlinkColor property, of document
        object, 422
voodoo coding, 377–378
VRML (Virtual Reality Modeling
        Language), 285

vspace property
  of `applet` element, 413
  of `image` object, 430

W

W3C. *See* World Wide Web
    Consortium (W3C)
web browsers
  browser sniffers, 36, 50
  browser-specific content, provided by
      Netscape, 48–50
  bug detector, 370
  button clicks, 253
  dealing with older, 10–11
  detection, 33
    example, 34
    methods for, 35–37
  Firefox-compatible, 49
  JavaScript and, 7, 8
  links when JavaScript is turned off, 57
  preloading images to cache, 63
  redirecting visitors based on, 45–46
  sending XML information to
      webserver, 318
  and user input to form text
      element, 245
  users, 412
  XML documents, 283
Webmonkey.com, 63, 88
  for cookie libraries, 225–226
  `WM_readCookie()` function, 229
web pages
  automatic update
    after server-side file change,
        325–329
    examples, 15, 16
  JavaScript location on, 9–10
web resources
  charity resources, 68
  for free JavaScripts, 2–3
  JavaScript and Ajax code
      examples, 407
  scripts for preloading images, 63
  tutorials, 405–406
webservers, 266
  advantages of programs, 302
  contacting third-party with Ajax and
      PHP, 308–309, 313–314
  for data storage, vs. cookies,
      300–301, 302
  file handling in PHP, 321–323

  on local computer, 271
    setup, 272
  for PHP programs, 304
  power of, 301–303
  secure, 360
  sending XML information from web
      browsers to, 318
  for sending XML to Internet
      Explorer, 291
website, *Book of JavaScript*
  brwsniff.js file, 36
  credit card script, 196
  date validation functions, 203
  `isValidUrl()`, 202
  `substring()` for checking credit card
      numbers, 202
websites, interactivity on, 2
`while` loops, 128–131, 150
  and arrays, 129–130
  vs. `for` loops, 132
white space in XML, 291–292
widgets, interactive, 276
width of screen, determining, 78
`width` property
  of `applet` element, 413
  of browser window, 72
  of `HTMLElement` object, 427
  of `image` object, 64, 430
  of `screen` object, 439
wildcard, dots (.) as, 204
`window` object, 448–454
  `document.the_form.elements.length`,
      131
  `document.write()` method, 19–20,
      30, 422
  `screen.availHeight` property, 78
  `screen.availWidth` property, 78
windows
  closing, 72–73
  function to open and center, 86
  manipulating appearance of, 70–72
  moving, 77–80
    to front or back of screen, 74
  as objects, 69
  opener property of, 75–77
  opening, 69–72
    example, 68
  resizing, 77
  status property of, 74–75
  swapping image in another, 81
  swapping image with link in
      another, 174

Electronic Frontier Foundation
Defending Freedom in the Digital World

Free Speech. Privacy. Innovation. Fair Use. Reverse Engineering. If you care about these rights in the digital world, then you should join the Electronic Frontier Foundation (EFF). EFF was founded in 1990 to protect the rights of users and developers of technology. EFF is the first to identify threats to basic rights online and to advocate on behalf of free expression in the digital age.

The Electronic Frontier Foundation Defends Your Rights!
Become a Member Today!
http://www.eff.org/support/

Current EFF projects include:

Protecting your fundamental right to vote. Widely publicized security flaws in computerized voting machines show that, though filled with potential, this technology is far from perfect. EFF is defending the open discussion of e-voting problems and is coordinating a national litigation strategy addressing issues arising from use of poorly developed and tested computerized voting machines.

Ensuring that you are not traceable through your things. Libraries, schools, the government and private sector businesses are adopting radio frequency identification tags, or RFIDs – a technology capable of pinpointing the physical location of whatever item the tags are embedded in. While this may seem like a convenient way to track items, it's also a convenient way to do something less benign: track people and their activities through their belongings. EFF is working to ensure that embrace of this technology does not erode your right to privacy.

Stopping the FBI from creating surveillance backdoors on the Internet. EFF is part of a coalition opposing the FBI's expansion of the Communications Assistance for Law Enforcement Act (CALEA), which would require that the wiretap capabilities built into the phone system be extended to the Internet, forcing ISPs to build backdoors for law enforcement.

Providing you with a means by which you can contact key decision-makers on cyber-liberties issues. EFF maintains an action center that provides alerts on technology, civil liberties issues and pending legislation to more than 50,000 subscribers. EFF also generates a weekly online newsletter, EFFector, and a blog that provides up-to-the minute information and commentary.

Defending your right to listen to and copy digital music and movies. The entertainment industry has been overzealous in trying to protect its copyrights, often decimating fair use rights in the process. EFF is standing up to the movie and music industries on several fronts.

Check out all of the things we're working on at http://www.eff.org and join today or make a donation to support the fight to defend freedom online.

ELECTRONIC FRONTIER FOUNDATION · 454 SHOTWELL STREET · SAN FRANCISCO, CA 94110 · 415.436.9333

WEBBOTS, SPIDERS, AND SCREEN SCRAPERS

by MICHAEL SCHRENK

The Internet is bigger and better than what a mere browser allows. *Webbots, Spiders, and Screen Scrapers* is for developers and business managers looking to unlock the competitive advantages of nontraditional online approaches. Readers will learn how to write stealthy webbots that read email, emulate online forms, auto-authenticate, manage cookies, and handle encryption. Sample projects reinforce these new skills so that readers can create more sophisticated webbots and spiders to track online prices, create anonymous browsing environments, bid on auctions in their closing moments, and more.

APRIL 2007, 352 PP., $39.95 ($49.95 CDN)
ISBN 1-59327-120-4 / 978-1-59327-120-6

CODE CRAFT
The Practice of Writing Excellent Code

by PETE GOODLIFFE

Code Craft teaches programmers how to move beyond writing correct code to writing great code. The book covers code-writing concerns such as presentation style, variable naming, error handling, and security. And it tackles broader, real-world programming issues like effective teamwork, developmental processes, and documentation. *Code Craft* is filled with language-agnostic advice that is relevant to all developers, and it's brought to you by an author with loads of practical experience.

DECEMBER 2006, 624 PP., $44.95 ($55.95 CDN)
ISBN 1-59327-119-0 / 978-1-59327-119-0

OBJECT-ORIENTED PHP
Concepts, Techniques, and Code

by PETER LAVIN

Object-Oriented PHP shows developers how to take advantage of the new object-oriented features of PHP. Working from concrete examples, the book begins with code compatible with PHP 4 and 5, and then focuses on object orientation in PHP 5. The author's practical approach uses numerous code examples, which will help developers get up to speed quickly, and show them how to apply what they've learned to everyday situations. All code samples are available for download on the book's companion site.

JUNE 2006, 216 PP., $29.95 ($38.95 CDN)
ISBN 1-59327-077-1 / 978-1-59327-077-3

WICKED COOL JAVA

Code Bits, Open-Source Libraries, and Project Ideas

by BRIAN D. EUBANKS

Wicked Cool Java contains 101 fun, interesting, and useful ways to get more out of Java. Full of example code and ideas for combining the code examples into useful projects, this book is perfect for hobbyists and professionals looking for tips and open-source projects to enhance their code and make their jobs easier. Topics include converting a non-XML text structure into XML using a parser generator, experimenting with a Java simulator for the Cell Matrix, creating dynamic music and sound in Java, working with open-source class libraries for scientific and mathematical applications, and many more.

NOVEMBER 2005, 248 PP., $29.95 ($40.95 CDN)
ISBN 1-59327-061-5 / 978-1-59327-061-2

THE CULT OF MAC

by LEANDER KAHNEY

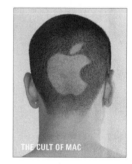

No product on the planet enjoys the devotion of a Macintosh computer. Famously dedicated to their machines, many Mac fans eat, sleep, and breathe Macintosh. In *The Cult of Mac*, Wired News managing editor Leander Kahney takes an in-depth look at Mac users and their unique, creative, and often very funny culture. From people who get Mac tattoos and haircuts, to those who furnish their apartments with empty Mac boxes, the book details Mac fandom in all of its forms. This paperback edition includes an all-new chapter about the iPod, updates throughout, and new photos that reflect current Apple technology.

NOVEMBER 2006, 280 PP., FULL COLOR, $24.95 ($30.95 CDN)
ISBN 1-59327-122-0 / 978-1-59327-122-0

PHONE:
800.420.7240 OR
415.863.9900
MONDAY THROUGH FRIDAY,
9 A.M. TO 5 P.M. (PST)

FAX:
415.863.9950
24 HOURS A DAY,
7 DAYS A WEEK

EMAIL:
SALES@NOSTARCH.COM

WEB:
WWW.NOSTARCH.COM

MAIL:
NO STARCH PRESS
555 DE HARO ST, SUITE 250
SAN FRANCISCO, CA 94107
USA

COLOPHON

The Book of JavaScript, 2nd Edition was laid out in Adobe FrameMaker. The font families used are New Baskerville for body text, Futura for headings and tables, and Dogma for titles.

The book was printed and bound at Malloy Incorporated in Ann Arbor, Michigan. The paper is Glatfelter Thor 60# Smooth, which is made from 50 percent recycled materials, including 30 percent postconsumer content. The book uses a RepKover binding, which allows it to lay flat when open.

UPDATES

Visit **http://www.nostarch.com/js2.htm** for updates and other information. Errata, additional resources, and all code samples and images included in the book are available at **http://www.bookofjavascript.com**.